GREAT MUSLIM ARMY COMMANDERS

Volume 2

THE CRUSADES (1095-1291)

S.E. Al-Djazairi

MSBN Books

S.E. Al-Djazairi: *Great Muslim Army Commanders,* Volume 2 – During the Crusades (1095-1291); Published by MSBN Books; 2020.

ISBN: 9781973460565

Website: msbnbooks.co.uk
Email: info@msbnbooks.co.uk

Cover: Saladin and Guy de Lusignan after the Battle of Hattin, 1187.
Author: Said Tahsine (1904-1985) Syria.

Design and Artwork: N. Kern

S. E. Al-Djazairi lectured and researched at the University of Constantine in Algeria. He also tutored at the Department of Geography of the University of Manchester, and worked as a research assistant at UMIST (Manchester) in the field of History of Science.
He has published papers on environmental degradation and desertification, politics and change in North Africa, and problems of economic and social development. He also contributed historical entries to various encyclopaedias.

Recently Published or Re-edited Works by the same author:
-*Our Civilisation*, 5 Vols, 2020.
-*The Destruction of the Environment in/of the Muslim World*, 2019.
-*Islam in China*, 3 vols, 2020.

CONTENTS

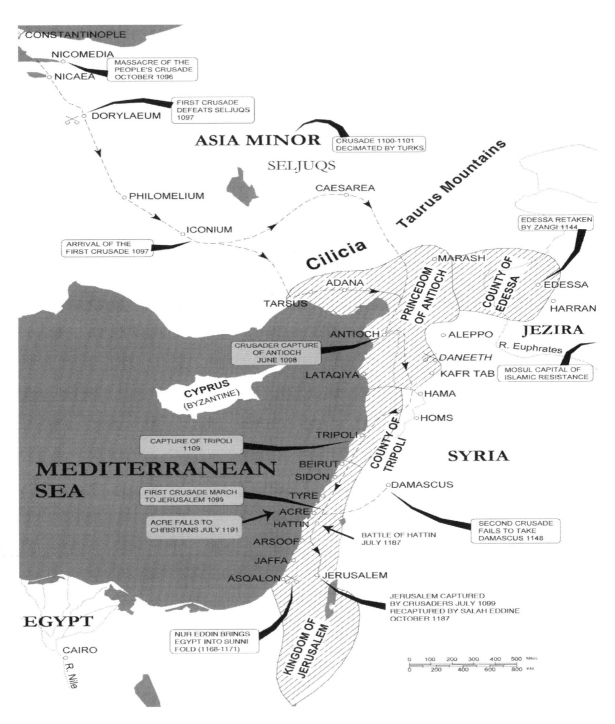

CONSTANTINOPLE

NICOMEDIA

NICAEA

MASSACRE OF THE
PEOPLE'S CRUSADE
OCTOBER 1096

DORYLAEUM

FIRST CRUSADE
DEFEATS SELJUQS
1097

ASIA MINOR

SELJUQS

CRUSADE 1100-1101
DECIMATED BY TURKS

PHILOMELIUM

CAESAREA

Taurus Mountains

ICONIUM

ARRIVAL OF THE
FIRST CRUSADE 1097

Cilicia

EDESSA RETAKEN
BY ZANGI 1144

ADANA

MARASH

PRINCEDOM
OF ANTIOCH

COUNTY OF
EDESSA

EDESSA

TARSUS

HARRAN

ANTIOCH

CRUSADER CAPTURE
OF ANTIOCH
JUNE 1098

ALEPPO

JEZIRA

R. Euphrates

DANEETH

LATAQIYA

KAFR TAB

MOSUL CAPITAL OF
ISLAMIC RESISTANCE

CYPRUS
(BYZANTINE)

HAMA

HOMS

CAPTURE OF TRIPOLI
1109

TRIPOLI

COUNTY OF
TRIPOLI

SYRIA

MEDITERRANEAN
SEA

BEIRUT
SIDON

DAMASCUS

FIRST CRUSADE MARCH
TO JERUSALEM 1099

TYRE

ACRE FALLS TO
CHRISTIANS JULY 1191

ACRE

HATTIN

SECOND CRUSADE
FAILS TO TAKE
DAMASCUS 1148

BATTLE OF HATTIN
JULY 1187

ARSOOF

JAFFA

ASQALON

JERUSALEM

JERUSALEM CAPTURED
BY CRUSADERS JULY 1099
RECAPTURED BY SALAH EDDINE
OCTOBER 1187

EGYPT

CAIRO

R. Nile

NUR EDDIN BRINGS
EGYPT INTO SUNNI
FOLD (1168-1171)

KINGDOM OF
JERUSALEM

0 100 200 300 400 500 Miles
0   200   400   600   800 KM

Overview of the first century of the crusades: 1095-1193.

INTRODUCTION

BACKGROUND TO THE CRUSADES

As well outlined by Stevenson:

> The Crusades (1095-1291) belong to a period nearly co-extensive with two centuries, the 12th and 13th. Many nationalities shared in this enterprise, but principally those of Western Europe. They joined together in the name of obedience to the Latin (Catholic) Church.... Western Europe was continuously at war with the Muslim East for nearly two centuries.... The crusades have been numbered as eight... But no expedition which went to help the Latins can be refused the name crusade. Together they form a continuous stream for the greater part of the 12th and 13th centuries.[1]

The crusades remain, indeed, to this day the longest conflict in history, this unique character being somehow misunderstood or not appreciated as crusade historians generally put their number at eight. This sets aside the fact that fighting was continuous between 1096 and 1291, with hardly any respite, the field of battle, stretching from Asia Minor through Syria-Palestine to Egypt, the daily scene of conflict, at times more violent and more deadly than others. Numbering the crusades at eight also fails to take note that many lesser, but still large expeditions, also took place. Just in the space of three years, 1269-1271, for instance, no less than three crusades were launched, and were led by three different Western rulers: the King of Aragon, the French King Louis IX, and the English Prince Edward. Historical narrative, as a rule, however, only speaks of the eighth crusade, lumping all three expeditions together.

Throughout the crusades, and from the time the Muslim coast of Palestine and Syria fell into Christian hands, early in the 12th century, its main ports: Acre, Tyre, Beirut, and other places became the scene of a ceaseless stream of incoming knights, ordinary foot soldiers and pilgrims, all ready to fight for the Christian cause, arrivals, which peaked in the summer season, when sea travel was safer.[2]

The crusaders arrived from all parts of Western Christendom, including Scandinavians and Normans, and from wherever there were churches, where the supposedly terrible plight of Eastern Christians was heard, and where the call to liberate the Holy Sites of Jerusalem was also heard.
 Men of the West were not alone in confronting the Muslims. From the early stages, the crusaders found strong allies in the local Armenian and Maronite Christians who hitherto had lived undisturbed, and free to practice their faith amongst

---

[1] W.B. Stevenson: *The Crusaders in the East;* Cambridge University Press; 1907; pp. 2-3.
[2] *Receuil des Historiens des Croisades;* Imprimerie Nationale; Paris; 1841 ff.; op cit; S. Runciman: *A History of the Crusades*; in 3 vols; Cambridge University Press, 1962; W.B. Stevenson: *The Crusaders;* op cit.

Muslims.[3] In the 13th century, when Western Europe could no longer afford all the manpower it could before, there came to its side an unlikely, but most powerful and even more welcome ally: the Mongols. After few ambassadorial exchanges, courtesy of the local Christian intermediaries, the Armenians principally, agreement was reached for a concerted onslaught from east and west against Islam. There were few mishaps at first as the attacks were not well coordinated, but when the mid 13th century Mongol onslaught took place (there had been an earlier one in 1219-1221,) it nearly finished off the Muslim presence itself. In 1258, following the capture of Baghdad by the Mongols, over a million Muslims were slain.[4]

Facing the crusaders and their allies were Muslim armies composed of Arabs, Turks and Kurds.[5] In the early stages, from 1096 till 1146, fighting on the Muslim side was led by the Seljuks, principally the Atabegs of Mosul and the Turks of Anatolia, the greatest leader amongst them: Imad Eddin Zangi.[6] In the subsequent period (down to the end of the 12th century), it was Nur-Eddin Zangi, followed by Salah Eddin, who led the fight from Aleppo and Damascus.[7] In the 13th century, precisely in 1250, the Mamluks of Egypt took over the anti crusader fight, and led by their great leader Baybars, they broke Crusader-Mongol power, before Baybars' successors expelled the last of the crusaders in 1291.[8]

The crusades did not take place in a vacuum. As the Damascus Imam-Scholar, al-Sulami, rightly understood, the crusades resulted from Christian success in the West (Spain and Sicily), and a decision to pursue the fight in the East.[9] Indeed, in 1085, the Christians took Toledo from the Muslims, followed by other major gains in the northern parts of Al-Andalus. From 1061 the Normans also began wresting Sicily from the Muslims. These two major successes emboldened Christianity to pursue the fight in the East, not just to capture the Holy Land, but also to terminate the caliphate. Christian attacks were primarily the result of Muslim weakness, itself the outcome of Muslim civil wars.

[3] Ibn al-Athir: *Kamil al-Tarikh*; ed., K.J. Tornberg; 12 vols; Leiden; 1851-72. W.B. Stevenson: *The Crusaders*; op cit. K.S. Salibi: The Maronites of Lebanon under Frankish and Mamluk rule; 1099-1516; *Arabica* IV; 1957.

[4] T. W. Arnold: Muslim Civilisation during the Abbasid Period; in *The Cambridge Medieval History*, Cambridge University Press, vol IV; edited by J.R. Tanner, op cit; pp. 274-298; at p. 279.

[5] Ibn al-Athir: *Kamil*; op cit. W.B. Stevenson: *The Crusaders*; op cit.

[6] Ibn al-Athir: *Tarikh al-Dawla al-Atabakiya Muluk al-Mawsil*; in RHOr; op cit; 11/ii; pp. 1-394. Ibn al-Athir: *Tarikh al-Dawla Al-Atabakiyya*; ed., Ab Al-Qadir Ahmad Tulaymat; Cairo; 1963.

[7] Kemal Eddin: *Zubdat al-Halab fi Ta'rikh Halab;* ed., S. Dahhan; Damascus; 1954. Ibn al-Qalanisi: *Dayl Tarikh Dimashk;* ed., H.F. Amedroz; Leiden; 1908.

[8] Al-Maqrizi: *Al-Suluk fi Ma'rifat Duwal al-Muluk;* tr., M. Qatremere as *Histoire des Sultans Mamluks de l'Egypte*; Paris; 1845. U and M.C. Lyons: *Ayyubids, Mamluks and Crusaders, Selection from the Tarikh al-Duwal wal Muluk of Ibn al-Furat*; 2 vols, W. Heffer and Sons Ltd, Cambridge, 1971.

[9] Al-Sulami: Un Traite Damasquin du debut du XIIem siecle, ed., E Sivan, *Journal Asiatique*, 1966, p. 207.

1. 10th Century Corrosion Of Islam Body Politics

The Muslim world, throughout its length and breath, was ridden with divisions and military conflict. The loss of Sicily and al-Andalus was the direct result of Muslim civil wars and Muslim alliance with invading Christian forces.[10] In the East, Ibn al-Athir says:

> Another story is that the Fatimids were afraid when they saw the Seljuk extending their empire through Syria as far as Ghaza, until they reached the Egyptian border and Atsiz (a Seljuk general) invaded Egypt itself. They (the Fatimids) therefore sent an invite to the Franks to invade Syria and to protect Egypt from the Muslims. But God knows best.[11]

Ibn al-Athir also notes:

> When the Franks, 'may God frustrate them, extended their control over what they had conquered of the lands of Islam and it turned out well for them that the troops and the kings of Islam were preoccupied with fighting each other, at that time opinions were divided among the Muslims, desires differed, and wealth was squandered.'[12]

Hillenbrand insists that 'the timing of the crusade attack could not have been more auspicious for the Europeans.'[13] Had the First Crusade arrived even ten years earlier, it would have met strong, unified resistance from the state then ruled by Malik Shah, the last of the three so called Great Seljuk Sultans.[14] Instead, when the Crusaders arrived, in 1096, the East was divided into innumerable principalities in conflict with each other.

To the 10th century, can be attributed the fatal developments responsible for this, namely the Carmathian rebellion, the upsurge of Buwayhid power, and that of the Fatimids; to the good fortune of Islam, their nefarious effect countered by the onset of Seljuk power.

In 900, the Carmathian rebellion broke out in Arabia. Operating from their base in the Kufa region, the Carmathians proclaimed the suspension of the *shari'a* (the sacred law of Islam), and gathered around them the peasants of southern Iraq and the tribes of the nearby desert.[15] From their new base in the Hasa, the Carmathians conducted repeated raids on Iraq, Syria, and in 904 invaded the Yemen and plundered Zabid, and between 911 and 915, a short lived Carmathian regime was established in Sana'a.[16] The Carmathian movement, Hitti insists, developed into a most malicious growth in the body politics of Islam, and to shed

---

[10] See Ibn al-Athir: *Kamil*; op cit; vol viii. J. D. Breckenridge: The Two Sicilies; in *Islam and the Medieval West*; S. Ferber Ed; op cit; pp. 39-59; at pp. 46-7. Rodrigo de Zayas: *Les Morisques et le racisme d'etat*; ed., Les Voies du Sud; Paris, 1992; p. 173. Ibn al-Idhari: *Al-Bayan al-Mughrib*; ed., A. Huici Miranda; Tetuan; 1963; pp. 381-5.

[11] Ibn al-Athir: *Kamil*; op cit; X; p. 186.

[12] Ibid; p. 256.

[13] C. Hillenbrand: *The Crusades, Islamic Perspectives*, Edinburgh University Press; 1999; p. 31.

[14] Ibid, p. 33.

[15] K. Salibi: *A History of Arabia*; Caravan; New York; 1980; p. 103.

[16] Ibid

the blood of their opponents, even if Muslims, the Carmathians considered legitimate.[17] Between the 10th and 11th centuries, the Carmathians kept Syria and Iraq drenched in blood.[18] Al-Tabari was contemporary with these events, and devotes considerable amounts of attention to this blood drenched era of Islamic history.[19] He narrates some of their many attacks on caravans including the massacres of pilgrims on their way to Makkah.[20] The Carmathian state fell subsequently, but its doctrine was passed on to the Fatimids of Egypt, and from one of them was to erupt the Ismaili or Assassin movement.[21] The Ismailis would play a crucial role during the crusades.

The early years of the 10th century were also marked by a succession of riots and military power struggles especially in the capital Baghdad, seat of the caliphate. One caliph was assassinated; the next was blinded by his own troops, who plundered his palace.[22] This came in 913, when western Persia was invaded by the Daylamites, a horde originating in the mountains at the southern end of the Caspian Sea.[23] They were extremely hostile to the Abbasid Caliph, and under their tribal chiefs, the Buwaihids, they occupied the whole of west Persia, establishing their capital in Shiraz.[24] In 945, Ahmed ibn Buwaih, whose father had claimed descent from the ancient Persian Sasanid kings,[25] marched out of Shiraz and occupied Baghdad unopposed. The Caliph Mustakil was obliged to recognise his authority and to bestow on him the honorific title of Muizz al-Dawlah (he who makes the state mighty.)[26] This was deemed not satisfactory, and on the fortieth day, Muizz al-Dawlah insisted that his name be mentioned in the Friday *khutba* (sermon), and his name stamped on the coinage.[27] The Buwaihids now roamed through the land at great will, and asserted their power forcefully. On 29 January, 946, at the audience of the ambassadors of Khurasan, and in front of a large crowd, the caliph was dragged from his throne to a dungeon, through the streets of his own capital beneath the blows and jeers of troops.[28] His palace was pillaged, and his eyes were put out. Throughout their century of supremacy (945-1055), the Buwaihids made and unmade caliphs at will.[29]

---

[17] P.K. Hitti: *History*; op cit; p. 445.
[18] *The History of al-Tabari (Tarikh al-rusul wa'l muluk;)* State University of New York Press; 1997; vol XXXVIII; (tr. F. Rosenthal) esp. pp. 81 ff.
[19] Ibid.
[20] Ibid.
[21] P.K. Hitti: *History*; op cit; p. 446.
[22] *The History of Al-Tabari*; op cit; vol xxxviii; pp. 190-1.
[23] P.K. Hitti: *History*; op cit; p. 470.
[24] E. Gibbon: *The Decline and Fall*; op cit; p. 54.
[25] Ibn Khallikan: *Wafayat al-Ayan wa-Anba Abna al-Zaman*, Biographical Dictionary, tr., M. De Slane Duprat, Paris and Allen & Co., London, 1843; vol 1; p. 98.
[26] J. Glubb: *A Short History*; op cit; p. 120.
[27] Ibn al-Athir: *Kamil*; op cit; vol viiii; p. 337.
[28] E. Gibbon: *The Decline and Fall*; p. 56; J. Glubb: *A Short History*; op cit; p. 120.
[29] P.K. Hitti: *History*; op cit; p. 471.

Meanwhile, in 1029, coming from the steppes, there appeared a tribe of Turkmen, the Ghuzz, who settled in the Bukhara region, where they embraced Sunni Islam.[30] Defeated by the Ghaznavid army, they did not return to the steppes, but dispersed into small groups, and continued to migrate west. The chiefs of the Ghuzz were members of the Turkish Seljuk family. A grandson of Seljuk, Tughril, marched west with his brother as far as Khurasan, and in 1037, the two brothers wrested Merw and Nishapur from the Ghaznavids, before quickly subduing Balkh, Jurjan, Tabaristan and Khwarizm, Hamadan, Ray and Ispahan.[31] This meant that a great part of eastern Islam had fallen under Turkish sway. Under Tughril's rule, this large territory was now well administered 'and the same hands which had been imbrued in blood became the guardians of justice and the public peace,' says Gibbon.[32]

In 1044, Caliph Qaim wrote to Tughril Beg, who was in Ray, to mediate between him and the Buwaihid prince of Baghdad.[33] It took some time, it would seem, but on December 18, 1055, Tughril Beg at the head of his armies stood at the gate of Baghdad.[34] Tughril was received by the Caliph with elaborate ceremonies, and was hailed as 'King of the East and of the West.'[35] For good reasons as Tughril had just restored the tottering power and status of the caliphate, threatened from all sides, most particularly by rising Fatimid power. However, taking advantage of Tughril's temporary absence from Baghdad on an expedition to the north, Al-Basari, the general in command under the Buwaihids, a supporter of the Fatimids, at the head of his Daylamite troops, forced Caliph al-Qaim to sign a document renouncing his right and the rights of all other Abbasids in favour of the Fatimids in Cairo, to whom he sent the emblems of the caliphate.[36] On his return, however, Tughril reinstated al-Qaim, and had al-Basari executed (1060). The Daylamite troops were disbanded and Buwaihid power was for ever crushed.[37]

The advent of the Seljuk Turks ushered a new and notable era in the history of Islam, Hitti notes.[38] When they first appeared from the east in the early part of the 11th century, the caliph's power did not stretch beyond his palace, and the Islamic land had been almost entirely dismembered. Such were the divisions, wars, each local prince 'waiting for an opportunity to fly at the throat of the other,' political and military anarchy prevailing everywhere, Shi'ite-Sunni conflict the order of the day, 'Islam seemed crushed,' says Hitti.[39]

---

[30] Ibid; p. 474.
[31] Ibid.
[32] E. Gibbon: *The Decline and Fall*; op cit; p. 232.
[33] J. Glubb: *A Short History*; op cit; p. 129.
[34] P.K. Hitti: *History*; op cit; p. 474.
[35] Ibn al-Athir: *Kamil*; op cit; vol ix; p. 436.
[36] P.K. Hitti: *History*; op cit; p. 474.
[37] Ibid; p. 475.
[38] Ibid; 473.
[39] Ibid.

"At the time of their appearance, Lane Poole says, 'the Empire of the Caliphate had vanished.' What had once been a realm united under a sole Muslim ruler was now a collection of scattered dynasties, not one of which was capable of imperial sway.[40]

> The prevalence of schism increased the disunion of the various provinces of the vanished empire. A drastic remedy was needed, and it was found in the invasion of the Turks. These rude nomads, un-spoilt by town life and civilized indifference to religion, embraced Islam with all the fervor of their uncouth souls. They came to the rescue of a dying State, and revived it. They swarmed over Persia, Mesopotamia, Syria, and Asia Minor, devastating the country, and exterminating every dynasty that existed there; and, as the result, they once more reunited Mohammedan Asia, from the western frontier of Afghanistan to the Mediterranean, under one sovereign; they put a new life into the expiring zeal of the Moslems, drove back the re-encroaching Byzantines, and bred up a generation of fanatical Mohammedan warriors to whom, more than to anything else, the Crusaders owed their repeated failure.[41]

Contemporary with the Seljuks were the Fatimids, who also played a central part in the history of the crusades. The Fatimid rise to power, Breckenbridge notes, did not just cause a major shift in the distribution of power in the 11th century, it laid seeds of changes within the Islamic world itself.[42] Nearly two centuries before their rise, when the Aghlabids of Tunisia took Sicily (in 827) the Muslim world was remarkably unified 'a chain of watchtowers along the North African coast could flash news from Alexandria to Gibraltar in a single day;' this was no longer the situation.[43] In 910 the Fatimids expelled the Aghlabids from Tunis.[44] The Aghlabids were the power in the Maghrib that then kept the Mediterranean in safe Muslim hands.[45] The Aghlabids were also the sponsors and promoters of the greatest civilisation that North Africa ever experienced.[46] Thus, by destroying the Aghlabids, and also meddling in Muslim Sicilian affairs, the Fatimids not only weakened the Maghrib, they also sowed the seeds of divisions which eventually undid the Muslim world. In 961, under their General Gawhar, a Sicilian Christian in origin, the Fatimids conquered Egypt; and in 969 moved their capital to Cairo.[47] A year later, they established control in Damascus, thus splitting the

---

[40] S. Lane Poole: *The Life of Saladin and the Fall of the Kingdom of Jerusalem*; J.P. Putnam's Sons, London, 1898, p. 10.

[41] Ibid.

[42] J. D. Breckenridge: The Two Sicilies; op cit; p. 45.

[43] Ibid. 35

[44] Ibn al-Idhari: *Al-Bayan al-Maghrib fi Akhbar al-Maghrib;* ed., R. Dozy; Leyden; 1848; vol 1; pp. 142-6.

[45] G. Iver: Kairawan; *Encyclopaedia of Islam*; first series; vol 4; pp. 646-9. H. Djait et al., *Histoire de la Tunisie* (le Moyen Age); Societe Tunisienne de Difusion, Tunis)

[46] See, for instance: H.H. Abd al-Wahab, '*Bait al-Hikma al-Tunusi, Baht Tarikhi fi Awwal Musasa Ilmiya jamia fi al-Bilad al-Ifriqiya,*" Majallat Majma al-Lugha al-Arabiya (Cairo) 30 (1963-4). H. Saladin: *Tunis et Kairouan;* Librairie Renouard; Paris; 1908.

[47] J. D. Breckenridge: The Two Sicilies; op cit.

Muslim world thoroughly. This gave rise to the greatest schism in Islamic history, and the eventual collapse of Muslim power.

2. 11ᵗʰ Century Disintegration

Precisely when the Spanish Christians and their French allies advanced deep into Islamic Spain to begin the `Reconquista' (from the middle 11ᵗʰ century onwards), Norman adventurers conquered Sicily, whilst Genoese and Pisan allies eliminated the Muslims from Sardinia and Corsica, and the first Crusaders began the conquest of Palestine and Syria.[48] This united Christian front reflects their awareness of that which undermined the Muslim world, and that it was their opportunity to crush the Muslim foe.

In Spain, Al-Mansur, at his death (1002), was succeeded by his son who ruled for six years before the Peninsula entered a period of chaos. As civil war erupted throughout the territory, Cordoba was burned down in 1018.[49] Muslim Spain disintegrated into the era of the 'party kings' (*reyes de taifas, muluk at-tawa'if*) (1009-1091), with thirty more or less independent rulers.[50] Intrigues and civil war soon invited northern Christian invasions.[51]

Throughout the rest of the Muslim world, the Fatimid rise became synonymous with decay and collapse. In North Africa, around 1051, and for years after, the Fatimids, in revenge against their former Zirid allies who had abandoned their cause, unleashed the Banu Hilal onto the region. In wave after wave, the invaders, followed by their families and herds, swept over Cyrenaica and Tripolitania into southern Tunisia, drawing others behind them, pilfering, burning, and destroying everything on their way.[52] The invaders spread havoc, the towns and cities were burnt down; the countryside was devastated; the whole of Ifriqya was turned into a vast empty, arid zone.[53] Much worse, the power and unity of the Maghrib were so shattered the region had now become unable to face Christian attacks.

The Fatimids had an equal role in the collapse of Muslim rule in Sicily. This began in 1061, with open warfare between the Kalbid Emir of Palermo and the Zirids of Tunisia.[54] The initial Norman invasion followed a local Muslim invitation,[55] and

---

[48] A.R. Lewis: The Moslem Expansion in the Mediterranean, op cit; p. 39.
[49] W. Durant: *The Age of Faith*, op cit; chap 13; p. 296.
[50] For the various principalities, their rulers, etc, see: Ibn Khaldun: *Kitab al-Ibar*; Edition Bulaq; 1868; vol iv; pp. 160-1.
-Al-Maqqari: *Nafh Al-Tib;* part tr., by P. De Gayangos: *The History of the Mohammedan Dynasties in Spain;* 2 vols; The Oriental Translation Fund; London, 1840-3; vol I; p. 288; Ibn al-Athir: *Kamil;* op cit; vol ix; pp. 203-4.
[51] J.J. Saunders: *Aspects of the Crusades*, University of Canterbury, 1962; p. 19.
[52] S and N. Ronart: *Concise Encyclopaedia of Arabic Civilization; The Arab West;* Djambatan; Amsterdam; 1966; p. 398.
[53] H. Saladin: *Tunis et Kairouan;* op cit; p. 107.
[54] See Ibn al-Athir: *Kamil;* op cit; vol viii.

under these auspices the Normans landed in Sicily in 1061 and began to advance at the expense of the Muslims.[56] The Normans who swept across South Italy and Sicily were a small band, but thanks to Muslim divisions, they were able to take hold of much territory.[57] When Bari fell, the final assault on the capital, Palermo, began, and in January 1072 it surrendered.[58] Less than twenty years later the Normans controlled the whole of Sicily. Following an initial period of co-existence, there began in the middle of the 12th century the persecution and mass elimination of Muslims on the Island.[59]

The Fatimid Caliph al-Hakem (996-1021), established in Egypt, went half mad with wealth and power so much so as to proclaim himself God; sending missionaries to establish his cult among the people.[60] As his emissaries were killed by the Egyptian population, he took Christians and Jews in favour, and persecuted Sunni Muslims before he was assassinated at the age of thirty six.[61] Another Fatimid ruler, Mustansir (ruled 1036-94) built for himself a pleasure pavilion, and lived a life of music, wine, and ease.[62] An inventory of his treasures by al-Makrizi includes precious stones, crystal vases, inlaid gold plates, parasols with gold and silver sticks, chess boards with gold and silver pawns, jeweled daggers and swords.[63] Yet this same caliph found it necessary in 1070 to send his daughters and their mother to Baghdad to escape starvation.[64] The Caliphs of Fatimid Egypt would openly side with the crusaders, as we shall see.

Further East, and yet again related to Fatimid upsurge and ideology, there erupted the Assassin movement, a break away Ismaili group formed in Iran.[65] In 1090 an Ismaili leader, Hassan ibn al-Sabbah (d. 1124), seized the fortress of Alamut in the Elburz Mountains of northern Persia.[66] Strategically situated on an extension of the Elburz Mountains, 10,200 feet above sea level, this eagle nest gave Ibn al-Sabbah and his successors a central stronghold of primary importance.[67] The Ismailis took by ruse or bribery a number of other mountain citadels in Syria,[68] eight of which

[55] M.L. de Mas Latrie: *Traites de Paix et de Commerce, et Documents Divers, Concernant les Relations des Chretiens avec les Arabes de l'Afrique Septentrionale au Moyen Age*, Burt Franklin, New York, originally Published in Paris, 1866; p. 42.
N. Daniel: *The Arabs and Medieval Europe*; Longman Librairie du Liban; 1975; p. 144.
[56] J. Glubb: *A Short History*; op cit; p. 148.
[57] J. D. Breckenridge: The Two Sicilies; op cit, pp. 46-7.
[58] Ibid.
[59] N. Daniel: *The Arabs*; op cit; p. 145.
[60] W. Durant: *The Age of Faith*, op cit; chap 13; p. 285.
[61] Ibid.
[62] P.K. Hitti: *History*; op cit; p. 626.
[63] Al-Maqrizi: *Kitab al-Khitat*, ed., Bulaq; partial French tr. by U. Bouriant and P. Casanova, Description topographique et Historique de l'Egypte, Paris, 1895-1900; vol I; pp. 414 ff. see also Ibn Taghri Birdi: *Al-Nujum al-Zahirah fi Muluk Misr wa'l Qahira*; ed., T.G.J. Juynboll; vol 2; Leyden; 1855; vol ii; pt. 2; pp. 181-2.
[64] P.K. Hitti: *History*; op cit; p. 626.
[65] See Ibn al-Athir: *Kamil*; op cit; vols ix and x.
[66] J.J. Saunders: *Aspects of the Crusades*; op cit. p. 25.
[67] P.K. Hitti: *History*; op cit; p. 446.
[68] Ibn Battuta: *Voyages d'Ibn Battuta*, Arabic text accompanied by French translation by C. Defremery and B.R. Sanguinetti, preface and notes by V Monteil, I-IV, Paris, 1968, reprint of the 1854 ed., vol I; p. 166.

9

they retained until towards the end of the crusades, two centuries later (when Baybars re-took them from them in 1270-3.)[69] From those fortresses, and during the two centuries of the crusades (1095-1291), the Ismaili Assassins launched a campaign of systematic murder of Islamic leadership that was unparalleled in history.[70] The Ismaili policy, Hillenbrand notes, was to murder prominent Muslim political and religious figures,[71] the impact of which was to ease considerably the task of the Christians. Only three years before the crusades, and in the space of less than two years, beginning in 1092, there was a clean sweep of all the major political leaders of the Muslim world from Egypt eastwards.[72] In 1092 the greatest figure of Seljuk history, Nizam al-Mulk,[73] de facto the ruler of the Seljuk empire for over thirty years, was murdered by the Ismailis.[74] Founder of the madrasa system, he had recommended religious rightness in people and ruler, considering no government secure without a religious base.[75] A month after Nizam, Malik Shah, the third Seljuk sultan, died in suspicious circumstances after a successful twenty year reign, his death followed closely by that of his wife, grandson and other powerful political figures.[76]

Leaderless, the Muslim East was ridden with internal strife. The two sons of Malik Shah, Barkyaruk and Mohammed were locked in a conflict, which consumed all military resources throughout the East.[77] The two brothers, rulers of Aleppo (Ridwan) and Damascus (Duqaq) were at war with each other, and their hostilities formed the central event of their reigns.[78] 11th century Syria, Lamonte notes, was 'a crazy quilt of semi independent states,' resulting from previous divisions of it made by the Byzantines and the Fatimid Caliphate of Cairo.[79] The Muslim world was, thus, in no position to fend off the attacks from Western Europe, which were about to occur.[80] The timing of the crusades, Hillenbrand notes, simply could not have been more propitious: 'Had the Europeans somehow been briefed that this was the perfect moment to pounce? Unfortunately there is little evidence on this in the Islamic sources, but seldom had the arm of coincidence been longer.'[81]

> A lucky star led the preachers of the First Crusade to seize an opportunity of which they hardly realized the significance. Peter the Hermit and Urban II chose the auspicious moment with a sagacity as unerring as if they had made a profound study of Asiatic politics. The Crusades penetrated like a

---

[69] Al-Maqrizi: *Kitab al-Suluk;* tr. R.J. C. Broadhurst as *History of Ayyubids and Mamluks;* Boston; 1980; p. 60.

[70] J.J. Saunders: *Aspects of the Crusades*; p cit, p. 25.

[71] C. Hillenbrand: *The Crusades*; op cit; p. 76.

[72] Ibid, p. 18.

[73] Ibn Khallikan: W*afayat al-Ayan*, (De Slane); op cit; vol I; p. 255.

[74] Ibid; p. 256.

[75] W. Durant: *The Age of Faith*, op cit; Chapter XIV; p. 309.

[76] C. Hillenbrand: *The Crusades*; op cit; p. 33.

[77] Ibid, p. 38.

[78] P.K. Hitti: *History*; op cit; p. 635.

[79] J.H. Lamonte: Crusade and Jihad: in *The Arab Heritage*, N.A. Faris editor; Princeton University Press, 1944; pp. 159-98; at p.163.

[80] C. Hillenbrand: *The Crusades;* op cit; p. 18.

[81] Ibid, p. 33.

wedge between the old wood and the new, and for a while seemed to cleave the trunk of Mohammedan empire into splinters [says Lane Poole.][82]

It was at Clermont in France that in 1095 Pope Urban II (Pope 1088-1099) made his call for the crusades. In his call to rally the Christians, he said:

> It is urgent for you to bring hastily to your brothers in the Orient the help so often promised and that is of pressing necessity. The Turks and the Arabs have attacked them...., and penetrating always further inside Christian countries, have on seven occasions beaten them in battle, and have killed and taken captive a great number, and have destroyed churches and devastated the kingdom.[83]

The pope, thus, used Muslim 'aggression' as an excuse for military invasion. However it was what has been seen, and also what is now to be seen, that were the true causes for the crusades.

3. At the Sources of the Crusades

At the main source of the crusades were the divisions of the Eastern and Western Churches, the divisions and conflicts within the Western Church itself, and the latter's conflict with Empire.

The two Churches of the East and West have been divided for centuries over doctrinal and other issues. These divisions, although little cited today, still remain as strong as ever. Some of these divisions concern the sacrament in the Greek rite, celebrated behind the iconostasis, the screen or wall separating the sanctuary from the body of the church, whilst the Roman Mass was a dramatic conjunction of priest and people.[84] In the 9th century (867) Photius (Patriarch of Constantinople 810-890) and the Emperor of Byzantium called a Church Council, which excommunicated the Pope and denounced the 'heresies' of the Roman Church- among them the procession of the Holy Ghost from the Father and the Son, the shaving of priestly beards, and the enforced celibacy of the clergy; 'from this usage,' said Photius, 'we see in the West so many children who do not know their fathers.'[85] For the Byzantines, the pope although an important personage of the Church could not claim to be God's representative on earth and to impose doctrine.[86]

These divisions grew worse following the schism between the two churches in 1054. But when the Seljuks threatened to overrun the Asiatic possessions of Byzantium, especially following the Seljuk victory at Manzilkert (in 1071), the Byzantine Emperor Alexius Comnenus appealed to Pope Urban II for help.[87]

---

[82] S. Lane Poole: *The Life of Saladin and the Fall of the Kingdom of Jerusalem*, J.P. Putnam's Sons, London, 1898, p. 25.

[83] Discours of Pope Urban II. It is re-transcribed by Fulcher of Chartres in Regine Pernoud: *Les Hommes et la Croisade*, Jules Tallandier, Paris, 1982.

[84] D. Hay: *The Medieval Centuries*; Methuen and Co; London; 1964; p. 20.

[85] W. Durant: *The Age of Faith*, op cit; Chapter 21; p. 529.

[86] S. Runciman: *The Fall of Constantinople*; op cit; pp. 7-8

[87] P.K. Hitti: *History;* op cit; p. 636.

Urban saw in this appeal a great opportunity for reuniting Eastern and Western Churches under, of course, Catholic sway.[88]

The Western Church itself was divided principally around the issue of priestly marriage. The Church, Durant explains, had long since opposed clerical marriage on the ground that a married priest, consciously or not, would put his loyalty to wife and children above his devotion to the Church; that for their sake he might accumulate money or property; or that he would try to transmit his see or benefice to one of his offspring; that an hereditary ecclesiastical caste might in this way develop in Europe; and that the combined economic power of such a propertied priesthood would be too great for the papacy to control.[89] Thus, it was ruled that the priest should be totally devoted to God, the Church, and his fellow men.[90]

The papacy, itself, was torn from within by a series of crises and scandals. In 891, Formosus was made pope, but his German alliances, throughout his papacy, aroused bitterness towards him.[91] Stephen VI (Pope 896-897) had the dead body of Formosus taken from the grave, clothed in the papal habillements, propped up in a chair, tried before a council, and having three of the fingers of the corpse cut off before it was cast into the River Tiber.[92] Stephen himself was eventually thrown into prison and strangled.[93] In five years, from 896 to 900, five popes were consecrated. Leo V., who succeeded in 904, was in less than two months thrown into prison by Christopher, one of his chaplains, who usurped his place, and who, in turn, was soon expelled from Rome by Sergius III, who, supported by a military force, seized the pontificate in 905.[94] A period followed when popes were made and unmade at the bidding of the papal treasurer and his wife.[95] Pope Sergius III's affair with the couple's daughter resulted in the birth of a future pope John XI (Pope 931-5); and subsequently the Roman court became the scene of faction fighting.[96] John X (Pope 914-928) was suffocated; Stephen VIII died of his injuries in prison, and Benedict VI was strangled by orders of his successor.[97] The papacy was supposed to be elected by the people and clergy of Rome, but the Roman nobility with its castles and powers exerted great pressure to ensure that members of their family were given the most lucrative positions in the Roman Church.[98] Powerful groups set up rival popes, the election of Benedict IX in 1032, for instance, was followed by the election of two anti popes.[99] The Emperor's intervention only added to the problem,

---

[88] Ibid.

[89] W. Durant: *The Age of Faith*, op cit; p. 542.

[90] Ibid.

[91] O.J. Thatcher; F. Schwill: *A General History of Europe;* John Murray Publisher; London; 1919.

[92] J.W. Draper: *A History;* op cit; vol 1; p. 379.

[93] Ibid.

[94] Ibid; vol II; p. 4.

[95] V. Green: *A New History of Christianity;* Fwd Rvd Lord Runcie; Sutton Publishing; Stroud; 1996; p. 64.

[96] Ibid.

[97] Ibid.

[98] R.H.C. Davis: *A History of Medieval Europe;* op cit; pp. 226-7.

[99] R.H.C. Davis: *A History of Medieval Europe;* op cit; pp. 227; V. Green: *A New History of Christianity;* op cit; p. 65.

resulting in a protracted conflict between Pope Gregory VII and Emperor Henry IV. At a Synod in Rome (21 February 1076), the Pope launched upon the Emperor a triple sentence of excommunication, anathema, and deposition, and on the following day released Henry's subjects from their oaths of obedience.[100] Henry responded by persuading the Bishop of Utrecht to anathematise Gregory- 'The perjured monk'. All Europe was shocked by the papal deposition of an emperor, and still more by the imperial deposition and Episcopal cursing of a pope.[101] Henry IV's expulsion was, however, much worse in effect, for a ruler expelled from the Church and in danger of eternal damnation, put his own kingdom under threat.[102] Following Henry's excommunication, German nobles met in conference to discuss his deposition and ruled that if within a year he were not free of the papal excommunication he would have to forfeit his crown.[103] The dissention led to armed conflict, eventually involving the powerful Normans of Sicily.

It seemed that Western Christendom was about to be torn apart, until it was realised that the best way to quell these quarrels was to avoid referring to whatever could give them life. And so a solution was found: cooperation elsewhere could create a situation of union; and the crusades against the Muslims could be the one such way out.[104] This was precisely one of the main reasons that led Pope Urban to call for the crusades in 1095. However, to stir the Christian armies into action, the Pope concocted a number of justifications for the crusades.

Depicting Muslims as threatening foes of Christendom before launching attacks against them has remained a dominant feature of Christian-Muslim history throughout the past ten centuries or so. Fabricated Muslim crimes, or isolated incidents, have been amplified so as to justify Christian attack and killing of Muslims. The crusades (1095-1291) were launched on the same premises.

Pope Urban II's call for the crusades made in November 1095 to an assembly at the French town of Clermont fervently dwelt on 'the terrible fate of Christians in the land of the infidels.'[105] One of the five versions of his speech is by Robert the Monk (Robertus Monachus):

> An accursed race, a race utterly alienated from God, a generation forsooth which has not directed its heart and has not entrusted its spirit to God, has invaded the lands of those Christians and has depopulated them by the sword, pillage and fire; it has led away a part of the captives into its own country, and a part it has destroyed by cruel tortures; it has either entirely destroyed the churches of God or appropriated them for the rites of its own religion. They destroy the altars, after having defiled them with their

---

[100] W. Durant: *The Age of Faith*, op cit; Chapter 21; p. 549.
[101] Ibid
[102] D.J. Geanakoplos: *Medieval Western Civilisation; and the Byzantine and Islamic Worlds*, D.C. Heath and Company, Toronto, 1979; p. 220.
[103] Ibid
[104] C. Cahen: *Orient et Occident au Temps des Croisades*, Aubier Montaigne, 1983; p. 60.
[105] Extracted from D.C. Munro: The Western attitude toward Islam during the period of the Crusades; *Speculum*, vol 6 No 4, pp. 329-43; pp. 329 fwd.

uncleanness. They circumcise the Christians, and the blood of the circumcision they either spread upon the altars or pour into the vases of the baptismal font. When they wish to torture people by a base death, they perforate their navels, and dragging forth the extremity of the intestines, bind it to a stake; then with flogging they lead the victim around until the viscera having gushed forth the victim falls prostrate upon the ground. Others they bind to a post and pierce with arrows. Others they compel to extend their necks and then, attacking them with naked swords, attempt to cut through the neck with a single blow. What shall I say of the abominable rape of the women? To speak of it is worse than to be silent.... Accordingly undertake this journey for the remission of your sins, with the assurance of the imperishable glory of the kingdom of heaven.[106]

Thus, according to Pope Urban, oncoming Christian armed response was in self-defence, a response to the dangers of extermination facing Christians. 'For the whole European community, it seemed a case of kill or be killed,'[107] Daniel remarks. The pope's exhortation was relayed and spread by priests and prelates who, Finucane says, exercised all the tricks of the orator's trade, 'cajoling, threatening, promising; using allegory, hyperbole, anaphora; rousing with revenge motifs.'[108] Hence, Balderic (Baldricus), archbishop of Dol says:

We have heard, most beloved brethren, and you have heard what we cannot recount without deep sorrow how, with great hurt and dire sufferings our Christian brothers, members in Christ, are scourged, oppressed, and injured in Jerusalem, in Antioch, and the other cities of the East..... Base and bastard Turks hold sway over our brothers.[109]

The Turks, according to Fulcher of Chartres:

Have killed and captured many, have destroyed the churches and devastated the Kingdom of God.[110]

'All atrocities,' which, as Munro observes, were 'highly spiced to suit the spirit of the time, and influence the Christians to take up arms, inciting many to take the Cross and flock to the Holy Land for revenge.'[111]

In truth, there were no Turkish atrocities and defilements of the Holy Sites; and far from being in danger of extermination the Christians were free to practice their faith and keep property and wealth, hardly disturbed by Muslims. Christians (like Jews) also occupied many positions of high status and power within the Islamic realm, and from the earliest times. Caliph Al-Mutasim (833-842), for instance, had

---

[106] In D. C. Munro, "Urban and the Crusaders", Translations and Reprints from the *Original Sources of European History*, vol 1:2, 1895, pp. 5-8.
[107] N. Daniel: *The Cultural Barrier*, Edinburgh University Press, 1975; p. 158.
[108] R. Finucane: *Soldiers of the Faith*; J.M. Dent and Sons Ltd; London, 1983; p. 30.
[109] In A.C. Krey, *The First Crusade: The Accounts of Eyewitnesses and Participants*, Princeton University Press; 1921; pp. 33-36.
[110] D.C. Munro: The Western attitude; op cit; at p. 329.
[111] Ibid.

two Christian ministers, one of whom was for finances.[112] In 1047 the Muslim traveller Nasir-i-Khosru saw Christians practicing freely their faith, and described the Church of the Holy Sepulchre as 'a most spacious building, capable of holding 8000 persons, and built with the utmost skill. The church interior is everywhere adorned with Byzantine brocade, worked in gold.'[113] This was but one of many Christian churches in Jerusalem, and Christian pilgrims had free access to the holy places.[114] In fact, the destruction of the Church of the Resurrection in Jerusalem in 1009, which the Pope used as the instance of Muslim desecration of Christian sites, was the work of the Fatimid king (Al-Hakem) (born in 985), gone mad; and the paradox, as Finucane notes, was that the king's chief secretary who drew up the document of destruction of the Church was a Christian, just like his vizier who signed it.[115] And even more importantly, this Fatimid ruler had put to death many of the respectable Muslim Sunnis.[116]

In truth, indeed, the Church's overriding ambition was to destroy the Muslim creed, to annihilate Islam.[117] The final decades of the 11th century offered the best conditions for this. Ibn al-Athir correctly assessed the situation:

> The power of the Franks first became apparent when in the year 478H/1085-86 they invaded the territories of Islam and took Toledo and other parts of Andalusia, as was mentioned earlier. Then they attacked and conquered the island of Sicily and turned their attention to North Africa, where they wrested from the Muslims certain parts, which were won back again, but they had other successes as you will see.[118]

Equally Saunders notes how the first crusade was launched in an atmosphere of intense religious emotion, and was conceived as a part of a grand counter offensive against Islam which was already being conducted on two fronts, in Spain and across the central Mediterranean towards North Africa.[119]

Whilst ridding itself of the traditional foe, the Church, by the means of the crusades could secure unity between the Greek and Latin Churches, and unity within Western Christendom itself. The schism between the Latin and Greek Churches (already referred to) had been steadily widening, and the Papacy sought to restore such lost unity.[120] Common interest and old association might be pleaded. 'Christianity,' as Stevenson also points out, 'was a bond of union, for the enemy were the Muslims.'[121] It was all the more an ideal opportunity, for the Byzantine

---

[112] T.W. Arnold: *The Preaching of Islam*. A History of the Propagation of the Muslim faith, Archibald Constable, Westminster, 1896 in Y. Courbage, P. Fargues: *Chretiens et Juifs*; op cit; p. 53.

[113] G. Le Strange: *Palestine under the Moslems*; Alexander P. Watt; London; 1890; p. 202.

[114] W. Durant; *The Age of Faith*; op cit; p. 585.

[115] R. Finucane: *Soldiers of the Faith*; op cit p. 155.

[116] C.R. Conder: *The Latin Kingdom of Jerusalem*; The Committee of the Palestine Exploration Fund; London; 1897; p. 231.

[117] C. Bennett: *Victorian Images of Islam*; Grey Seal; London; 1992; p. 6.

[118] Ibn Al-Athir: *Kamil*; op cit; X; p. 185.

[119] J.J. Saunders: *A History of Medieval Islam*; Routledge; London; 1965; p. 158.

[120] J.J. Saunders: *Aspects of the Crusades*; op cit; p. 20.

[121] W.B. Stevenson: *The Crusaders*; op cit; p. 6.

Emperor sought the help of the Western brethren to gain security from the Seljuk Turks, whilst the pope's aim was to gain the Eastern Church. The references in Urban's speech to 'the Churches of the East do hint that a grand reunion of the Christian body was envisaged as a consequence of the defeat of the Muslim 'infidel.'[122]

Pope Urban also sought unity amongst Western Christians in his own realm, and stressed the ideological aims of the crusade: peace among Christians and death to the enemies of the faith.[123] Peace that would mean that local feudal internal wars were now repressed, and men's military ardour was diverted to the crusades.[124] Perhaps most pressing of all, Brundage points out:

> There was the history of the past twenty years in Europe, the record of a consuming internecine strife between Empire and papacy. Would not a successful military venture in the East under papal auspices and papal leadership, tend to bolster papal prestige and power against the Western enemies of the papacy?[125]

The challenge to Christendom to forget its private feuds in one great effort for God and Christ, this skilful allusion to the glories of the old Frankish race produced an immediate result. As the voice of the Pope died away there went up one cry from the assembled host:

'Deus Vult! Deus Vult! Deus Vult! (God wills it!) (God wills it!)[126]

A vivid picture of the immense fervour of the next few months has been preserved. In the highways and the cross-roads men would talk of nothing else; layman and priest alike took up the cry and urged their fellows to start for Jerusalem.[127]

Crusader enthusiasm was further enhanced by the promise of remission of sins for the participants. In the words of Urban II:

> ... To all those who will depart and die on route, whether by land or sea, or lose their life in fighting the pagans, the forgiveness of their sins will be granted. And this I grant to those who participate to this voyage in accordance with the authority that I hold from God.[128]

'When the pope himself promised the crusaders full remission of sins and an increase of eternal salvation, for example (the words of Innocent III at the fourth Lateran Council, 1215),' Finucane notes, 'this filtered down to the ordinary man in the crowd as a promise of instant heaven, if he died on the crusade-or while travelling to the Holy Land. Everyone, whatever his evil past, might therefore

---

[122] J.J. Saunders: *Aspects of the Crusades*; op cit; p. 20.

[123] J.H. Lamonte: *Crusade and Jihad* in N.A. Faris ed., *The Arab Heritage*, Princeton University Press, 1944; pp. 159-98; p. 161.

[124] W. Durant: *The Age of Faith*, op cit; p. 829.

[125] J.A. Brundage: *The Crusades*; The Marquette University Press; 1962; p. 6.

[126] T.A. Archer: *The Crusades* T. Fisher Unwin; London; 1894; p. 31.

[127] Ibid; p. 34.

[128] A. Bouamama: l'Idee de croisade dans le monde Arabe hier et aujourd'hui, in *De Toulouse a Tripoli*, AMAM, Colloque held between 6 and 8 December, 1995, University of Toulouse; 1997; pp. 211-9; at p. 212.

wipe the slate clean and perhaps even qualify for martyrdom. It was, indeed, a new form of salvation.'[129]

Pope Urban had promised 'eternal wealth,' but had also argued that the 'wealth of the Orient' contrasted with the 'poverty of the Western world.'[130] The powerful trading cities of Pisa, Genoa, Venice, and Amalfi also had great plans to extend their rising commercial power and capture Islamic wealth for themselves. Once the Normans captured Sicily from the Muslims (1062-1091), and Muslim rule was partly broken in Spain (1085 ff.), the western Mediterranean was freed for Christian trade; the Italian cities grew richer and stronger, and planned to end Muslim ascendancy in the eastern Mediterranean, and open the markets of the Near East to Western European goods.[131] 'We do not know how close these Italian merchants were to the ear of the Pope,' Durant notes,[132] 'but it is difficult to imagine the contrary,' for subsequently a great partnership developed on the ground. In return for trading privileges in the towns and cities that would be captured by the Christians, the Italian merchant cities gave the crusaders their firm support, and the role they were to play in the capture of the sea-port towns was to be of vital importance.[133] Without them, Stevenson points out, Syria could neither have been conquered nor held for a single year.[134]

The Church's sanctification of the crusading idea is undeniable and the Papacy's wealth and power were, indeed, greatly enhanced by its support.[135] Eventually, following the Christians' conquests, the Church would grow immensely rich as countless towns and villages in Palestine and Syria, their trades, farms, and riches became its property.[136]

The leaders of the crusades, themselves, had great dreams of making fortunes in the East. Godfrey of Bouillon, one of the principal leaders, was accompanied by a brother, Baldwin, and Bohemond, another leader, by a nephew, Tancred, who hoped to make their fortunes overseas.[137]

'Instead of fratricidal war in Christendom, and the ruin of Christian trade,' Conder remarks, 'a new ambition was offered to Bohemond by Peter the Hermit and the Pope: an Asiatic principality, to be won with the sword.'[138]

Raymond of St. Gilles, the third most important leader, likewise, had an eye for the fair lands of Syria.[139] As Stevenson notes:

---

[129] R.C. Finucane: *Soldiers of the Faith*; op cit; p. 36. On indulgences, see Robert Somerville: The Council of Clermont and the First Crusade,' *Studia Gratiana* XX, (1976); p. 329.

[130] R. Pernoud: *Les Hommes de la Croisade*, op cit; in Y. Courbage, P. Fargues: *Chretiens et Juifs dans l'Islam Arabe et Turc*, Payot, Paris, 1997; p. 85.

[131] W. Durant: *The Age of Faith*, op cit; p. 586.

[132] Ibid.

[133] W.B. Stevenson: *The Crusaders*; op cit; pp. 5-6.

[134] Ibid.

[135] C. Bennett: Victorian Images of Islam; op cit; p. 6.

[136] Regesta, No 420-425; see Quarterly Statement, Palestine Exploration Fund; January, 1890. There are fifty documents in the Cartulary of the Holy Sepulchre, referring to property in Palestine and in Europe. Plus see: C.R. Conder: *The Latin;* op cit; pp. 194 fwd.

[137] D. Hay: *The Medieval*; op cit; p. 91.

[138] C.R. Conder: *The Latin Kingdom*; op cit; p. 17.

The aim of the leaders stamps its character on the crusades. Effectively it was an enterprise for the conquest and partition of Syria. Only in this light can we understand the history of the invasion.[140]

The same incentives held for the masses. The depressed condition and perhaps, almost hopeless misery, made it a relief for most to leave their homes, and not a sacrifice, also notes Stevenson.[141] The crusade offered a way of escape from starvation and oppression, and 'promised temporal as well as spiritual blessing,' he adds.[142] All in all, as Durant sums up:

> Extraordinary inducements brought multitudes to the standard. A plenary indulgence remitting all punishments due to sin was offered to those who should fall in the war. Serfs were allowed to leave the soil to which they had been bound; citizens were exempted from taxes; debtors enjoyed a moratorium on interest; prisoners were freed, and sentences of death were commuted, by a-bold extension of papal authority, to life service in Palestine. Thousands of vagrants joined in the sacred tramp. Men tired of hopeless poverty, adventurers ready for brave enterprise, younger sons hoping to carve out fiefs for themselves in the East, merchants seeking new markets for their goods, knights whose enlisting serfs had left them labourless, timid spirits shunning taunts of cowardice, joined with sincerely religious souls to rescue the land of Christ's birth and death. Propaganda of the kind customary in war stressed the disabilities of Christians in Palestine, the atrocities of Moslems, the blasphemies of the Mohammedan creed; Moslems were described as worshiping a statue of Mohammed... Fabulous tales were told of Oriental wealth and of dark beauties waiting to be taken by brave men. Such a variety of motives could hardly assemble a homogeneous mass capable of military organization. In many cases women and children insisted upon accompanying their husbands or parents, perhaps with reason, for prostitutes soon enlisted to serve the warriors.[143]

Neither were the most desperate robbers, murderers, and violent men to be denied 'a share in the holy work-room for repentance and for good services.'[144] Even the animal world joined the crusades, and as leaders (like the inspired goose and the perspicacious goat).[145]

This was the force, in the hundreds of thousands, setting off from Europe in the years 1095-96, and descending on the Muslim world.

---

[139] J.H. Lamonte: *Crusade and Jihad*; op cit; p. 162.
[140] W.B. Stevenson: *The Crusaders;* op cit; pp. 10-11.
[141] Ibid; p. 5.
[142] Ibid.
[143] W. Durant: *The Age of Faith*; op cit; pp. 588-9.
[144] C.R. Conder: *The Latin Kingdom;* op cit; p. 25.
[145] R. Finucane: *Soldiers of the Faith*; op cit. p. 117.

IMAD EDDIN ZANGI

Following Urban's speech (in 1095) from throughout Europe there descended on the Islamic East hordes of armed men; knights and peasants, vagrants, murderers and priests, noble women and prostitutes; 'a big army and workmen of all sorts, thousands and tens of thousands without end.'[146]

The van of the crusades consisted of two hundred and seventy five thousand men, accompanied by eight horses, and preceded by a goat and a goose, 'into which someone had told them that the Holy Ghost had entered,' says Draper.[147] This people's army, Oldenbourg describes, was

> Made up of wretches who had nothing more to lose, fanatics resolved to risk everything, voluntary martyrs, marauders, repentant sinners and adventurers of all descriptions, and even of secular saints motivated by simple charity, marched under the banner of miracles, putting their whole trust in the God whose emblem they wore sewn on their garments. The heavenly and the earthly Jerusalem were so thoroughly confused in their minds that they apparently understood the pope's appeal to mean that paradise could be seized on earth by force.[148]

Disappointment and famine drove the hordes to madness, adds Draper, and 'in their ignorance, that every town they came to must be Jerusalem- in their extremity they laid hands on whatever they could. Their track was marked by robbery, bloodshed, and fire.'[149] In Byzantium, their xenophobic, violent, behaviour made Emperor Alexius only too happy to be rid of them; 'such a rabble at the gates of Constantinople was not a pleasant prospect.'[150] Once reaching Muslim territory, in October (1096), the crusaders were met at Nicea by the Seljuk Turks under Kilij Arslan, who drew this army into an ambush, and then slaughtered them on the seashore so decisively that barely three thousand-one man for every hundred who set out-'escaped to tell the tale.'[151] Their bones piled into mounds outside Nicea, and may have been used by a later wave of crusaders to build part of a fortification.[152] A contemporary said: The 'bodies of all the warriors who had been slain, which lay around, were brought together, they made, I will not call it a great heap nor yet a mound, nor even a hill, but as it were a high mountain of considerable size.'[153]

---

[146] The First and second Crusades from an Anonymous Syriac Chronicle; tr., by A.S. Tritton; with notes by H.A.R. Gibb; *Journal of the Royal Asiatic Society (JRAS)* 1933; pp. 69-101; at p. 69.

[147] J.W. Draper: *A History*; vol ii; op cit; pp. 22-3.

[148] Z. Oldenbourg: *The Crusade* tr., from the French by A. Carter; Weinfeld and Nicolson; London; 1965; p. 50.

[149] J.W. Draper: *A History*; op cit; pp. 22-3.

[150] R. Finucane: *Soldiers of the Faith*; op cit; p. 21.

[151] C.R. Conder: *The Latin Kingdom of Jerusalem*; op cit; p. 26.

[152] R. Finucane: *Soldiers of the Faith*; op cit; p. 104.

[153] Anna Comnena: *Alexiad*; IV; ch 6.

Soon after, the main crusade armies began to reach Byzantium. Godfrey of Bouillon, the main leader, reached Constantinople at the end of December of 1096, months ahead of the others. Bohemond did not reach Constantinople until after Easter, Raymond of St Gilles towards the end of April, and the French in early May.[154] By May 1097 the crusading army was complete. It was made up of four great armies: the men of Lorraine under Godfrey of Bouillon; the Normans from Italy under Bohemond; the Provencal contingent under Raymond of Saint Gilles, Count of Toulouse, and the papal legate Adhemar of Monteil; and the French and the vassals of the King of France under the Duke of Normandy and the Count of Flanders and Blois.[155] This was the first time that the main armies of the First Crusade had come together. Franks, Greeks and the Muslims, alike, were awestruck by the spectacle. One Byzantine contemporary described the crusaders as: 'A countless multitude of locusts, so great as to resemble clouds and overcast the sun when it flew.'[156]

A Latin eyewitness recalled,

> Then the many armies there were united into one, which those who were skilled in reckoning estimate at 600,000 strong for war. Of these there were 100,000 fully armed men [and a mass of] unarmed, that is clerics, monks, women, and little children.[157]

This huge army set off from Constantinople marching onto and through Asia Minor. In May, the Crusaders besieged Nicea, and despite the siege and fierce assaults, the city resisted, before it was ceded to the Byzantines.[158]

On the first of July 1097, the crusaders inflicted a severe defeat on the troops of Kilij at Dorylaeum (northwest Anatolia).[159] The Turks of Anatolia who met the crusaders were fierce and effective fighters, but were few in number.[160] They could not prevail in fixed encounters against superior numerical forces, especially as the Franks kept pouring in across Asia Minor.[161] Seljuk power was sapped further by internal enemies, most notably the Armenians, who allied themselves with the 'Franks'.[162] Before the conquest of Antioch (Autumn 1097), the Turkish garrison of 'Maressa' (Marata) fled at the approach of the crusaders for fear of the (Christian) native population, and at Artah (Artesia) the Armenians massacred all the Turks inside the city even before the crusaders arrived, and then flung open the gates to welcome their Christian brethren with great rejoicing.[163] In their

---

[154] Z. Oldenbourg: *The Crusades;* op cit; p. 68.

[155] Ibid.

[156] T. Asbridge: *The First Crusade*; Oxford University Press; 2004; p. 122.

[157] Quotation from John Zonoras' *Epitome*, taken from an unpublished translation by R. Macrides and P. Magdalino; Fulcher of Chartres, p. 183.

[158] P.K. Hitti: *History*; op cit; p. 637.

[159] Ibid.

[160] C. Hillenbrand: *The Crusades*, op cit; p. 42.

[161] Ibid.

[162] W. Durant: *The Age of Faith*, op cit; p. 590.

[163] Z. Oldenbourg: *The Crusades*; op cit; p. 114.

advance, the crusaders were also provided guides and recruits by the Maronite Christians of Lebanon.[164] Wherever the Frankish army successfully carried Muslim strongholds, it owed some of this success to the support of local Christians to whom the crusaders appeared 'as saviours.'[165] These fellow Christians, Oldenbourg remarks

> Had come 'to the ends of the earth' to drive out the Turks; and in spite of countless reasons for mutual dissatisfaction, some of the Christians of these provinces-the Armenians-were to remain on friendly terms with the Franks for a long time.[166]

So welcoming the Armenians were, in the course of a few months they proclaimed Baldwin, Godfrey's brother, their sovereign in the captured city of Edessa, which had a strong Armenian population.[167]

The Fatimids, too, soon sympathised with the crusaders against the Seljuks.[168] The Vizier of Malik al-Afdal sent the Christian leaders offers as soon as they entered Syria, and his envoys brought a friendly message.[169] Stephen of Blois wrote to his wife to tell her that: 'The Emperor of Babylon [al-Afdal] also sent Saracen messengers to our army with letters, and through these he established peace and concord with us.'[170]

The Christian chronicle the *Gesta* says that the crusaders presented 100 Turkish heads to Fatimid ambassadors camped nearby.[171] These envoys appear to have stayed in the Christian camp for almost a month, and when they left they were accompanied by Frankish ambassadors.[172] In the exchange of embassies, the Fatimids had, Gibbon says, declared that 'their sovereign was the true and lawful commander of the faithful, who had rescued Jerusalem from the Turkish yoke.'[173]

The Fatimids also sent gifts of horses and silk robes, of vases, and purses of gold and silver, and said that 'In his (the Fatimid ruler) estimate of their merit or power, the first place was assigned to Bohemond, and the second to Godfrey (the two main crusader leaders).'[174] To the princes, they offered to join them in fighting the Turks.[175]

---

[164] P.K. Hitti: *History;* op cit; p. 639.

[165] Z. Oldenbourg: *The Crusades*; op cit; p. 114.

[166] Ibid.

[167] Von Sybel: *The History and Literature of the Crusades*, London, Chapman; 1861; p. 34.

[168] H Lamarque: La Premiere Traduction du Koran; in *De Toulouse a Tripoli*, Colloque held between 6 and 8 December, 1995, University of Toulouse; AMAM, Toulouse, 1997; pp. 237-46; op cit; p. 239.

[169] *Archives*, I, p. 162; *Regesta*, No 4; in C.R. Conder: *The Latin;* op cit; pp. 41-2.

[170] T. Asbridge: *The First Crusade*; op cit; pp. 186-7.

[171] R. Finucane: *Soldiers of the Faith*; op cit. p. 198.

[172] T. Asbridge: *The First Crusade*; op cit; pp. 186-7.

[173] E. Gibbon: *The Decline and Fall of the Roman Empire*; vol 6; Methuen and Co; 1898; p. 307.

[174] Ibid.

[175] C.R. Conder: The *Latin Kingdom*; op cit; pp. 41-2.

The first crusader detachments reached Antioch on October 20, 1097. Antioch, a large cosmopolitan city on the Orontos River and the Mediterranean coast, was the key to Syria and Palestine. Nothing in the West could compare with it for size and wealth.[176] 'Magnificently fortified, it was equipped with all the latest developments of military techniques. The outer walls were over six miles long, and with its four hundred towers, its citadel towering well over six hundred feet above the lower quarters of the town, and its mountainous hinterland, it was very nearly impregnable.'[177]

For the crusaders, if they had any chance to progress south, the city had to be captured.[178] Whilst the odds seemed against them, they still led siege to the city, pitching their camp, closing the roads to those who would go out, and soon began to mount raids, killing and plundering in all the surrounding districts.[179] They received further support from the Armenian population, who, whenever feeling strong enough, stormed the outlying castles dependent on Antioch and surrendered them to the crusaders.[180] In the city itself, Yaghi Siyan, the ruler, sought help from other Muslim principalities close by. Ridwan of Aleppo was not ready to help, but was rather inclined to make an alliance with the Fatimids of Egypt, who were then negotiating with the crusaders.[181] The city of Antioch also included a considerable Christian minority, and Yaghi Siyan had guaranteed their security, as Ibn Al-Athir says, 'not allowing a hair of their heads to be touched.'[182] However, one such Christian subject was to cause the city to fall to the crusaders.[183] This Armenian, Phirouz, had acquired the favour of the emir and the command of three towers, 'disguising' in the words of Gibbon, 'his foul design of perfidy and treason.'[184] He possibly made the first contact with Tancred's men posted nearby, but more than likely contact was initiated and maintained via Armenian traders passing in and out of the city.[185] In the end, Phirouz and the crusaders agreed a plan to let them into Antioch.[186] One night, the French and Normans ascended the scaling-ladders that were thrown from the walls by the Armenians, and opened the gates to their comrades. Soon the army rushed through the gates, and the Muslims

---

[176] Z. Oldenbourg: *The Crusades*; op cit; p. 94.

[177] Ibid

[178] Ibid.

[179] The First and second Crusades; op cit; p. 70.

[180] W.B. Stevenson: *The Crusaders*; op cit; p. 25.

[181] Ibid, p. 26.

[182] Ibn al-Athir: *Kamil*; op cit; X, 187.

[183] The First and second Crusades; op cit; p. 71.

[184] E. Gibbon: *The Decline and Fall;* op cit; p. 301.

[185] Anna Comnena: *Alexiade*; ed., and tr. B. Leib; 3 vols (Paris 1937-76); tr., into English: *The Alexiad of Anna Comnena*; tr. E.R.A. Sewter; Hammondsworth; 1969; vol. 3, pp. 20-21; *Gesta Francorum et aliorum Hierosolimitanarum;* ed., and tr. R. Hill; London; 1962; p. 44; Raymond of Aguilers: *Le Liber de Raymond of Aguilers*; ed., J. Hill and L.L. Hill (Paris; 1969), p. 64; Fulcher of Chartres, pp. 230-33; Albert of Aachen, IV.15; Ralph of Caen: Gesta Tancredi in expeditione Hierosolymitana, RHC Occ; III; pp. 587-716; pp. 651-3; H. Hagenmeyer: Dei *Kreuzzugssbriefe aus den Jahren 1088-1100;* Innsbruck; 1901., pp. 159; William of Tyre: *Chronique*; ed. R.B.C. Huygens, Corpus Christianorum, 62-63 A; 2 vols; Turnhout; 1986; tr. Into English: *A History of Deeds Done beyond the Sea by William of Tyre*; tr. E.A. Babock and A.C. Krey; 2 Vols; new York; 1943; pp. 285-7; Matthew of Edessa, p. 170; Ibn al-Qalanisi, p. 45; Kemal ad-Din, p. 580; Ibn al-Athir, p. 192. For an analysis of contemporary source variation see: France, *Victory in the East*, pp. 257-8.

[186] E. Gibbon: *The Decline and Fall*; op cit; p. 301.

inside quickly found 'that although mercy was hopeless, resistance was impotent.'[187] On hearing this news, Yaghi Siyan fled the city, and when he saw him, his army commander did the same by another gate.[188] This was of great help to the Franks as Ibn al-Athir remarks: 'if he had stood for an hour, they (the Franks) would have been wiped out.'[189] Some three thousand Muslim men still fortified themselves in the citadel of Antioch and put out a stout resistance.[190] In the city, meanwhile, the Christians entered the homes, and the Muslim population was overwhelmingly massacred or mutilated.[191] The crusaders 'spared neither sex nor condition and paid no respect to age... killed the servants... mothers of families and the children of nobles.'[192] Oldenbourg notes how after the fall of the city, the crusaders (helped by the native Christians) killed all the Turks they could find inside the city, believing 'that a massacre of this kind was pleasing to God.'[193] An eyewitness noted:

> All the streets of the city on every side were full of corpses, so that no one could endure to be there because of the stench, nor could anyone walk along the narrow paths of the city except over the corpses of the dead.[194]

From the time of their arrival, the crusaders showed an excessive brutality not experienced before in the region. For months, they ravaged the countryside around the Orontes, pushing their raids further and further afield. When they fell on a town with a Muslim population, they slaughtered the men and took women into slavery.[195] This was the least that could happen to them. The Norman leader, Bohemond, had Muslim prisoners killed and their heads roasted on spits.[196] Outside Antioch, just as at Nicea earlier, before the city was taken, some 500 Muslim heads were carried back to the camp, and about 200 of them were shot into the city and the rest set up on stakes in view of the defenders to add to their distress.[197] On this occasion, a contemporary, Stephen of Blois wrote to his wife that the heads had been brought into camp so that everyone could share in the rejoicing; for a Bishop who was present, 'the impaled heads furnished a joyful spectacle for the people of God.'[198]

[187] Ibid.
[188] Ibn al-Athir: *Kamil*; op cit; X, 188.
[189] Ibid
[190] Abu Shama: *Kitab al-Rawdatayn;* ed. M.H. M. Ahmad; 2 vols; Cairo; 1954.; I; p. 175.
[191] Ibn al-Qalanisi: *Dayl Tarikh Dimashk;* ed. H.F. Amedroz; Leiden; 1908, p. 220.
[192] R. Finucane: *Soldiers of the Faith*; op cit; 1983.
[193] Z. Oldenbourg: *The Crusades*; op cit; pp. 116-7.
[194] Albert of Aachen: *Historia Hierosolymitana*; RHC Occ; IV;.22-3; *Gesta Francorum*, pp. 47-8; Raymond of Aguilers, p. 65; Fulcher of Chartres, pp. 233-5. Ibn al-Qalanisi: *The Damascus Chronicle...* tr H.A.R. Gibb; London; 1932; p. 44; remarked that the number of Antiochene's 'killed, taken prisoner and enslaved . . . is beyond computation'.
[195] Z. Oldenbourg: *The Crusades;* op cit; p. 112.
[196] William of Tyre: *Historie Liber Secundus;* in Receuil des Historiens Occidentaux; I; p. 190.
[197] William of Tyre: *A History of the Deeds Done Beyond the Sea*; tr. E. Babcock and A.C. Krey; 2 vols; Columbia; 1941; I; pp. 227-8.
[198] Ibid; Fulcher of Chartres: *A History of the Expedition to Jerusalem; 1095-1127*, tr. F. Ryan; ed., H. Fink; University of Tenessee Press; 1969; p. 94.

Muslim rulers seemed little, if at all, concerned by the crusaders' inroads deep into Muslim territory, or their massacres and cruelties, nor did they seem aware of the dangers facing them.[199] They were, instead, busy quarrelling over territorial possession, much more important in their eyes.[200] The Fatimids in particular seemed much happier with the new situation. Just when the various Turkish armies were trying to retake Antioch from the Christians, the Fatimids treacherously took Jerusalem from the Turks.[201] Ibn Taghribirdi (d. 1469-70) also blames the Fatimids for the Muslim defeat at Antioch and specifically blames al-Afdal (who, although Muslim, was of Armenian origin), the vizier of Egypt, for not sending out the Fatimid armies to join the Syrian commanders: 'I do not know the reason for his not sending them out, with his strength in money and men.'[202] He repeats this observation at the very end of his account of the defeat at Antioch: 'All this and still the armies of Egypt did not prepare to leave.'[203]

The Turkish armies, which sought to retake Antioch, were themselves ineffective and disorderly, a condition caught by Ibn al-Athir, who insists on the disunity, lack of purpose, and fickleness amongst some of their leaders, most particularly.[204]

Following Antioch, the crusaders marched south, and arrived in front of Ma'arrat an-Nu'man, and set siege to the city. The notables of Ma'arrat made contact with Bohemond, the new master of Antioch, who was in command of the Christians. He promised to spare the lives of the inhabitants if they would stop fighting and withdraw from certain buildings.[205] Desperately placing their trust in his word, the families gathered in the houses and cellars of the city and waited all night in fear. The Franks arrived at dawn. It was carnage.[206] The slaughter lasted three days; the crusaders, it is said, killed more than 100,000 people.[207] Robert the Monk says:

> Our men walked through the roads, places, on the roofs, and feasted on the slaughter... They cut into pieces, and put to death children, the young, and the old crumbling under the weight of the years... Streams of blood ran on the roads of the city; and everywhere lay corpses.[208]

Radulph of Caen said how:

> In Maarra our troops boiled pagan adults in cooking pots; they impaled children on spits and devoured them grilled.[209]

---

[199] A.M. Nanai: L'Image du croise dans les sources historiques Musulmanes: in *De Toulouse a Tripoli*; op cit; pp. 11-39; at p. 13.

[200] Z. Oldenbourg: *The Crusades*; op cit; p. 113.

[201] C.R. Conder: *The Latin Kingdom*; op cit. p. 47.

[202] Ibn Taghribirdi: *Al-Nujum al-Zahirah fi Muluk Misr wa'l Qahira;* Cairo; 1939.

[203] Ibid; V, p. 148.

[204] Ibn al-Athir: *Kamil*; op cit; X, pp. 188-90.

[205] A. Maalouf: *The Crusades Through Arab Eyes;* tr. J. Rothschild; Saqi; London 1984; p. 38.

[206] Ibid.

[207] Ibn al-Athir: *Kamil;* op cit; X, pp. 188-90.

[208] Robert the Monk, in G. Le Bon: *La Civilisation*, op cit; p. 248.

[209] In Janet Abu Lughod: *Before European Hegemony*; Oxford University Press; 1989; p. 107.

In fact, as the chronicler, William of Tyre, notes, it was a common practice for the crusaders to roast and eat the flesh of the Muslims they slew.[210] The daughter of the Byzantine Emperor, Anna Comnena, accused Peter the Hermit's followers of slicing up babies and impaling others on spits to roast over fires, while the elderly were subjected to a variety of tortures.[211]

At Ma'arrat, to avoid such a fate, many Muslims were said by a Christian writer to have jumped down wells to their deaths.[212] For Muslim chroniclers, the massacres of Ma'arrat were yet another sign of the ferocity of the enemy.[213]

Following the capture of Ma'arrat an-Nu'man, the armies under Raymond of Toulouse, the most powerful count of France, pushed southward.[214] They occupied the fortress of Hasn al-Akrad,[215] which commanded the strategic pass between the plains of the Orontes and the Mediterranean. They then besieged Arqah on the western slope of northern Lebanon and occupied Antartus (present day Tartus) on the coast.[216]

The crusaders kept progressing south in direction of Jerusalem. The city had been initially left in the hands of two Seljuk vassals, Turcoman chiefs of the Artuqid family: Sukman and his brother, Il-Ghazi.[217] However, before the crusaders arrived, in the year 491H/1097-8, and whilst the Turkish armies were busy trying to relieve Antioch, the Fatimid army under the personal leadership of al-Afdal, the vizier and de facto ruler of the empire, attacked and seized it from the Turks.[218] This was a 'real betrayal of Islam,' according to Lamarque.[219] 'The humour of history', Durant says, 'meant that when the crusaders arrived in front of Jerusalem in 1098, the Turks whom they had come to fight had been expelled from the city by the Fatimids a year before (1097).'[220] This did not pre-empt or change Christians' aims. They put the city under siege and began to batter its walls. On July 15, 1099, after a strenuous siege, the city fell, and the crusaders made their entry. Jerusalem was held for the Fatimids by Iftikhar ad-Daula (The pride of the Nation,) who, with his entourage and his army, were allowed to leave the city under safe crusader conduct.[221] The population on the other hand was put to the sword. The Christians butchered more than 70,000 Muslims.[222] For seven days riot

---

[210] C.R. Conder: *The Latin Kingdom*; op cit. p. 45.

[211] *The Alexiad of Anna Comnena*, tr. E.R. A. Sewter; Harmondsworth; 1969; pp. 311; 437.

[212] R. Finucane: *Soldiers of the Faith*; op cit; p. 106;

[213] A.M. Nanai: L'Image du croise; op cit; p. 18.

[214] P.K. Hitti: *History*; op cit; p. 638.

[215] Ibn Khaldun: *Kitab al-Ibaar;* Bulaq; 1868; vol 5; p. 187.

[216] P.K. Hitti: *History*; op cit; p. 638.

[217] Al-Nuwayri: *Nihayat al-Arab fi funun al-Adab*; XXVIII; ed. S.A. Al-Nuri; Cairo; 1992; pp. 46-7, Ibn Khallikan: *Wafayat al-Ayyan, Biographical Dictionary*, tr., M. De Slane Duprat, Paris and Allen & Co., London, 1843; I, 160.

[218] C. Hillenbrand: *The Crusades*, op cit; p. 44.

[219] H. Lamarque: La Premiere Traduction Latine du Coran; op cit; p. 239.

[220] W. Durant: *The Age of Faith*, op cit; p. 591.

[221] B. Z. Kedar: The Subjected Muslims; op cit; p.143. On the dumping of corpses, see e.g., *Gesta Francorum et aliorum Hierosolimitanorum*, ed. K. Mynors, tr. R.Hill; London, 1962, p. 92.

[222] Ibn al-Athir: *Kamil*; vol x, pp. 193-5 in F. Gabrieli: *Arab Historians*; op cit; p. 11

and carnage continued. 'Men forgot their vows, forgot the Sepulchre and Calvary, hastening to gather spoil, revelling and exulting, and claiming for their own the empty houses which they seized.'[223] Even priests were not slow to ask their share. Arnold, as Latin patriarch, claimed the treasures of the Mosque, which Tancred and Godfrey had shared between them.[224] The Muslim dead were split open or burnt so that the gold they had, or supposed to have, swallowed, could be more easily recovered from the ashes.[225] The chronicler, Humbert of Romans, delighted on 'The splendid occasion when the blood of the Arabs came up to the horses' knees, at the capture of Jerusalem in 1099.'[226] To complete their deeds, the Christians desecrated the Al-Aqsa Mosque: pigs were installed in the sanctuary (Mihrab), and a church was erected in place of one of its oratories.[227] Imad Eddin speaks of the mihrab of the mosque full of pigs and excrement.[228]

The Muslim populations reacted with terror and horror to the massacres of Ma'arrat an-Nu'man, Jerusalem, Antioch and other places, which put them in 'a state of emergency.'[229] Writing from Baghdad, the historian Ibn al-Jawzi (d. 597H/1200) notes in his record for the year 491/1097-8, that is even before the fall of Jerusalem: 'There were many calls to go out and fight against the Franks and complaints multiplied in every place.'[230]

The ruling elites, however, stood by, too absorbed by their own preoccupations to react.[231] Whilst history blames the Fatimids most for the betrayal of the Muslim cause, others were to blame, too, as local courts and princes shared in the same passive attitude towards the Christian onslaught. Songs about the sufferings of Jerusalem were sung in every Muslim court in the East, since at that time songs and verses took the place of newspapers and propaganda talks; the Abbasid Caliph of Baghdad and the Fatimids of Cairo welcomed the refugees, but the fugitives' appeals to Muslim solidarity fell on deaf ears.[232] Not once did Muslim states unite for concerted action against the crusaders.[233] When the Franks:

> May God frustrate them [Ibn al-Athir exclaimed] extended their control over what they had conquered of the lands of Islam and it turned out well for them that the troops and the kings of Islam were preoccupied with fighting each other, at that time opinions were divided among the Muslims, desires differed, and wealth was squandered.[234]

---

[223] C.R. Conder: *The Latin Kingdom;* op cit; p. 67.
[224] Ibid.
[225] Fulcher of Chartres: *A History of the Expedition to Jerusalem; 1095-1127;* op cit; p. 122; 154-5.
[226] In N. Daniel: *The Arabs,* op cit; p. 253.
[227] Abu Shama: *Kitab al-rawdatayn,* Beirut, II, p. 96.
[228] In C. Hillenbrand: *The Crusades,* op cit; p. 301.
[229] C. Cahen: *al-Sharq wa'l-gharb:* Beirut: 1995, p. 112.
[230] Ibn al-Jawzi: *Al-Muntazam fi Tarikh al-Muluk wa'l umam;* Hyderabad; 1940; vol IX, 105.
[231] C. Hillenbrand: *The Crusades,* op cit; p. 257.
[232] Z. Oldenbourg: *The Crusades;* op cit; pp. 155-6.
[233] G.E. Von Grunebaum: *Islam,* op cit. p. 61.
[234] Ibn al-Athir; *Kamil;* x; op cit; p. 256.

The crusaders were, thus, assisted not only by their own religious zeal and cupidity, but above all by Muslim divisions amongst themselves.[235] Even amidst the massacres of Muslim populations, some of the leaders were prepared to enter in alliance with the Christians against Muslim rivals.[236] The crusaders were supplied goods, food, and much else by Muslim local rulers who wished only to keep their kingdoms safe.[237] In the meantime, the Ismailis were continuing their policy of terror striking down any leader seeking to rally the resistance against the crusaders, whilst the local Christians, both Armenians and Maronites, were considerably serving the crusader cause.

Amidst this generalised Muslim state of utter decrepitude, chaos and betrayal, only the Seljuks reacted. They took the lead in the fight, but they counted in their ranks, besides their Turkish troops, Muslim Arabs and Kurds as well as the religious elites (imams, qadis, muftis, and others).

1. Events From 1099 Until the Fall of Tripoli (1109)

In the midst of the chaos which had engulfed the Muslim world in the early phase, the Turks registered victories which, without a doubt, saved the Muslim entity from extinction. In the year 1100, the Seljuk Danishmand cut Bohemond's army to pieces and took Bohemond prisoner.[238] The following year, 1101, four large armies departed from Europe with the aim of building on the successes of the First Crusade, and widening the crusader presence in the East.[239] The arrival of these fresh Christian armies united the hitherto divided Turkish armies, and, together, Malik Ghazi and Qilij Arslan crushed the crusaders.[240] One great army was wiped out by the Turks near Angora.[241] Fifteen thousand Latin, under the Counts of Nevers and Bourges, perished near Erekli on the way to Tarsus.[242] William IX of Acquitaine and Welf, Duke of Bavaria were defeated by Qilij Arslan and Qaraja, the Emir of Harran, as they sought to reach Cilicia.[243] In total, tens of thousands from the invading armies perished on the field of battle, which amounted to a very decisive Muslim victory, as it prevented the Christians from widening their hold on the East.[244]

---

[235] R. Finucane: *Soldiers of the Faith*; op cit; p. 8.
[236] W.M. Watt: *Muslim Christian Encounters;* Routledge; London; 1991; p. 81
[237] S. Runciman: *A History of the Crusades*, op cit; vol i, p. 399.
[238] The First and second Crusades; op cit; p. 74.
[239] See: J.L. Cate: The Crusade of 1101, in *A History of the Crusades;* ed., by K.M. Setton; University of Pennsylvania Press; 1955; vol 1; pp. 343-67.
[240] Ferdinand Chalandon: The Earlier Comneni: in *The Cambridge Medieval History,* Vol IV: Edited by J. R. Tanner, C.W. Previte; Z.N. Brooke, Cambridge; 1923; pp. 318-350; at pp. 340-1.
[241] C.R. Conder: *The Latin Kingdom;* op cit; p. 71.
[242] Ibid.
[243] Ferdinand Chalandon: The Earlier Comneni; p. 340.
[244] Z. Oldenbourg: *The Crusades;* op cit; pp. 174-5; C.R. Conder: *The Latin Kingdom*; op cit; p. 71.

Despite their victories and resilience, the Seljuks faced formidable obstacles. On one hand they could not prevent or even slow the uninterrupted supply of men and provisions to the crusaders who had now established a very strong presence on the coasts of Syria and Palestine. The coastal towns and cities formed, in fact, the backbone of the Crusader East, and every year, large numbers of fighters poured in, especially in the spring and summer seasons.[245] Most of the arriving pilgrims, even when not intending to stay permanently, were willing to lend assistance to the armies of the emerging Latin states, and so provided an important reserve of manpower.[246] All parts of Europe sent fighters, including regions as far as Norway, which on one occasion sent sixty ships full of fighting men.[247]

The second major obstacle hampering Seljuk efforts were Muslim divisions, as princes and local rulers kept fighting each other, each of them capitalising on the difficulties of their neighbours who were attacked by the Franks.[248] The contemporary chronicler, Ibn al-Qalanisi, remarks how between October 1101 and October 1102, the people of Khurasan, Iraq, and Syria were in a state 'of constant bickering and hatred, wars and disorder, and fear of one another, their rulers involved in mutual warfare.'[249] Muslim ruling elites, Nanai points out, showed 'a humiliating incapacity to understand the nature and the real objectives of the massive outbreaks of the Franks in Syria and Palestine,'[250] but, as a general rule, Nanai also notes, the Muslim layman has always been more perceptive than his ruler in understanding the hatred the Franks held towards Muslims.[251] It was for this reason that the resistance to the invader in the first half of the 12th century was stronger and more effective coming from the people than from the rulers.[252] Imams and other religious elites also made a considerable contribution to the anti crusade movement. Qadi Ibn al-Khashab of Aleppo, most particularly, before he was murdered by the Ismailis, not content to sit back in the mosque or madrasa and to preach and teach jihad, was also closely involved in the running of affairs in Aleppo at a time when the city was extremely vulnerable to external attacks.[253] Unlike their rulers, these scholars also considered the Frankish invasion a terrible calamity upon Islam and Muslims.[254] The solution to this calamity, they held, was in the recovery of the true spirit of Islam and Jihad. Al-Sulami, who preached in the Umayyad mosque of Damascus in the early years after the fall of Jerusalem, held

[245] C.R. Conder: *The Latin Kingdom*; op cit; p. 114.
[246] J.A. Brundage: *The Crusades;* The Marquette University Press; 1962; p. 75.
[247] C.R. Conder: *The Latin Kingdom;* op cit. p. 90.
[248] J.H. Lamonte: Crusade and Jihad: in *The Arab Heritage*, N.A. Faris ed; Princeton University Press, 1944; pp. 159-98; p. 168.
[249] Ibn al-Qalanisi: *The Damascus Chronicle of the Crusade*, extracted and tr, from The Chronicle of Ibn al-Qalanisi, extracted and tr., by H.A. R. Gibb; London, Luzac and Co, Ltd, 1932, pp. 46-59; reprinted in A.R. Lewis: *The Islamic World*; op cit; pp. 47-53 at p. 51.
[250] A.M. Nanai: L'Image du croise; op cit; p. 14.
[251] Ibid; p. 19.
[252] Ibid.
[253] C. Hillenbrand: *The Crusades*, op cit; p. 109.
[254] Ibn Al-Qalanisi: *Dayl tarikh Dimashq*, Damascus, 1983, p. 218.

that Muslims ought to rally against their enemy, the crusaders.[255] Al-Sulami's solution to this dire predicament lies first 'in moral rearmament to end the process of Muslim spiritual decline.' The Christian attacks, according to him, were 'a punishment as well as a Divine warning to Muslims to return to 'the Right Path.' Jihad against the infidel, he insists, 'is a hollow sham if it is not preceded by the greater Jihad (al-Jihad al-Akbar) over one's baser self; personal spiritual struggle becoming an absolute requirement before conducting war against the Franks.'[256] Muslims' defeat, argues al-Sulami, was God's punishment for abandoning their religious duties, their indifference to the Frankish presence, and, above all, for their neglect of Jihad.[257]

In contrast with the divided Muslims, the Christians showed great unity of purpose. The local Christians, in particular, manifested great zeal towards the crusader cause, most fervent of all being the Armenians and the Maronites.[258] When the Mongols subsequently (as to be seen) overran the caliphate, other Christian communities in Syria and Iraq also showed great zeal and support for the Mongols and their crusader allies, often taking the lead in the massacre of Muslims. Very certainly the only reason other Christian communities such as the Copts did not show the same zeal was because the Crusaders did not overwhelm Egypt. The Maronites of Mount Lebanon did not hesitate and gave a good welcome and great loyal support to 'their co-religionists from the West.'[259] The early crusaders had the line of their march pointed out by friendly Maronites coming down from the mountain villages to meet the princes.[260] Maronite support to the Count of Tripoli was particularly helpful to him in resisting the Turks.[261]

The most effective support, though, was from the Armenians.[262] Armenia, Saunders insists, is a classic example 'of the evils of what may be called theological nationalism, that identity of a people's culture with a special body of sectarian beliefs, which has been the curse of Christianity in the East.'[263] In countless sieges of Muslim cities, the Armenians played the main part in support for the crusaders.[264] At the siege of Antioch in 1097, the Muslims offered a stubborn resistance, and the position of the besieging crusaders was no better than that of the besieged Muslims.[265] Fortunately for the crusaders they were let into the city by the Armenian Phirouz, and local Armenians also provided a supply of provision.[266]

---

[255] Al-Sulami in C. Hillenbrand: *The Crusades*, op cit; p. 104.

[256] In E. Siwan: La Genese de la contre croisade; *Journal Asiatique*; 254 (1966); pp. 199-204.

[257] Al-Sulami: Un Traite Damasquin du debut du XIIem siecle, ed., Siwan, *Journal Asiatique*, 1966, p. 207.

[258] J.J. Saunders: *Aspects*; op cit; p. 39.

[259] C. Cahen: *Orient et Occident au temps des Croisades*, Aubier Montaigne, 1983; p. 73.
K.S. Salibi: The Maronites of Lebanon under Frankish and Mamluk Rule; 1099-1516; *Arabica* IV; 1957.

[260] C.R. Conder: *The Latin Kingdom*; op cit; p. 57.

[261] Jacques de Vitry: ed. Bongars, p.1093; in A. Hoteit: Les differentes communautes de Tripoli et leur attitude envers les Croises, in *De Toulouse*, op cit; pp. 41-58; at p. 52.

[262] J.J. Saunders: *Aspects of the Crusades*, op cit; p. 39.

[263] Ibid; p. 40.

[264] W.B. Stevenson: *The Crusaders*; op cit; p. 26.

[265] Ibid. 26

[266] Ibid.

Then and subsequently, the Armenians not only fought side by side with the crusaders against the Muslims, Lesser Armenia also acted as a most useful base for the crusaders in the north eastern corner of the Mediterranean, besides serving as a screen to protect the Frankish principalities of northern Syria against the Turks.[267]

Although considerably hindered, the Turks managed to meet the crusaders' challenges, and even if unable to repulse them, they were at least able to prevent their territorial progress. By their victory at the decisive battle of Harran in 1104, the Turks were able to thwart the Christian attempt at controlling the whole of Syria and reaching Islam's main stronghold: Mosul.

From the time of the Muslim victory at Harran, 1104, the fighting became continuous, and the fortunes of war shifted from one side to another. Ibn al-Qalanisi, who wrote the Chronicles of Damascus, speaks of many such encounters.[268] In April 1105, Zahir Eddin Tughtekin, the Atabeg of Damascus (1104-1128), after recovering from illness that nearly took him, set out for the district of Hims, marching on Rafaniya, before he was joined by another Muslim contingent. Together they attacked Rafaniya, slaying its defenders and the Frankish garrison. The castle was also captured together with other forts, and all their occupiers put to the sword.[269] In March-April 1105, Aleppo's army was crushed by Tancred. The Muslim infantry first held the ground, but the cavalry was routed, and the foot-soldiers were killed en masse by the Christians, all three thousand of them.[270] The same year, in August, a combined army of Damascus, and on this very rare occasion, of Fatimid Egypt, were crushed by the Franks between Yafa and Ascalon.[271] In the following year, 1106, in the month of February, Khalaf B. Mula'ib of Afamiya was murdered by the Ismailis. This was soon followed by Tancred's march on the town torn by Muslim factional conflict, forcing it to capitulate.[272] In 1107, Tughtekin advanced on a castle near Tiberias, captured it and slew its Frankish garrison.[273] In the same year, and the year after, conflict tore the Muslim camp, and as a result, Qilij Arslan was killed fighting a fellow Muslim emir: Jawali Saqawa. Jawali Saqawa forced Mosul into submission, driving out most of the population, and committed every kind of excess. In response, the sultan sent against him the newly emerging leader of the Muslim armies: Mawdud. Mawdud entered Mosul in 1108 and crushed the armies of Jawali.[274] Then, the first decade of the crusader presence was completed by the capture of the mighty city of Tripoli (in 1109) by the army of Raymond St Giles.

---

[267] J.J. Saunders: *Aspects*; op cit; pp. 42-3.
[268] Ibn al-Qalanisi: *The Damascus Chronicles;* (Gibb); op cit; pp. 66 ff.
[269] Ibid; 69.
[270] Ibid; p. 70.
[271] Ibid; p. 71.
[272] Ibid; pp. 72-4.
[273] Ibid; p. 75.
[274] Ibid; p. 75ff.

2. From Mawdud to the Death of Il-Bursuqi (1110-1127)

Mawdud, the Seljuk Atabeg of Mosul was one of the greatest Muslim leaders to emerge in the early stages of the crusades. He began to prepare for his first campaign in December 1109.[275] Then, in April 1110, he moved against Edessa with the support of the Ortoqid Il-Ghazi and the Emir of Mayafaraqin, Soqman al-Qutbi.[276] Mawdud could not take Edessa, though, as renewed dissentions in Muslim ranks hampered his mission. In 1113, he crossed the Euphrates in direction of Syria, then with Tughtekin prepared to launch an attack to retake Jerusalem, and liberate the Holy Land. By this, he was anticipating the aspirations of Nur Eddin Zangi and Salah Eddin by half a century or so.[277] Mawdud's successful leadership was cut short, though. He fell to the daggers of the Ismaili Assassins, murdered at the Friday prayers in October 1113.[278]

 By the time they had killed Mawdud, the Ismailis had already murdered most of the Muslim leaders fighting the crusaders, including the Emir of Homs, Janah al-Dawla, in 1103, and the Emir of Apamea, Khalaf ibn Mula'b in 1106; the latter's death profiting the Franks of Antioch, most particularly.[279] Il-Bursuqi, the successor of Mawdud, was also to fall to the daggers of the Ismailis at the Friday prayers in 1126.[280] Also to be murdered by the Ismailis was Ibn al-Khashab, the Qadi of Aleppo, who in 1111 led people in riots against the inept Caliph of Baghdad to demand intervention against the Franks. Ibn al-Khashab also played an important part in the great Muslim victory at Balat in 1119.[281] The impact of Ismaili killings of Muslim leadership was a decisive factor in the early victories of the Franks.[282] And so were the dissentions amongst Muslim leadership. When the Seljuk Sultan, Mohammed, sponsored attacks on Edessa between 1108 and 1113, his efforts were fraught by opposition from local rulers.[283] In Aleppo, following the assassination of Alp Arslan in 1114, his successor adopted a policy of friendship towards the crusaders.[284] Another attempt on Edessa by Il-Bursuqi (Mawdud's successor) in May 1114, with a large army, which included in its ranks Sultan Mohamed's own son, and a young officer with a great future, Imad Eddin Zangi,[285] also failed. So did a subsequent attempt in 1115, routed by an alliance of Christian and Muslim forces at the battle of Danith.

[275] Sibt al-Jawzi: *Mira't Ezzaman;* in RHOr; vol iii; p. 537.
[276] S. Runciman: *A History of the Crusades,* in 3 vols; Cambridge University Press, 1962; vol ii; p. 115.
[277] W.B. Stevenson: *The Crusaders in the East,* op cit, p. 96.
[278] Ibn Khalikan: *Wafayat al-Ayan;* (De Slane); op cit; i. p. 227.
[279] S. Runciman: *The Crusades,* op cit, p. 120.
[280] The First and second Crusades; op cit; p. 86.
[281] C. Hillenbrand: *The Crusades,* op cit; p.110.
[282] J.J. Saunders: *Aspects of the Crusades*; op cit; p. 22.
[283] C. Hillenbrand: *The Crusades,* op cit; p. 21.
[284] Ibn al-Qalanisi: *The Damascus Chronicles*; op cit; pp. 148-9; Kemal Eddin: *Zubdat*; RHOr; iii; op cit; pp. 605-6.
[285] S. Runciman: *A History*; op cit; vol ii; p. 128.

Amidst thoroughly broken Muslim ranks, only the appeal for Jihad could bring any semblance of unity and rebuild lost effectiveness in the field of war. On 27 June 1119, fired up by calls for Jihad, although he was not himself particularly devout, Il-Ghazi, an Ortoqid Turk, fought the combined forces of Roger of Antioch, Baldwin of Jerusalem and Galeran at the battle of Balat (also known as the field of blood).[286] Before the battle, Qadi Ibn al-Khashab of Aleppo, one of the moving spirits behind Il-Ghazi's rise to power, gained his permission to preach the Jihad through the army.[287] His ardour, Hindley remarks, soon infected even the skeptical mercenaries; strong men wept openly.[288]

'Then, says,' the contemporary historian of Aleppo, Kamel Eddin, 'Tugha Arslan Ibn Dimlaj (emir of Arzan in the Jazira, and vassal of Il-Ghazi) led the charge, and the army swept down on the enemy tents, spreading chaos and destruction. God gave victory to the Muslims. The Franks who fled their camp were slaughtered. The Turks fought superbly, charging the enemy from every direction like a man. Arrows flew as thick as locusts, and the Franks, with missiles raining down on infantry and cavalry alike, turned and fled.... Roger was killed, and so were 15,000 of his men... A signal of victory reached Aleppo as the Muslims were assembled for the noon prayer in the Great Mosque.'[289]

So great were the losses amongst Christians that only two men of baronial rank escaped alive; the ruler of Antioch, himself, fell fighting in the midst of his finest knights.[290] Il-Ghazi, Hillenbrand notes, might have been swayed by the eloquence of the Qadi of Aleppo, Ibn al-Khashab, but did not have the personality around which other Muslim military commanders could congregate under the banner of Jihad.[291] Il-Ghazi's victory at Balat, however, proved that Ibn al-Khashab, who was preaching Jihad with great fervour, had shown the way.[292]

In 1124, Aleppo was besieged by Baldwin, St Giles of Tripoli, Jocelyn Count of Edessa and the armies of Dubais ibn Sadaqa, an ally of the Christians.[293] The siege lasted nine months. Aleppo was reaching the verge of starvation when it was rescued in January 1125 by Il-Bursuqi, the governor of Mosul, who forced the Franks and their Muslim allies to retreat to Antioch.[294] When Il-Bursuqi arrived, the last extremity had been reached: the walls of the city were defended by men who had risen from sick beds.[295] Following this success, Il-Bursuqi, with the support of Zahir Eddin Tughtekin, and also Kirkham of Hims, went on the offensive.[296] He

[286] C. Hillenbrand: *The Crusades*, op cit; p. 21.
[287] G. Hindley: *Saladin*, Constable, London, 1976, p. 36.
[288] Ibid.
[289] Kemal Eddin: *Zubdat al-Halab fi Ta'arikh Halab*; Dahan edition II; pp. 187-90.
[290] H.E. Mayer: *The Crusades*; tr. J. Gillingham; Oxford University Press; 1990; p. 73.
[291] C. Hillenbrand: *The Crusades*, p. 110.
[292] Ibid.
[293] Ibid; The First and second Crusades; op cit; p. 96.
[294] Ibid.
[295] W.B. Stevenson: *The Crusaders*; op cit; p. 112.
[296] Ibid; p. 116.

captured Kafr al-Tab, before investing Ezaz.[297] On 11 June, 1125, though, he was defeated by King Baldwin (who had been released following his earlier capture.)[298] Undaunted, Il-Bursuqi reacted with great vigour the following year, besieging Atharib, and making substantial territorial gains.[299] His counter offensive was cut short on 26 November 1126, when he was stabbed to death by the Ismailis.[300]

Following the murder of Il-Bursuqi, Imad Eddin Zangi was appointed in his place as commander of the east. Zangi's career was to run a full course of twenty years.

3. Zangi From Youth to Atabeg (1094-1127)

In the words of Ibn al-Athir:
> Had not God, most high, been gracious to the Muslims and made the Atabeg ruler of the lands of Syria, the Franks would have overrun it completely.... The last Muslim leader Zahir Eddin Tughtekin had died in this year 1128, Syria was left completely at their mercy with no-one to defend its inhabitants, but God in his mercy to the Muslims was pleased to raise to power Imad Eddin Zangi.[301]

Likewise, Archer notes:
> (King) Fulk (the crusader ruler of the North Eastern crusader states) had been a successful ruler of his little kingdom, and had well maintained it if he had not indeed extended its power. Yet his reign had witnessed a slow though momentous change that was pregnant with disaster for the Franks. One by one the 'Mohammedan' lords on the Orontes and Euphrates had acknowledged the supremacy of the Viceroy at Mosul, and abandoned their mutual discords. This unification of the power of the Muslims, which was the first step towards stemming the tide of Latin conquest, was mainly the work of one man: Zangi, the Atabek of Mosul.[302]

When his father died, Zangi was aged ten. He grew up amongst the Seljuks of Mosul who gave him protection.[303] Zangi's father, Aq Sunqur, played a leading role in the politics of the Seljuk state and enjoyed a remarkable relationship with the Seljuk leader, Malik Shah, and his entourage. It is even mentioned that Aq Sunqur's wife was the wet nurse of Malik Shah.[304] As court chamberlain, Aq Sunqur, was very

---

[297] Ibid; pp. 116-7.
[298] Kemal Eddin: *Zubdat* in RHOr; iii; p. 651.
[299] Ibid; pp. 652-3; Fulchert of Chartres, in *Receuil Historiens occidentaux*; iii; 55.
[300] S. Runciman: *A History*; vol ii; op cit; p. 175.
[301] Ibn al-Athir: *Kamil*; op cit; x; p. 458.
[302] T.A. Archer: *The Crusades*; op cit; p. 197.
[303] C. Hillenbrand; Abominable Acts: The Career of Zengi; in *The Second Crusade*; edited by J. Phillips and M. Hoch; Manchester University Press; 2001; pp. 110-31; p. 112.
[304] Ibn al-Adim: *Bughyat al-talab*; partial ed., Ali Sevim, Ankara; 1976; p. 104.

much trusted by his royal master, and enjoyed the special privilege of standing at his right hand at all public levees and councils of state.[305] Later, as governor of the province of Aleppo, his rule was humane and enlightened; his name became a proverb for loyalty and uprightness; and he died for his loyalty to his old master's son (1094).[306] When he died he left a ten year old son, Zangi, surnamed Imad Eddin or "Pillar of the Faith", round whom the household rallied.[307] More importantly, the young Zangi had found a powerful protector and patron in Kerbogha (Kerbugha).[308] Kerbogha, the greatest man then ruling in Mesopotamia was lord of Mosul and many other cities, a vassal-in-chief of Malik Shah's son and successor, and he had not forgotten his old friend the "Gyrfalcon" (Aq-Sunkur), and he summoned Zangi and his Mamluks to his court.[309] "Bring the lad," he wrote, "for he is the son of my comrade in arms, and it behooves me to see to his nurture".[310] Accordingly, in 1094, Zangi was called to the court at Mosul, where he lived a favoured courtier under successive rulers, 'For thirty years, a notable squire of the fighting lords who held the borderland between the Crescent and the Cross.'[311]

In their armies he won a reputation for bravery and resourcefulness which even the Christians honoured.[312] Once near Amid, when the issue of a battle was in the balance, Kerbogha embraced Zangi before the army, and then consigned him to his own Mamluks, saying: "Behold the son of your old master; fight for him!"

They closed round the boy and set-to with such fury that the day was won. This was Zangi's first battlefield, and he was then about fifteen.[313]

Zangi had grown tall and distinguished looking, 'of swarthy complexion and piercing eyes, and his character was as upright as his carriage.'[314] Up to his thirty-eighth year he continued to play a secondary part in the wars and politics of Mesopotamia. Five great barons, one after the other, held the government of Mosul with the defence of the marches, and each of them treated him like a son, granted him rich fiefs, and gave him high command in their constant expeditions against the Franks.[315]

Zangi's first campaigns against the Franks were at the service of Mawdud, by his side in all his campaigns from 1108-09.[316] With Mawdud he was present at the great battle near Tiberias, where he distinguished himself by a conspicuous deed of

---

[305] S. Lane Poole: *The Life of Saladin and the Fall of the Kingdom of Jerusalem*, J.P. Putnam's Sons, London, 1898, p. 35.
[306] Ibid, p. 35.
[307] G. Hindley: *Saladin*, op cit, p. 30.
[308] Ibid.
[309] S. Lane Poole: *The Life of Saladin*, op cit, p. 35.
[310] Ibid, p. 36.
[311] G. Hindley: *Saladin*, op cit, p. 30; S. Lane Poole: *The Life of Saladin*, p. 36.
[312] G. Hindley: *Saladin*, op cit, p. 30.
[313] S. Lane Poole: *The Life of Saladin*, op cit, p. 36.
[314] Ibid.
[315] Ibid.
[316] N. Elisseeff: *Nur Ad Din: Un Grand Prince Musulman de Syrie au Temps des Croisades*, Damascus, 1967, Vol 2, p. 299.

valour.[317] At the head of his men he had repulsed a sortie of the garrison, and pursued them to the gate of the city, which he struck with his lance. Then turning around, he found he was alone; his men had halted after the engagement, and left him to follow the enemy single-handed.[318] For some time he maintained his precarious position, and kept the Franks busy, hoping his men would come up and join in an assault; but when none appeared, he reluctantly turned round, and slowly returned to the lines unhurt. The story of this exploit spread abroad and he was known thereafter by the name of al-Shamy, "the Syrian".[319]

Following his services under Mawdud and in the wake of the latter's assassination by the Ismailis, Zangi in the years 1114-5 fought under the command of the new governor of Mosul, Aq Sunqur al-Bursuqi.[320] In 1118-9, Zangi was serving under yet another Seljuk leader, Masu'd.[321] Zangi, in fact, served under all successive governors of Mosul.[322] During all these campaigns, Elisseeff remarks, Zangi was able to acquire a vast military experience and also a profound knowledge of the lands and territory where the fighting took him.[323] Both experience and knowledge would subsequently prove very useful and to great effect in his jihad against the Franks and in the defence of Mosul.[324] Serving in the ranks of the Mosul army, Zangi participated in the many sieges of Edessa; crossed many times the whole of the Jazira region and Syria, and also fought in Tiberias, therefore all his subsequent campaigns were located in territories he was well accustomed with.[325]

In 1122, Zangi was rewarded by the Seljuk Sultan, Mahmud, for his military services by the gift of his first direct government, the fief of Wasit, then a large and important city, together with the post of warden of Basra.[326] The Sultan greatly appreciated Zangi's person and his courage most of all. On one occasion the Sultan rode forth to play polo, attended by his court. When it came to choosing partners, he singled out Zangi and handed him the chogan mall, saying "Come and play". After the match he turned to the other courtiers and up-braided them for their jealousy: "Are ye not ashamed?" he asked. "Here is a well-known man, whose father held an exalted place in the state, and not one of you has so much as offered him a gift, or bidden him to his table! By Allah, if I have left him so long without providing for his charges or allotting him a fief, it was only that I might see what ye would do". Then to Zangi: "I give you to wife Kundughly's widow, and my people shall supply you

[317] T.A. Archer: *The Crusades*; op cit; p. 198.
[318] S. Lane Poole: *The Life of Saladin*, op cit, p. 37.
[319] Ibid.
[320] Ibn al-Athir: *Kamil*, op cit, p. 351.
[321] Ibid; p. 378.
[322] Ibn Wasil: *Mufarrij al-Kurub*; ed., Jamal Eddin El-Shayyal; Cairo; 1953; vol 1; pp. 28-9.
[323] N. Elisseeff: *Nur Ad Din*, op cit, p. 299.
[324] Ibid, pp. 299-300.
[325] Ibid, p. 300.
[326] S. Lane Poole: *The Life of Saladin*, op cit, p. 37.

with gold for the wedding.'[327] Kundughly had been the richest noble of the court, and his widow was endowed like a king's daughter.[328]

The Sultan's favour to Zangi extended even further. Following his reassertion of power in Baghdad, the monarch needed a strong personality to represent him in the Iraqi capital.[329] This personality needed to retain the respect of the emirs, as well as the affection of the population. The unanimous opinion, Elisseeff remarks, was that only one man had all the required qualities: this was Zangi b. Aq Sunqur.[330] And so, in 1126, the Sultan appointed him as the Sihna of Baghdad and Iraq.[331] Zangi was also permitted in his new position to keep his fiefs in Wasit and Basra which he had received previously.[332]

Soon these appointments far from the field of battle proved of little substance. The Christians had, following the murder of Al-Bursuqi in 1127, began to exert extreme pressure on both Syria and the Jazira, their audacity increasing immensely and their destructiveness also equally high.[333] Meanwhile a deputation of notables from Mosul to Baghdad asked sultan Mahmud to appoint Zangi as their governor.[334] The deputies insisted that the succession to Al-Bursuqi was to be that of a very powerful figure, a firm and decisive character able to lead the war against the Franks, and that person could only be Zangi.[335] And so, in that year, Zangi was appointed governor of Mosul.[336] Sultan Mahmud furthermore entrusted the upbringing of his two sons (Alp-Arslan and Farruk Shah) to Zangi, hence his title Atabeg (tutor) traditionally attached to his name.[337]

The new position placed Zangi at the forefront of the struggle with the crusaders, 'The champion of the Faith against the Franks,' says Lane Poole.[338] The rise to power of Zangi was one of the most stupendous events in the history of Islam, coming at a time of great emergency. For the first time in centuries the Muslim world had no leader of any calibre, the last great figure, Tughtekin of Damascus, having died in the year 1128. This was at a time when the crusaders were making powerful forays into the Muslim land. A contemporary Muslim author, quoted by Archer, says:

[327] Ibid, p. 40.
[328] Ibid.
[329] N. Elisseeff: *Nur Ad Din*, op cit, p. 328.
[330] Ibid, p. 329.
[331] Ibn al-Athir: *Kamil*, op cit, VIII, 323.
[332] N. Elisseeff: *Nur Ad Din*, op cit, p. 329.
[333] Ibid, p. 331.
[334] H.A.R. Gibb: Zangi and the Fall of Edessa; in K. Setton: *History of the Crusades;* University of Pennsylvania Press; vol 1, edited by M.W. Baldwin; Philadelphia; 1955; pp. 449-462; at p. 454.
[335] N. Elisseeff: *Nur Ad Din*; op cit; 331.
[336] Ibn al-Athir: *Tarikh al-Dawla Al-Atabakiyya;* ed. Ab Al-Qadir Ahmad Tulaymat; Cairo; 1963; p. 34.
[337] Ibn Khaliqan: *Wafayat al-Ayan*; (De Slane); op cit; vol 1; p. 540.
[338] S. Lane Poole: *The Life of Saladin*, op cit, p. 41.

The Franks were spread far and wide; their troops were numerous and their hands extended as if to seize all Islam. Day after day their raids followed one another; through these they did the Muslims much mischief, smiting them with desolation and ruin. Thus was the happy star of the Muslims darkened, and the sun of their prosperity dimmed.

The Frankish possessions stretched from Mardin and Chabakhtan to El-Arish on the Egyptian frontier, with hardly a break, except for a few strong cities such as Aleppo, Emesa, Hamah and Damascus. Their incursions were pushed as far as Diar-Bekr, and the district round Amida. They spared neither those who believed in the unity of God nor those who denied it. From Upper Mesopotamia to Nisibis and Ras al-'Ain they robbed the folk of money and of goods; at Harran they weighed down the inhabitants with scorn and oppression. In their misery men longed for death. Commerce was interrupted, and the roads to Damascus save that which passed by Rakka and the desert left deserted. Even those towns not actually conquered had to pay tribute in return for their freedom. Frankish agents visited Damascus itself, passed the slave markets in review, and set free all Christian captives from Asia Minor, Armenia, and elsewhere.[339]

Elisseeff further explains the precarious condition of the Muslim world at the time of Zangi's appointment. The Christians were militarily far superior to the Muslims, and they could assemble, much faster, and more effectively, much larger armies. The Muslims, due to the lack of a capable military leader, were prey to bloody internal feuds. The Franks controlled vast territories that stretched as far as Egypt, and also controlled the whole coastline of Palestine and Syria. All the ports were in their hands, and so they received constant reinforcements from overseas, besides keeping Muslim trade through the Mediterranean under their dictate. Only the hinterlands were in Muslim hands, but even then, Muslims suffered from constant Frankish incursions. Damascus was constantly prey to attacks by the knights from Jerusalem, and its commerce could only pass through the desert, and even then faced regular Bedouin attacks. Aleppo, Hama, Homs, and all Muslim cities suffered continuous raids by Frankish armies, and chaos and fear thus ruled in such places. Even to the furthest north, places such as Dyar al-Bakir, likewise, suffered constant Frankish raids, and the Franks were so powerful as to impose their terms on Muslim localities. Aleppo had to pay half its yearly revenue to Christian Antioch, whilst Damascus permitted the crusaders to come into the city and release any Christian prisoner held there. Anarchy and chaos, and local feuds characterised much of Egypt, Syria and Mesopotamia. This was the context in which Zangi became Atabeg.[340]

---

[339] T.A. Archer: *The Crusades;* op cit; pp. 198-9.
[340] N. Elisseeff: *Nur Ad Din*, op cit, pp. 332-3.

Zangi, however, Elisseeff remarks, 'a man full of great energies and talent, but also harsh dispositions', was going to begin the methodical reconquest of Muslim territory.[341]

It was Zangi's destiny, Archer insists,

> To change all this; to inspire his people with courage; to lead them to their first successes, and thus to pave the way for his son's (Nur Eddin) conquest of Egypt, and for his third successor's (Salah Eddin) conquest of Jerusalem. To Muslims of a later generation it seemed as though Zangi were God's special servant chosen by Him to accomplish the protection of His people.'[342]

More importantly, as Hindley notes, Zangi was the first Muslim leader of any stature to present himself as fighting the Holy War on any long term basis.[343] Indeed, of both concepts of Jihad and long term planning, it was the second that Muslims were deficient of mostly.

4. Zangi's Military Campaigns (1127-1143)

One of Zangi's first concerns was to try at least to lessen, if not to remove, divisions amidst Muslim ranks.[344] Following his reorganisation of the army of Mosul, he marched on Jazirat Ibn Omar.[345] Zangi first offered a substantial reward to the local commander to submit, but when the latter refused, Zangi used force.[346] His troops crossed the Tigris either on small vessels or by swimming across, and took position on the opposite side. The local garrison made a sortie but was repulsed, and following this debacle the local emir sued for peace.[347] This accord, Elisseeff remarks, was providential for Zangi, for the following night, a sudden flood of the Tigris swept through the area where Zangi's army was concentrated. Without the rapid submission of the local emir, the whole of Zangi's army could have been swept away by the floods.[348] Following Jazirat-ibn-Omar, Zangi captured Nisibis and Sinjar.[349] Here a fresh danger awaited him. The cities commanding the upper course of the Euphrates, Edessa, Saruj, Bira, and other places, formed Christian outposts, and, in the hands of Joscelin de Courtenay, their garrisons were a powerful force. They could not be left safely in the rear without precautions.[350] Zangi met the difficulty by arranging a truce with Joscelin, who was probably glad enough to postpone a struggle with so formidable an adversary; and the Atabeg was left free

---

[341] Ibid, p. 333.
[342] T.A. Archer: *The Crusades*, op cit, p. 199.
[343] G. Hindley: *Saladin*, op cit, p. 30.
[344] N. Elisseeff: *Nur Ad Din*, op cit, p. 334.
[345] T.A. Archer: *The Crusades*, op cit, p. 199
[346] N. Elisseeff: *Nur Ad Din*, op cit, p. 334.
[347] Ibid.
[348] Ibid.
[349] T.A. Archer: *The Crusades*, op cit, p.199
[350] S. Lane Poole: *The Life of Saladin*, op cit, p. 49.

to advance into Syria.[351] Whilst Zangi was engaged in establishing order in his new territories he received an appeal from Aleppo for deliverance from the exactions of the Franks.[352] At this time Aleppo was so weak that its inhabitants paid half their revenue to the Franks down to a mill hardly twenty paces from the town.[353] He straightway crossed the Euphrates (1128), passed through Manbij, and whilst on his way, the Franks retired, thus allowing Zangi to enter the town peacefully, welcomed with thanksgivings at Aleppo in June of the same year, thus restoring the union of Mosul with Aleppo.[354] The only Syrian lord who had been able to stand against the Crusaders was Tughtekin, the Atabeg of Damascus; and he was just dead. Thus, the arrival of Zangi onto Syrian ground was perfect in timing, to take his place and to champion the 'despairing Muslims against the infidels.'[355] The following year, Zangi took Hamah which had been left without strong defence.

Zangi's attempts at forming a strong Muslim front against the crusaders were constantly being thwarted by the Ismailis, in particular. On Tughtekin's death the Ismailis at Banyas resumed their assassination activities, under the shelter of the vizier at Damascus.[356] In 1129, they engaged in secret talks with the Franks so as to cede to them the city of Damascus.[357] The plan was that, on the last Friday of Ramadan, 13 September 1129, the Christians would station themselves at the doors of the city whilst the Ismailis would guard the doors of the Great Mosque, where the authorities and notables would be gathered for Friday prayers.[358] The two sides would act together, and capture the city. The plot was uncovered, which caused great public outrage amongst Muslims, and after the Ismailis lost their protector in Damascus, the vizier Al-Mazdaghani (after he had been removed by the Atabeg Taj al-Mulk Buri), the people slaughtered every Ismaili in the city.[359] Regardless, the Christians still advanced on Banyas, and, having received its surrender, proceeded to Damascus and encamped nearby at the end of November 1129. Battle was joined in the Marj as-Suffar, some miles southwest of the city, and the Muslims won a great victory.[360] Winter rains and fog, which now set in, made military action impossible, and thus the Franks abandoned their project and retreated in December with their rearguard closely pressed by Muslims.[361] Although they failed to capture Damascus, the Christians still held the important town of Banyas.[362]

[351] Ibid.
[352] Ibid.
[353] T.A. Archer: *The Crusades*, op cit, p. 199.
[354] Ibid.
[355] S. Lane Poole: *The Life of Saladin*, op cit, p. 49.
[356] H.A.R. Gibb: Zangi and the Fall of Edessa; in K. Setton: *History of the Crusades;* University of Pennsylvania Press; vol 1, edited by M.W. Baldwin; Philadelphia; 1955; pp. 449-462; at p. 455.
[357] N. Elisseeff: *Nur Ad Din*, op cit, p. 340.
[358] Ibid.
[359] S. Runciman: *The Crusades*; op cit; p. 179.
[360] R.M. Nicholson: The Growth of the Latin State; 1118-1144; in K.M. Setton: *The Crusades*; vol 1; op cit; pp. 410-48; p. 430.
[361] Ibid; p. 431.
[362] Ibid.

In 1130, Zangi resumed his campaign by the assault on Atharib, a frontier fortress which, Ibn Al-Athir says, 'held the Muslims as it were by the throat.'[363] Its garrison was full of picked warriors, and from its position and the strength of its defenders it was one of the most formidable of the Latin strongholds.[364] According to the later legend when King Baldwin heard of the siege he called his council together. Some thoughtless warriors did not show any alarm, disdaining their Muslim foe. One, however, took a different view:

'Was not this the young warrior who had ridden up to the gate of Tiberias? Had we not better scatter his forces before they grow great?[365]'

These words decided Baldwin to relieve Atharib. He marched "with his horsemen and foot, his banners and crosses, his princes, knights, and counts", to meet the *Lion of Tiberias*.[366] Zangi's officers and counselors advised a retreat to Aleppo, but he dismissed their counsel: "Let us put our trust in God, and meet them". Instead of waiting for a relieving army, he went forth to the encounter, and a furious battle ensued.[367] Zangi at the head of his men kept charging the enemy again and again, shouting the words of the Prophet, "Take a taste of Hell!" The issue was never doubtful. "The swords of God," in Ibn Al-Athir's expressive words, "found their scabbards in the necks of His foes." Zangi 'waded through a sea of blood, trampling down the Franks.'[368] They turned to fly, but what could avail when "the bottle was hung on the peg, and the locust had ended its song?" No quarter was given; Zangi plunged through 'a sea of blood, cleaving heads and laying bones bare, till the field was covered with mangled corpses and severed limbs.' Only those escaped who hid under the heaps of slain, or "mounted the camel of night."[369] Deprived of its last hope, Atharib was taken by assault by Zangi; he had its fortifications razed to the ground, whilst the garrison was enslaved or put to the sword. The chronicler Ibn al-Furat, two centuries later, remarking that Atharib had remained in ruins until his time.[370] After making terms with the neighbouring fortress of Harim, Zangi returned to Mosul by now, already, celebrated as the most famous leader in Islam. His deeds were acclaimed over the land, and his name became a proverb for valour and ferocity. 'The "*Sanguineus*" the Christians wrote his name, and he had signed it in blood on the field of Atharib.'[371] His exploits are recited in rhyming prose:

> He ravaged the Franks in the midst of their domain; and wreaked revenge for the true believers' pain; till the crescents of Islam waxed full, after their wane; and the suns of faith, of late extinct, flashed forth again; and the Muslims trod proudly, arrayed in victory's dress; and drank of the ever-

[363] Ibn al-Athir in T.A. Archer: *The Crusades*; op cit; p. 199.
[364] S. Lane Poole: *The Life of Saladin*, op cit, p. 50.
[365] T.A. Archer: *The Crusades*; op cit; p. 200.
[366] S. Lane Poole: *The Life of Saladin*, op cit, p. 51.
[367] Ibid.
[368] In T.A. Archer; *The Crusades;* op cit; 200.
[369] S. Lane Poole: *The Life of Saladin*, op cit, p. 51.
[370] Ibn al-Furat: *Tarikh al-Duwal wal Muluk;* ed. M. F. El-Shayyal; unpublished Ph.d.; University of Edinburgh; 1986; IV; p. 30.
[371] S. Lane Poole: *The Life of Saladin*, op cit; p. 52.

> flowing wells of success; deprived the Trinitarians of keep and fortress; and dealt back their lies and wickedness: so the worship of the One was restored in the Island and Syrian regions; and there flocked to the cause of Islam defenders in legions.[372]

This was yet only the beginning of a great fighting career.

The death of sultan Mahmud in September 1131 was a serious setback to Zangi's war effort, diverting him away from the Syrian front for more than three years. The death of the sultan was, indeed, followed by a struggle between his brothers for the succession to the sultanate of Iraq, into which Zangi was inevitably drawn as a partisan of sultan Mas'ud. At the height of the struggle he was defeated by the forces of the caliph al-Mustarshid, who had been drawn into battle, the caliph a few months later besieging Mosul (August-October 1133).[373] Zangi survived the attack, and realising the futility of such involvement, and that the focus should be on Syria and the war against the crusaders, he henceforth abstained from Iraq's affairs.

To wage the *Jihad* with success, it was essential to have possession of Damascus, which was at the heart of Syria, once the former glorious Umayyad capital, but now little better than an outpost of the Franks.[374] If Damascus was under his control, Lane Poole remarks, he would then mass the armies of Syria and the Jazirah (Island), and he would drive the "dogs of Christians" into the sea.[375] Zangi's dream was meant never to be realised by himself, though it did after his death, at the hands of his son, Nur Eddin, just over two decades later.[376] This campaign for the acquisition of Damascus began favourably for him, though, following a series of fortuitous events. In June 1132, the ruler of Damascus, Buri, died as the result of wounds inflicted by the Ismailis, and was succeeded by his son, Shams-al-Muluk Ismail. After a successful start with the recapture of Banyas (December 1132) and of Hamah (August 1133), followed by a devastating raid on the county of Galilee in retaliation for a Christian attack on the Hauran (September 1134), he alienated by his tyrannical conduct both his troops and his subjects. Realising, apparently, their growing exasperation, he wrote secretly to Zangi urging him to come with all speed to receive the surrender of Damascus, and threatening to deliver it up to the Christians if he should delay.[377] As Zangi began his march, the local nobility removed Shams al Muluk, and his brother Mahmud was proclaimed in his place, but only nominally. The statesman who governed Damascus in the name of a series of nominal lords, Muin Eddin Anar (the Ainardus of the Latin chroniclers), rather than

[372] Ibid; p. 41.
[373] H.A.R. Gibb: Zangi and the Fall of Edessa; op cit; p. 456.
[374] S. Lane Poole: *Saladin*; op cit; 52
[375] Ibid.
[376] N. Elisseeff: *Nur Ad Din*, op cit, p. 340; T.A Archer: *The Crusades*, op cit; Ibn al-Qalanisi: *The Damascus* Chronicles, op cit.
[377] H.A.R. Gibb: Zangi and the Fall of Edessa; op cit; p. 457.

making an alliance with Zangi, instead, made common cause with the Christians.[378] The Christians themselves dreaded Zangi, 'the champion of Islam,' in Lane Poole words, and were glad to ally themselves with Anar in checking his advance.[379] The alliance was strong enough to thwart Zangi's attempts on the city.

In the Spring of 1135, Zangi resolved to attack the crusader strongholds which still lay in the very neighbourhood of Aleppo. His campaign was a triumphal progress. The Christians were taken by surprise, and no army resisted his advance.[380] He captured Kafr al-Tab and Ma'rrat an-Nu'man, one of the earliest conquests of the crusaders.[381] Now all the country between Hama and Aleppo was restored to Islam. Then, he turned his attention to the liberation of Homs by delivering relentless attacks on the city.[382] During this campaign he was diverted further east for a whole year (as noted already) to be involved in the wars between the Seljuk Sultan and the Abbasid Caliph. In his absence, his lieutenant, Sawar, fell on the crusader realm of Antioch in an invasion the like of which was not experienced in its previous history.[383]

In 1137, Zangi re-launched his offensive, beginning with an attack on the Castle of Bar'in (Montferrand). The Arab historians describe the fortress as "high as the crest of Orion, loftier than the mountain-peaks", 'the giddy summit of which was unattainable by the weary-winged birds;' and the Franks thought it impregnable.[384] When they heard of Zangi's move, and his besieging the castle, Raymond, Lord of Tripoli was joined by King Fulk of Anjou to relieve the siege, but Zangi heard of their approach. He carefully prepared his battle plan, and very quickly, in a short fight, Raymond was taken prisoner, and Fulk took refuge in the castle and became one of the besieged.[385] Before Zangi could move to invest Montferrand, King Fulk sent messengers to the Patriarch of Jerusalem, to the Count Edessa, and to the Prince of Antioch, begging for immediate relief.[386] The Christians: kings, counts and barons, assembled their cavalry and infantry and set out together.[387] Anticipating their arrival, Zangi mounted an audacious counter attack, and in the ensuing battle, the Christians were routed, and fled, closely pursued by the Muslims.[388] The Atabeg then cut off all means of communications with the fort.[389] Zangi knew that the possession of Montferrand would prevent the Franks from penetrating into the upper Orontes valley, and that it was also admirably situated to control Hama and

[378] S. Lane Poole: *The Life of Saladin*, op cit, p. 52.
[379] Ibid, p. 53.
[380] W.B. Stevenson: *The Crusaders;* op cit; p. 134.
[381] Ibid. Kemal Eddin: *Zubdat*; in RHOr; iii; p. 671.
[382] Ibid.
[383] W.B. Stevenson: *The Crusaders;* op cit; p. 134.
[384] S. Lane Poole: *The Life of Saladin*, op cit, p. 53.
[385] W.B. Stevenson: *The Crusaders*, op cit, p. 137.
[386] S. Runciman: *A History*; op cit; vol 2; p. 203.
[387] Ibn al-Athir: *Kamil;* op cit; xi; p. 33.
[388] Ibid.
[389] Ibid.

the city of Homs.[390] Likewise the Christians realized the strategic value of the place. Priests and monks dispersed in a vast campaign, raising armies, declaring that if Zangi took Montferrand and the Christians inside it, he would overrun all their lands in no time, for there would be no one to defend them.[391] Inside Montferrand, the King was growing desperate. He was cut off from news of the outside world; his supplies were running out, and day and night Zangi's ten great mangonels pounded at the walls of the castle.[392] (A mangonel or stone-sling was a machine for throwing stones worked by means of twisted ropes. The other chief siege-engine of the day, the catapult (balista), resembled a huge arbalest or crossbow).[393] At last, King Fulk sent a messenger to Zangi to ask for his terms.[394] Zangi demanded and obtained the cession of Montferrand, and the king might go free with all his men.[395] The Atabeg presented King Fulk— "ab hoste satis humane tractatus" as William of Tyre admits—with a robe of ceremony, and the exhausted and dispirited garrison was allowed to leave the castle with the honours of war.[396] With his capture of the place, Zangi was in control of a greatly strategic position for his future campaigns, but it was his forbearance in releasing his Christian prisoners, as Runciman notes, which never ceased to astonish historians.[397]

In 1138, Zangi learned that strong reinforcements from Europe were landing in Syria, and hastily patching up a truce with Damascus he retreated to Mosul. In fact a formidable coalition was gathering to finish him once and for all.[398] The Byzantine Emperor John Comnenus brought an army into Syria, and was joined not only by the army of the Crusading states, but also by Anar, the lord of Damascus and its dependencies.[399] John began by exchanging friendly embassies with Zangi, and we read of gifts of falcons and hunting-leopards, and a treaty that guaranteed the immunities of Aleppo. But such facts 'were not worth their parchment in days when Christian ecclesiastics laid down the rule that an oath to an infidel was null and void,' Lane Poole remarks.[400] The Emperor next took Bizaa and Kafar Tab, and then laid siege to Shayzar, the fortress on the Orontes, in April, 1138. Zangi was called to the rescue, and pressed on with forced marches. Though not strong enough to drive the enemy from their position on the heights, he harassed the Byzantines, and then using some skilful diplomacy and some payment in cash, he managed to change the Emperor's mind, which was already disgusted at:

> The indifference and frivolity of the Latin princes; for on the twenty-fourth day of the siege "the Dog of the Romans" departed, abandoning his siege-

---

[390] S. Runciman: *A History of the Crusades*; pp. 203-5.

[391] Ibn al-Athir: *Kamil;* op cit; vol xi; p. 33.

[392] S. Runciman: *A History of the Crusades*; op cit; pp. 203-5.

[393] S. Lane Poole: *The Life of Saladin*, op cit, p. 53.

[394] S. Runciman: *A History of the Crusades*; op cit; 203-5

[395] Ibid.

[396] S. Lane Poole: *The Life of Saladin*, op cit, p. 53.

[397] S. Runciman: *A History of the Crusades*; op cit; 203-5

[398] S. Lane Poole: *The Life of Saladin*, op cit, p. 53.

[399] Ibid, p. 54.

[400] Ibid.

train, including eighteen huge mangonels, which Zangi instantly appropriated. "It was thus", said Ibn-al-Athir, that *"God sufficed the faithful in the fight"*.[401]

Like his predecessors, however, Zangi was operating against a background of Muslim divisions and hostility mostly aimed against himself. Earlier in his role as Atabeg, in 1129, he fought Dubais who was seeking to become Emir of Mosul.[402] The Abbasid Caliph Mustarshid was also bent on the capture and execution of Zangi, who, on one particular occasion, was rescued from the caliph by the Kurdish governor of Tikrit, Najm Eddin Ayyub.[403] This happened in the year 1132, when Zangi had become embroiled in the affairs of Iraq, following Sultan Mahmud's death, and the war between his brothers. Seeking to unite the Eastern front, Zangi found himself faced by the caliph, whose military power was not dented by armed conflict with the crusaders, and thus had remained strong. Zangi was defeated, and was now being pursued:

> A broken army, flying before its pursuers, reached the left bank of the Tigris. On the other side, upon a steep cliff, stood the impregnable Fortress of Tekrit, defended landwards by a deep moat and accessible only by secret steps cut in the rock and leading from the heart of the citadel to the water's edge. The one hope of the fugitives was to attain the refuge of the castle, and their fate turned upon the disposition of its warden. Happily he chose the friendly part, and provided a ferry by which they crossed to safety. The ferry boats of the Tigris made the fortunes of the house of Saladin. The flying leader who owed his life to their timely succour was Zangi, the powerful lord of Mosul; and in later days, when triumph returned to his standards, he did not forget the debt he owed Tekrit, but, ever mindful of past services, carried its warden onward and upward on the wave of his progress. This warden was Saladin's father: Ayub.[404]

The Ismailis were an even greater threat than the caliph and the local warlords, and Zangi was extremely fortunate to escape their daggers. Zangi's ally, Taj al-Mulk Buri, ruler of Damascus, was less fortunate, though, and was murdered by them in 1132.[405] The Ismailis had by now managed to 'honeycomb' Persia, Iraq and Syria with their cells.[406] In 1140 they captured the Castle of Masyaf, near Aleppo in northern Syria, and turned it into a second Alamut.[407] From there they maintained their attacks against Muslim leadership, and thus weakened Muslim ranks considerably.

---

[401] Ibid.

[402] T.A. Archer: *The Crusades;* op cit; p. 201.

[403] S. Runciman: *A History*; vol ii; op cit; p. 194.

[404] S. Lane Poole: *The Life of Saladin*, op cit, p. 3.

[405] The First and second crusades from an Anonymous Syriac chronicle: tr., by A.S. Tritton and notes by A.H. R. Gibb: *JRAS*: Part two: April; pp. 273-305; at p. 273.

[406] J.J. Saunders: *Aspects of the Crusades*; op cit; p. 26.

[407] Ibid.

Egypt was still under Fatimid rule, and thus remained at peace with the crusaders, absorbed in its own domestic preoccupations. The Fatimid Caliph had appointed his son Hassan as vizier in 1135, but the young man had shown himself to be almost insanely ferocious.[408] After forty emirs had been beheaded on a trumpery charge, there was a revolt. The caliph only saved himself by poisoning his son, and handing over the corpse to the rebels.[409] He then appointed as vizier an Armenian, Vahram, who was more interested in enriching his friends and fellow Christians than in aggressive action against the Franks.[410]

Damascus, which was essential to the Muslims in the anti crusader fight for obvious strategic and other reasons was, however, out of the reach of Zangi. For some time, already, he tried to conciliate the rulers of the Syrian capital by marrying the widowed mother of the reigning lord of the city, and giving his own daughter to the emir himself, Shihab Eddin Mahmud.[411] The young man, who was much better disposed to Zangi, was, however, murdered soon after, in 1139.[412] The Murderers, including an Armenian, had thus removed Zangi's ally, who was soon replaced by his brother Mohammed, but only nominally, as Anar took the situation in the city under his firm control.[413] Indignant at the murder of her son, the princess invited Zangi to Damascus.[414] On his way, Zangi captured Baalbek of which the new ruler, Mohammed, was the governor, and after refortifying it, he withdrew to the Biqa Valley and tried to negotiate the surrender of Damascus.[415] On the rejection of his demands, he blockaded the city from December until the following May, without result. During the siege, Prince Mohammed fell ill and died, and Anar set up his young son Abak in his place without opposition.[416] Anar, this time, negotiated with the Christians a more radical solution, offering to pay 20,000 pieces of gold for their expedition against Zangi, besides offering the strategic centre of Banyas.[417] In his negotiating bid, he kept emphasising to them the gravity of the situation to themselves should Zangi take over the city.[418] When the Christians began to assemble at Tiberias, Zangi retired to the Hauran (May 4), before they and the Damascenes could join forces. In his absence the allies besieged Banyas and captured it.[419] Anar delivered the castle to King Fulk, but before he could return to Damascus Zangi appeared in the Ghutah and devastated it for three days.[420] He returned northwards but a week later attempted a sudden surprise attack at dawn

---

[408] Ibn al-Athir: *Kamil*; in RHOr; i; pp. 405-8.
[409] Ibid.
[410] Ibid.
[411] S. Lane Poole: *The Life of Saladin*, op cit, pp. 54-5.
[412] N. Elisseeff: *Nur Ad Din*, op cit, p. 367.
[413] Ibid; pp. 367-8.
[414] H.A.R. Gibb: Zangi and the Fall of Edessa; op cit; p. 459.
[415] Ibid.
[416] Ibid.
[417] Ibid, 460; Elisseef, op cit; p. 370.
[418] Elisseef 370.
[419] H.A.R. Gibb: Zangi and the Fall of Edessa; op cit p. 460.
[420] Ibid.

and when it failed, he finally withdrew.[421] Facing a strong block, Zangi's plans in Syria were defeated, and his only course of action was to place Salah Eddin's father, Ayub, as warden of Baalbek in reward for his long and tried services, whilst himself left Damascus in his foe's hands and repaired to Mosul.[422]

Zangi now planned an attack upon the Crusaders from a different quarter. Repulsed in the south, he would swoop upon them from the mountains of the north. His preparations were deliberate.[423] He protected his rear and flank by seizing Shahrzur and Ashib (which he rebuilt and named after himself el-Imadiya, Amadia, as it is called to this day).[424] Then he gradually advanced towards the enemy. One after the other, the towns of Diyar-Bekr fell into his hands, until his army stood before the strong walls of Amid, to which he began to lay siege. But Amid was not his objective; his eyes were elsewhere; and as the Eastern chronicler says, he "but coquetted with Amid to conceal his desire for Edessa".[425]

So long as his old antagonist, Joscelin de Courtenay, held the famous episcopal city, Zangi did not dare to approach it. The restless Count had been a terror throughout Diyar-Bekr and Syria: a very "devil amongst unbelievers", the Muslim historians called him; and Edessa had been the strongest outpost of the Christian state.[426] But Joscelin was dead, and a second and very different Joscelin sat in his seat. Valiant like his father, but only rarely, ordinarily sluggish and pleasure-seeking, Joscelin II preferred the comfortable ease of his fief at Tell Bashir (Turbessel) to the rigours of the hill-country of Edessa, and Zangi's ruse of a siege of Amid was quite enough to decide the Count to go away to his pleasant Syrian estate.[427]

Now that Joscelin had been lured away, Zangi could launch his major offensive against his most important objective to date: Edessa.

[421] Ibid.
[422] S. Lane Poole: *The Life of Saladin*, op cit, p. 55.
[423] Ibid.
[424] Ibid.
[425] Ibid, p. 56.
[426] ibid.
[427] Ibid.

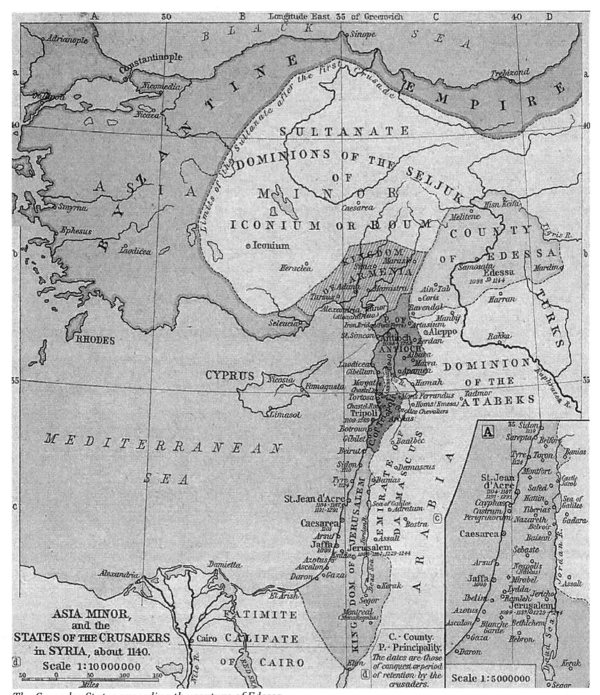

The Crusader States preceding the capture of Edessa

5. Zangi's Capture of Edessa

The strategic importance of Edessa is caught by Stevenson:

> For nearly fifty years, Edessa was the bulwark of the Latin states. A glance at
> the map shows the importance of its position. It stood like a rampart
> opposite Mosul and nearest the capital of the caliphs (Baghdad). It

commanded the roads from Mosul to Aleppo and penetrated like a wedge between Muslim Syria and the Emirates of Mesopotamia. By menacing east and south it isolated Aleppo and protected the Syrian crusaders. Aleppo was weakened even more than the crusaders were strengthened. It was almost encircled by Edessa and the adjoining state of Antioch. With its best allies in Mesopotamia it depended for safety on communication with the east. But the line of march from Mosul to Aleppo was never free from peril as long as the crusaders held Edessa. In the country from Harran to Rakka there was danger of attack at any moment, and those who passed through safely left a dangerous enemy in the rear.[428]

It was in 1144 that Zangi launched the decisive assault on Edessa. In order to do that he resorted to many stratagems. It is probable, Belloc notes, that the fight he was conducting at that time with Muslim rivals was exaggerated in order to make the Christians believe him to be too much occupied to act, but in fact his name had become an inspiration to all Islam in those parts.[429] Zangi's apparent campaign against the Ortoqid Turks in Dyar al-Bekr was indeed aimed at diverting crusaders' attention.[430] Zangi, Ibn al-Athir writes, was aware that if he made a direct attack on Edessa, as soon as first news of his march was known by the Franks, they would rally to fight him back. They would concentrate there to defend it, and it was too well fortified to be an easy conquest.[431] Hence, he made it look that he had scores to settle in Dyar al-Bekr. When the Christians saw that war was starting again between him and the Ortoqids and other princes, they lost their apprehensions, and Jocelyn, the ruler of Edessa left the city, crossed the Euphrates for his other possessions on the western side of the river.[432]

Zangi had already written to the tribes of Turkmen, calling upon them to give support and assistance and to carry out the obligation of the Holy War, and large numbers amongst them had now joined him.[433] Zangi had also mustered considerable siege equipment to bombard the strong fortifications of the city. His army also included Syrians from Aleppo and men from as far as Khurasan who were experts in mining and sapping defences.[434] Once this done, with great speed, he hastened to encamp before the city, soon to be joined by a numerous army.[435] The Syriac (Abul'Faraj?) source says that Zangi arrived in front of the city at dawn on the Thursday (28 November 1144) with an army 'as numerous as the stars,' which filled all the plain round the town.[436] In earnest Zangi assigned the officers of his

---

[428] W.B. Stevenson: *The Crusaders*; op cit; p. 153.
[429] H. Belloc: *The Crusade;* Cassell and Company Ltd; London; 1937; p. 238.
[430] R. Grousset: *Histoire*; op cit; vol 2; p. 179.
[431] Ibn al-Athir: *Kamil*; xi; pp. 64-6; in F. Gabrieli: *Arab Historians*; op cit; p. 51.
[432] Ibn al-Athir; pp. 443-4; in R. Grousset: *Histoire;* op cit; vol 2; p. 179.
[433] Ibn al-Qalanisi: *The Damascus Chronicle* (Gibb); op cit; pp. 266-7.
[434] Ibn al-Athir; p. 686; in R. Grousset: *Histoire*; p. 183; Ibn al-Qalanisi: *The Damascus Chronicle* (Gibb); p. 267.
[435] Ibn al-Qalanisi: *The Damascus Chronicle* (Gibb); op cit; pp. 266-7.
[436] The First and second Crusades from an Anonymous Syriac chronicle; at p. 281.

legions to appropriate stations, and dug in.[437] In the shortest time, the city was thoroughly surrounded. 'Even the birds could scarcely approach the city in fear of their lives from the unerring shafts and watchfulness of the besiegers,' says Ibn al-Qalanisi.[438] The siege was to last three weeks.[439]

Even though it lay in a valley, Edessa was a difficult city to take, for its powerful triangular walls were solidly anchored in the hills ringing the town.[440] In the upper town there were high towers and down below there was the lower town where the citizens could take refuge that is should the city itself be taken.[441] For its defence, Edessa had been entrusted to the Latin Archbishop Hugh II with support of the Armenian Bishop John, and the Jacobite Bishop: Basil.[442] The Syriac source also says that three bishops were in the town, the Frank Papias who took command, the Syrian Basilius son of Shumana a native of the town, and the Armenian Ahnanius.[443] Zangi, it is thought, had hoped to find the Christians disunited, that the local Christians would dissociate themselves from the Franks, but quite the reverse, the Syrian Bishop, Basilius Bar Shumana, as well as the Armenian Ananias (Ahnanius), both strongly sided by the Franks.[444] In the fight that would soon ensue, they would all resist stoutly and fight to the bitter end.[445]

On the 1st day of Kanun, writes Michael the Syrian, Zangi ordered the beginning of the attack with all means and manners. Seven ballistas hurled stones at the defences, and battered the wall violently.[446] As their mangonels unceasingly bombarded the city, the Muslims engaged in constant and persistent fighting with the besieged.[447] At the same time a shower of arrows was descending on the city 'like raindrops,' says Michael the Syrian.[448] Every citizen, old, young, man, woman, monks and others were present on the walls fighting on the front line.[449] When Zangi saw these people fighting stoutly, he ordered the sappers to begin digging a mine under the wall.[450]

As the digging proceeded, Muslim bombardment became fiercer by the day. The catapults and siege engines battered the fortifications, whilst the continual shooting of arrows tormented the citizens incessantly, giving them no respite.[451] Despite the

---

[437] William of Tyre: *Historia*; XVI; pp. 4-5; PL., CCI; 642-5; in J.A. Brundage: *The Crusades;* op cit; p. 81.

[438] Ibn al-Qalanisi: *The Damascus Chronicle* (Gibb); pp. 266-7.

[439] Ibn al-Athir: *Kamil*; xi; pp. 64-6; in F. Gabrieli: *Arab Historians*; op cit; p. 51.

[440] A. Maalouf: *The Crusades;* op cit; p. 134.

[441] William of Tyre: *Historia*; XVI; pp. 4-5; PL., CCI; 642-5; in J.A. Brundage: *The Crusades*; op cit; p. 81.

[442] S. Runciman: *A History;* op cit; p. 235.

[443] The First and Second Crusades; op cit; p. 282.

[444] R. Grousset: *Histoire*; op cit; vol 2; p. 179.

[445] The First and Second Crusades; op cit; p. 282.

[446] Michael the Syrian; III; ii; pp. 260-1; in R. Grousset: *Histoire*; op cit; p. 181.

[447] Ibn al-Qalanisi: *The Damascus Chronicle* (Gibb); p. 267.

[448] Michael the Syrian in R. Grousset: *Histoire*; op cit; p. 181.

[449] Ibid.

[450] Ibid.

[451] William of Tyre: *Historia*; XVI; pp. 4-5; PL., CCI; 642-5; in J.A. Brundage: *The Crusades;* op cit; p. 81.

tight blockade, the inhabitants managed to send news of the Muslim attack to the rest of the crusader kingdom.[452]

Hearing of the attack on his city, Joscelin rushed a messenger to Jerusalem to seek assistance from Queen Melisende, regent of Jerusalem, and the Prince of Antioch, Raymond of Poitiers, to help him save his city.[453] The Queen, who had charge of the kingdom's government, on the advice of the council of the nobles, agreed to send a great army with all speed to Edessa that 'they might give the Lord Count and the suffering citizens the comfort which they desired.'[454] The troops marched as fast as they could, but the distance to Edessa was considerable and Winter had arrived.[455]

Zangi was aware that reinforcements could be arriving any time and relieve the city, and so he put every resource in the fight, and urged his army to press the siege and to undermine the defences with greater vigour.[456] The Muslims dug mines under the fortress, on the north side under the bridge outside the Gate of Hours and reached the foundations. In the meantime above them the fighting was going on constantly.[457] As they dug passages beneath the walls, they buttressed these with posts.[458] Before ordering the wood to be set alight, Zangi made offers to the besieged:

'We will give you two men who will go inside the tunnel, and we want you to send two of yours to go with them and see the mining of the wall. Surrender the city before you are conquered by the sword. I don't want you to be killed.'[459]

The Syriac source adds:

'He (Zangi) sent proposals of peace (to the defenders but they did not listen) for he wished a surrender so that the town should not be destroyed and the inhabitants killed. He said to them: "Fools, you see that there is no hope of saving your lives, why do you watch and hope? Have mercy on yourselves, your sons and daughters, your wives and houses, and your city, that it be not laid waste and empty of inhabitants.'[460]

When from inside the city, he saw that Muslim sappers were tunneling under the ramparts, Abu'l-Faraj suggested writing a letter to Zangi proposing a truce, and the Frankish Bishop agreed.[461] However, the bishop's proposal for a truce, according to the Syriac source, was made with the hope that it would delay the Muslim attack until Christian reinforcements arrived.[462] Just then, however, according to the Syriac source, something unexpected happened:

---

[452] Ibid.

[453] R. Grousset: *Histoire*; op cit; p. 182.

[454] William of Tyre: Historia; XVI; pp. 4-5; PL., CCI; 642-5; in J.A. Brundage: *The Crusades*; op cit; p. 81.

[455] R. Grousset: *Histoire*; op cit; p. 182.

[456] Ibn al-Athir: *Kamil*; xi; pp. 64-6; in F. Gabrieli: *Arab Historians*; op cit; p. 51.

[457] The First and Second Crusades; op cit; at p. 282.

[458] William of Tyre: *Historia;* XVI; pp. 4-5; PL., CCI; 642-5; in J.A. Brundage: *The Crusades*; op cit; p. 81.

[459] Michael the Syrian; ed. Chabot; III; ii; pp. 260-1; in R. Grousset: *Histoire;* op cit; p. 184.

[460] The First and Second Crusades; op cit; p. 282.

[461] A. Maalouf: *The Crusades;* op cit; p. 135.

[462] The First and Second Crusades; op cit; at p. 283.

'Then an ignorant silk merchant named Hasnun put out his hand and tore the letter; there was a great commotion and this wise plan was foiled. Although Zangi said, "If you want a truce we will grant it. If help come- and if not, surrender and be safe." He did not want the town to be ruined but when he saw that persuasion was useless, as Scripture says "The Lord hardened Pharaoh's heart to his destruction." They were left to ruin and a bad end, and answered Zangi rudely with insults and abuse, foolishly, beyond all measure.'[463]

There was no Christian force approaching Edessa, though, not even Joscelin, who was much nearer to his city. Although he had been informed of the offensive against his capital, he did not dare fight the Atabeg. He preferred to camp at Tel Bashir, expecting that troops from Antioch or Jerusalem would come to his aid.[464] As he waited, the Muslim siege advanced to its final stages. The Muslims had by now dismantled the foundations of the northern wall, and in their place had erected great quantities of wood, joists and beams. They filled the interstices with naphtha, animal fat, and sulphur, so that fire would spread more easily and the wall would collapse. Then, on Zangi's orders, the fire was started.[465] The heralds of Zangi's camp gave the call to prepare for battle, telling the soldiers to rush in through the breach as soon as the wall collapsed.[466] The fire devoured the oil and sulphur and began on the beams, while a north wind blew the smoke into the faces of the garrison.[467] Soon the wood and melted fat were in flames. Just then, the Muslims launched the assault:

'The air was darkened by thick smoke, the knees and the hearts trembled to the sound of the trumpet, of the troops thrusting forward and the shouts of the population,' says Michael the Syrian.[468]

When the wood was consumed, the wall and the two towers collapsed. Just then, the Muslims discovered a second wall standing in front of them.[469] The temporary rampart proved to be too short at both ends, for the part that fell was longer than what the Christians had built.[470] Hastily, the besieged filled the breach with corpses of both Christians and Muslims.[471] The Muslims pressed forth, but the besieged fought stoutly in the two gaps from dawn till the third hour on the eve of the feast of the 'Mother of God,' 24th December.[472] The Armenian source says that the Christians first repulsed the Muslim assault:

'The brave fighters resisted the attackers and pushed them back. Happy I would be if my narration ended here,' said the narrator.[473]

[463] Ibid.
[464] A. Maalouf: *The Crusades;* op cit; p. 135.
[465] Ibid.
[466] Ibid.
[467] The First and second Crusades; op cit; at p. 284.
[468] Michael the Syrian; ed. Chabot; III; ii; pp. 260-1; in R. Grousset: *Histoire;* op cit; p. 184.
[469] Ibid.
[470] The First and Second Crusades; op cit; p. 284.
[471] Michael the Syrian; III; ii; pp. 260-1; in R. Grousset: *Histoire;* op cit; p. 184.
[472] The First and Second Crusades; op cit; p. 284.
[473] N. Shnorhali: Elegie sur la Prise d'Edesse; in *Doc Armeniens*; op cit; I; pp. 247-55.

Muslims were as resilient as their Christian foes. They launched a strong assault and managed to put scaling ladders against the walls, fighting hard to break into the city.[474] In a final and violent push, they erupted inside the city. The Syriac source says that when many defenders had been killed, the Turks forced their way in (God was angry with the inhabitants, it says) 'and slew with the sword, sparing none.'[475] Women, children, and young people fled toward the upper citadel, only to find that the gate was shut, the fault of the Catholic Bishop, who had told the guards, 'Do not open the gate unless you see my face!' Groups of people climbed up in succession.[476] Disaster followed. The crowd, rank after rank, from fear of death and captivity, pushed upwards, treading on one another-a pitiable sight and full of terror-they were squashed and crushed into a solid mass, and some five thousand were, thus, suffocated.[477] In the meantime, fighting was raging not far from the citadel. The Frankish bishop was killed by an axe on the road to the citadel and many priests, deacons, and monks were also slain.[478] It was then that Zangi came near the citadel, and when he saw those who had been crushed to death he was deeply affected, and at once gave order to stop hostilities.[479] The city had now fallen to the Muslims but the citadel still remained in Christian hands. Zangi gave order to his officers to lay siege to it.[480] He then advanced to the gate of the citadel, and spoke peaceably to the defenders asking them to surrender, promising to spare their lives. Some of them came out to ask security for the Franks in it. Among them was the priest Barsama of Ishmael. By his power of talk he had made himself prominent in the citadel. Zangi gave him a sworn promise that their lives would be spared, and so, two days after the capture of the town, the citadel surrendered.[481]

Following the taking of Edessa, Cox says, the Christians expected Muslim deeds of blood and cruelty as 'they (the Muslims) might be apt pupils in the horrible school in which the Christians had attained a standard of ideal excellence.'[482] Instead, as the Anonymous Syriac source says:

> When the upper fort was taken and they received the promise of their lives, Zangi fetched the metropolitan Basilius who was in the keeping of a soldier, and they began to bring out the Franks from the citadel with their women and children, and priests and deacons, with much gold, vessels of silver, and raiment. Many of the townsmen had joined them to go with them for Zangi had sworn to take them across the Euphrates that they might go where they wished. The next day Zangi reviewed the prisoners from all the camps, some were selected and sent into captivity. They set guards that no Turk might

---

[474] Michael the Syrian; III; ii; pp. 260-1; in R. Grousset: *Histoire;* op cit; p. 184.
[475] The First and Second Crusades; op cit; p. 284.
[476] A. Maalouf: *The Crusades*; op cit; p. 135.
[477] The First and Second Crusades; op cit; p. 284.
[478] Ibid.
[479] Ibid.
[480] Ibn al-Athir: Kamil; xi; pp. 64-6; in F. Gabrieli: *Arab Historians;* op cit; p. 52.
[481] The First and Second Crusades; op cit; p. 284.
[482] G.W. Cox: *The Crusades*; Longman; London; 1874; p. 83.

hurt the townsmen and at the gates that none might enter the town. The men of Edessa went to their homes and Zangi gave them what they needed, fodder, etc., and cheered them. They dwelt in their homes.[483]

6. Following Edessa and the Death of Zangi

When news of the re-capture of Edessa spread, the Muslim world regained much of its lost enthusiasm. From Baghdad to North Africa the victory was greeted with jubilation.[484] The most ambitious projects were now being attributed to Zangi, the refugees from Palestine and the many coastal cities already speaking of the recovery of Jerusalem.[485] The poet Qaysarani wrote:

> Tell the rulers of the infidels to flee the territories they pretend to hold, for this land is the land of Zangi.[486]

Edessa, in the words of a Muslim historian, was:

> The conquest of conquests: the stoutest prop of the Latin Kingdom was uprooted; Saruj and the other satellites of the great city immediately surrendered; and the valley of the Euphrates was finally freed from the oppression of the infidel.[487]

The caliph, in Baghdad, lost no time in heaping prestigious titles upon the hero of the moment: al-Malik al-Mansur, 'Victorious King'; 'Ornament of Islam'; 'Protector of the Prince of the Faithful'.[488]

Whatever their pompous character, these titles nevertheless reflected the leading place Zangi now held in the Muslim world, whilst the Franks trembled at the very mention of his name.[489] Their disarray was all the greater because King Fulk had died shortly before the fall of Edessa, leaving two children who were both minors. His wife, who acted as regent, quickly sent emissaries to the Christian West to bring news of the disaster that 'had just befallen his people.'[490] In all their territories, Ibn al-Qalanisi writes, calls were issued 'for people to assemble for an assault on the land of Islam.'[491] 'Zangi had knocked the coping-stone from the Christian edifice in Palestine, it seemed only a matter of moments the whole building should crumble.'[492] As if to confirm Christian fears, Zangi returned to Syria after his victory, giving rise to rumours that he was preparing a large scale offensive against the main

---

[483] The First and Second Crusades; op cit; p. 285.
[484] G. Hindley: *Saladin*, op cit, p. 33.
[485] A. Maalouf: *The Crusades*; op cit; p. 136.
[486] Al-Qaysaran quoted in E. Siwan: *L'Islam et la Croisade*, 1968, p. 46.
[487] S. Lane Poole: *The Life of Saladin*, op cit, p. 58-9.
[488] A. Maalouf: *The Crusades*; op cit; p. 137.
[489] Ibid.
[490] Ibid.
[491] Ibid.
[492] G. Hindley: *Saladin*, op cit, p. 33.

crusader strongholds.[493] Forty days after the siege of Edessa Zangi sent his army to Saruj. Reacting in panic the Christians fled to al-Bira, and the Muslims took Saruj.[494]

After staying in Aleppo for a year Zangi came to Edessa, leaving his troops on the river Jullab between Kasas and Harran on the stream. With his governors, chiefs, commanders, and other councilors, he came to the town, in the middle of Pentecost. The Metropolitan, priests, deacons, and all the Christians as well as the Muslims who had gathered from all quarters, all came to see him.[495] Zangi entered by the north gate, the Gate of Hours, went towards the Church of St. John, went down to the springs, and inspected everything carefully. He greeted the Christians and saluted the Metropolitan.[496] He said that he had come for their sake to give them whatever they were in need of. The Muslims had rebuilt the breaches and the seven towers which the war engines had destroyed a year earlier at the siege, a work even stronger than the foundations, and had carved on them in Arabic the story of the capture of the city and the ruler's name.[497] Zangi gave orders that a great hostel should be built for the convenience of the sick and suffering who came there and endowed it with the fields nearby.[498]

> Zangi [the Syriac source says] visited our Syrian churches, examined their beauty, ordered two great bells to be given them and hung on them, as was the custom in the time of the Franks, and got ready to go. He told the metropolitan to be zealous in guarding the town and not to betray his government.[499]

In Edessa, however, Grousset remarks, things did not go as Zangi wanted. If the Syriac population and its leader, Basilius bar Shumana, remained loyal, the Armenians, on the other hand, did not show the same loyalty.[500] In fact the Armenians began conspiring with the Franks to kill the small Turkish garrison and let the Franks in again.[501] And so, in January 1146, just as his preparations for a spring offensive seemed complete, Zangi, who was south of Edessa, found himself forced to change his plans, and turn north again. His spies had informed him that a plot to massacre the Turkish garrison had been hatched by Jocelyn of Edessa and some of his Armenian friends who had remained in the city.[502] This plot was crushed by Kutchuk Ali of Irbil,[503] and Zangi had the Armenian plotters crucified.[504] Zangi still spared the Christian population, only ordering the ringleaders to be

[493] A. Maalouf: *The Crusades*; op cit; p. 137.
[494] The First and Second Crusades; op cit; p. 286.
[495] Ibid; p. 289.
[496] Ibid.
[497] Ibid.
[498] Ibid; p. 290.
[499] Ibid; p. 291.
[500] R. Grousset: *Histoire*; vol 2; p. 195.
[501] Ibid.
[502] A. Maalouf: *The Crusades;* op cit; p. 137.
[503] Michael the Syrian; iii; pp. 267-8; Ibn al-Qalanisi: *The Damascus Chronicles* (Gibb); op cit; p. 270.
[504] Kemal Eddin; p. 687; in R. Grousset: *Histoire;* op cit; p. 195.

executed. He had part of the Armenian population exiled, and replaced them with three hundred Jewish families.[505]

This alert, however, convinced Zangi that it would be better to temporarily put on hold plans for further attacks against the Christians, and instead, consolidate the territory he has so far liberated. An emir who controlled the powerful fortress of Ja'bar, situated on the Euphrates along the main route from Aleppo to Mosul, had, however, refused to recognise Zangi's authority.[506] This act of insubordination seriously threatened communications between Zangi's two capitals, and so he decided to lay siege to Ja'bar in June 1146. Zangi hoped to take it in a few days, but the enterprise proved more difficult than expected, and three long months passed as the besieged refused to surrender.[507] Zangi harassed the castle with incessant assaults as he had sworn not to turn aside till he had taken it. However, on the night of 4th September, as he lay asleep without care, two of his eunuchs killed him in his bed.[508] Elisseeff says that the assassin, named Yaranqas, was a slave of Christian origin, who pierced the Sultan's couch with his dagger.[509] A number of the Atabeg's foes might have commandeered the murder as Elisseeff points out.[510] The murderer(s) fled to the castle; and soon, on that night, it became known that he had been killed.[511] Ibn al-Athir writes:

> In this year (541 H) on 5 Rabi' II/4 September 1146, the Atabeg Imad Eddin Zangi ibn Aq Sunqur, martyr for the Faith, ruler of Mosul and Syria, was killed while he was besieging Ja'bar as we have narrated. He was killed at night, murdered by a group of his courtiers. They fled to the fortress, whose inhabitants joyfully shouted the news to the (besieging) camp. When Zangi's servants came to his bedside they found that there was still a spark of life in him. One of Zangi's close friends, recalled: 'I went straight to him; he was still alive, and when he saw me, clearly wanting to make an end of it he made a sign to me with his fingers imploring me to take pity on him. At the very suggestion I fell to the ground and said: "My Lord, who has done this?" but he was beyond speech, and yielded up his soul, may the Lord have mercy on him.
> Zangi was a handsome man, with a swarthy complexion, fine eyes, and hair that was beginning to go grey. He was more than 60 years old, for he had been a baby when his father was killed, as has been narrated. After his death he was buried at Rakka.'[512]

Ibn al-Qalanisi comments on the event in verse:

> 'At his death did his enemies ride forth, grasping the swords

[505] Ibid.
[506] A. Maalouf: *The Crusades;* op cit; p. 138.
[507] Ibid.
[508] The First and Second Crusades; op cit; p. 291.
[509] N. Elisseeff: *Nur Ad Din,* op cit, p. 385.
[510] Ibid.
[511] The First and Second Crusades; op cit; p. 291.
[512] Ibn al-Athir: *Kamil*: xi; op cit; pp. 72-3; in F. Gabrieli: *Arab Historians*; op cit; pp. 53-4.

they dared not brandish while he lived.'[513]
The wise old chief, Salah Eddin, as soon as he heard of the murder of Zangi, took Zangi's son Mahmud (Nur Eddin) and the other chiefs who followed him, went quickly to Aleppo, and installed him as ruler. He seized the treasure with the great wealth that was stored up there for safe keeping.[514]

It is said that a great authority on genealogies and biographies tells the following story:

> The King of Sicily (Roger) sent a naval expedition that ravaged Tripoli in North Africa. Now there was in Sicily a learned, God-fearing Muslim whom the King held in great respect, relying on his advice rather than that of his own priests and monks; so much so that the people used to say that the King was really a Muslim. One day, as the King was standing at a window overlooking the sea, he saw a small boat come into the harbour. The crew told him that his army had invaded Muslim territory, laid it waste and returned victorious. The Muslim sage was dozing at the King's side. The King said to him: 'Did you hear what they said?' 'No.' 'They told me that we have defeated the Muslims in Tripoli. What use is Muhammad now to his land and his people?' 'He was not there,' replied the old man, 'he was at Edessa, which the Muslims have just taken.' The Franks who were present laughed, but the King said: 'Do not laugh, for by God this man is incapable of speaking anything but the truth.' And a few days later news came from the Franks in Syria that Edessa had been taken.' Certain honest and godly men have told me that a holy man saw the dead Zangi in a dream and asked him: 'How has God treated you?' and Zangi replied, 'God has pardoned me, because I conquered Edessa.'[515]

Men looked back on his reign as the turning point of the tide against the Christians. He and his son, Nur Eddin, brought the Turkish regimes in Syria to the pinnacle of their prestige, and their renown was to overshadow Saladin for years [adds Hindley.][516]

*****

Zangi was dead, but his legacy, most particularly the capture of Edessa, was stupendous, marking a significant turning point in Muslim fortunes. The whole state of Edessa with its towns and defences had now been regained for Islam, and this also meant relief to Aleppo. The gains were threefold: its communication with the

[513] In A. Maalouf: *The Crusades*; op cit; p. 139.
[514] The First and Second Crusades; op cit; p. 292.
[515] Ibn al-Athir: *Kamil*; xi; pp. 64-6; in F. Gabrieli: *Arab Historians*; op cit; pp. 52-3.
[516] G. Hindley: *Saladin*, op cit, p. 30.

east was secured; its enemy was now in front, no longer in the rear as well; and it, in turn, began to encircle what was left of crusader territory.[517]

To the Christians, however, the loss of Edessa was a disaster. It roused a sudden and violent emotion all over Western Europe.[518] According to Grousset:

> The retaking of Edessa caused a terrible stir in Christendom. Frankish Syria was now dismantled by the fall of this Mesopotamian bastion. Without a doubt it was only a limited re-conquest, and the bulk of crusader land was not directly threatened, and the line of the Euphrates constituted a strong frontier. However, the crusade was now in retreat. The fall of Edessa began the wave of the Muslim return. This was how it was seen in the West.[519]

It was the first sensational bad news to reach the West out of the East; the first dramatic evidence that what had been universally taken in Europe as 'the fixed triumph of the Cross was now imperilled.'[520]

St Bernard (1090-1153), a leading preacher, saw the Muslim conquest of Edessa as the prelude to an attack on Jerusalem.[521] In earnest he began rousing Western Christendom for a new crusade.

---

[517] W.B. Stevenson: *The Crusaders;* op cit; p. 153.

[518] H. Belloc: *The Crusade;* Cassell and Company Ltd; London; 1937; pp. 239.

[519] R. Grousset: *Histoire;* op cit; p. 208.

[520] H. Belloc: *The Crusade;* op cit; p. 239.

[521] In V. G. Berry: The Second Crusade; in *A History of the Crusades;* ed., by K.M. Setton; University of Pennsylvania Press; 1955; pp. 463-512; pp. 471-2.

NUR-EDDIN ZANGI
(1147-1174)

To his subjects [Lane Poole writes] Nur Eddin was a model of all virtue, the embodiment of Moslem piety, "a second Omar ibn Abd-al-Aziz" (the pious Umayyad ruler,) as religious, just, and clement a king as ever ruled. Even the Crusaders bore witness to his chivalrous character, and William of Tyre admits that, in spite of his race and creed, "Noradinus was a just prince, wise, and religious", though a great oppressor of Christians. Justice was the quality he valued next to—indeed as a part of—godliness. He would himself appear in the Qady's court to answer the process of a subject, and he insisted on no favor being shown to his rank. He remitted all customs, dues and tithes throughout his dominions, and lived simply and frugally on his private means, without touching the public revenue.

When his wife complained of her poverty, and disdained his offer of three shops at Emesa, belonging to his estate, and worth about twenty gold pieces a-year, he rebuked her: "I have nothing more, for all the rest I hold only in trust for the people". In pursuance of that trust he built citadels for their defense, and founded many colleges, convents, hospitals, and caravanserais, for their spiritual and bodily welfare. No man delighted more in the conversation of the learned and devout. None was more diligent in the observance of the minutest rules of his religion. There was a holy calm in the grave but gentle eyes, which relieved the massive brow and ennobled the swarthy, almost beardless, face. He possessed the dignity and serenity of the true Eastern gentleman; in his presence there was silence and stillness.[522]

Nur Eddin succeeded his father straight after the latter's death. This happened just as in Europe a new crusade was being preached. St. Bernard of Clairvaux (1090-1153), the main preacher, promised absolution and a heavenly reward to all those who took up the cross.[523] He proclaimed that:

> The soldier of Christ carries a sword not without reason, for he is the minister of Christ for the punishment of evil-doers, as well as for the praise of good men. Clearly when he kills a malefactor he is not a homicide but as I should say a malicide, and he is simply considered the avenger of Christ on those who do evil and the protector of Christians..... The Christian glories in the death of the pagan, because Christ is thereby glorified.[524]

[522] S. Lane Poole: *The Life of Saladin*, op cit, pp. 131-2.
[523] R. Payne: *The Crusades*; Wordsworth Editions; 1986; p. 156.
[524] St Bernard: *Opera*; ed., Mabillon; Vol I; col. 549. Also in Milman *Latin Christianity*, IV, p. 251.

Hundreds of thousands responded to the call for the crusade, so many, according to a contemporary, that it left the cities and castles empty, and scarcely one man for seven women.[525] Three hundred and ninety five thousand men reached the capital of the Greeks, Constantinople.[526] It seemed with this new crusade that the Christian West would prevail, especially as the conditions in the Muslim world looked precarious following Zangi's death. His sudden disappearance was welcome news to his enemies, who hoped that the dynastic disputes that usually followed the death of Muslim princes would disrupt his realm.[527] The eldest of his sons, Saif Eddin Ghazi, hurried to Mosul to take government there, and Nur Eddin went to be proclaimed in Aleppo. The division of the realm was the signal for the foes to invade or prepare to invade. Faster than any other, Anar sent his troops from Damascus, which reoccupied Baalbek, and in the centre, Raymond of Antioch led a raid.[528] However, soon, the sons of Zangi came to agreement: Saif Eddin would send help if need be to Nur Eddin without any desire to annex his share of the family lands.[529] A third brother, Nusrat Eddin, was established as Nur Eddin's vassal at Harran, while the youngest of the family, Qutb Eddin, was growing at his oldest brother's court at Mosul. Secure from danger from his fellow Muslims thanks to the unity of his family, Nur Eddin could now begin the mission for which his father had already initiated him. Nur Eddin, who had accompanied his father in many military campaigns, and who thus had acquired a great prestige amongst the military, was the rightful heir to Imad, indeed. Now, as the Atabeg of Aleppo, aged 29, he was about to begin Islam's counter offensive.[530] Nur Eddin, who, Lane Poole says, 'was a bold and fearless warrior, a splendid horseman, ready to expose himself in the front of every battle.'[531]

1. Nur Eddin Zangi (b. 1118-)

'In the Sultan of Aleppo (Nur Eddin Zangi),' Cox notes, 'we have a man to whom the chronicles of the time and of later ages delighted to ascribe the magnanimity and simplicity of Omar.'[532] His 'narrow' piety, according to Runciman, won him the respect of his subjects and of his enemies.[533] Austere, seldom smiling, living simply, something he forced on his own family, his wife most of all, devoting the revenues instead to charity, and also defence of the realm, he was a careful and watchful administrator 'and his wise government consolidated the realm that his sword had

[525] G.W. Cox: *The Crusades*; op cit; p. 93.
[526] The First and second crusades; Part two: op cit; p. 298.
[527] S. Runciman: *A History of the Crusades*; op cit; Vol 2; p. 239.
[528] Ibid.
[529] Ibid; p. 244.
[530] Ibid. N. Elisseeff: Nur Ad Din, p. 389.
[531] S. Lane Poole: *The Life of Saladin*, op cit, p. 132.
[532] G.W. Cox: *The Crusades;* op cit; p. 100.
[533] S. Runciman: *A History of the Crusades*; vol 2; op cit; p. 398.

won.'[534] It is said that his career at war and peace, of all the rulers and leaders of Islam, came the nearest to that of the First Four Caliphs.[535] Under his rule, he would gradually unite the once divided Muslim world, add the kingdom of Damascus to that of Aleppo, and wage a long and successful war against the crusaders. He would expand the Muslim front from the Tigris to the Nile, and force the crusaders

> To own the wisdom and courage, and even the justice and piety, of this implacable adversary [says Gibbon.][536]

Nur Eddin's first deed on succeeding his father, Imad, was to re-assert Muslim authority over Edessa. There, profiting from Imad Zangi's death, Jocelyn, its former ruler, sought to reoccupy it. His agents made contact with the Armenians in the city and won over the local Jacobite Christians.[537] Together with reinforcements from Beaudouin of Maraash, a baron with very pro-Armenian feelings, they crossed the Euphrates, in the vicinity of Al-Bira, and following a pre-conceived plan, reached the walls of Edessa at night.[538] On 27 October, 1146, thanks to the Armenians, who guarded two towers, the crusaders were thrown down ladders and ropes, and thus were able to climb up the defences of the city.[539] The Muslims were caught by surprise, some were slain but many escaped to the citadel. At dawn the four gates were opened to the invading forces, and Jocelyn entered the city, whilst the Crusaders and the Armenians spread through the streets hunting Muslims who could not reach the citadel and butchering them.[540] The Muslim garrison of the citadel, however, put up a strong resistance, and Jocelyn was unable to storm its fortifications. As messengers had reached Nur Eddin at Aleppo, he counter attacked with ten thousand horsemen, marching with all speed night and day, and on 2 November appeared before Edessa.[541] Nur Eddin put in place a siege, and his miners began to sap the walls, whilst mangonels submitted the city to intense bombardment.[542] Inside the situation rapidly deteriorated for the Christians, and the Muslim garrison in the citadel affected sorties, causing great loss amongst the foe. Famine soon spread, and the siege lengthened.[543] Jocelyn's situation grew desperate as he was caught between Nur Eddin and the citadel, and so resolved on a plan of escape. The Armenian citizens, rather than face the vengeance of Nur Eddin, resolved to share Jocelyn's fortunes.[544] At night, they set the city on fire, and made their attempted escape; the sudden irruption of flood of people surprised the Muslim besiegers, and thanks to the chaos thus created, the horsemen amongst the

---

[534] S. Runciman: *A History of the Crusades*; vol 2; op cit; p. 398.

[535] E. Gibbon: *The Decline and Fall*; op cit; vol 6; p. 336.

[536] Ibid.

[537] S. Runciman: *A History of the Crusades*; vol 2; op cit; p. 240.

[538] N. Elisseeff: *Nur Ad Din*, op cit, p. 396.

[539] Ibid, p. 397.

[540] Ibn al-Qalanisi: *The Damascus Chronicles* (Gibb); op cit; p. 274; S. Runciman: *The Crusades*; vol 2; op cit; p. 240; N. Elisseeff; p. 397.

[541] Ibn al-Qalanisi: *The Damascus Chronicles*; op cit, p. 274.

[542] N. Elisseeff: *Nur Ad Din*, op cit, p. 397.

[543] Ibid.

[544] T.A. Archer: *The Crusades;* op cit; p. 205.

Christians managed to cut through Muslim lines.[545] Following a moment of surprise the Muslims reacted, and as the Christians filed through the gates, the Turks from the citadel fell upon them in the rear while Nur-Eddin's army barred all progress in front.[546] The slaughter was terrible amongst the Armenians, in particular, and only the more able amongst them managed to escape with the Frankish host.[547] Jocelyn and his army, meanwhile, and large numbers of native Christians, made their way towards the Euphrates.[548] Nur Eddin followed on their heels, until the following day when the two sides met and engaged in a fierce fight. The Christian counter-attack was driven back, and the Frankish army broke up in panic.[549] Baldwin of Marash was killed on the field, whilst Jocelyn, wounded in the neck, escaped with his bodyguards.[550] The Armenian bishop John was captured and taken to Aleppo. Many native male Christians, deserted by the Franks, were massacred, and their wives and children enslaved, and the whole Christian population was driven into exile.[551] Nur Eddin's severe retribution was in reaction to the slaughter of the Muslim population by Jocelyn and his allies. Also, months before, in May 1146, when his father Imad was still alive, a first attempt had been made by the Armenians to restore the city to Jocelyn, an attempt which was crushed by Kutchuk Ali of Irbil.[552] Zangi had spared the Christian population, only ordering the ringleaders to be executed, and part of the Armenian population to be exiled.[553] This lenient Muslim reaction had obviously failed to make the point; this time, Nur Eddin went further. Nur Eddin also understood that should Edessa fall into Christian hands, again, Aleppo would be under immediate threat, especially now that the arrival of a new crusade was imminent.

The new crusade had been ardently preached in the Christian West. St Bernard, the main preacher, saw the Muslim conquest of Edessa as the prelude to an attack on Jerusalem 'and the very shrine of the Christian religion' unless his hearers worked to prevent it:

> What are you brave men doing? What are you servants of the cross doing? Will you thus give a holy place to dogs and pearls to swine? [He demanded; declaring that God] was making a trial of the Christians and giving them an opportunity for salvation in His service.[554]

St Bernard exhorted his audience to receive the blessed arms of the Christian zealously.[555] And after preaching in France, he aimed for Germany, to him, the

---

[545] N. Elisseeff: *Nur Ad Din*, op cit, p. 397.
[546] T.A. Archer: *The Crusades;* op cit; p. 205.
[547] Ibid.
[548] S. Runciman: *A History of the Crusades*; vol 2; op cit; p. 240.
[549] Ibid.
[550] Ibid.
[551] Ibn al-Qalanisi: *The Damascus Chronicles*; pp. 274-5; S. Runciman: *The Crusades;* vol 2; op cit; p. 240.
[552] Michael the Syrian; iii; pp. 267-8; Ibn al-Qalanisi: *The Damascus Chronicles*; Gibb; p. 270.
[553] Ibid.
[554] In V. G. Berry: The Second Crusade; op cit; pp. 471-2.
[555] Ibid.

Germans, who had so far shown little interest in fighting in the Holy Land, should be introduced to the 'delights' of battling against the infidels.[556]

The pope, Eugenius III (Pope 1145-1156), for his part, moved by the pleas of the Eastern lord, Hugh of Jabala, and by the Armenian bishops, who had come to see him, and who had proposed to unify the Roman and Armenian churches, issued a bull: *Quantum pradecessores* from Vetralla on December 1, 1145.[557] He addressed the French king 'his dear son, Louis, the illustrious and glorious king of the Franks, and his cherished sons the princes and all the faithful living throughout Gaul.'[558] Eugenius recalled Urban's summons for the First Crusade, which resulted in the conquest of Jerusalem and other sites in the Holy Land, and the retention of those places and additions to their number until 'the sins of the faithful' had brought about the recent capture of Edessa, and he exhorted the powerful nobles in particular to emulate their forefathers and

> Gird themselves courageously to oppose the multitude of unbelievers which
> is rejoicing that it has obtained a victory over us.... to snatch from their hands
> the many thousands of captives who are our kinsmen.[559]

To those vowing to go on the crusade he promised remission of penance, protection of wives, children and possessions, freedom from legal action from the time of taking the cross until their return or death, cancellation of the obligation to pay interest on debts, and much else.[560]

Whilst the Christians were being fired up to join the new crusade, events unfolding in the East in the year 1147 were about to play a major part in the objective of this next crusade. Damascus at the time was ruled by Anar who was on friendly terms with the Christians. Early in 1147, one of Anar's lieutenants, Altuntash (an Armenian convert to Islam) governor of Bosra and Sarkhad in the Hauran, declared his independence of Damascus and came to crusader Jerusalem for support, offering to hand Bosra and Sarkhad to the Franks if they would set him up in a lordship in the Hauran.[561] Queen Melisende summoned her Council to discuss the suggestion. To support Altuntash would mean the rupture of the alliance with Damascus, but it was a tempting offer.[562] The population in the Hauran was largely Christian Melkite, of the Orthodox rite, and with this Christian help it should be easy to colonise the Hauran; and its control would put Damascus at the mercy of the Franks.[563] Moreover, the control of this rich farming region would secure Jerusalem great supplies of food and goods, and would place greater strains on Damascus.[564]

[556] R. Payne: *The Crusades*; op cit; p. 156.
[557] On the bull, see Jaffe-Wattenbach: *Regesta Pontificum Romanurum;* II; no 8796. For the text, cf. Otto of Freising; *Gesta,* I, 36; M. Villey: *La Croisade: Essai sur la Formation d'une Theorie Juridique;* Paris; 1942; pp. 106-205.
[558] V. G. Berry: The Second Crusade; op cit; pp. 466-7.
[559] Ibid; p. 467.
[560] On the bull, see Jaffe-Wattenbach: *Regesta Pontificum Romanurum;* II; no 8796; etc.
[561] S. Runciman: *A History of the Crusades*; vol 2; op cit; p. 241; Ibn al-Qalanisi: *The Damascus Chronicles*; op cit; p. 276.
[562] S. Runciman: *A History of the Crusades*; op cit; p. 241.
[563] Ibid.
[564] N. Elisseeff: *Nur Ad Din*, op cit, p. 404.

So the decision to invade Damascus was taken. In May 1147, the Christian army, which included Templar and Hospitalliers, set for Damascus, crossing the Jordan with the King at their head, and marched into the Jaulan.[565] The ruler of Damascus, Anar, most certainly greatly disturbed by this act from his allies, sought to dissuade the Christians, proposing a large financial indemnity, and most of all warning them that should they advance on his realm, this would bring Nur Eddin into action against them, besides capturing Damascus for himself.[566] The Christians saw that as sign of weakness on the part of Anar, and did not believe in Nur Eddin's intervention at all, judging him too weak to be able to mount a prompt response.[567] Their overt confidence proved wrong. Early in their march, they were attacked by bands of Turks, who kept harassing their less protected ranks, whilst Nur-Eddin, who was called for help by Anar, arrived with his armies from Aleppo.[568] When the Christians reached Bosra, the combined armies of Nur Eddin and Damascus fell on them. Ibn al-Qalanisi narrates:

'The combatants drew up eye to eye, and their ranks closed up to one another, and the Askar of the Muslims gained the upper hand over the polytheists. They cut them off from watering place and pasture ground, they afflicted them with a hail of shafts and death dealing arrows, they multiplied among them death and wounds, and set on fire the dried herbage on their roads and paths. The Franks, on the verge of destruction turned to flight, and the Muslim knights and horsemen, seeing favourable opportunity presented exterminating them, made speed to slay and to engage in combat with them. Mu'in Eddin (Anar), however, endeavoured to restrain the Muslims and prevent them from attacking and pursuing the Franks on their retreat, for fear of a rally on their part and a counter attack upon the Muslims.'[569]

In fact, as Runciman and Elisseeff point out, Anar did not want the destruction of the Christian army, for he feared Nur-Eddin and sought to maintain a Christian presence to check Nur Eddin's power.[570] Thus, the Franks were able to cross back into Palestine, but their expedition had proved quite costly and pointless.[571]

Anar was not alone to dread Nur Eddin's power. Both the caliph in Baghdad and the Fatimids in Egypt sent their support to Anar in order to reinforce him against Nur Eddin whom they judged as growing far too powerful.[572]

Nur Eddin, himself, had just learnt that first units of crusaders from Europe had crossed the Bosphorous, further north in Byzantium, and were on their way down. In a preventive action, he captured late May 1147 Artah, soon to be followed by

---

[565] S. Runciman: *History of the Crusades*, op cit, p. 241; N. Elisseeff: *Nur Ad Din*, op cit, p. 404.
[566] N. Elisseeff: *Nur Ad Din*, op cit, p. 404.
[567] Ibid.
[568] Ibn al-Qalanisi: *The Damascus Chronicles*; op cit; p. 277; S. Runciman: *A History of the Crusades*; vol 2; op cit; p. 242.
[569] Ibn al-Qalanisi: *The Damascus Chronicles*; op cit; pp. 277-8.
[570] S. Runciman: *History of the Crusades*, op cit, p. 241; N. Elisseeff: *Nur Ad Din*, op cit, p. 405.
[571] William of Tyre: *Historia,*; xvi; 8-13; pp. 715-28.
[572] N. Elisseeff: *Nur Ad Din*, op cit, p. 406.

Basuta, Batriki and Mamul and Sih al-Hadid.[573] Having thus severed the links of communication between Antioch and the North, Nur Eddin went on in October 1147 to establish his control over the routes linking up Antioch to the south, and thus captured Hab, or Hisn Hab and Basarfut, both of which were strategically positioned fortresses.[574] Then, the following month, November, he reduced Jabal Ulaym, and captured the fortress of Kafarlata, thus securing his communications with the city of Hama.[575]

Meanwhile, in the West, whilst some crusaders had begun their journey in April, others followed throughout late spring of the same year. Men from Flanders, Frisia, Normandy and Cologne set out for England, where they were joined by Scottish and English crusaders, and they all left Darthmouth on May 19, their first destination: Portugal, where the Iberian crusade was reaching its apex.[576] They reached Portugal in the summer, and became involved in the bloody siege and capture of Lisbon from its Muslim defenders.[577] It ought to be remembered that this phase corresponded precisely with the decline of Almoravid power, and Western Christendom had used the opportunity to seize their realm, whether in the Iberian peninsula, or in North Africa. Whilst northern crusaders wrested one place after the other in both Spain and Portugal, the Maghrib was prey to Norman attacks. In 1146 a fleet of 200 ships under the command of George of Antioch captured the city of Tripoli after three days of fighting, followed by several days of plunder.[578] This was one of many such attacks, and the Normans were about to subdue the whole region before a subsequent counter offensive by the Almohads would dislodge them.[579]

It was in this context of initial Christian successes in the west that the main crusader armies headed East. What it meant was that if this crusade succeeded, the Muslim world would be entirely surrounded and broken apart. The enterprise looked rather promising. The new leader of the Muslim world, Nur Eddin, was young and without any power-base, whilst the armies advancing against him were not only numerically strong, they also included the flower of Western Christendom. Amongst those who had enrolled, other than the French King, Louis, were his queen, Eleanor of Aquitaine, a niece of Raymond of Antioch; the Bishops of Noyon, Langres and Lisieux; Thierry of Alsace, Count of Flanders; Henry, son of Count Palatine Theobald of Blois; Robert, Count of Perche and Dreux; Count Alfonso Jordan of Toulouse; the Counts of Nevers, Tonnere, Borbon, Soissons and Ponthieu;

[573] Kemal Eddin: *Zubdat al-Halab fi Ta'arikh Halab;* tr., as Histoire d'Alep de Kamal Ad-Din by E. Blochet; in *Revue de L'Orient Latin* (ROL); Vols 3-6; iii; pp. 515-6. N. Elisseeeff: Nur Ad Din, p. 409.
[574] N. Elisseeff: *Nur Ad Din*, op cit, pp. 409-10.
[575] Ibid, p. 410.
[576] V. G. Berry: *The Second Crusade*; op cit; pp. 481-2.
[577] Felipe Fernandez Armesto: *Before Columbus;* MaCMillan Education; London, 1987; p. 64.
[578] H. Wieruszowski: The Norman Kingdom of Sicily and the Crusades; in *Politics and culture in medieval Spain and Italy*; ed., H. Wieruszowski; Edizioni di Storia e Letteratura (Roma; 1971), p. 26.
[579] D. Abulafia: The Norman Kingdom of Africa and the Norman Expeditions to Majorca and the Muslim Mediterranean; in D. Abulafia: *Italy, Sicily and the Mediterranean 1100-1400;* Variorum Reprints; London; 1987; pp. 27-49.

William of Warenne, Earl of Surrey; barons like Enguerrand of Coucy, Godfrey of Rancom, Hugh of Lusignan, and William of Courtnay; Everard of Barres, later Grand Master of the Temple; and many other nobles and knights, 'and throngs of lesser folk.'[580] The King of Germany, Conrad III von Hohenstaufen, was joined by his nobles and troops; bishops, princes, and magnates, and was advancing with fully equipped troops to include at the other extreme not only those with equipment or money, but also the robbers and other criminals whose enlistment had been hailed 'as a special sign of divine grace.'[581] The papal legate Hubald had also carried the bull to Denmark, and the Danes were now involved in this enterprise 'to accomplish their vows and expiate their crimes.'[582] The objective for these armies was going to be Damascus.

2. Damascus (1148-1154)

The 'Second' Crusade armies followed the same route as the first crusades fifty or so years earlier: through Byzantine territory. Byzantium at the time was under Manuel Comnenus, a man who had genuine sympathy and understanding for the West, and who employed Latins in his government.[583] The Byzantine Emperor greeted with courtesy both armies led by the French King, Louis, and that of Conrad of Germany; both rulers, though, despised the Byzantines, and thought longingly of sacking Constantinople.[584] Understandably, the Greeks acted with caution. The Greeks, 'Tainted with perjury,' as one Latin wrote, 'shut their cities and fortresses and sent their merchandise down to us on ropes suspended from the walls.'[585]
The crusaders responded by plundering the countryside and local villages for their food.[586]

The Germans crossed first into Asia Minor. The Byzantine Emperor had advised the crusaders to avoid the interior land, and to instead follow the coastal route, but Conrad, certainly distrusting the Emperor, dismissed the advice.[587] At Dorylaeum, on 26 October 1147, where the first crusade had defeated Qilij Arslan, this time Emperor Conrad's army meeting a large Turkish force was so badly beaten that hardly any one Christian in ten survived.[588] The booty captured by the Muslims on

---

[580] Odo of Deuil: *De profectione*; p. 8; in V.G. Berry: the Second Crusade; op cit; p. 469.
[581] Otto, Gesta, I; p. 46; Bernhardi: Konrad III; pp. 596 ff. in V. G. Berry: The Second Crusade; op cit; p. 483.
[582] P. Riant: *Expeditions et pelerinages des Scandinaves en terre sainte au temps des croisades;* Paris; 1865; p. 225, in V.G. Berry: The Second Crusade; op cit; p. 481.
[583] R. Payne: *The Crusades*; op cit; p. 157.
[584] Ibid.
[585] R. Finucane: *Soldiers of the Faith;* op cit. p. 59.
[586] Ibid.
[587] N. Elisseeff: *Nur Ad Din*, op cit, p. 413.
[588] W. Durant: *The Age of Faith*; op cit; p. 595.

this occasion, of slaves and goods, was sold in the bazaars of the Near East for many months.[589]

In the meantime, French barons, led by Louis VII, reached Constantinople, then crossed into Asia Minor, and learnt at Nicea, the disaster met by Conrad.[590] The survivors from that crusade joined the French, and all decided this time to follow the coastal route.[591] The French King's army, two days beyond Laodicea, met a great disaster at a pass between the snow covered mountains. The Turks, on the higher slopes, fired arrows down at the Christians, then hurled down heavy stones and tree trunks.[592] After that, the Turks descended to cut down the survivors: it was another massacre.[593]

The remnants of the Christian armies that subsequently joined with the local crusaders were thus considerably weakened. On arriving, their leaders met in council with the local Christians to decide between two objectives. Raymond of Antioch and the northern states advocated attacking Nur Eddin, whilst the Jerusalem crusaders supported the attack on Damascus even if the city's ruler, Anar, was in peace terms with them.[594] Conrad who had landed in the south agreed with the attack on Damascus, whilst Louis, who was residing in Antioch, left it partly, because of Raymond's intrigues with Louis' wife, Eleanor, and he, too, agreed with the plan for the attack on Damascus.[595] Another major factor that prompted the attack on Damascus was that the arriving Christians were far more interested in the city's riches,[596] and these reminded their brethren that Damascus, a city referred to in the Scriptures, ought to be retaken from the 'Infidels.'[597] The losses suffered by their armies whilst crossing Turkish territory had also rendered an assault on Aleppo a much riskier enterprise.[598] As Ross Burns also explains, few amongst the newcomers appreciated the important role Damascus had previously played in fending off a united Muslim front.[599] Its name was also more familiar to them and its hinterland was crucial in securing the future of the Crusader kingdom.[600] Also, if Damascus was captured, this would neutralize the corridor running from Aleppo to Cairo.[601]

Whilst the Christians gathered their forces and began to prepare their attack, more troops kept arriving from Europe via the coastal ports of Palestine.[602] For very long,

[589] R. Payne: *The Crusades*; op cit; p. 157.
[590] N. Elisseeff: *Nur Ad Din*, op cit, p. 413.
[591] Ibid.
[592] R. Payne: *The Crusades*; op cit; p. 157.
[593] Ibid.
[594] R. Finucane: *Soldiers of the Faith*; p. 23; W.B. Stevenson: *The Crusaders;* op cit; p. 159.
[595] W.B. Stevenson: *The Crusaders*; op cit; p. 159.
[596] R.H.C. Davis: *A History*; op cit; p. 277; S. Runciman: *A History*; op cit; p. 281.
[597] N. Elisseeff: *Nur Ad Din*, op cit, p. 418.
[598] R. Payne: *The Crusades;* op cit; p. 158, refers to the French king's reluctance to lose more knights in an attack on the city.
[599] R. Burns: *Damascus, A History;* Routledge; London; 2005; p. 152.
[600] Ibid.
[601] Ibid.
[602] N. Elisseeff: *Nur Ad Din*, op cit, p. 417.

Elisseeff remarks, there has not been noted such large gathering of princes and barons in the Kingdom of Jerusalem.[603]

In July 1148, the large Christian army assembled at Tiberias, from whence it crossed the Galilee, passing trough Banias, south of The Hermon, and emerged in the Plain of Wad al-Ajam, south west of Damascus.[604] The Christians made a halt at Kiswa, on the side of the river, one stage away from Damascus, from thence, the armies of Louis, Conrad, and Baldwin slaughtered their way to the outskirts of the city.[605] The Damascene scholar, Ibn Al-Qalanisi, who was living at the time says that the Franks approached the city and made for the site known as Manazil al-Asakir, but finding no water there, since the supply had been cut off from it, they proceeded to al-Mizza, owing to its proximity to water, and advanced on the town with their cavalry and foot soldiers.[606] The Muslims drew up in face of them on Saturday 24 July and battle was joined between the two forces. A great number joined in the struggle, the Muslim army 'composed of the levies and the death dealing Turks, the town bands, volunteers and ghazis.'[607] The Christians, however, took the upper hand owing to the superiority of their numbers and equipment. They gained control of the water, spread throughout the orchards, and encamped in them.[608] After that they moved close up to the city and occupied a section of it 'which no troops either in ancient or recent times had succeeded in holding'.[609] The situation was grave, but the Muslims fought fiercely. There was stalemate until on 26 July, the tide began to turn in the favour of Muslims as reinforcements of Turcoman, Bedouins and Turkish volunteers of Ghazis, as well as country-people, joined in with the urban militia.[610] The following morning the Muslims made an early attack upon the Christians, 'With their confidence renewed and their fears dissipated. They held their ground in face of the Franks and discharged upon them shafts of fate and arrows of wounding, which fell without intermission upon footman or knight, horse and camel in their camp,' Ibn al-Qalanisi says.[611] 'During this day,' he adds, 'there arrived from the Biqa' and elsewhere large numbers of bowmen, by whom the numerical strength of the Muslims was increased and their military equipment redoubled.... In the following day, Tuesday, the Muslims advanced for attack, and spread havoc at the barricades, which the Franks had constructed with trees from the orchards, by a hail of arrows and bombardment of stones.... A large number of Muslim foot soldiers of the town bands and men of the villages became emboldened against them (the Franks), and made a practice of lying in wait for them on the roads, when

---

[603] Ibid.

[604] Ibid, p. 418.

[605] Abu Shama: *Kitab ar-Rawdatin*; 2 vols in one; Cairo; 1287-88 (H) (1870-1); p. 52.

[606] Ibn al-Qalanisi: *The Damascus Chronicles*; op cit; pp. 282 ff.

[607] Ibid.

[608] Ibid.

[609] Ibid.

[610] N. Elisseeff: *Nur Ad Din*, op cit, p. 418.

[611] Ibn al-Qalanisi: *The Damascus Chronicles*; op cit; pp. 282 ff.

they suspected no danger, and killing all those whom they captured, and bringing their heads to claim rewards for them. A large number of heads were brought in.'[612] The Christians then decided to change tactics, and move out of the orchard area, and contouring Damascus from the south their troops installed themselves on the eastern side from where they could better locate their Muslim foes and avoid any surprise attack. This however created further problems, for there was a scarcity of both water and fodder there, and the Christians were moreover facing the stronger side of the defences.[613] Meanwhile Muslim reinforcements were pouring into the city. Reports began to reach the Franks speaking of the rapid advance of fresh Muslim armies, and so they became convinced of the imminence of disaster.[614] They realized that should Nur Eddin make a sweep against them, not only would they be defeated, but also the city would fall under his sway, and would lead to what they dreaded most of all, the unification of Syria.[615] Nur Eddin's army coming from the north, would also outflank them in the position they were in at present, and that would mean utter disaster, indeed.[616] The Christians, thus, decided to raise the siege, and march back to Jerusalem. The retreat was a disaster:

'When the Muslims learned this,' says Ibn al-Qalanisi, 'and the signs of the retreat of the Franks became clear to them, they moved out to attack them on the morning of the same day and hastened towards them, pursuing them with arrows, so that they slew a large number of men, horses, and other animals in their rear files. In the remains of their camps, moreover, and along their highroads there were found such uncountable quantities of burial pits of their slain and of their magnificent horses, that there were stenches from their corpses that almost overcame the birds in the air. The people rejoiced at this mercy which God had bountifully bestowed upon them, and multiplied their thanks to Him for having vouchsafed to them an answer to the prayers they had offered up without ceasing during the days of this distress, and to God be praise and thanks therefore.'[617]

So considerable were the Christian losses, 'the stench of their corpses polluted the plains for many months to come.'[618]

The attack on Damascus had not just been a disaster for the Christians, it had also proved to the Muslims, and to the Damascenes, most particularly, that the Franks could not be trusted.[619] The principal features of the situation now, Stevenson notes, are the enthusiastic confidence of the Muslims, and the fact that Islam and Christendom had measured arms and the followers of Islam had been victorious.[620] The armies of Christendom, he adds, had, in Muslim view, 'been impotent against

---

[612] Ibid.
[613] N. Elisseeff: *Nur Ad Din*, op cit, p. 421.
[614] Ibn al-Qalanisi: *The Damascus Chronicles*; op cit; pp. 282 ff.
[615] N. Elisseeff: *Nur Ad Din*, op cit, p. 422.
[616] Ibid.
[617] Ibn al-Qalanisi: *The Damascus Chronicles*; op cit; pp. 282 ff.
[618] S. Runciman: *A History;* op cit; p. 284.
[619] R. Finucane: *Soldiers of the Faith;* op cit; p. 23.
[620] W.B. Stevenson: *The Crusaders*; op cit; Note 2; pp. 163-4.

the swords and prayers of the true believers.' The religious dimension was further enhanced by the fact that when Damascus was hard pressed Anar moved its citizens by religious appeals and the exhibition of 'Uthman's Qur'an.[621]

On the Christian side, however, it must have seemed deplorable to many, Stevenson concludes, that an expedition worthy to be compared in equipment with the first crusade should return home having accomplished absolutely nothing.[622] It was proposed that Ascalon should be attacked, so that the memory of the expedition might be somewhat redeemed in the judgment of posterity by one important capture.[623] The idea was soon abandoned amidst Christian disillusions. Embittered by their defeat, the two Western sovereigns, Louis and Conrad, left the East back for home in 1148, soon to be followed by the rest of the nobility.[624]

When the news of the disaster reached Europe, people were stunned by the scale of losses:

> The fathers, husbands and sons or the brothers of many women would see their homes no more.[625]

People began to ask how it was that the Almighty allowed His defenders to be so humiliated. St Bernard who had preached the Second Crusade was attacked as a reckless visionary who had sent men to their death, and skeptics even called in question the most basic tenets of the Christian faith.[626] St-Bernard himself lamented:

'He (the Lord) has not spared His people; He has not spared even His own name, and the gentiles say: 'Where is their God?' We promised success, and behold desolation!'[627]

He also said: 'It seems that the Lord, provoked by our sins, has forgotten His pity and has come to judge the earth before the appointed time.'[628]

Failure, which St Bernard also attributed to the iniquity of allowing thieves and murderers to take part in an enterprise that ought to be for the devout alone.[629] St Bernard also, and together with Abbot Suger, put most of the blame on Byzantium and its Orthodox Church, which they sought to annihilate for the 'Glory of Rome,' (the Catholic Church.)[630]

The failure of the Second Crusade marked a decisive turn in the life of the states of the Levant, Elisseeff remarks.[631] Muslim power was now rising, and was being organized under Nur Eddin. He was first to bring about political and moral unity in

---

[621] Ibid; p. 163.
[622] Ibid.
[623] William of Tyre; *Historia,;* xvii; p. 7.
[624] W. Durant: *The Age of Faith*; op cit; p. 595.
[625] G.W. Cox: *The Crusades;* op cit, p. 93.
[626] W. Durant: *The Age of Faith*, op cit; Chapter 23; p. 595.
[627] St Bernard in R.H.C. Davis: *A History*; op cit; p. 277.
[628] Ibid.
[629] G.W. Cox: *The Crusades*; op cit; p. 93.
[630] N. Elisseeff: *Nur Ad Din*, op cit, p. 423.
[631] Ibid, p. 426.

Syria before extending his authority upon Egypt, and victoriously attack the crusaders.[632]

****

In September 1148, Nur Eddin resumed his operations. He attacked the Castle of Araima, which was instantly destroyed, and Bertram, its lord, was carried prisoner to Aleppo.[633] Following that success, Nur Eddin captured Al-Barra, west of Ma'arat an Nu'man, thus threatening the road between Apamia and Antioch.[634] However, before the year was out, a crusader-Ismaili coalition was led against him, the two forces having come to the agreement that Nur Eddin was their common enemy.[635] In November 1148, the coalition caught him by surprise in his camp at Yagra.[636] Nur Eddin could only manage to extirpate himself with great difficulty, but his army suffered heavily. This setback was welcomed with rejoicing amongst the Ismailis in particular, which would prompt Nur Eddin to launch attacks against them early in 1149.[637] Then, after being joined by the troops of Damascus, he laid siege to the castle of Anab, not far from Sarmin in June 1149.[638] Raymond of Antioch came to the rescue of the fort, and left reinforcements there. The Ismailis advised the Count to retire speedily, but deceived by a seeming retreat of Nur Eddin, Raymond did not heed their advice, and instead, with his army moved south east and camped five kilometers from Anab.[639] Aware of their move, Nur Eddin encircled them, and at dawn on 29 June 1149, gave the signal of attack.[640] The Christians sought to charge the Muslims, who first let them through, and then formed a circle around them, and slew them in large number.[641] Raymond, himself, was slain, it was said by Shirkuh (a Kurdish general, who was to play a leading role in the ensuing phase (the bringing of Egypt into the Sunni fold.)[642] The slaying of one of the crusade leaders was soon followed by the removal of yet another: Jocelyn of Tell Bashir. This occurred probably early in 1150, during a fresh attempt by Jocelyn and his army on Edessa.[643] In the battle, Jocelyn's army was annihilated, and he fell in the hands of Nur Eddin's viceroy in Aleppo, Ibn al-Daya.[644] Nur Eddin who had a grudge against Jocelyn, probably since the Edessa days, had him blinded and left to languish in a dungeon at Aleppo till his death nine years later.[645] Jocelyn's captivity was soon

---

[632] Ibid.
[633] Abu Shama: *Kitab al-Rawdatin*; (Cairo); op cit; p. 55.
[634] N. Elisseeff: *Nur Ad Din*, op cit, p. 426.
[635] Ibid, p. 427.
[636] Ibid.
[637] Ibid, p. 428.
[638] Ibn al-Athir in RHOr, I, 476
[639] N. Elisseeff: *Nur Ad Din*, op cit, p. 431.
[640] Ibid.
[641] Ibid, p. 432.
[642] Kemal Eddin: *Zubdat*; (ROL) iii; p. 521; Abu Shama: *Kitab*; (Cairo); 55.
[643] T.A. Archer: *The Crusades;* op cit; p. 205.
[644] Kemal Eddin: *Zubdat;* (ROL); iii; p. 524.
[645] T.A. Archer: *The Crusades*; op cit; p. 205.

followed by the loss of all that remained of his once prosperous county.[646] Nur-Eddin made gains in the districts neighbouring Aleppo, and Ezzaz, his first objective, was captured after a long siege on 15th July 1150.[647] In October-November he besieged Tell Khalid and defeated a Christian relieving force near Tell Bashir; Tell Bashir itself fell to him after a series of attacks in July 1151.[648]

Nur Eddin's victories were accomplished despite unfavourable conditions, most notably Muslim disunity and plotting against him. Earlier in his rule, soon after he succeeded his father, he faced alliances of Christians, Muslim princes, and the Ismailis.[649] The Ismailis, in particular, showed strong common cause with the crusaders.[650] This was obvious in the combined Ismaili-Christian attacks which occurred in 1148 and which inflicted a serious defeat on Nur Eddin.[651]
Nur Eddin also found himself in conflict with the new ruler of Damascus, Mujir Eddin (Anar had died in August, 1149). Following Anar's death, Nur Eddin sought to bring Damascus into the anti-Crusader fold again. In May 1151, he made yet another strong attempt in that direction. Positioning himself south of the city, he called upon the population, declaring:

> I only want the well being of the Muslims, wage the Holy War against polytheists and secure the freedom of the Muslims who are their prisoners. If we fight together, if we work together in the name of the Holy war (victory would follow...)[652]

However, the chronicler adds, he did not get the reply he sought. The Damascene leadership sought the alliance of the Franks instead, and thus called on them to assist them in exchange of considerable payment.[653] In response, the Christians poured into the city, thus ending Nur Eddin's latest attempt.

In the Autumn of 1152, the Ortoqid prince, Timurtash of Mardin, appeared with a Turcoman army and asked Mujir Eddin for his support for a surprise attack on Jerusalem so as to profit from the divisions amongst the crusaders.[654] Although Mujir Eddin refused the request; the Turcoman army still attacked; the Franks, however, made a sudden sortie and crushed the Turcomen.[655] The refusal by Mujir Eddin to assist fellow Muslims dented his prestige amongst his people. The following year, Ascalon, which was besieged by the Christians, called for Muslim help. The Fatimids remained passive, whilst Nur-Eddin and Mujir Eddin mobilised an army to give it assistance. About May of 1153, the two chiefs approached the

---

[646] Ibid.
[647] Kemal Eddin: *Zubdat*; (ROL); op cit; iii: p. 524.
[648] Abu Shama: *Kitab al-Rawdatin;* RHOr; iv; 67 ff.; and 73; Kemal Eddin: *Zubdat*; (ROL); iii; p. 524.
[649] R. Finucane: *Soldiers of the Faith*; op cit; p. 198.
[650] H.A.R. Gibb: The Career of Nur Eddin; in *The Crusades* (Setton ed); pp. 513-27 at p. 515.
[651] S. Runciman: *A History;* vol ii; op cit; pp. 325-6.
[652] Ibn al-Qalanisi; op cit; 313; Le Tourneau, *Damascus de 1075 a 1154*, 1952, p. 319.
[653] Ibid.
[654] S. Runciman: *History of the Crusades*, op cit, p. 337.
[655] Ibid.

town of Banyas together, but once there, Mujir Eddin decided to attack Banyas rather than march on Ascalon.[656] This change of plan by Mujir Eddin and the dispute that ensued caused the collapse of the effort aimed at helping Ascalon. The two armies, Ibn al-Qalanisi says, retired in 'disorder before a single Frank had struck a blow at them or any Frankish troops had come up with them.'[657] Consequently, Ascalon, the last Muslim stronghold in Palestine, also called the Bride of Syria, fell to the crusaders.[658] Once more, Mujir Eddin's failure to provide assistance when it was needed, besides his dispute with Nur-Eddin caused deep resentment in Damascus.[659] This was made worse by Mujir Eddin's relationship with the Christians. The Franks, under King Baldwin, moved up to the city, where many of them were allowed to visit the bazaars within the walls, while Mujir Eddin paid a cordial visit to the King in the Christian camp.[660] Mujir Eddin hastened to assure Baldwin of his devoted friendship, and he agreed to pay him a yearly tribute. While Frankish lords journeyed and raided as they pleased over Damascene territory, Frankish ambassadors came to the city to collect the money for their king.[661] To Mujir Eddin and his counselors, mindful of their own safety, a Christian protectorate was preferable to their fate should Nur Eddin become their master, but to the ordinary citizen of Damascus 'the insolence of the Christians was unbearable, and the rulers were proving themselves traitors to the faith.'[662]

It was not long before the city's population rose in revolt. Mujir called his Christian allies for help, but in vain.[663] Before they could organize their expedition, Nur Eddin was already in front of the city, together with his leading officers, including Shirkuh.[664] The troops camped around the city, and on 18 April 1154, Nur Eddin launched his first attack.[665] Fighting was soon joined between the opposing armies, lasting a whole week, until, finally, on 25 April, near Bab Kaysan, the army of Nur Eddin made its way into the city.[666] Ibn al-Qalanisi narrates:

'Nur Eddin's soldiers hoisted a standard, and planting it on the wall shouted *Ya Mansur!* (O Victorious one); whereupon the troops and citizens ceased to make further resistance owing to the affection which they entertained for Nur-Eddin, and his justice and good reputation. One of the woodcutters hastened with his axe to the East Gate and broke its bolts; the gate was thrown open, and Nur Eddin's soldiers entered it with ease and confidence, and proceeded swiftly through the main streets. Not one man put up any resistance to their advance. The Thomas Gate also

[656] Abu Shama: *Kitab al-Rawdatin* (Cairo); p. 90; p. 130.
[657] Ibn al-Qalanisi: *The Damascus Chronicle*; op cit; p. 316.
[658] Beha Eddin: *Al-Nawadir al-Sultaniya*; in RHOr; iii; p. 99. W.B. Stevenson: *The Crusaders;* op cit; pp. 171-2.
[659] W.B. Stevenson: *The Crusaders;* op cit; p. 172.
[660] S. Runciman: *A History of the Crusades;* vol ii; p. 336.
[661] Ibn al-Qalanisi: *The Damascus Chronicles*; (Gibb); op cit; pp. 306-7; Ibn al-Athir: *Kamil* in RHOr; 1; p. 496; and Atabegs (RHOr) ii; p. 189.
[662] S. Runciman: *A History of the Crusades*; op cit; p. 340.
[663] Ibid p. 341.
[664] N. Elisseeff: *Nur Ad Din*, op cit, p. 486.
[665] Ibid.
[666] Ibid.

was opened, and the troops entered through it. Thereafter, Nur Eddin himself and his domestic officers entered the city to the joy of all the people and troops.'[667]

Nur Eddin's entry into Damascus was a major landmark in crusade history, uniting the two main Muslim strongholds: Aleppo and Damascus. This came in addition to Edessa and to the lands re-conquered by himself and his father. Now, there was a semblance of united Muslim territory, which contrasted with the former disunity, which had made the existence of the crusader states possible.[668] This was a grandiose accomplishment, well summed up by Elisseeff:

'The road towards Syrian unity was reached by stages, and each step forward helped towards the renewal of Sunni Islam and the Holy War against the Franks. Nur Eddin spent eight years to accomplish this dream of unity, which his father, Imad, had nurtured all his life. First Nur Eddin had to assert his position in Aleppo, then he had to fight Shi'ite power, and give renewed vigour to Sunni Islam... Nur Eddin pushed the frontier of his realm west, and by his capture of Harim secured a plentiful supply of farm products; his capture of Appamea secured protection from a Frankish attack through the Orontes, whilst the occupation of Azaz gave him the key to the route beyond Aleppo towards the North. Nur Eddin now controlled the eastern part of the crusader principality of Antioch. His success at Inab and Appamea, allowed him to install himself on the right side of the Orontes thus preventing the Count of Tripoli from moving eastwards, and also secured circulation between Aleppo and Damascus. Having neutralized the Franks, Nur Eddin, after his third major attempt, secured Damascus.'[669]

Grousset, likewise, remarks that Nur Eddin's entry in Damascus was a determining event in history, accomplishing the unification of Muslim Syria.[670] In contemporary Muslim view, such as Ibn al Athir's, previous Burid rulers not only favoured Ismaili action, but also had to bow to the Crusader protectorate.[671] Now, instead, Muslim power stretched along the crusader border, and Nur Eddin could strike as he pleased. The barrier between Jerusalem and the sultan of the north, Stevenson notes, was broken. 'The old scourge of Antioch and Edessa came near Jerusalem, and when the Muslim sultan judged that the time had come, the way was open for an attack on the Holy City.'[672]

---

[667] Ibn al-Qalanisi: *The Damascus Chronicles*; (Gibb); op cit; pp. 319-20.
[668] W.B. Stevenson: *The Crusaders*; op cit; pp. 173.
[669] N. Elisseeff: *Nur Ad Din*, op cit, p. 489.
[670] R. Grousset: *Histoire*, op cit, II, 365.
[671] Ibn al-Athir: *Atabegs*, op cit; 191-2.
[672] W.B. Stevenson: *The Crusaders in the East*, op cit, pp. 173-4.

3. From Damascus to Egypt (1154-1161)

Despite their failure in front of Damascus, Christian forces kept arriving in Palestine in ever great numbers.[673] These arrivals that could have had a determining impact years before proved less effective now. Nur Eddin had skillfully built a much stronger power-base. He had under his command the Kurdish general, Shirkuh and his nephew Salah Eddin, a united leadership ever animated by the chief desire 'to rid the land of the infidels.'[674] Nur Eddin had also made his army much more effectual by promoting a new spirit in the midst of his soldiers and officers. Jihad had now become a rallying cry for the Muslims, and the alliance between the religious classes and the military leadership had become quite strong.[675] To bolster the spirit of jihad, Nur Eddin included in his army religious men who were actually prepared to fight in the ranks.[676] Also in the ranks were prayer leaders, Qur'an readers, preachers, and judges, who enhanced the religious dimension of the military conflict.[677] On one occasion, Nur Eddin was urged to spend more money on preparation for war and less on religious institutions and devotees. He replied that the prayers offered for Islam were its best weapons.[678]

In praise of Nur Eddin's spirit of jihad, Imad Eddin al-Isfahani wrote:

'Nur Eddin asked me to write a two line poem on his tongue about the meaning of jihad, so I said:

'My zeal is for campaigning and my delight is in it. I do not have any other wish in life except it.

The successful outcome of seeking is by serving and by jihad.

Freedom from care is dependent on exertion (in the path of God.)'[679]

In another poetic extract, Al-Isfahani grants these lines to Nur Eddin:

'I have no wish except Jihad,

Repose in anything other than its exertion for me.

Seeking achieves nothing except by striving.

Life without the striving of Jihad is an (idle) pastime.'[680]

Whilst inspired by the spirit of Jihad, Nur Eddin also displayed a remarkable political astuteness. Following his capture of Damascus, he understood he needed years of calm so as to organise his larger realm and assert his firm authority.[681] The resources at his disposal did not permit him to fight on two different fronts, and so he sought to secure the neutrality of his neighbours, and whenever a new enemy

---

[673] C.R. Conder: *The Latin Kingdom;* op cit; p. 115.
[674] J.H. Lamonte: Crusade and Jihad: op cit; p. 171.
[675] C. Hillenbrand: *The Crusades*, op cit; p. 131.
[676] N. Elisseeff: *Nur al-Din: Un Grand Prince*, op cit, Vol 3; p. 735.
[677] C. Hillenbrand: *The Crusades*, op cit; p. 120.
[678] W.B. Stevenson: *The Crusaders in the East*, op cit, p. 163.
[679] Imad Eddin al-Isfahani: *Kharidat al-Qasr*, Cairo 1951; p. 43.
[680] Ibid; p. 72.
[681] N. Elisseeff: *Nur Ad Din*, op cit, p. 495.

arose, Nur Eddin sought to isolate him, and this way he could face only one foe at a time.[682]

After years of calm, fighting with the crusaders resumed in February 1157 following the break of the truce by King Baldwin.[683] Nusrat Eddin, Nur Eddin's brother, defeated a large detachment of Hospitallers and Templars together with their Muslim allies in April of that year.[684] On that occasion, Nusrat's troops pretended flight pursued by the knights who fell in an ambush.[685] The slaughter inflicted on the Christians was immense, and considerable numbers of prisoners were subsequently paraded in the streets of Damascus.[686]

Not long after this, Nur Eddin himself went on the military path. Following a meticulous preparation, and the addition of considerable amount of equipment, including mangonels, and in the company of many religious figures, Nur Eddin left Damascus on 11 May 1157 in direction of Banyas, then in crusader hands.[687] A siege was soon put in place, and whilst it was in progress, Nur Eddin crushed a company of Hospitallers near the town. Banyas itself submitted to a fierce bombardment, and soon was forced to surrender.[688] The Muslim victory was short lived as a very powerful army led by King Baldwin also made its way towards the town forcing Nur Eddin to retreat.[689] Nur Eddin's evacuation, however, proved to be a well laid trap. He allowed Baldwin and his troops to enter Banyas, and then, as the king and his army were returning south down the Jordan, he fell on them just north of the Sea of Galilee, and won a great victory on 19 June 1157.[690] In the fight, the Muslims first showered the crusaders with a barrage of arrows, before attacking them, causing carnage in their ranks.[691] The number of the slain and prisoners was considerable, and the chronicler William of Tyre gives an impressive list of the names of those of baronial ranks who lost their lives or their freedom on that day.[692] The king, himself, barely escaped to the castle of Safed.[693] The king waited there until the Muslims had passed the Jordan River before retiring to Acre.[694] Ibn Al-Qalanisi describes the triumphal return of the Muslims to Damascus:

'The prisoners and the heads of the slain reached Damascus on the Monday following the date of the victory. They had set the Frankish horsemen in pairs upon camels, each pair being accompanied by the one of their standards unfurled, to

---

[682] Ibid.

[683] S. Runciman: *A History*; vol 2; pp. 342-3.

[684] N. Elisseeff: *Nur Ad Din*, op cit, p. 507.

[685] Ibn al-Qalanisi: *The Damascus Chronicles*; op cit; pp. 330-1.

[686] W.B. Stevenson: *The Crusaders*; op cit; p. 177.

[687] N. Elisseeff: *Nur Ad Din*, op cit, p. 508.

[688] William of Tyre: *Historia*, XVIII, xii, 212-3. Abu Shama: *Kitab al-Rawdatin;* (Cairo); p. 107. W. B. Stevenson: *The Crusaders*; op cit; p. 177.

[689] Abu Shama: *Kitab al-Rawdatin;* (Cairo); p. 107. W. B. Stevenson: *The Crusaders*; op cit; p. 177.

[690] Abu Shama: *Kitab al-Rawdatin;* (RHOr); iv; p. 88; W.B. Stevenson: *The Crusaders*; op cit; p. 177.

[691] N. Elisseeff: *Nur Ad Din*, op cit, p. 511.

[692] William of Tyre: *Historia,* op cit, XVIII, xiv, 215.

[693] W. B. Stevenson: *The Crusaders;* op cit; p. 177.

[694] N. Elisseeff: *Nur Ad Din*, op cit, p. 511.

which were attached a number of skins of their heads with their hair. Their leaders and the commanders of their fortresses and provinces were set each one upon a horse, each wearing his coat of mail and helmet and with a standard in his hand, while the foot-soldiers, sergeants and Turcopoles were roped together in threes, or fours, or fewer, or more. An accountable number of the townsfolk-old men, young men, women and children-came out to see what God (exalted His name) had granted to the whole body of Muslims in this brilliant victory, and they multiplied their praises and glorification to God, and their fervent prayers for al-Malik al-Adil Nur Eddin, their defender and protector.'[695]

On either side of this military episode, a series of dramatic events took focus away from the battlefield. A succession of earthquakes devastated the region, causing extensive damage to cities and considerable human losses.[696] Profiting from the ensuing chaos, the crusaders, newly reinforced by arrivals from Europe, advanced in the summer of 1157 in the direction of the Orontes.[697] However, no sooner the Christians found that Nur Eddin had assembled a strong army and was marching against them, they decided to retreat.[698] Later that same year, Nur Eddin fell gravely ill.[699] When it seemed his death was imminent, he made arrangements, nominating as his successor his brother Nusrat Eddin.[700] As his condition worsened, alarming rumours spread, the Muslim armies dispersed, and the provinces were thrown again into a state of confusion.[701] Emboldened by these events, the Christians went on the attack, again. They called for reinforcements from the Armenian ruler of Cilicie, who hurried to join them.[702] The Christians first failed in their attempt against Shayzar, but were more successful in capturing a number of Muslim defences, including the Castle of Harim.[703] In March 1158, a crusader expedition ravaged the district of Hauran, and penetrated as far as Dariya, near Damascus.[704] Christian optimism for the capture of the city was soon dashed by the news that Nur Eddin was recovering, and was about to lead his army against them, thus prompting a crusader retreat.[705]

In the Spring (April) of 1158, Nur Eddin, now completely recovered from his illness, resumed the military offensive. From May to August, he conducted operations in the district of Suwad.[706] Then, on 15th July 1158, he fought the near fatal battle by the 'Wooden Bridge' (which crossed the Jordan just below the Lake of Tiberias). At the

[695] Ibn al-Qalanisi: *The Damascus Chronicles* (Gibb); op cit; p. 337.
[696] Ibid; p. 328 ff.
[697] N. Elisseeff: *Nur Ad Din*, op cit, p. 516.
[698] R. Grousset: *Histoire des Croisades*, op cit, II, p. 379.
[699] Ibn al-Qalanisi: *Damascus Chronicles*, op cit, p. 341.
[700] Ibid.
[701] Ibid.
[702] William of Tyre: *Historia*, op cit, xviii, 221; R. Grousset: *Histoire*, op cit, II, p. 38.
[703] W.B. Stevenson: *The Crusaders*; op cit; p. 178; Ibn al-Qalanisi: *The Damascus Chronicles* (Gibb); p. 342; 344.
[704] W.B. Stevenson: *The Crusaders*; p. 179.
[705] N. Elisseeff: *Nur Ad Din*, op cit, p. 524.
[706] Abu Shama: *Kitab al-Rawdatin;* (RHOr) iv; pp. 97 ff.

battle, Nur Eddin was deserted by some of his emirs, and only a small band of personal attendants remained by his side.[707] As he hurriedly made his way away from his troubled situation, the Christians, fearing this retreat could be a Muslim ploy to drag them into an ambush, failed to take advantage of the situation.[708]

Soon after, in December 1158, Nur Eddin fell gravely ill again. This time, he nominated his other brother, Kutb Eddin of Mosul, as his successor.[709]

Nur Eddin recovered once more. This time, though, his mind was on pilgrimage to Makkah. As Stevenson notes, two illnesses in successive winters were a warning to the sultan that he must not delay to perform this duty of the faithful, and the pilgrimage month of 1161 fell at the close of the year.[710] With a truce momentarily achieved, and another to follow, Nur Eddin was able to pay his religious duty.[711] During his pilgrimage, he showed great generosity towards the people of the two Holy cities; built wells, strengthened their defences, and restored many edifices.[712] Nur Eddin also granted a considerable amount of money and supplies to the Sherif of Madinah before returning to Syria in February 1161.[713]

Coinciding with Nur-Eddin's absence, events of great bearing occurred simultaneously in the Crusader Kingdom and in Egypt. In late 1161, Queen Melisinde died. Her death was soon followed (February 1162) by that of King Baldwin, her son.[714] This opened the way for the succession of Baldwin's brother: Amalric. Amalric had ambitions and a character suited to the situation now evolving in Egypt. There, a bitter struggle for power had arisen amongst the Fatimid ruling elites. This followed the death from illness of the young caliph, Al-Faiz on July 23 1160.[715] His successor, aged only nine, was, of course, incapable of resolving the intense rivalries and struggles for power.[716] The storm, Ibn Al-Athir says was brewing.[717] As the power struggle proceeded in Egypt, Amalric who had long before set his sight on the country, assumed power. At the same time Nur Eddin had reached the peak of his power, too. The combination of these circumstances in all three kingdoms: Jerusalem, Egypt and Syria was soon to result in an event of great magnitude: the return of Egypt to the Sunni-anti crusader fold, which itself would have a decisive impact on events in the following century (13th).

---

[707] W.B. Stevenson: *The Crusaders*; op cit; p. 179.
[708] Ibn al-Qalanisi: *The Damascus Chronicles* (Gibb); op cit; p. 347.
[709] Ibid; pp. 349-51.
[710] W.B. Stevenson: *The Crusaders*; op cit; p. 184.
[711] Ibid.
[712] N. Elisseeff: *Nur Ad Din*, op cit, p. 559.
[713] Ibid.
[714] W.B. Stevenson: *The Crusaders*; op cit; p. 184.
[715] N. Elisseeff: *Nur Ad Din*, op cit, p. 564.
[716] Ibid.
[717] Ibn al-Athir: *Kamil*, op cit, IX, p. 75.

Nur Eddin and the Return of Egypt to the Anti Crusader Fold:

> For two centuries [says Lane Poole] Egypt had suffered the rule of a dynasty of heretical Caliphs who boasted a descent from Fatima, the daughter of the Prophet Mohammed, and were hence known as the Fatimids. They professed the peculiar mystical philosophy of the Shiites, maintained the incarnation of the Divine Reason in the Imams sprung from Ali and Fatima, and believed in the coming of the Mahdy, the last inspired leader of the same elect descent.... Their wealth was fabulous, if we may credit the amazing inventory of jewels and treasure recited by the Arab historians; the luxury and prodigality of their court were the wonder of foreign envoys...
>
> Egypt has proved herself the Capua of more than one conquering race. The Fatimid Caliphs, abandoning the simplicity of their early days, when they ruled as missionaries among the simple hardy Berbers of Qayrawan, reveled in the wealth and luxury of their beautiful palaces at Cairo, and were content after a while to devote themselves to the unique pursuit of pleasure, and to leave the obnoxious labor of government to their servants. Their viziers gradually usurped all sovereign powers, and even assumed the title of King, whilst the Fatimid pontiff, buried in the cushions of his harem, retained only the mysterious spiritual authority with which the "true Imam" was invested.[718]

The Fatimids had either allied themselves to the crusaders, or at best only given faint support to the Muslim cause.[719] Abandoning Jerusalem in 1099, and its population to be slaughtered by the Christians was not going to be forgotten or forgiven by the people. On the few occasions the Fatimids sent armies to fight the Christians, these were only token gestures.[720] When, at last, in 1153, one of the Egyptian generals, Ibn Al-Sallar, became vizier, and prepared for the relief of Ascalon (which was then besieged) with goods, equipment and men, he was assassinated.[721] The naval force that was subsequently sent returned home whilst the city was still under siege.[722] Fatimid lukewarm attitude to the crusades played no little part in their eventual downfall. This downfall began with the rise of the crusader king, Amalric.

The rise of Amalric signaled a considerable shift, opening a new period in history, as Stevenson points out.[723] Fired by youth and ambition, he aimed at extending his dominions indulging in far reaching dreams of conquest.[724] The Christians had by

---

[718] S. Lane Poole: *The Life of Saladin*, op cit, pp. 77-8.

[719] Ibn Taghribirdi: *Nujum al-Zahira fi Muluk Misr wa'l Qahira;* Cairo; 1938; V, p. 148.

[720] Ibn Zafir: *Akhbar al-Duwal al-Munqati'a;* ed. A. Ferre; Cairo; 1972; p. 82.

[721] P.K. Hitti: *An Arab-Syrian Gentleman and Warrior in the Period of the Crusades. Memoirs of Usamah ibn Munqidh,* Columbia University, New York, 1929; pp. 40-3; Ibn al-Qalanisi: The Damascus Chronicles; op cit; p. 314.

[722] Ibn al-Qalanisi: *The Damascus*; op cit; p. 315.

[723] W.B. Stevenson: *The Crusaders;* op cit; p. 185.

[724] Ibid.

now lost all hope for the conquest of Syria and for the recapture of the territories which the Muslims had recovered: Nur Eddin had by now set up a powerful state, against which the crusader states could only at best defend themselves.[725] It was then that the King of Jerusalem, Amalric, realising the progressive weakening of Fatimid power, began to be interested more and more in Egypt.[726] Coincidently, William of Tyre (1130-90), a chancellor of the Kingdom of Jerusalem of Amalric, was frequently in charge of diplomatic missions to the Fatimids.[727] During such missions, he became better acquainted with the divisions amongst the ruling elites.[728] Such divisions encouraged Amalric in his objective to wrest Egypt for himself. Amalric also had in his sight the great wealth and treasures of the Fatimids. Cairo was one of the wealthiest cities in the world, and William of Tyre's account of the caliph's reception of the Frankish ambassador (Hugh of Caesarea) shows that even an austere churchman could not help but be overwhelmed by the almost fairy tales splendour of the caliph's palace.[729] The inner part of the palace is described by William of Tyre:

> Curtains embroidered with pearls and gold, which hung down and hid the throne, were drawn aside with marvellous rapidity, and the caliph was revealed with face unveiled. Seated on a throne of gold, surrounded by his privy counsellors and eunuchs.[730]

Events unfolding in Egypt seemed all set to help Amalric's designs. In August 1163, Ibn Ruzzik, the vizier of the caliph, died. The contest for his succession arose between the two emirs, Dirgham and Shawar. Shawar was compelled to flee from the country for Damascus in the first days of September to seek help from Nur Eddin.[731] Nur Eddin was at first hesitant, not having full trust in Shawar. He had, moreover, been seriously weakened militarily a short while before, so serious military setback in fact, it nearly ended both his reign and his life. On that occasion, in late Spring 1163, that is a few months before Shawar came to solicit his aid, he had invaded the crusader territory of Tripoli, and had camped at the foot of the mighty fortress of Krac des Chevalliers.[732] He was completely unaware that very substantial reinforcements had arrived from Europe.[733] On a hot day of May, at midday, whilst the Muslim camp was at rest, the Christians suddenly erupted, and attacked the camp.[734] In the ensuing battle Nur Eddin's army was crushed, and he barely escaped with his life.[735] According to Muslim historians, the Christians surprised and attacked his camp, and Nur Eddin had his life saved by a faithful

[725] N. Elisseeff: *Nur Ad Din*, op cit, p. 563.

[726] Ibid.

[727] M. Rodinson: *Europe and the Mystique of Islam*; tr. R. Veinus; I.B. Tauris and Co Ltd; London; 1988; p. 9.

[728] Ibid.

[729] William of Tyre, R.H.C.Oc., I. pp. 910-11.

[730] W of Tyre: *A History of Deeds done*; op cit; 319-21.

[731] W.B. Stevenson: *The Crusaders*; op cit; p. 186.

[732] William of Tyre,: *Historia*, XIX, vii, 262-3; Ibn al-Athir: Kamil, IX, pp. 82-3.

[733] T.A. Archer: *The Crusades;* op cit; p. 242.

[734] N. Elisseeff: *Nur Ad Din*, op cit, p. 563.

[735] T.A. Archer: *The Crusades;* op cit; p. 242.

Kurdish soldier who cut the rope tying his horse before falling victim to the devotion of his leader, the Christians dashing towards him (Nur Eddin) just too late.[736]

Events, in Egypt, however, moved too fast for Nur Eddin's prudence. There, just after Shawar had gone to see Zangi, Dirgham, the new strong man, quarreled with Amalric over the yearly subsidy, and the new King of Jerusalem with prompt decision invaded Egypt in September, 1163, to exact the usual tribute.[737] Dirgham, after suffering a severe defeat near Bilbays, ingeniously avoided total destruction of his army and capture of the country by breaking down the dams and causeways and flooding the country with the imprisoned waters of the Nile, then at its height. Amalric had already retired to Palestine, when Dirgham, hearing of Shawar's negotiations at Damascus, perceived his mistake in not befriending the crusader King, and hastened to propose to him an eternal alliance, to be cemented by increased tribute.[738] Nur Eddin then decided to intervene, supported by his general, Shirkuh, who had faith in the Egyptian people that they would prefer a Muslim sultan to Christian rule.[739] If, moreover, Egypt and Syria were united, crusader Jerusalem would be caught between two fires.[740] More importantly, because of the sorry state of Egypt, Byzantium, too, had begun thinking of taking it over, and this threat, Newby points out, was all the greater because the Byzantine emperor was pro Catholic, and thought of getting help from the knights of the Kingdom of Jerusalem to help him assert his power.[741] If Amalric and the Byzantine emperor joined in an attack on Egypt and succeeded in turning it into a united Catholic Christian power base, all Islam would then be threatened. Damascus, Aleppo, even the Holy cities in the Hedjaz and the trade routes with the Far East through Yemen and Aden would have to face attacks with devastating results.[742] Nur Eddin had to act.

In April 1164, a column commanded by Shirkuh left for Egypt. As the expedition marched, Nur Eddin made an incursion into the territory of Jerusalem to divert attention away from the expedition as it passed the Christian borders, and so the march was accomplished safely.[743] Reaching Egypt, and profiting from the ineffective opposition, Shirkuh swiftly eliminated Dirgham and had Shawar reinstated in May 1164.

Shawar, once back in power, however, sought to rid himself of Shirkuh. He cautiously excluded Shirkuh from the fortified city of Cairo, and kept him in the suburbs. Then safe, as he thought, within his own strong walls, he defied his ally,

---

[736] Abu Shama: *Kitab al-Rawdatin* (RHOr); iv; p. 123 ff; Ibn al-Athir: *Kamil;* (RHOr); i; p. 530.
[737] S. Lane Poole: *The Life of Saladin*, op cit, p. 81.
[738] Ibid.
[739] Ibn al-Athir: *Kamil* (RHOr); op cit; i; pp. 546-9.
[740] Ibid.
[741] P.H. Newby: *Saladin in His Time*, Faber and Faber, London, 1983, p.45.
[742] Ibid.
[743] W.B. Stevenson: *The Crusaders*; op cit; p. 187.

broke all his promises, and refused to pay the indemnity.[744] Shirkuh was not the man to either forego his rights nor condone broken faith; he sent his nephew, Salah Eddin to occupy Bilbeys and the eastern province.[745] Now Shawar decided to send a secret invitation to King Amalric of Jerusalem inviting him to drive Shirkuh out.[746] In return, Amalric was to receive 400,000 gold pieces, half to be paid immediately, and another half to be paid once Shirkuh was eliminated together with his army.[747] Amalric responded favourably, and sent the same army with which he had intended to support Dirgham against the very man whom he was now to protect. The tables were thus turned: the Franks were now the allies of their former enemy, and the savior of the Egyptian vizier, Shirkuh, had become his foe.[748] Shirkuh now had to face a very strong Fatimid-crusader alliance, which threatened to overwhelm his force. Events elsewhere saved the day for him. Nur Eddin no sooner he had heard that the Franks had left Jerusalem for Egypt, decided to open a second front against them.[749] He marched in direction of Aleppo where he received reinforcements from northern Syria and Mosul so as to compensate for the shortfall of troops that had accompanied Shirkuh.[750] Following that, Nur Eddin marched on to the stronghold of Harim, put on a siege against it and submitted it to an intense bombardment.[751] The most powerful crusade princes after the king, Bohemond of Antioch and Raymond of Tripoli, reinforced by contingents of Armenians and Greeks, as well as Templars and Hospitalliers, forced him to raise the siege.[752] Nur Eddin feigned retreat pursued by the Christians, until he drew them to the terrain that he decided was most favourable to him for battle.[753] As the Christians directed their blows at the Muslim right wing made of the troops of Aleppo and Hisn Kayfa, the latter pretended defeat and left the field of battle hurriedly. Seeing this, the Christian cavalry set off in their pursuit away from their infantry.[754] It was then that the Mosul contingent fell on the poorly defended crusader foot, and slew them in considerable numbers. When the Christian cavalry returned from its chase, it was in its turn decimated by the Muslim archers.[755] The same tactics would be used by Salah Eddin twenty or so years later at the Great Battle of Hattin (1187). This great battle was won by Nur Eddin on 20 Ramadan 559/11 August 1164.[756] Following that Nur Eddin advanced and took Harim.[757] From this position he was now able to threaten Antioch, and he soon took Banyas in October 1164.[758] These resounding

---

[744] S. Lane Poole: *The Life of Saladin*, p. 83.
[745] Ibid.
[746] J. Glubb: *A Short History*; op cit; p. 172.
[747] G.W. Cox: *The Crusades*; op cit; p. 97.
[748] S. Lane Poole: *The Life of Saladin*, op cit, p. 83.
[749] N. Elisseeff: *Nur Ad Din*, op cit, p. 590.
[750] Ibn Al-Athir: Atabegs, 219-20; William of Tyre, XIX, viiii, 264.
[751] N. Elisseeff: *Nur Ad Din*, p. 592.
[752] T.A. Archer: *The Crusades;* op cit; p. 242.
[753] N. Elisseeff: *Nur Ad Din*, op cit, p. 593.
[754] Ibid.
[755] Ibid.
[756] Ibid.
[757] Ibn al-Athir: *Tarikh al-Dawla* (RHOr); ii; p.223; William of Tyre; xix. 9.
[758] Ibn al-Athir: *Kamil;* RHOr; i. p. 541.

victories spelled crusader disaster, and as a result, Amalric was forced to concede favourable terms to Shirkuh in Egypt.[759] Consequently both crusaders and Shirkuh agreed to evacuate Egypt together in October 1164.[760] On the 27th of October, the Syrians marched out of their camp and filed off between the lines of the allied Crusaders and Egyptians, Shirkuh himself, battle-axe in hand, bringing up the rear.[761] A Frankish officer, surprised at this warlike attitude, asked the old warrior whether he was afraid that the Christians would attack him in spite of their pledge. "Let them try!" said Shirkuh as he passed on.[762] In accordance with the agreement, the army returned to Damascus, where they found that Nur-Eddin's victories had been crowned by the surrender of Banias in mid October, and the capture of Bohemond Prince of Antioch, Raymond Count of Tripoli, with Hugh of Lusignan, and other noted knights, who were led in chains to Aleppo.[763] Thus, by creating a second major front, Nur Eddin had not just managed to save Shirkuh and the Egyptian campaign from disaster, he had also registered one of the most notable victories of crusade history.[764]

Shirkuh advocated another attempt on Egypt, which Nur Eddin agreed to. And so in January 1167, at the head of picked men he set out once more for Egypt.[765] The allied forces of the Fatimids and the crusaders were, however, waiting for him. Crusaders and Fatimids had signed a pact, which put Egypt directly under Christian protectorate for the first time in the history of the crusades.[766] Soon after, in Alexandria, banners of Amalric and the Fatimids waved together on the city walls in a common effort against Shirkuh.[767] 'We can see' Lamarque notes, 'this stupefying spectacle for the era, a Muslim army fighting alongside a Christian army another Muslim army.'[768] Shirkuh and his men were, however, bold and confident, and many in Egypt supported his enterprise.[769] And just as before, whilst Shirkuh occupied crusader attention to the south, Nur Eddin was busy capturing Christian territories to the north. He first took Munaitera west of Baalbek.[770] Then, he devastated the region around Arka, and destroyed the fortresses of Safitha and Araima,[771] and the castle of Hunain.[772] Nur Eddin's campaign, once more, forced the Franks and Fatimids to compromise in Egypt, and both crusaders and Shirkuh withdrew from the country in late summer 1167 after a protracted campaign.[773]

---

[759] T.A. Archer: *The Crusades*; op cit; p. 242.

[760] W.B. Stevenson: *The Crusaders;* op cit; p. 188.

[761] S. Lane Poole: *The Life of Saladin*, op cit, p. 84.

[762] Ibid.

[763] Ibid.

[764] N. Elisseeff: *Nur Ad Din*, op cit, p. 589.

[765] Ibn al-Athir: *Kamil* (RHOr); i. 546; Beha Eddin: *Al-Nawadir* (RHOr); iii; p. 44.

[766] A.S. Atiya: *Crusade, Commerce and Culture*; Oxford University Press; London; 1962; p. 74.

[767] G.W. Cox: *The Crusades;* op cit; p. 97.

[768] Henri Lamarque: La Premiere Traduction Latine du Coran; op cit; p. 239.

[769] W.B. Stevenson: *The Crusaders*; op cit; p. 191.

[770] Ibn Khalikan: *Wafayat al-Iyan* (De Slane); iv; p.487.

[771] Imad Eddin in Abu Shama: *Kitab al-Rawdatin* (RHOr); iv; p. 154.

[772] Abu Shama: *Kitab al-Rawdatin*; (Cairo); op cit; p. 144.

[773] Abu Shama: *Kitab* (RHOr); iv; p. 133.

In 1168, Amalric, whose ambitions over Egypt had not dimmed, and not happy with the mere payment of tribute by the Egyptian Sultan, descended on Egypt with the support of a large army of Knight Templars, this time with the intention of definitive conquest.[774] In open violation of his word, and without any excuse, he now entered as an enemy where before he had been considered as an ally.[775] Arrived at Bilbays (Pellisium) on the 3rd of November, 1168, he committed a wholesale massacre, sparing neither age nor sex.[776] This, Cox notes, only increased the reputation of the Christians for merciless cruelty.[777] For the contemporary Muslim historian, Abu Shama: 'If the Franks had behaved with humanity toward the inhabitants of Bilbeis, they would have certainly taken Fustat and Cairo afterwards, but it was God who, for His own ends, drove them to act thus.'[778]

'They were fighting for their lives, their land, and their liberty... they were honestly defending their wives and their little children whom these faithless dogs would slaughter to the last one if they succeeded in taking the city.'[779] These are the words of William of Tyre, and the city he is talking about is Cairo, which was put under the siege by Amalric's army in 1168.[780]

Terror and panic forced the Fatimids to act prior to calling for Nur Eddin's help again.[781] They took advantage of the Christians' foolish loitering, to marshal their forces and strengthen their defences. The old city of Fustat, for three hundred years the metropolis of Egypt, and still a densely populated suburb of Cairo, was by Shawar's orders set on fire, that it might not give shelter to the Franks (12 November, 1168).[782] The fire burnt so intensely, 'the people,' Lane Poole says, 'fled as from their very graves, the father abandoned his children, the brother his twin; and all rushed to Cairo for dear life. The hire of a camel for the mile or two of transit cost thirty pieces of gold.'[783] The capital itself was in a tumult of preparation for the attack. Amalric did not keep it long in suspense, but he was forced to abandon the usual camping ground (the Birket-al-Habash) on account of the suffocating smoke from Fustat.[784] The assault, however, was postponed by the negotiations which Shawar conducted in order to buy off this greedy Christian. At the same time, he was sending messengers to Damascus to implore Nur Eddin's assistance.[785] The young Caliph of Egypt himself wrote the request, and even enclosed some of his wives' hair as a supreme act of supplication which 'no gentleman could resist.'[786]

---

[774] W.B. Stevenson: *The Crusaders*; op cit; p.193; A.S. Atiya: Crusade; op cit; p. 75.

[775] S. Lane Poole: *The Life of Saladin*, op cit, p. 92.

[776] Ibid.

[777] G.W. Cox: *The Crusades*; op cit; p. 98.

[778] Abu Shama: *Kitab* (RHOr); iv; p. 114.

[779] *Estoire d'Eracles*, R.H.C.Occ., II, p. 953.

[780] Z. Oldenbourg: *The Crusades*; op cit; p. 522.

[781] Ibn al-Athir: *Kamil* (RHOr); i; p. 557.

[782] S. Lane Poole: *The Life of Saladin*, p. 93.

[783] Ibid.

[784] Ibid.

[785] Ibid.

[786] Ibid.

Shirkuh, accompanied by his nephew Salah Eddin, and 8,000 of Nur Eddin's best men, descended on Egypt, again, late in 1168 (December). To keep Amalric at bay until Shirkuh arrived, the Fatimids convinced the crusader king that the promised sum of money needed time to be collected.[787] It was then that the powerful Muslim army led by Shirkuh arrived. Suddenly facing the old warrior and his great army, the crusaders beat retreat back to Palestine.[788] On the 8th of January 1169, Shirkuh made a triumphal entry into Cairo.[789] Shawar, inwardly devoured by jealousy and fear, rode out daily to the Syrian camp, and there showed great signs of devotion to the cause, seemingly performing his engagements to Nur-Eddin, but was actually plotting the arrest of Shirkuh and his officers at a friendly banquet.[790] Once the plot was discovered Shirkuh ordered the execution of the scheming and unreliable Vizier.[791] Before that Shirkuh had suggested to Shawar that he united with Nur Eddin against the Franks for the triumph of Islam, Shawar had answered: 'No, for they are not Firenj (Franks), but Firej (salvation.)'[792] Shirkuh then stepped in his place as the caliph's vizier and thus became the true ruler of Egypt.[793]

Soon after his success, Shirkuh died. A quote from the Qur'an by Ibn al-Athir reads: 'When they rejoice in what they have received, We take them away.'[794]

Shirkuh, Lane Poole rightly notes, had the grace to die at the right moment; the way was now open for Salah Eddin.[795]

Salah Eddin, Shirkuh's nephew, was accepted and acknowledged by the Fatimid caliph as his successor, and this was the beginning of his rise to the great man he was to become. It is remarkable, Lane Poole observes, how Salah Eddin, months earlier, did his best not to be involved in this third Egyptian campaign that is now propelling him to the height of power. At the time, in face of his nephew's reticence, Shirkuh, in the presence of Nur Eddin, had said:

"Now, Yusuf (Salah Eddin), make ready for the march."

Salah Eddin answered: "By Allah, if the sovereignty of Egypt were offered me, I would not go: what I endured at Alexandria (during the previous campaign when he was besieged for months there) I shall never forget."

Then Shirkuh said to Nur Eddin, "Needs he must come with me."

Nur- Eddin turned to the young man and repeated the words, "Needs must that you go with your uncle".

In vain Salah Eddin pleaded his aversion to the campaign and his lack of means; Nur Eddin would not listen, but supplied him with horses and arms and bade him make ready:

---

[787] G.W. Cox: *The Crusades*; op cit; p. 98.

[788] W.B. Stevenson: *The Crusaders*; op cit; p. 194.

[789] Ibid.

[790] S. Lane Poole: *The Life of Saladin*, p. 95.

[791] W.B. Stevenson: *The Crusaders in the East*, op cit, p. 194.

[792] Z. Oldenbourg: *The Crusades;* op cit; p. 366.

[793] W.B. Stevenson: *The Crusaders*; op cit; p. 194.

[794] Sura vi; 44.

[795] S. Lane Poole: *The Life of Saladin*, p. 97.

"So I went", said Salah Eddin, recounting the scene in later years, "I went like one driven to my death.'

Thus were accomplished the words of the Qur'an:

'Perchance ye hate a thing although it is better for you and perchance ye love a thing although it is worse for you: but God knoweth and ye know not.'[796]

In 1171 the Fatimid Caliph died. The mass of the Egyptian population hardly mourned the end of Fatimid rule.[797] There was so little disturbance that, as the Muslim historian Abu'l Fida (Abul Feda, and other spellings) puts it, 'not even two goats locked horns.'[798]

The end of Fatimid rule had a momentous impact, though. Now, as Lamonte notes, the religious schism between the Sunnite and Shi'ite caliphs, which had materially aided the Christians in their earlier conquests, was ended, and Christendom was now confronted with a technically united Islam.[799] From the island of resistance of the early crusades: Mosul, now the Muslim front stretched from Anatolia to Egypt, passing by Syria, a whole united territory facing the crusaders for the first time since they arrived. The way was open for the next great ruler of Islam to continue the task of Nur Eddin. This next ruler was Salah Eddin, governor of Egypt, representing Nur Eddin. No sooner Salah Eddin's power began to ascend, Nur Eddin died (1174).

Nur Eddin's death was felt with great sorrow. According to Gibbon:

> In his life and government the holy warrior revived the zeal and simplicity of the first caliphs. Gold and silk were banished from his palace; the use of wine was also banned from his dominions; the public revenue was scrupulously applied to the public service; and the frugal household of Noureddin was maintained from his legitimate share of the spoil which he vested in the purchase of a private estate. His favourite sultana sighed for some female object of expense. "Alas," replied the king, "I fear God, and am no more than the treasurer of the Moslems. Their property I cannot alienate; but I still possess three shops in the city of Hems: these you may take; and these alone can I bestow." His chamber of justice was the terror of the great and the refuge of the poor. Some years after the sultan's death, an oppressed subject called aloud in the streets of Damascus, "O Noureddin, Noureddin, where art thou now? Arise, arise, to pity and protect us!" A tumult was apprehended, and a living tyrant blushed or trembled at the name of a departed monarch.[800]

Nur Eddin's funeral elegy written by al-Isfahani reads:

---

[796] S. Lane Poole: *The Life of Saladin*, p. 94.

[797] J.H. Lamonte: Crusade and Jihad: op cit; p.176.

[798] Abu'l Fida; vol iii; p. 53; in P. K. Hitti: *History of the Arabs;* op cit; p. 646.

[799] J.H. Lamonte: Crusade and Jihad: op cit; p. 176.

[800] E. Gibbon: *The Decline and Fall;* op cit; Vol 6; p. 336.

'Religion is in darkness because of the absence of his light (this is a pun on the name of Nur Eddin=The Light of Religion).

The age is in grief because of the loss of its commander.

Let Islam mourn the defender of its people

And Syria mourns the protector of its kingdom and its borders.'[801]

4. The building of the Muslim State by Imad and Nur Eddin Zangi

According to Stevenson:

Imad Eddin Zangi in his new position was destined far to surpass the achievements of his predecessors. His career had already marked him as one well capable of consolidating the power placed in his hands. He possessed most of the qualities of a good soldier and capable ruler. He was a man of clear purpose, which is the first condition of success, and swift in the execution of his plans. He was unscrupulous and cruel in his treatment of his enemies but his friends and subjects were the gainers. He was feared doubtless more than loved; yet his soldiers were attached to him, for he shrank from no danger and he made their interests his own. The power he gained was to the advantage of his people, for he sought to establish order and security in the states he governed. The even handed justice which he administered is the mark of a strong ruler in the East. His conception of a state may still be read in his own words; it is: 'a garden surrounded by a hedge into which those who are outside fear to enter.'[802] The significance of Zangi's rule lies in the fact that he erected a barrier against the crusaders' progress, and forged a weapon for their destruction.[803]

Whilst he was a great military leader, the first to break crusader hold on Muslim territory, Imad also knew that true power and success depend upon discipline and law and order. Oppression and license were never permitted among his officers, and no one in that age more rigorously punished assaults upon women.[804] The wives of his soldiers, he held, were under his special protection, and no man insulted them with impunity during their husbands' absence at war.[805] He discouraged his followers from acquiring property.

So long as we hold the country [he said] what boosts your estate, when your military fief serves as well? If the country be lost to us, your estates go too.

[801] Imad Eddin al-Isfahani: *Kharidat*; op cit; p. 42.
[802] W.B. Stevenson: *The Crusaders*; op cit; p. 123.
[803] Ibid; p. 124.
[804] S. Lane Poole: *The Life of Saladin*, op cit, p. 44.
[805] Ibid.

> When a Sultan's followers own lands, they oppress and harass and despoil the folk.[806]

He never allowed his armies to transgress public order in any form or manner. According to Kemal Eddin, when Zangi's troops left Aleppo 'they seemed to be walking between two ropes,' so careful were they not to trample the crops. They knew from experience that the Atabeg was not a man to be trifled with.[807]

No soldier was permitted to take even a truss of straw from a peasant without paying for it. Acts of violence were rigorously punished by crucifixion. He was lenient in his taxation towards the poor, but rich cities like Aleppo were heavily mulcted for the cost of his campaigns. After all he gave them a good return for their money.[808] His subjects and his army went in awe of him; under his government the strong dared not harm the weak.[809]

> My father [says Ibn al-Athir] told me about the occasion when Zangi arrived in the Jazira one winter, one of his chief emirs, 'Izz ad-Din ad-Dubaisi, who held the city of Daquqa as a fief from him, billeted himself on a Jew. The Jew appealed to the Atabeg, who sympathised with him. He had only to give ad-Dubaisi a look to make him pack his bags and move.[810]

The effects of his severe and resolute rule were seen in the security and prosperity of his dominions, and especially in the revival of his capital, Mosul. The father of Ibn-al-Athir relates, again:

> Before he (Zangi) came to power the absence of strong rulers to impose justice, and the presence of the Franks close at hand, had made the country a wilderness, but he made it flower again. The population increased, and so did its prosperity. My father told me that he had seen Mosul in such a state of desolation that from the cymbal-makers' quarter one could see as far as the old Great Mosque, the *maidan* and the Sultan's palace, for not a building in between remained standing. It was not safe to go as far as the old Great Mosque without an escort, so far was it from human habitation, whereas now it is the centre of a mass of buildings, and every one of the areas mentioned just now is built up.[811] … But as the Martyr's reign went on, the country enjoyed protection, the designs of the wicked were frustrated, and the powerful were restrained from tyranny. The tidings of improvement spread abroad, and the folk flocked into his territory and settled there. Verily Generosity breeds attachment. Buildings multiplied at Mosul and the other towns, insomuch that the very cemeteries vanished under new suburbs.[812]

---

[806] Ibid.
[807] In F. Gabrieli: *Arab Historians*; op cit; note 2; p. 54.
[808] S. Lane Poole: *The Life of Saladin*, p. 44.
[809] Ibn al-Athir: *Kamil*: xi; pp. 73-4.
[810] Ibid.
[811] Ibid.
[812] S. Lane Poole: *The Life of Saladin*, op cit, p. 45.

Zangi was also keen to surround himself with excellent administrators and thus secured prosperity in the territory under his control. He built the great Government House, doubled the height of the ramparts, deepened the fosse, and erected the gate called after him al-Bab al-Imadi.[813] The stability and unity of the vast domain that he constituted between Mosul and Aleppo was a crucial accomplishment in his war against the crusaders.[814]

As he pushed the battlefield further to the west, Zangi managed to encourage the development of a thriving farming sector in the region of Mosul.[815] The rich farming plains which stretched at the foot of the chains of the Sabahtan yielded rich cereal crops, whilst around the towns there grew thriving orchards.[816] Before his time Mosul was so poor in fruits that when a merchant sold grapes he cut off little bunches with scissors to make the weight exact; but when Zangi restored its prosperity, fertile gardens grew up around it, pomegranates and pears, apples and grapes abounded, insomuch that last year's gathering was hardly exhausted before the new crop was ready to be plucked.[817]

Thanks to Zangi, Sunni Islam was on the ascendency again, owing primarily to the vigour and authority with which the Atabeg led the Holy War, which permitted him to contain the Frankish advance, and to give nascent Sunni Islam sufficient strength to contain the Shiite and Ismailis.[818]

When Imad Eddin Zangi died in September 1146, the way was open to his successors; the objectives to be reached remained:

> On one hand the restoration of the Sunna of the Prophet so as to create the indispensable psychological and religious climate without which no war is accepted by men, and the other hand the expulsion of the crusaders who had installed themselves for half a century in the North of Syria and Palestine.[819]

******

Nur Eddin, Imad Eddin's son, was a remarkable leader, who Ross Burns remarks, rose above the petty power play of other leaders of the time, constantly jockeying for advantage and ready to play the Crusaders' game.

> By a steadiness of purpose and clarity of vision that surpassed his predecessors of many centuries, he kept to a path that integrated the military, political and religious dimensions of his vision.... His vision was taken further by Saladin but not enhanced. Nur al-Din brought an integrity

---

[813] Ibid.
[814] N. Elisseef: *Nur Ad Din,* op cit, pp. 386-7.
[815] Ibid.
[816] Ibid.
[817] S. Lane Poole: *The Life of Saladin,* op cit, p. 45.
[818] N. Elisseeff: *Nur Ad Din,* op cit, p. 388.
[819] Ibid.

and sense of purpose to the Muslim world that it had long lacked. Later, Saladin may have carried his aims forward by retaking Jerusalem for Islam but he could not better his mentor's vision of a just society firmly based on core Islamic traditions.[820]

Nur Eddin was extremely pious and devout, and strongly reinforced the place of religion in his realm. Religious men played a central part in his policies. They gave oratory speeches all over the realm, and had a profound effect in exalting the religious feelings of the people.[821] The main force that united Muslims, in the end, was the revival of the spirit of Jihad. From the time of Nur Eddin, in particular, the faith of Islam took a decisive place in the life of an army on the move; prayers were conducted in the open, and not just for purposes of ideology and morale but also for the reinforcement of corporate discipline.[822] Jihad 'had been restored from the state of somnolence into which it had fallen and thus to permit it to assume to the full the role that the theoricians of Islamic law had given it in their books,' notes Hillenbrand.[823] So devout was Nur Eddin, Ibn al-Qaysarani described him as being engaged in two holy wars, one against the Franks and another in his own soul against the forces of evil.[824] Nur Eddin, as Newby remarks, was the first Muslim ruler to see that the Holy War against the Franks could only be successful if the Muslim states were united, and that this unity must be based on the acceptance of the basic Sunni ideology.[825] The concept of Holy War was thus reinforced, and it so happened that the pressure of the population for the Jihad played a considerable part in discouraging defections amongst army officers and also in rallying the princes who showed a certain degree of hesitancy.[826] It was also the spirit of jihad which united the Muslims regardless of their different ethnicity. The ease with which ethnic divisions between Arabs and Turks could be overridden, Ross Burns remarks, was thanks to the common belief in the preservation of the supremacy of Islam.[827] This was evident in the vehemence with which the citizens of Damascus responded to the call of Jihad during the 1148 crusader attack on the city. It was enough for the Qur'an of Caliph 'Uthman to be held up in the Great Mosque when the crusaders were already at the city's gates to inspire the citizens to the resistance which in the end led to the humiliating retreat of three Christian armies.[828] It was this spirit which in the end would secure the decisive successes such as the retaking of Jerusalem. It was in Nur Eddin's time, Newby points out, that grew the idea of recovering Jerusalem so that it could be purified of the unbelievers.[829] Nur Eddin

[820] R. Burns: *Damascus, A History*; op cit; p. 162.
[821] N. Elisseeff: *Nur Ad Din*, op cit, p. 578.
[822] W. Durant: *The Age of Faith*; op cit; p. 516.
[823] C. Hillenbrand: *The Crusades*, op cit; p. 195.
[824] P.H. Newby: *Saladin in His Time*, op cit, p. 55.
[825] Ibid.
[826] N. Elisseeff: *Nur Ad Din*, op cit, p. 578.
[827] R. Burns: *Damascus, A History;* Routledge; London; 2005; p. 157.
[828] J.M. Mouton: *Damas et sa Principaute sous les Seljouks et les Bourides 1076-1154*; Cairo, Institut Français d'Archeologie Orientale;1994; p. 84; p. 379.
[829] P.H. Newby: *Saladin in His Time*, op cit, p. 22.

ordered a pulpit to be made against the day he entered Jerusalem in triumph and could install it in the Al-Aqsa Mosque.[830] He did not fulfill this dream, but laid the foundations for it.

Nur Eddin's attachment to justice for all and protection against the whims of princes was demonstrated by his decision on the day he assumed his rule to give concrete form to the Muslim concept of *Dar al-Adl*, a form of Supreme Court, which he had constructed.[831]

The Place of Education and Learning:

'In spite of its military character and the truculence of many of its leaders, nothing is more remarkable in Seljuk civilization than the high importance attached to education and learning,' says Lane Poole.[832] 'Many of the great soldiers of that age,' he adds, 'delighted in the society of men of culture; and though the victorious Atabeg (Zangi) might exclaim that to him "the clash of arms was dearer far than the music of sweet singers, and to try conclusions with a worthy foe a greater delight than to toy with a mistress," yet he loved the company of his wise counselor el-Jawad.[833]

The Atabeg Zangi of Mosul, with all his vast energy and military talent, could scarcely have held the reins of his wide realm without the aid of his Vizier and right-hand-man Jamal-al-din, surnamed el-Jawad, "the Bountiful", whose grand-father had been keeper of the coursing leopards in Sultan Malik Shah's hunting stables.[834] So ably did he administer the several governments successively put under his charge, and so charming were his manners and conversation, that Zangi received him into the intimacy of his friendship and advanced him to the post of Inspector-General of his principality and President of the Divan or Council of State.[835] His salary was a tenth of the produce of the soil and he spent his wealth in boundless charity. He lavished his wealth on pilgrims at Makkah and Madinah, built aqueducts and restored mosques. He kept a gigantic roll of pensioners, and on the day he died, "the air resounded with the lamentations of widows and orphans and of the countless poor who had hailed him benefactor."[836]

---

[830] Ibid.
[831] R. Burns: *Damascus, A History*; op cit; p. 165.
[832] S. Lane Poole: *The Life of Saladin*, op cit, p. 18.
[833] Ibid, p. 20.
[834] Ibid, p. 19.
[835] Ibid.
[836] Ibid.

The madrasa system led to a revolution in learning, and the system developed so much as to lay the very foundations of our modern system of higher learning.[837] These colleges (madrasas) were first founded in the middle decades of the 11th century by Nizam al-Mulk (1018-1092), prime minister under the Seljuks. His network of madrasas stretched throughout the lands of the eastern caliphate.[838] Nizam example was followed by the Turkish leaders, including Imad and Nur Eddin.

> To found a college was as much a pious act among Seljuk princes, as to build a mosque or conquer a city from the infidels [Lane Poole notes.][839]

Professors travelled from college to college, just as medieval scholars wandered from university to university. Many of these learned men and ministers of state (the two were frequently united) were descendants or household officers of Seljuk Sultans.[840]

Nur Eddin made a particular effort to make education free and to support the students.[841] Al-Nuriyyah al-Kubra, founded by him, was an authentic example of a school for which endowment was given. It allowed for the upkeep of the school and for the stipends of teachers and students. It was one of his favours,' says Ibn Jubayr, that he endowed a Maliki Zawiya in the mosque of Damascus occupied by Maghribi students with many endowments some of which were: two flour mills, seven orchards, land, baths and two shops. 'I was told,' says Ibn Jubair, 'by a Maghribi who was directing this endowment that its income was 500 dinars a year.'[842]

Nur- Eddin was very devoted to the society of the learned, and poets and men of letters gathered round his Court.[843] It is well known, that in the presence of a scholar or man of religion, he would rise to his feet and invite him to sit next to him.[844]

Under Nur Eddin, Damascus' Golden Age began. There took place in the city a period of building that has remained unmatched in any century of the city's history.[845] Other than the madrasas and other governmental edifices, Nur Eddin also founded hospitals, most reputed of which was the al-Nuri hospital of Damascus, where teaching and discussions on topics related to medicine were conducted by people of great renown.[846] When he built the Damascus hospital (Al-Nuri), he appointed as the director Abul Majd al-Bahilli. This physician went regularly to the hospital to examine patients and to give the necessary instructions

---

[837] S.M Hossain: A Plea for a Modern Islamic University: Resolution of the Dichotomy; pp. 91-103. *Aims and Objectives of Islamic Education*: Edited by Syed Muhammad al-Naquib al-Attas; Hodder and Stoughton King Abdulaziz University, Jeddah; 1977; p. 100.

[838] F. Wustenfeld: *Geschichte der Arabichen Aertze und Naturforscher*; Gottingen; 1840, iii; 240; 319.

[839] S. Lane Poole: *The Life of Saladin*, op cit, pp. 18-9.

[840] Ibid, p. 19.

[841] Al-Nu'imi: *Tarikh al-Madaris*; I; p. 100.

[842] Ibn Jubayr: *Rihla;* op cit; p. 285.

[843] S. Lane Poole: *The Life of Saladin*, p. 20.

[844] P.H. Newby: *Saladin in His Time*, Faber and Faber, London, 1983, p. 55.

[845] R. Burns: *Damascus, A History*; op cit; p. 157.

[846] Ibn Abbi Ussaybi'ah: '*Uyun al-anba' fi Tabaquat al-Attiba*, edited by A. Mueller (Cairo/Konigsberg; 1884, reprint, 1965), vol 3, pp. 256-7.

to the attendants and servants working under his direction. Then, he visited the citadel to examine the sick amidst the dignitaries before returning to the hospital to give his lectures.[847] As places of learning, hospitals were also richly endowed with libraries, and Nur Eddin constituted into waqf a large number of books on medicine for the Al-Nuri Hospital.[848] This collection was located in two specified spots at the entrance of the *Iwan,* and a group of physicians and hospital employees sat in front of Abu Majd al-Bahili, who then distributed the books for reading.[849] The lecture and exchange between students took place following the reading of such works for as long as three hours.[850]

Nur Eddin's strong belief was that the chief protector of Islam and its lands was not himself but God, the one true God,[851] and he carried on war against the crusaders as a religious duty.[852]

> He was also a social reformer who led a simple life, who embellished and improved the towns under his sway; endowed public institutions to promote religion, built hospitals to care for the sick and diseased, and for the advantage of travellers. The courts of justice were administered with equity and he himself gave an example of submission to them. By such means as much as by deeds of arms, he created the Syrian power which in the hands of Saladin, along with Egypt, completed the overthrow of the Latin (crusader) states.[853]

The Character of Nur Eddin
(by T.A. Archer)[854]

'Nur Eddin was one of the greatest princes that ever ruled in Syria. The Christians themselves acknowledged his valour and success; to the Muslims of this century and the next he was a model of every virtue. "Though so great a persecutor of Christians," writes William of Tyre, "he was a just ruler, wise, and religious, so far as the traditions of his race permitted." It was for his justice above all that his subjects loved him; he would take no unjust tax from his vast dominions, but like any private man lived of his own; when his wife complained of her poverty, and slighted a gift of three shops in Emesa as insignificant, "I have nought else, for all I have I hold only as treasurer for the faithful," was his reply. He once left his game of ball to appear before the cadi at the suit of a private person, and when the decision was given in his favour, resigned his claim in favour of his opponent. His justice enticed strangers to his dominions, one of whom, after his death, having appealed to Salah Eddin in vain, went in tears to the tomb of

[847] A. Whipple: *The Role of the Nestorians and Muslims in the History of Medicine*. Microfilm-xerography by University Microfilms International Ann Arbor, Michigan, U.S.A. 1977; p. 89.
[848] Y. Eche: *Les Bibliotheques Arabes, Publiques et Semi Publiques en Mesopotamie, en Syrie et en Egypte au Moyen Age*. Damascus: Institut Francais; 1967, p. 235.
[849] Ibid.
[850] Al-Safadi: *Al-Wafi bi'l wafayat;* Ms of Ahmad III; Istanbul; No 2920; I. V., 12 r.
[851] Ibn al-Athir: *Al-Dawala al-Atabakiya* (RHOr); ii; p. 307.
[852] W.B. Stevenson: *The Crusaders*; op cit; p. 155.
[853] Ibid, p. 156.
[854] T.A. Archer: *The Crusades*; op cit; pp. 239-41.

Nur-Eddin. The popular sympathy forced Salah Eddin at last to make recompense; the man then wept again, and when Salah Eddin asked his reason, the man replied that he wept for a ruler who could do justice even in the grave.

Though himself a skillful warrior, and like his father careful of his soldiers' rights Nur-Eddin would permit no plundering. Yet his followers loved him, and stood firm in battle, for they knew that if they perished their master would be true to their children. When some of his soldiers grumbled at his bounty to the dervishes, he rebuked them saying, "These men have a right to live at the public expense; I am grateful to them for being content with only a part of what they might justly claim. So, too, when an emir slandered a learned doctor from Khorassan, Nur-Eddin replied, "If you speak ill of him, I shall punish you severely, even though you tell the truth. His good qualities are enough to cover his faults, whereas you and your like have vices many times greater than your virtues."

Nur-Eddin was a great builder, and provided for the refortification of the chief cities of Syria, especially after the earthquake of 1169. He raised mosques everywhere, and founded hospitals in various towns. Many years after, Ibn El-Athir, disgusted with his paid physician sought advice from the hospital at Damascus; he would have paid for the service done him, but his gift was refused, with the remark, "Doubtless you are rich enough to pay, but here no one is too proud to accept the gifts of Nur-Eddin."

The Islamic law as regards food, drink, and dress was carefully observed by Nur-Eddin, who unlike previous rulers enforced the same obedience on his subjects. His court was marked by a strictness of etiquette, which did not suffer any one to sit in his presence, except Ayyub, the father of Salah Eddin. Very different was that of Salah Eddin, where a visitor found himself unable to make the Sultan hear through the babble of so many voices all talking at once; "At Nur-Eddin's court," he exclaimed, "Nur-Eddin's sight alone made us as motionless as if we had a bird perched on our heads; in silence we listened when he spoke, and he in turn lent attention to our speech."

One amusement alone did Nur-Eddin permit himself, namely, the game of "ball on horseback," (polo) a pastime which appealed to him as a rider of unusual skill. When reproached for this, he replied: "I do not play to amuse myself, but for needful recreation, since a soldier cannot always be fighting. Moreover, while playing at this game, we have our horses ready against a sudden attack by the foe. Before God this is my only reason for playing." "Rarely," says Ibn Al-Athir, "has a prince made of his very amusements an act of high devotion."

There was much of high religious feeling in Nur-Eddin's character, and this feeling permeated his whole life of active warfare against the Christian intruder. When told how his brother had lost an eye in fighting for the Holy Cause, Nur-Eddin refused to offer his condolence, "for could my brother but see what Allah hath in store for him in Paradise, he would willingly lose his other eye in such a cause." Nor was Nur-Eddin any more regardful of his own safety. One day a friend rebuked him for his carelessness, bidding him consider what would become of Islam should its chief defender fall. Nur-Eddin's noble reply was: "Who is Mahmud (*i.e.,* himself) that you should speak thus of him. Our country and religion have a defender better than me, and that defender is God."[855]

---

[855] Ibid.

SALAH EDDIN

Nur Eddin's heir was his son, Malik Shah Ismail, a boy of eleven, who had been with him at Damascus. There, the emir al-Muqaddam seized the regency; an act which was followed by declarations of independence in various parts of the realm.[856] This apparent collapse of Muslim unity offered the Christians a chance. Initially, when the Muslims were victorious in Egypt, all that remained for the crusaders was to put their hopes on the rivalry between the new master of Egypt (Salah Eddin) and the powerful Atabeg of Syria (Nur Eddin). This explains the unexpected sympathy the Christians initially showed towards Salah Eddin, who, however warlike he appeared, was still a lesser threat, and much weaker, than Nur Eddin.[857] However, after Nur Eddin died, on May 15, 1174, and he left his estates to his eleven year son, Malik Shah Ismail, King Amalric shifted his support to the young prince against Salah Eddin, and subsequently a truce was signed between Amalric and Al-Muqaddam.[858] In June 1174, Amalric marched on Banyas, and Al-Muqaddam came out from Damascus to meet him and, probably as Amalric intended, at once proposed to buy him off with the promise of a large sum of money, the release of all Christian prisoners in Damascus, and an alliance in the future against Salah Eddin.[859] However, by a strike of fortune, on his way back, Amalric, who was beginning to suffer from an attack of dysentery, arrived in Jerusalem seriously ill. On 11 July 1174, he died at the age of thirty-eight.[860]

The deaths of Nur Eddin and Amalric in the space of a few months from each other opened the gateway for Salah Eddin and his victories to come.[861] He was destined to be one of the greatest legends in Muslim history. Salah Eddin's rise, however, cannot be detached from the story, or his links with the Zangids. It was to the close relationship between Salah Eddin's father Ayub and his uncle, Shirkuh, and their alliance with Imad and Nur Eddin Zangi, that Salah Eddin owes his rise.

1. From the Early Years Till the Eve of Hattin

As noted earlier, it was Ayyub, Salah Eddin's father, who rescued Imad Eddin Zangi when the latter found himself in a perilous situation in 1132, when he was being pursued by the Abbasid Caliph troops intent on killing him. This was never forgotten by either Imad or his son, Nur Eddin, who looked after Ayyub, his

---

[856] S. Runciman: *A History*; op cit; pp. 398-9.
[857] Z. Oldenbourg: *The Crusades;* op cit; p. 371.
[858] Ibid; p. 374.
[859] Ibn al-Athir: *Kamil* (RHOr); i; p. 611.
[860] S. Runciman: *A History*; op cit; p. 399.
[861] Ibid.

brother Shirkuh and Salah Eddin with the greatest of care and devotion. In 1138 Ayyub and his brother, Shirkuh, following some local incident, left the castle of Tikrit, tradition says on the night Ayyub's third son, Salah Eddin Yusuf, was born.[862] Both probability and historical opinion, Hindley points out, are against this tale, though.[863] What is certain is that the two brothers traveled to Zangi's Mosul, and were not disappointed of their welcome. The Atabeg, Zangi had not forgotten the rescue of six years earlier, and was never the man 'to turn away a good sword either.'[864] The two brothers served in his armies in many wars, and when Baalbek fell in October 1139, Ayyub was appointed as the governor of the conquered city.[865] To be placed in command of so great and prosperous a city was a convincing proof of Zangi's confidence, especially when it happened to be the southernmost outpost, distant only thirty-five miles from what was then hostile Damascus.[866] Just as Zangi placed his trust in the family of Ayyub, the latter repaid it by serving assiduously, Shirkuh being wholly devoted to Nur Eddin, and his most trusted general till the end of his life.[867] Ayyub showed similar attitude. It is told that in 1171, after Salah Eddin succeeded the Fatimid Caliph as the governor of Egypt, Nur Eddin called on him to assist with his Egyptian army in an expedition against the Franks.[868] Salah Eddin failed to act, and not just that, some of his officers even declared they were ready to go to war against Nur Eddin.[869] Ayyub, when he heard this, called on his son, and said the following:

'Well,' said the father, [Ayyub to his son, Salah Eddin] I declare that if your uncle (Shirkuh) and I, saw Nur Eddin, we would get off our horses, and prostrate ourselves in front of him. Even if he gave us the order to cut your head off, we would do it without hesitation.'[870]

Salah Eddin understood the message and until Nur Eddin died in 1174, he showed no resentment or rebellious aptitude, thus maintaining the united Muslim front.

Return must be made to Salah Eddin's childhood, to a world, which Hindley claims, was a place of cosmopolitan cities in which Armenians, Kurds and Turks, Syrians, Arabs and Greeks, Christians as well as Muslims competed in commerce and learning and the business of government.[871] It was a world where, and Salah Eddin's father and uncle proved the point, any man with talent, regardless of his nationality or origins could hope to rise in the services of the throne.[872] It was in

[862] G. Hindley: *Saladin*, Constable, London, 1976, p. 47.
[863] Ibid.
[864] S. Lane Poole: *The Life of Saladin*, op cit, p. 65.
[865] Ibid.
[866] Ibid, p. 66.
[867] Ibn al-Athir: *Tarikh al-Dawla Al-Atabakiyya*; ed. A.A. Tulaymat; Cairo; 1963. Ibn al-Athir: Tarikh al-Dawla; in *RHC Or* vol ii. Abu Shama: *Kitab al-Rawdatayn;* in (RHC Or); vols iv-v. N. Elisseeff: *Nur Ad Din*, op cit.
[868] N. Elisseeff: *Nur Ad Din*, op cit, pp. 672-3.
[869] Ibid.
[870] Ibn Al-Athir: *Atabegs*, p. 287.
[871] G. Hindley: *Saladin*, op cit, p. 23.
[872] Ibid.

Baalbek that Salah Eddin spent some years of his childhood between 1139 and 1146. No doubt he received the usual education of a Muslim boy; probably as the son of the commandant he had the best teaching available. Ayyub was particularly devout, and his son was doubtless taught for years in the study of the Qur'an.[873] Other courses must have included Arabic grammar, elements of rhetoric, poetry, and theology.[874]

Salah Eddin entered the army service at the age of fourteen, when in 1152 he left Damascus to join his uncle at Aleppo; here he received a military 'fief' in the service of Nur Eddin.[875] Four years later, aged eighteen, he was appointed to a post in the administration of Damascus and shortly after that entered the personal entourage of Nur Eddin as a liaison officer 'never leaving him whether on the march or at court.'[876] We are informed that he showed himself a youth of "excellent qualities", that he learned from Nur Eddin how "to walk in the path of righteousness, to act virtuously, and to be zealous in fighting the infidels".[877] As the favoured governor's son, he naturally enjoyed a privileged position, but, far from exhibiting any symptoms of future greatness, he was evidently a shining example of that tranquil virtue which shuns "the last infirmity of noble minds,' says Lane Poole.[878] This is all we are told of Salah Eddin up to the age of twenty-five. The Syrian nobles, and those with high ranks like Salah Eddin, spent their youth in study, and their manhood in war and hunting and the cultivation of letters.[879]

It was in the year 1164 that Shirkuh led the first expedition against Egypt, and it was in his final and successful expedition, late in 1168, that he dragged his unwilling nephew, Salah Eddin, into Egypt. Salah Eddin was then just one of the many officers, most ranking higher than him, and yet, it happened that it was he who was chosen by the Fatimid Caliph as his successor, and it was he who, following the premature deaths of both his uncle and the Caliph found himself, so unexpectedly, with the governorate of Egypt.

As soon as he took power, Salah Eddin faced a series of challenges. The first threat came from Sicily, when, in 1174, reacting to the fall of the Fatimids, the Sicilian monarch, William, sent a vast and well equipped fleet to attack Alexandria. Conservative estimates put the force at 30,000 men, intending to link up with the armies of Amalric (just before he died).[880] Fatimid supporters were to

[873] S. Lane Poole: *The Life of Saladin*, op cit, p. 66.
[874] Ibid, p. 67.
[875] G. Hindley: *Saladin*, op cit, p. 49.
[876] Beha Eddin: *La Vie de Saladin*, in *Receuil des Historiens Orientaux*, 1895, vol 3, p. 43.
[877] S. Lane Poole: *The Life of Saladin*, op cit, p. 72.
[878] Ibid.
[879] Ibid.
[880] H. Wieruszowski: The Norman Kingdom of Sicily; op cit; pp. 40-1.

stir the population to revolt as soon as the Christian fleet appeared.[881] The plot was, however, uncovered by Salah Eddin, who had the ring leaders decapitated; the expedition failed, and the expeditionary corps was annihilated by the Alexandrian population.[882] This hardly discouraged William who in 1175-6 sent two more expeditions against the commercial centre of Tinnis, near the Nile Delta.[883] These expeditions equally failed.

From his early time in power, Salah Eddin found himself, just as his predecessors, battling internal Muslim foes who had formed alliances with the crusaders. At the Battle of Hama, in 1175, he crushed the armies of the Emir of Aleppo, as well as the Ismailis and the Franks who had formed an alliance against him.[884] The Ismailis remained a great threat, though, especially with the accession of Rashid al-Din Sinan, the 'Old man of the Mountain.' He reigned for thirty years (1163-93) during which he pursued a campaign of terror against Sunni Islam.[885] Even before Salah Eddin's rule (during Nur Eddin's), Sinan had begun a more active policy, and had sent messages to Amalric suggesting a close alliance against Nur Eddin.[886] Nur Eddin survived an assassination attempt by the Ismailis.[887]

> This redoubtable secret society [writes Lane Poole] partly religious, still more political, had spread abroad from its cradle at the castle of Alamut in the mountains on the south of the Caspian Sea. Its corps of *fidawis*, or emissaries, trained to murder as a fine art, had used their daggers to some purpose in the wars which had tormented Syria, and the Society had been rewarded by the gradual acquisition of nine forts among the Ansariya Mountains, forming an almost impregnable chain of fortresses from Valenie (taken in 1125), on the coast, to Masyaf inland. These "Assassins"—*Hashshashin* or smokers of hashish (their name among the vulgar), more properly Ismailis, or Batinis, "Esoterics"—had taken firm root in Syria at the time of Saladin's invasion, and were the terror of the country. Nur-al-Din had vainly attempted to subdue them, and had gained nothing by his endeavor except the unpleasant discovery of a warning pinned to his pillow by a poisoned dagger. In Egypt they had supported the lost cause of the Fatimids, from whose sect they were derived.... The Master was therefore willing enough to send his fanatics to murder Saladin in his camp.[888]

Salah Eddin survived attacks by the Ismailis in 1175-1176, and in 1185.[889] On the second attack, which occurred on 22nd May 1176, Salah Eddin was resting in the

[881] Ibid.
[882] Ibid.
[883] Ibid; p. 41.
[884] J.H. Lamonte: Crusade and Jihad; op cit; p. 178.
[885] J.J. Saunders: *Aspects of the Crusades*; op cit; p. 26.
[886] S. Runciman: *A History of the Crusades*; op cit; p. 397.
[887] P.K. Hitti: *History of the Arabs*; op cit; p. 646.
[888] S. Lane Poole: *The Life of Saladin*, op cit, pp. 138-9.
[889] Imad al-Din: *Sana al-Barq al-Shami*; summarised by al-Bundari; ed. F. al-Nabarawi; Cairo; 1979; p. 100.

tent of one of his captains, when the first assailant rushed in upon him and struck at his head with a knife.[890] The cap of mail which the Sultan wore under his *tarbush* saved him for the moment. He gripped the assassin's hands; but, seated as he was, he could not prevent his going on stabbing at his throat.[891] The second blow to the neck cut through the collar of the thick riding tunic he was wearing but was stopped by the mail shirt underneath.[892] All this was the work of an instant, and in another, his personal guard had grasped the knife by the blade and held it, though it sawed his fingers, until at last the assassin was killed, with the knife still clenched in his hand.[893] Another cut-throat followed, and fell dead; and yet a third; but the guard was now on the alert.[894] His war, as 'a defender of Islam,' Salah Eddin is reported to have said, was to wage a threefold war against 'Frankish infidels, political traitors and Ismaili heretics.'[895] He was to succeed a long way with the first two, but with the third, the Ismailis, he largely failed, and their threat was to remain until they were destroyed by Sultan Baybars of Egypt in 1270. Until this Ismaili menace had been finally removed, Saunders notes, it was not possible for the Muslims to undertake seriously the ejection of the Franks from Syria.[896]

> The long survival of the crusading states in the Levant would be inexplicable if it was not for the Ismailis, for the crusaders confronted the Muslim enemy who was forced to fight with one hand tied behind his back [adds Saunders.][897]

Salah Eddin, however, had circumstances which were in his favour more than his predecessors. Divisions in the Muslim world of the Near East (between Shia Fatimids and Sunnis), Edburry notes, had contributed to the success of the First Crusade and its aftermath, but the fall of the Fatimids in 1171, and Salah Eddin's control of both Egypt and Damascus meant that for the first time, a single Muslim ruler governed all the lands adjacent to the Christian held territories.[898] Salah Eddin's army was also much stronger, composed of large contingents of his fellow Kurds, Turks and Arabs.[899] More decisively, even, the Muslims had taken the ideological edge over the Franks, that is, they had recovered the concept of Jihad, something they had long lacked.[900] Just as under Nur Eddin, the Muslim armies were now regularly accompanied by the 'ulama' who read to them and preached to them, and the call for Jihad was extremely powerful in uniting the Muslims at war as

---

[890] G. Hindley: *Saladin*, op cit, p. 87.

[891] G. Hindley: *Saladin*, op cit, p. 87; S. Lane Poole: *The Life of Saladin*, op cit, p. 145.

[892] Ibid.

[893] Ibid.

[894] S. Lane Poole: *The Life of Saladin*, op cit, p. 145.

[895] J.J. Saunders: *Aspects of the Crusades*; op cit; p. 27.

[896] Ibid.

[897] Ibid.

[898] P. W. Edbury: *The Conquest of Jerusalem and the Third Crusade*, Scholar Press, 1996; p. 1.

[899] C. Hillenbrand: *The Crusades*, op cit; p. 445.

[900] Ibid, p. 191.

in peace.[901] Salah Eddin himself was personally and publicly committed to jihad.[902] Beha Eddin writes:

> If one said that Salah Eddin had gone forth on the Holy War he did not spend a dinar or a drachma except on the war or in gifts and donations one would speak the truth and one's statement would be accurate. The Holy War and the suffering involved in it weighed heavily on his heart and his whole being in every limb; he spoke of nothing else, thought only about equipment for the fight, was interested only in those who had taken up arms, had little sympathy with anyone who spoke of anything else or encouraged any other activity. For love of the Holy War and on God's path he left his family and his sons, his homeland, his house and all his estates, and chose out of all the world to live in the shade of his tent, where the winds blew on him from every side-so much so that on one stormy night on the plain of Acre his tent fell down, and if he had not happened to be in the turret he would have been killed. All this only increased his zeal, constancy and passion. Anyone who wanted to ingratiate himself with him had only to encourage him in his efforts and recount some anecdote of the war.[903]

The crusader kingdom, on the other side, had now regained some of the strength that Nur Eddin had broken. In 1177, a powerful lord of northern France, Philip Count of Flanders, landed in the Holy Land with a substantial army.[904] This was followed in November of the same year by Christian attacks on the Valley of the Orontes, Hama being their main objective, before the offensive was diverted on Harim.[905] Then, a short time after, Salah Eddin suffered a much more serious setback. He was crossing a stream with his army, when he was caught by a company of Templars and foot soldiers, and encumbered by his baggage, he was easily defeated.[906] At first he retired fighting, and tried to get his men into order of battle; but his bodyguard was cut to pieces around him, and he was himself all but taken prisoner.[907] Seeing that the day was lost, he turned at last, and mounting a swift camel rode for his life.[908] His army, already confused by the surprise attack, was pursued for twelve miles, and suffered terrible losses, those who saved themselves did so only by escaping to Egypt, reaching it on the 8th of December, Salah Eddin amongst them.[909]

---

[901] W.M. Watt: *Muslim Christian Encounters*; op cit; p. 81.
[902] C. Hillenbrand: *The Crusades*, op cit, p. 191.
[903] Beha Eddin: *An-Nawadir* (RHOr); iii; in F. Gabrieli: *Arab Historians;* op cit; pp. 99-100; p. 105.
[904] Z. Oldenbourg: *The Crusades*; op cit; p. 390.
[905] Imad Eddin in Abu Shama: *Kitab* (RHOr); iv; p. 191.
[906] Ibn al-Athir: *Kamil* (RHOr); i. p. 628.
[907] S. Lane Poole: *The Life of Saladin*, op cit, p. 155.
[908] Ibid.
[909] Imad Eddin in Abu Shama: *Kitab* (RHOr); iv; p. 188. W.B. Stevenson: *The Crusaders*; op cit; pp. 217-8.

Having survived this setback, Salah Eddin went on the offensive. On June 10, 1179, he met a large Christian force led by the King on the plain of Marj Ayun, and decided to attack them before the Count of Tripoli and the Templars could make a junction with the king.[910] At first the Christians took the upper hand, but deceived by the easy Muslim defeat they started rushing for the spoils and after some Muslim fugitives. Taking advantage of this, Salah Eddin rallied his fleeing troops, and calling upon them for a great effort, made one of his furious charges.[911] The enemy, who had thought they had won the day, were taken by surprise; and burdened by the spoils had no time to form up.[912] The Muslims inflicted on them a shattering defeat. The crusader kingdom lost half of its knights, dead or captive; one of the prisoners on that day was the Grand Master of the Temple, Odo of Saint Amand.[913]

Two months later Salah Eddin besiege the Castle of Jacob's watchtower. To break the defence before the assault the Muslims dug mines and set fire under the walls. 'The flames spoke a language that all understood and none required to ask the news,' says al-Fadil.[914] At dawn the castle was stormed, Muslim prisoners were released, and the great part of the defenders of the castle slain.[915] After the capture of the castle, the districts of Sidon, Beirut and Tyre, all in Christian hands, were ravaged. On the night of the 13th October, the Egyptian fleet made a successful attack on Akka (Acre).[916]

In the spring of 1180, Salah Eddin was about to open a vigorous campaign. King Baldwin wisely chose the prudent course, and sent messengers to propose peace. Salah Eddin could not disagree, for droughts and bad harvests were seriously hampering his supplies.[917] In the summer he consented to a truce for two years by sea and land, for natives and new-comers alike, and it was confirmed by solemn oaths. For the Christians it was a humiliating concession: never before had they set seal to a treaty drawn up on equal terms which reserved no advantage for themselves.[918] The war ceased for a while.

More truces followed, and generally held, although constantly broken on the Christian side, until 1187 when, yet one more truce, was broken by the French lord, Reynald of Chatillon. Reynald had made himself sovereign in the great castle of Kerak beyond the Jordan, and repeatedly violated the truce arranged between the Christians and Salah Eddin.[919] Reynald was planning to make himself the master of all pilgrim roads to Makkah.[920] In early 1183, he organised a large offensive

---

[910] Z. Oldenbourg: *The Crusades;* op cit; p. 393.

[911] S. Lane Poole: *The Life of Saladin*, op cit, p. 158.

[912] Ibid.

[913] Z. Oldenbourg: *The Crusades*, op cit, 393.

[914] Al-Fadil; in Abu Shama: *Kitab* (RHOr); iv; pp. 206-7.

[915] W.B. Stevenson: *The Crusaders*; op cit; p. 221; Imad Eddin in Abu Shama: *Kitab* (RHOr); iv; p. 203.

[916] Imad Eddin and al-Fadil in Abu Shama: *Kitab* (RHOr); iv; p. 209; p. 210.

[917] S. Lane Poole: *The Life of Saladin*, op cit, p. 161.

[918] Ibid.

[919] W. Durant: *The Age of Faith*, op cit; p. 596.

[920] Z. Oldenbourg: *The Crusades*; op cit; p. 401.

against Arabia, having armed a fleet which sailed down the Red Sea coast from the Gulf of Akaba, pillaging and spreading terror among the coastal cities.[921] On one occasion, he sought to invade Arabia, destroy the tomb of the Prophet at Madinah, and smash the Kaaba at Makkah to ground.[922] His small force of knightly adventurers sailed down the Red Sea, landed at el-Haura, and marched to Madinah. They were surprised by an Egyptian detachment, and all were cut down except a few who escaped with Reynald, and some prisoners who were taken to Makkah and slaughtered instead of goats at the annual pilgrimage sacrifice (1183).[923] Four years later, in 1187, Reynald seized the caravan with Salah Eddin's sister, breaking yet another truce, which resulted in many Muslim prisoners, including Salah Eddin's sister.[924] 'Since they trusted in Mohammed,' said Reynald 'Let him come and save them.' Salah Eddin, infuriated, swore to kill Reynald with his own hand,[925] which he would eventually do after the Battle of Hattin (1187). His refusal to return both caravan and sister triggered Salah Eddin's anger, and resulted in the Battle of Hattin.[926]

2. The Battle of Hattin (4th July 1187)

In 1187 Salah Eddin, after having cut short the borders of the Christians in many quarters, resolved to risk an attack on the centre of their strength, by a direct attack on the Crusader Kingdom of Jerusalem.[927] In the spring of 1187 the call to the Holy War went out, and while the troops from various parts were arriving, preparations went ahead.[928] Salah Eddin first dispatched a considerable force to execute a raid in the northern parts of the crusader kingdom. It was put in charge of Modhaffer Eddin, Prince of Edessa and Harran, who crossed the Jordan, harried the hill-country of Galilee, and at a bloody encounter of Saffuriya (May 1), cut to pieces the knights of the Temple and the Hospital who had come forth against him.[929]

In the meantime, the Muslims were gathering, the rendezvous was Tell 'Ashtera, in the Hauran, near the borders of the Holy Land, east of the Lake of Tiberias. By the third week in June even the late-comers had arrived.[930] Salah Eddin had now gathered all his disposable forces from Egypt, Syria, and Mesopotamia at

[921] Ibid.
[922] S. Lane Poole: *Saladin and the Fall of the Kingdom of Jerusalem*; Beirut; Khayats; 1964; p. 175.
[923] W. Durant: *The Age of Faith*, op cit; p. 596.
[924] Ibid; p. 597.
[925] Ibid.
[926] P. W. Edbury: *The Conquest of Jerusalem;* op cit; p. 29.
[927] C. Oman: *A History of the Art of War*; Methuen; London; 1898; p. 322.
[928] M.W. Baldwin: *Raymond III of Tripolis and the Fall of Jerusalem (1140-1187)*; Princeton University Press; 1936; p. 99.
[929] C. Oman: *A History of the Art of War in the Middle Ages*; 2 vols; London; 1924; p. 322.
[930] M.W. Baldwin: *Raymond III*; op cit; p. 100.

'Ashtera.[931] On the 24th of June the emirs in council gave their decision to attack the Crusader Kingdom. Troops were passed in review, regulars and auxiliaries, a total probably of 60-70,000 men, about the same as that to be mustered by the Christians.[932] No chronicler gives any particulars as to the kind of troops Salah Eddin had assembled, but judging from the tactics they employed during the battle, there must have been the usual predominance of horse archers. All accounts, Christian and Muslim, emphasise the effectiveness of their arrows throughout the engagement.[933] His army was made of Arabs, Kurds, Turks, and volunteers from various parts of the Muslim world. There were ten thousand mailed Mamluks of the regular army, beside the innumerable contingents of the provinces.[934]

Following Salah Eddin's pious custom, the camp was broken two days later, Friday 26th of June, on the day of worship and at the hour of prayer. The next day he crossed the Jordan south of Lake Tiberias and took up a position near the river banks.[935] He encamped at Seennabra, close to the bridge of El-Kantara, which crosses the river a mile south of the point where it issues from the Sea 'of Galilee'.[936] Three days later he passed the stream, and advanced into Christian territory.[937]

Meanwhile in Jerusalem, the Christians had begun assembling in great strength, although Mudhaffer Eddin's raid had seriously disturbed them.[938] They had also heard that Salah Eddin was concentrating his army in the Hauran, and they had resolved to draw together in full force.[939] King Guy summoned in all his barons and knights; the military orders put all their available men into the field.[940] The towns sent contingents even larger than they were bound to furnish.[941] Nor did they forget the spiritual aid of precious wood of the 'Holy Cross.' 'The True Cross' was fetched out from the Church of the Holy Sepulchre and sent to the front, in charge of the Bishop of Lydda.[942] By the end of June, the Christian army finally assembled was the largest in many years and one of the largest in the history of the Crusades.[943]

---

[931] C. Oman: *A History of the Art of War*; op cit; p. 322.
[932] W.B. Stevenson: *The Crusaders*, op cit; p. 243. C.W.C. Oman: *A History of the Art of War*; gives sixty to seventy thousand. 1, p. 324.
[933] M.W. Baldwin: *Raymond III*; op cit; p. 100.
[934] C. Oman: *A History of the Art of War;* op cit; p. 322.
[935] W.B. Stevenson: *The Crusaders;* op cit; pp. 243-4; RGKJ, p. 430.
[936] C. Oman: *A History of the Art of War;* op cit; p. 322.
[937] Ibid.
[938] Ibid.
[939] Ibid.
[940] Ibid.
[941] Ibid.
[942] L'Estoire de Eracles Emperor (*Eracles*); in *(RHC Occ)* II; p. 46; and the *Chronique d'Ernoul;* ed. L. de Mas Latrie; Societe de l'Histoire de France; Paris; 1871 (Ernoul), pp. 155-6.
[943] *Brevis Historia Regni Hierosolymitari* (SS, XVIII) (Brevis); p. 53. *Libellus*, p. 208. *Eracles*, p. 47.

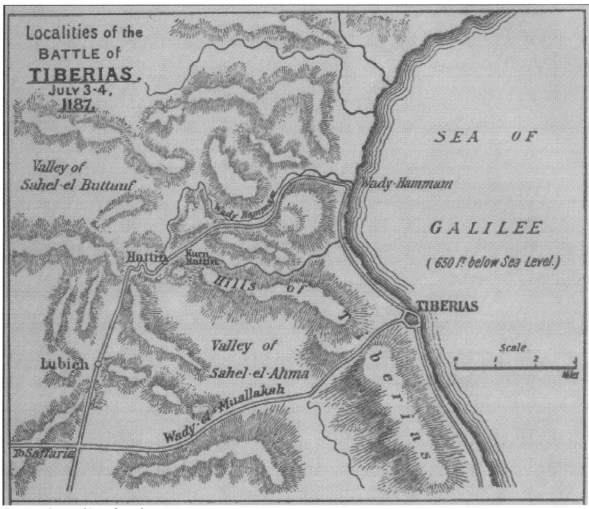

Source: Oman (Art of war)

On Thursday July 2, Salah Eddin, now deep in Crusader Kingdom, first posted the main part of his army on the high ground under the ridge west of Tiberias where it blocked the direct route to the town, but still controlled the passes and the water supply for itself. It could also, as appeared later, command access to the other pass. But his army was nevertheless situated where a Muslim defeat would mean disaster. With the lake and the Jordan behind, retreat would be out of question.[944] Defeat in such a position would thus mean Muslim forces hurled down the slopes and driven into the lake.[945] This, most certainly, was what prompted the Christians to move against him despite some risks, for they had great confidence in the size of their army, and also the knowledge that defeating Salah Eddin now would mean eliminating the whole Muslim army at a stroke, and

---

[944] Abu Shama: *Kitab; (RHC Or)* IV, pp. 282-3 clearly describes the location of Salah Eddin's camp. There can be no doubt, however, that his army was posted under the ridge blocking the passes when the Crusaders marched out.
[945] S. Lane Poole: *The Life of Saladin*, op cit, pp. 206-7.

thus opening the roads of Syria and Egypt to themselves.[946] But in order to attack, the Christian army had to cross the waterless plain.[947]

Just as Salah Eddin was besieging the castle of Tiberias in order to stir the Christians into action, their army began to march. On the small hours of the morning of Friday 3 July, drawn up in three divisions, they advanced in his direction. In the advance guard was Raymond, Count of Tripoli, on account of his rank and because the march was through his territory.[948] The rest followed, whilst the Templars guarded the rear of the huge army. Abu Shama states that Salah Eddin heard the news of the Christian advance at the hour of prayer just as his men were making a breach in the citadel of Tiberias.[949] As soon as the news was verified the Sultan confirmed that his decision, based on his earlier judgment, was accurate, and rejoiced to hear that they were on the march.[950]

The Franks had marched about nine or ten miles out of Saffuriya, when they began to be surrounded by Muslim skirmishers. Salah Eddin did not display his main force, but sent against the crusaders his horse-bowmen, whose orders were to make the march slow and painful by showering them with arrows.[951] By the time the host drew near the deserted village of Marescallia, it was terribly weary and harassed by Muslim attackers.[952] Accounts differ as to how much actual fighting took place on Friday.[953] It is evident, however, that the Christians and especially the Templars in the rear were busy all day beating off bands of Muslim skirmishers, which caused considerable strains.[954] As the day advanced, the Muslim pressure on all sides became so great that the Christians could proceed no further. Fearing that the Templars would be cut off if any further advance was made, and eluding the attack on the formidable bodies of Muslims holding the hilltops, King Guy bade the trumpets sound for halt and encampment.[955] The Christians stopped on top of a hill called Qarn Hattin.[956]

---

[946] Thus, modern historians' claim that the crusader advance was foolish only say so in light of the subsequent crusader defeat. Had the crusaders won at Hattin, their advance against Salah Eddin would have been depicted much more favourably.

[947] S. Lane Poole: *The Life of Saladin*, op cit, p. 208.

[948] *Libellus*, p. 222; According to *Eracles*, p. 64, Ernoul, p. 169, Raymond made the first charge on Saturday because the battle was in his barony.

[949] Abu Shama: *Kitab al-Rawdatyn*; (*RHC Or*), op cit; p. 287.

[950] Imad Eddin al-Isfahani: *Al Fath al-Qusi fi 'l Fath al-Qudusi*; in F. Gabrieli: *Arab*; op cit; p. 130.

[951] C. Oman: *A History of the Art of War;* op cit; p. 325.

[952] Ibid.

[953] *Fratres Hospitalis Ultramarine Archumbaldo, Magistro Hospitalis Italiae*, 1187 (SS, N.s.V, 2-4; RH doc 661 (Archumbaldo), p. 2.

[954] M.W. Baldwin: *Raymond III;* op cit; p. 118; note 58.

[955] C. Oman: *A History of the Art of War;* op cit; p. 236.

[956] *Eracles*, p. 62, mentions the "Valley of Barof" which RGKJ, p. 433, n. 5, identifies with the modern Sahel el-Buttauf. This, however, would be too far to the north and not on the direct route to Tiberias. *Eracles*, p. 64, also speaks of the plain of Barof as the location of Saturday's battle whereas all other accounts agree in locating the latter near the Horns of Hattin. On the other hand, it also refers to the pass over the hills near the Horns as not far away to the left. It is impossible to locate the place exactly, but it cannot have been far from the Horns since the army seems not to have moved far the next morning.

See also Ernoul, pp. 167-8; Ralph of Coggeshall, *chronicon Angliconum*, ed., J. Stevenson; London; 1875; p. 21; Roger of Wendover: *Liber Qui dicitur Flores Historiarum*, ed H.G. Hewlett; London; 1886; 1, 140; RGKJ, p.433 n.. 6.

The decision had been made, and the Christians now faced the prospect of a night under arms with no hope of obtaining water. The Muslims had thwarted their attempt to reach lower ground. To retrace their steps through the waste was unthinkable. The jaws of the trap had closed on them.[957] The crusaders were surrounded on all sides by the Muslims who were so close that they could talk back and forth, so close, it was said, that a cat could not have escaped from the Christian army. All night long the Christians listened to the calls of, "Allah is Great! There is no other god but Allah!" Little rest they found; 'as their hopes sank their courage diminished.'[958]

The Muslim situation was not much easier than their foes': with the lake at their back, retreat was impossible, and the formidable Christian army was still intact.[959] Defeat for the Muslims, in the now unavoidable battle of the following day, would mean the loss of their whole army and territory. Nevertheless, this night preceding the battle, the Muslims had lost their fear of the enemy and were in high spirits.[960] This was the 27th night of Ramadhan, *Laylat al-Qadr* (the Night of Power/Glory), a particularly important event for the Muslims. A Muslim chronicler remembers the exultation of that night:

> It was the night of Qadr, night to be preferred to a thousand months, during which the angels and Gabriel descend to the earth, night whose dawn announced the victory that the morning was to bring to pass. Great was our happiness during that glorious night, for we were among those of whom God has said: "God gives them a reward in this world and one more beautiful in the next." [Koran iii, 141] On that night, heaven showed itself to us with the holy law to be accomplished. The cupbearers of the heavenly river were in readiness, the eternal gardens promised us their fruits, the source of life opened before us, happiness turned toward us, proofs of a Divine intervention manifested themselves. God was protecting Islam and preparing its victory.[961]

On the morning of Saturday, July 4th,[962] both sides were ready for the fight; both knew that the fate of the crusader kingdom depended on the outcome. In this battle Salah Eddin was joined by members of his family, including his son, al-Afdal, and also his nephew, Taki Eddin, who were able military emirs.[963] Ahead of the Muslim troops, the Sultan had drawn up his battalions.[964] He particularly kept a

---

[957] M.W. Baldwin: *Raymond III;* op cit; p. 118.

[958] *Eracles*, pp. 63-4; Ernoul, p. 568. According to the *Libellus*, p. 223.

[959] C. Oman: *The Art of War;* op cit; p. 326.

[960] Ibn al-Athir: *Kamil;* vol xi; pp. 351-5; in F. Gabrieli: *Arab Historians;* op cit; p. 121.

[961] Imad Eddin in M.W. Baldwin: *Raymond III;* op cit; p. 120.

[962] All the sources agree on Saturday as the final day of battle. *Eracles*, p. 64; Ernoul, p. 168; *Libellus*, p. 224; Archumbaldo, p. 2; Ibn al-Athir, p. 683.

[963] Beha Eddin: *Al-Nawadir (RHC Or);* iii; p. 92.

[964] Imad Eddin al-Isfahani: *Al Fath al-Qusi fi 'l fath al-Qudusi;* in F. Gabrieli: *Arab Historians;* op cit; p. 131.

watch on the Christian vanguard in case they should charge, and also made sure to cut off their access to water.[965]

The main forces of both armies engaged each other on the plain just south of the Horns of Hattin,[966] at about nine o'clock.[967] Although all sources agree on the main aspects and outcomes of the battle, they all differ on some details regarding the fighting and on some particular incidents of the day. The reason for these differences is simple: like other battles involving large armies, Hattin's battlefield stretched over a large area, and different eye-witnesses saw different incidents.

Soon, along the whole battle line, fighting raged furiously, both sides putting up a tenacious fight.[968] From the start, Salah Eddin, himself, rode up and down the Muslim lines encouraging and restraining his troops where necessary. The whole army obeyed his commands and respected his prohibitions.[969] In Taki Eddin and Mudhaffer Eddin, the Muslim army had very able generals, who were not only stout fighters but also gifted military tacticians, who attacked and retreated at the most appropriate moments.[970]

A crucial factor explaining Muslim successful stand (and eventual victory,) was the date of battle. It was fought in Ramadhan, just as other great Muslim battles (Badr, Guadalete, Ain Jalut,), and this had a powerful psychological effect, stirring Muslim resilience and hardiness. Their assaults against Christian lines were full of resolve and none shrank from his duty. On one occasion, the Muslims charged the enemy lines with such a fury they almost broke through, slaying many Franks in the process.[971] Muslim tactics were also most effective, aiming to isolate horse from foot, and destroy them separately.

As fighting raged, and throughout the length of the front line, the two armies struck at each other with all their might and fury.[972] The Christians stood stoutly but could not resist the fierce Muslim thrusts coming from every direction, and the showers of arrows aimed at weakening their cavalry.[973] The main source of Christian strength was their heavy cavalry charges, but the terrain where Salah Eddin had locked them in did not allow that. Being surrounded from all sides, the Franks could not beat off their foe, nor could they advance. None of them could escape, except for those for whom the Muslims opened a corridor so as to break Frankish unity and compactness. For the rest, 'Not even an ant could have escaped, and they could not defend themselves by charging.'[974]

---

[965] Ibid.

[966] *Eracles*, p. 266, MS. D; Ernoul, p. 169.

[967] According to the *Continuation, loc. cit.*, the Muslims, after the first backward movement and the setting of the fire, held their position until "haute tierce." *Fratres Hospitalis Archumbaldo*, p. 2, describes the master of the Temple beginning battle about the third hour.

[968] Ibn al-Athir: *Kamil*; vol xi; pp. 351-5; in F. Gabrieli: *Arab Historians*; op cit; pp. 121-2.

[969] Ibid; p. 121.

[970] Any reading of the battle proves this point, and the successful maneuvering of the Muslim armies.

[971] Ibn al-Athir: *Kamil*; vol xi; pp. 351-5; in F. Gabrieli: *Arab Historians*; op cit; pp. 121-2.

[972] Ibid; p. 122.

[973] Ibid.

[974] Imad Eddin al-Isfahani: *Al Fath al-Qusi*; (Gabrieli); op cit; p. 133.

The battled raged for many hours before the Muslims were successful in splitting the cavalry from the foot. Once that happened, the slaughter began as the cavalry was destroyed by the shower of arrows, whilst the infantry, left unprotected, was slain en masse on the ground.[975] Realising the issue was lost, many crusaders deserted the field of action, and to affect Christian morale even worse, the Holy Cross was lost to them.[976]

As the battle neared its end, the Franks dismounted and sat down on the ground and the Muslims fell upon them, pulled down the king's tent and captured every one of them, including the King, his brother, and Prince Arnat of Karak (Reynald of Chatillon), Islam's most hated enemy. They also took the ruler of Jubail, the son of Humphrey (of Toron), the Grand Master of the Templars, one of the Franks' greatest dignitaries, and a band of Templars and Hospitallers.[977] They were too despondent over the loss of the 'Holy Cross' even to attempt escape, and were captured in droves.[978]

Of the huge Christian army that had entered the field of battle, only 200 of the knights and foot-soldiers escaped together with Raymond, Count of Tripoli, the Lord Balian, and Reynald of Sidon, whilst the rest were either dead, badly wounded, or were now in Muslim hands.[979]

> The number of dead and captured was so large that those who saw the slain could not believe that anyone could have been taken alive, and those who saw the prisoners could not believe that any had been killed [says Ibn al-Athir.][980]

Amongst the prisoners was the flower of the crusader state, including the King, the Master of the Temple, the Constable, and so many barons and knights.[981] 'The devil and his crew were taken,' says Imad Eddin, and the Sultan sat to review his chief prisoners, who came forward stumbling in their fetters 'like drunken men.'[982] The Grand Master of the Templars was brought in 'in his sins,' and many of the Templars and Hospitallers with him. King Guy and his brother Godfrey were escorted in, with Hugh of Jubail, Humphrey, and Prince Reynald of Chatillon, 'who was the first to fall into the net.'[983]

Salah Eddin had all the knight Templars and Hospitallers executed. The lives of the countless others he spared, including the king and many distinguished knights, who were all treated honourably as prisoners of state and taken to Damascus.[984] The battlefield itself was a revolting shambles; covered with corpses of slain men

---

[975] C. Oman: *The Art of War;* op cit; p. 326 ff.

[976] R. Grousset: *Histoire des Croisades,* II, 799 ff.; S. Lane-Poole: *Saladin,* op cit; pp. 214ff.

[977] Ibn al Athir: *Kamil,* in F. Gabrieli: *Arab Historians,* op cit, p. 123.

[978] R. Grousset: *Histoire des Croisades,* II, 799 ff.; S. Lane-Poole: *Saladin,* op cit; pp. 214ff.

[979] P.W. Edbury: *The Conquest of Jerusalem and the Third Crusade,* Scolar Press, 1996; p. 161.

[980] Ibn al-Athir: *Kamil;* vol xi; pp. 351-5; in F. Gabrieli: *Arab Historians;* op cit; p. 123.

[981] P.W. Edbury: *The Conquest;* op cit; p. 47.

[982] Imad Eddin al-Isfahani: *Al Fath al-Qusi;* (Gabrieli); op cit; p. 134.

[983] Ibid.

[984] *Eracles,* pp. 64-5; Ernoul, p. 170; W.B. Stevenson: *The Crusaders;* op cit; pp. 247-8; RGKJ, pp. 437ff.; Grousset: *Histoire,* op. cit., pp. 797-9.

and horses, disclosed by the dust as it settled and victory became clear.[985] Thus was the tragic fate of the great army the Christians had assembled.[986] A year afterwards the heaps of bleaching bones could be seen from afar, and the hills and valleys 'were strewn with the relics of the horrid orgies of wild beasts.'[987] According to Baldwin, this battle sounded the death knell of the Kingdom of Jerusalem. Not only had its entire army been destroyed, but its castles and towns had been denuded of their best defenders. Without army, leaders, or adequate garrisons, it soon succumbed.[988]

3. After Hattin, and the Recapture of Jerusalem

Salah Eddin's triumph soon reverberated throughout the land. There were thousands of Muslim slaves in the cities who awaited with joy their liberation at his hands.[989] Even the scattered Christian sects had less to fear from 'the generous Sultan than from the rapacity and tyranny of their Christian masters, to whom heresy was almost as hateful as Islam itself,' says Lane Poole.[990] With the people to support him, and no one to oppose, save a desperate garrison here and there, Salah Eddin's progress through Palestine was an almost uninterrupted march of triumph.[991] The castle of Tiberias surrendered the following day after Hattin; Acre opened its gates within five days of the victory; in three weeks, the strong Castle of Toron in Upper Galilee surrendered.[992] The Muslims took Jaffa and Mejdel Yaba, whilst Haifa, Caesarea and Arsuf, Nazareth, Sebastieh and Nablus submitted to Muslim detachments sent against them.[993] The forts south of Saffuriya were taken, including Fuleh and Deburieh, Lejeun, and Beisan. Then from Toron, Salah Eddin marched on Sidon, and took it after subduing Sarafend. Beirut fell on the 8th of August, whilst Gebal was given up to a Muslim force a week later.[994] Ascalon was besieged by the Muslims on 23 August, and on the 4th of September it capitulated.[995] Three months after Hattin the Latin kingdom of Jerusalem ended nearly a century of existence, surviving in name only.[996] There only remained in crusaders hands a few castles, such as Belfort and Safed still held by Templars, and Hunin and Belvoir garrisoned by knights of the Hospital;

---

[985] Imad Eddin al-Isfahani: *Al Fath al-Quds* (Gabrieli); op cit; pp. 135.

[986] M.W. *Baldwin: Raymond III;* op cit; p. 129.

[987] S. Lane Poole: *The Life of Saladin*, op cit, p. 215.

[988] M.W. *Baldwin: Raymond III;* op cit; p. 132.

[989] S. Lane Poole: *The Life of Saladin*, op cit, p. 218.

[990] Ibid.

[991] Ibid.

[992] Al-Maqrizi: *Kitab al-Suluk;* tr., into Fr as: L'Histoire d'Egypte de Makrizi by E. Blochet; in *Revue de l'Orient Latin* (ROL); vols xiii-xi; here ix; 24 ff. See also C.R. Conder: *The Latin Kingdom*; op cit; pp. 154-5.

[993] P.W. Edbury: *The Conquest;* op cit; p. 161; C.R. Conder: *The Latin;* op cit; pp. 154-5.

[994] C.R. Conder: *The Latin;* op cit; p. 155,

[995] Ibn Khalikan: *Wafayat* (De Slane); op cit; iv; p. 518.

[996] W. B. Stevenson: *The Crusaders*; op cit; pp. 249 ff.; RGKJ; pp. 441 ff.

the two cities of Tyre and Ascalon on the coast; and the Holy City itself.[997] Tyre escaped by 'a hair's breadth.' Had Salah Eddin attacked Tyre directly after Acre, it would have capitulated, for the Prince of Antioch, who succeeded to the County of Tripoli, had not reinforced its small garrison.[998] Afterwards it was too late. Salah Eddin's failure to do that was going to have severe repercussions subsequently as the town became a bridgehead for Crusader resurgence. Yet, by late summer only the county of Tripoli and the principality of Antioch remained as Latin Christian colonies in the Levant.[999] And of course, there also remained the choicest prize: Jerusalem.

The city now became the central focus of the Holy War. For a century Muslims had to suffer the pain and humiliation of seeing it in Christian hands with mosques and Muslim shrines turned into churches or secular buildings,[1000] often sullied with pigs and excrement. Salah Eddin had himself, during a serious illness, pledged that he would devote himself to recovering Jerusalem whatever the cost, an illness, which according to his biographer, Imad Eddin, 'was sent by God to Salah Eddin to wake him from the sleep of forgetfulness.'[1001]

The Sultan was, however, anxious to spare the city the misery of a siege.

"I believe", he told its people, "that Jerusalem is God's abode, as you also believe. It would be much against my will to lay siege to the House of God or put it to the assault.'[1002] To obtain it in peace and without bloodshed he offered to leave the inhabitants free to fortify the city and cultivate the land for five leagues round, and even to supply them plentifully with money and food, until the following Pentecost, on condition that when Pentecost came, 'if they saw a prospect of being rescued, they should keep the Holy City; but if they saw no chance of succor, then they must surrender Jerusalem, and he would conduct them and their possessions safely to Christian soil.'[1003]

> The offer [says Lane Poole] was chivalrous, even quixotic, when the notorious bad faith of the Crusaders is remembered, and the lack of any security for their keeping a promise. But the delegates from Jerusalem refused it without hesitation. If God pleased, they said, they would never surrender the city where the Savior died for them. So Saladin, pleased at their devotion, promised them on his oath that he would never take it except in the honorable way, by the sword. The Sultan's chivalry is the more remarkable, since Jerusalem itself had lately presented a signal example of bad faith. After Balian of Ibelin had escaped from the field of Hattin, he sent to Saladin, begging him to give him a safe-conduct to go to

---

[997] S. Lane Poole: *The Life of Saladin*, op cit, p. 220.
[998] Ibid.
[999] M.W. Baldwin: *Raymond III;* op cit; p. 133.
[1000] C. Hillenbrand: *The Crusades,* op cit; p. 150.
[1001] Abu Shama: *Kitab*; op cit; (Cairo); II; p. 65.
[1002] G. Hindley: *Saladin*, op cit, p. 2.
[1003] S. Lane Poole: *The Life of Saladin*, op cit, p. 224.

Jerusalem and bring his wife and children back to Tyre. The petition was at once granted, on the conditions that Balian should only stay one night in the city, and should never more bear arms against the Sultan. When he arrived at Jerusalem he was welcomed with delight as a deliverer, for there were no knights of rank there, and he was made commander and guardian of the city by universal acclamation. In vain he protested that he had given his oath to Saladin and could not honorably stay or help in the defense. "I absolve you"," said the Patriarch, "from your sin and your oath, which it were a greater sin in you to keep than to break; for it were a perpetual disgrace upon you to leave Jerusalem in this strait and go away, nor should you ever have honor again whithersoever you went". So Balian stayed, and since there were but two knights in the place, who had also fled from Hittin, he knighted thirty burghers. The Patriarch opened the treasury for him, and the garrison went out and bought provisions for the siege. Fugitives had come in from all sides, and there were reckoned to be 60,000 men in the city, besides women and children.[1004]

Salah Eddin's patience and forbearance were not dented even after this act of bad faith. Perhaps he believed that Balian could not help himself; and far from showing rancour, he gave him a fresh proof of his confidence.[1005] Balian again sent to him at Ascalon to beg him to give another safe-conduct, to take his wife and children to Tripoli; he explained that he was forcibly withheld from keeping his former promise. Instead of reproaches, Salah Eddin sent an escort of fifty horse, who carried out his wishes.[1006]

In the end, in face of persistent Christian bad faith and refusal to agree to the sultan's peace terms, Jerusalem was besieged by Muslim armies on 20 September 1187. Then the attacks against the city's defences began. After a while it became obvious that until the early afternoon, Muslim attackers were blinded and dazzled by the sun rising slowly up the eastern sky behind the Christian bowmen and the artillery on the battlements.[1007] After five days Salah Eddin called off the action, and on the evening of 25 September, the defenders saw the Muslim army strike camp and begin to move off northward.[1008] That night the sounds of the distant chanting of the Christians could be heard across the hillsides, the Churches of Jerusalem, full with worshippers, giving thanks for this victory; some even thinking that the Muslims had withdrawn.[1009] Salah Eddin, however, had merely shifted the point of attack, and on the morning of 26 September the citizens awoke to find that the Muslim banners were now on Mount Olive and that the mangonels were already in

---

[1004] Ibid, pp. 224-5.
[1005] Ibid, p. 226.
[1006] Ibid.
[1007] G. Hindley: *Saladin*, op cit, p. 3.
[1008] Ibid.
[1009] Ibid.

position for an attack on the weaker northern and eastern walls.[1010] The attack resumed with ferocity, and the defenders themselves put up a brave fight. On 29 September the props under the foundation were fired, the weakened wall fell, and a great breach was opened up. Despite a brave stand, Christian resistance could only amount to a small period of time. On the final moments, Ibn al-Athir writes:

> When the Franks saw how violently the Muslims were attacking, how continuous and effective was the fire from the ballistas and how busily the sappers were breaching the walls, meeting no resistance, they grew desperate, and their leaders assembled to take counsel. They decided for safe conduct out of the city and to hand Jerusalem over to Salah Eddin. They sent a deputation of their lords and nobles to ask for terms, which were eventually accepted, and the city surrendered on Friday 27 Rajab/2 October 1187, a memorable day on which the Muslim flags were hoisted over the walls of Jerusalem.[1011]

The surrender of Jerusalem to the Muslims occurred nearly a century after it was first taken from them. Salah Eddin's terms were accepted, says a learned Christian, 'with gratitude and lamentation'; perhaps some learned Christians compared these events of 1187 with those of 1099.[1012] 'By a strange coincidence,' Lane Poole remarks, 'it was the 27th of Rejeb, the anniversary of the blessed Leylat el-Miraj, when the Prophet of Islam ascended to heaven and 'visited in his sleep the Holy City which his followers had now recovered after ninety years of Christian occupation.'[1013]

No massacre or violence were perpetrated, the entry of Salah Eddin more 'like that of (Caliph) Omar (in 637-638) (peaceful) rather than that of Godfrey (1099) (followed by the massacre of the Muslim population).'[1014] Salah Eddin's brother al-Adil asked for the gift of a thousand slaves from the still un-ransomed Christian poor; it was granted and he freed them.[1015]

Most of the Christians left Jerusalem. Salah Eddin allowed those who so wished to remain, on condition that they paid a capitation tax.[1016] According to the evidence of the contemporary Christian chronicler, Ernoul, those of Salah Eddin's soldiers who had been ordered to escort the hosts of refugees behaved admirably throughout the journey, taking care of the sick and those exhausted by the march, themselves carrying children and giving up their horses to old men and women.[1017]

> Then I shall tell you [says the Squire of Balian] of the great courtesy which Saladin showed to the wives and daughters of knights, who had fled to

---

[1010] Ibid.

[1011] Ibn al-Athir: *Kamil;* op cit; vol xi; pp. 361 ff; in F. Gabrieli: *Arab Historians*; op cit; p. 142.

[1012] W. Durant: *The Age of Faith*, op cit; p. 598.

[1013] S. Lane Poole: *The Life of Saladin*, p. 230.

[1014] C.R. Conder: *The Latin Kingdom;* op cit; pp. 156-7.

[1015] W. Durant: *The Age of Faith*, op cit; p. 598.

[1016] Z. Oldenbourg: *The Crusades*; op cit; p. 431.

[1017] Ibid; p. 432.

Jerusalem when their lords were killed or made prisoners in battle. When these ladies were ransomed and had come forth from Jerusalem, they assembled and went before Saladin crying mercy. When Saladin saw them he asked who they were and what they sought. And it was told him that they were the dames and damsels of knights who had been taken or killed in battle. Then he asked what they wished, and they answered for God's sake have pity on them; for the husbands of some were in prison, and of others were dead, and they had lost their lands, and in the name of God let him counsel and help them. When Saladin saw them weeping, he had great compassion for them, and wept himself for pity. And he bade the ladies whose husbands were alive to tell him where they were captives, and as soon as he could go to the prisons he would set them free. (And all were released wherever they were found.) After that he commanded that to the dames and damsels whose lords were dead there should be handsomely distributed from his own treasure, to some more and others less, according to their estate. And he gave them so much that they gave praise to God and published abroad the kindness and honor which Saladin had done to them.[1018]

'Blessed are the merciful, for they shall obtain mercy' was a forgotten beatitude when the Christians made shambles of the Holy City (in 1099), [says Lane Poole.] Fortunate were the merciless, for they obtained mercy at the hands of the Moslem Sultan.

'The greatest attribute of heaven is Mercy;

And it is the crown of justice, and the glory,

Where it may kill with tight, to save with pity.'

If the taking of Jerusalem were the only fact known about Saladin, it were enough to prove him the most chivalrous and great-hearted conqueror of his own, and perhaps of any, age [adds Lane Poole.][1019]

The Patriarch left Jerusalem with all his own wealth and a good deal of that belonging to the churches of Jerusalem, and set sail for Europe. However unworthy and discredited he might be, his title gave him certain obligations, and so he travelled first to Rome and from there made a tour of the capitals of Christendom, describing 'the suffering of Jerusalem' and preaching a fresh crusade.[1020]

The news of the Muslim capture of Jerusalem struck the hearts of Western Christendom. It was in the time of the papacy of Urban II that Jerusalem was taken from the Muslims, and it was in the time of Urban III that it was retaken by the Muslims. Pope Urban III who was at Ferrara died of grief when he heard the

[1018] Ernoul 229-230; S. Lane Poole: *The Life of Saladin*, op cit, pp. 232-3.
[1019] S. Lane Poole: *The Life of Saladin*, op cit, p. 234.
[1020] Z. Oldenbourg: *The Crusades*; op cit; p. 432.

news.[1021] When Clement III became pope, he sent his messengers to all the great men of Christendom- emperors, kings, counts, and marquises- and to the knights and sergeants telling them that:

> He would take upon himself and acquit before God all the sins of those who would bear the sign of the cross to go to recover the Promised Land provided that they had confessed and were truly penitent.[1022]

He also announced that he would grant the tithe to all those who wished to have it so that they might do God's service.[1023] And so was launched the Third Crusade in 1189.

From the time Jerusalem was captured until the arrival of the Third Crusade, Salah Eddin attempted to capture crusader positions. In November 1187, the Muslim armies besieged the town of Tyre; ten ships blockading the port.[1024] In the early morning, one day, they were surprised by a Christian fleet and were destroyed, one ship only escaping, and the Muslims were forced to retire in failure.[1025] After that, Salah Eddin focused his attention on the fortresses. Hunin, one of the chief fortresses of Upper Galilee fell on 26 December, 1187, whilst Kerak was taken after a fierce battle by Salah Eddin's brother in October 1188.[1026] Safed, the Hospitallers' fortress was surrendered on 6th of December after heavy bombardment; Belvoir, high over the Jordan Valley, south of Tiberias, held until 5 January 1189; Shobek (Montreal) held until May; Belfort, north west of Bana, yielded on 3 May 1190.[1027] In less than three years, Salah Eddin recaptured most of Palestine and Syria, which had been won in sixty years by the crusaders.[1028] It is important to note that many of his victories occurred on Friday, a day he chose because in all the mosques, prayers were made for his success.[1029]

Whilst he was busy recovering such territories, the armies of the 'Third Crusade' were either on their way, or preparing for the march, the whole of the Christian West rising together as seldom seen.

4. The 'Third Crusade' (1189-1192):

'The fall of Jerusalem had acted as a spark to a train which had been laid and all Christendom was aflame again,' says Stevenson.[1030]

[1021] P.W. Edbury: *The Conquest*; op cit; p. 47.

[1022] Ibid; p. 75.

[1023] Ibid.

[1024] Imad Eddin quoted in Abu Shama: *Kitab (RHC Or)*; op cit; iv; 343.

[1025] Beha Eddin: *Nawadir (RHC Or)*; op cit; iii; p. 103.

[1026] S. Runciman: *A History*; op cit; vol 2; pp. 468-9.

[1027] Ibid.

[1028] C.R. Conder: *The Latin Kingdom*; op cit; pp. 158-9.

[1029] Ibid. p. 151.

[1030] W.B. Stevenson: *The Crusaders*; op cit; p. 260.

Englishmen, Italians, Germans, Scandinavians, every man was now in the service of God. National rivalries and differences which existed in Europe were in theory subordinated to the interests of religion, remarks Oldenbourg.[1031] Ever fervent crusaders, a number of great French barons set out for the East between 1188 and 1190 without waiting for the Kings. These included the Count of Bar, the Count of Champagne, and the Count of Brienne, not to mention lords of lesser importance from the north and south of France. In fact, the whole body of French Chivalry rose, and the majority soon left for Palestine.[1032] Fleets from Pisa and Genoa first, and then Normans from the Mediterranean, English, Danes, Norwegians, and Flemings all joined the call.[1033]

The three largest armies to set for the East were led by the principal rulers of Europe, Richard Coeur de Lion of England, Philip August of France, and the German Emperor. The armies of France, Italy and the Nordic countries took the sea route, whilst the German Emperor, Frederick of Hohenstaufen, found it more practicable to travel through Hungary and the Balkans, and then via Constantinople.[1034] Frederick, known as Barbarossa, was accompanied by his bishops and his vassals.[1035] When he reached Asia Minor, however, his army was decimated nearly entirely by the Turks, and Frederick himself drowned in a stream.[1036] Out of 200,000 who left Germany, not more than five thousand followed Frederick of Swabia, his son and successor, by the coast road to Acre.[1037] Richard and Philip came by sea in the year 1191, Richard capturing for himself Cyprus on his way. Then a fleet arrived bringing ten thousand men, mostly from Flanders and Denmark.[1038]

Acre, in Muslim hands, was going to be the objective of the incoming crusaders. When he heard the news that the Emperor of Germany, the King of France and the King of England and all the high barons overseas were coming against him, Salah Eddin had Acre strongly garrisoned and fortified with all means that were then available, he pledged, besides, to support the town in case of Christian attack.[1039] Just as he had foreseen, Acre was the crusader objective, and quite understandably. It was the port of landing, of course, but even more, the siege of the town had already begun even before the main Christian armies arrived, on Monday 28th August 1189. It would last until 12th July 1191.[1040] The siege was in fact at first quite fortuitous, and again quite revealing of both Christian mentality, and Salah Eddin's

[1031] Z. Oldenbourg: *The Crusades*; op cit; p. 443.
[1032] Ibid; p. 446.
[1033] Ibid.
[1034] Ibid; p. 447.
[1035] Ibid.
[1036] S. Runciman: *A History*; op cit; vol 3; p. 15.
[1037] Jeoff De Vinsauf, I, Chs. 14-7; Jacques de Vitry, p. 103. English tr.
[1038] J. Glubb: *A Short History*; op cit; p. 178.
[1039] Peter W. Edbury: *The Conquest;* op cit; p. 76.
[1040] Beha Eddin: *Nawadir* (RHOr); iii; p. 133.

quixotic attitude. The siege began when Guy de Lusignan, one of Salah Eddin's former prisoners, was freed after Hattin, and managed to acquire a following of hundreds of knights and sergeants newly arrived from France, or escaped from captured castles, and then went on to lay siege to the city.[1041] Salah Eddin was taken aback by Guy's audacity in marching on Acre. The fact that Guy was in breach of his solemn oath did not really surprise him (the word of Christian, Newby points out, he now recognized meant nothing even when sworn on the Gospel) but he was surprised by the large force Guy had put together, about 9,000 men, not counting the Pisans.[1042] Salah Eddin wanted to intercept Guy as he came along the coastal road but his war council disagreed. 'Let them take up their position before Acre and we will cut them to pieces one day,' said an emir.[1043] Events were to prove Salah Eddin right and his emirs wrong.[1044] When he realised that Acre was under siege, and he arrived with his troops, the Franks had already dug themselves into a fortified camp as impregnable to the army from outside as it was to the men of the garrison. The Christians completely invested the town by the side of the land, and fortified their position by entrenchments.[1045] The Muslims took up their position facing the Franks, and pitched Salah Eddin's tent on Tel Kaisan.[1046] Just then Salah Eddin was struck by a serious illness, which seriously undermined the Muslim war effort.[1047] In the meanwhile, Christian reinforcements were arriving by sea. Whilst it is difficult to account precisely the numbers of those who landed at Acre in the spring of 1189, and during the siege, this can be reckoned at over 100,000 men, 'to judge by the numbers of Genoese fleets bringing a succession of Genoese, Venetian, and Pisan Crusaders (from April 1189), and later on Danes, Frisians, men of Champagne (in September), the North Italians and Germans at the end of the same month, the French from all parts of the country, Italians, and Scandinavians (in October).'[1048] Then in the summer of 1190, the armies of the Count of Champagne and his chief vassals arrived, followed by those of the King of France and the Count of Flanders, and lastly of the King of England. With these must be included the forces led by Frederick of Swabia, who despite the disaster in Asia Minor, had managed to keep with him his knights.[1049] Caught between the besieged city on one hand, and Salah Eddin's army on the other, this monstrous camp, overflowing with people and 'crawling like an ant hill,' became the rallying point for the military forces of the whole European chivalry.[1050]

[1041] Z. Oldenbourg: *The Crusades;* op cit; p. 436.
[1042] P.H. Newby: *Saladin in His Time*, Faber and Faber, London, 1983, p. 135.
[1043] Ibid.
[1044] Ibid.
[1045] Imad Eddin; in Abu Shama: *Kitab* (RHOr); iv; p. 428.
[1046] Beha Eddin: *Nawadir;* op cit; p. 22.
[1047] Ibn al-Athir: *Kamil* (RHOr); ii; p. 14.
[1048] Z. Oldenbourg: *The Crusades*; op cit; p. 451.
[1049] Ibid.
[1050] Ibid; 447.

The Muslim garrison inside Acre resisted aware that Salah Eddin's army was in the field helping them. The sultan made repeated attempts to relieve the city, seeking to draw out the Christians in his direction, and causing them considerable losses.[1051] The defenders themselves showed exceptional bravery and resilience, stirred as they were by a powerful belief in their cause. When a man from Damascus amongst the besieged Muslims compounded explosives and burned three of the besiegers towers, was offered a reward by Salah Eddin, he turned it down in favour of Allah's reward.[1052] Despite the Christian tightening siege, links with the besieged were kept by carrier pigeons and swimmers. One such swimmer drowned while attempting to make the passage into the besieged city, and as his body was washed ashore, and the Muslims of Acre obtained the money and letters that Salah Eddin had sent them, the biographer, Beha Eddin, was prompted to remark: 'never before we have heard of a man receiving a trust in his lifetime and delivering it after his death.'[1053]

During the siege, Salah Eddin was deeply upset by the conduct of many around him, including his nephew, Taqi Eddin, who had greatly distinguished himself at Hattin. Taqi Eddin decided to leave the siege around Acre for the Jezireh and Armenia to expand his own fiefs.[1054] Departing with his own army, there, against his uncle's orders, he engaged in wars against local rulers who were allies to his uncle.[1055] This compounded an already tense situation. Yet, when he learnt by letter that Taqi Eddin had died from illness in Armenia, he wept profusely, and those around him did, too. At that moment Beha Eddin, the Qadi, said 'Ask God for forgiveness for allowing yourselves to give way in this manner. Remember Almighty God and submit to what has been determined and pre-ordained.'[1056]
Salah Eddin replied: 'I ask pardon of God.' When some years earlier he learnt the death of his son, his reaction was much less than that. But now, he had grown much older and more exhausted.[1057] Taqi Eddin was a great general, too, and Salah Eddin believed that he would have returned to the Holy War with new recruits, but God had decided otherwise. Perhaps 'He had willed the death of Taqi Eddin as a way of rebuking True believers for their shortcomings. Perhaps this great new wave of crusaders from Europe was a solemn warning, too. The only way possible for the faithful was prayer, the waging of Holy War, and total submission to the will of God.'[1058] Salah Eddin bathed his eyes in rose water and ordered a meal to be served which all present would share.[1059]

[1051] P W. Edbury: *The Conquest;* op cit; p. 95.
[1052] Ibn Khaldun: *Kitab al-Ibar;* op cit; vol iv; p. 321.
[1053] Beha Eddin: *Al-Nawadir al-Sultaniya*; Cairo 1317 (H); p. 120; tr., as *Saladin;* London; 1897; p. 206.
[1054] P.H. Newby: *Saladin in His Time*, op cit, pp. 148-9.
[1055] Ibid, p. 149.
[1056] Ibid, p. 150.
[1057] Ibid.
[1058] Ibid.
[1059] Ibid.

After a two year siege, too long to describe here, Acre was taken by the crusaders. Beha Eddin narrates the final stages of the event:

'Repeated attacks by Muslim contingents were still able at this stage to turn the enemy attack away from the siege, even after the city was wide open to be taken. But the defenders grew weaker, the number of breaches in the walls increased although the defenders built up in place of the broken wall another internal wall from which they fought when the vulnerable section finally collapsed.

On Friday 17 Jumada II/12 July 1191, the Muslims surrendered the city.

The Franks all together gave a mighty shout, and struck a heavy blow into Muslim hearts. Great was our affliction; our whole camp resounded with cries and lamentations, sighs and sobs. The Marquis took the King's standards into the city and planted one on the citadel, one on the minaret of the Great Mosque-on a Friday! One on the Templars' tower and one on the Battle Tower, each one in place of a Muslim standard. The Muslims were all confined to one quarter of the city.'[1060]

Acre had fallen, its tower in ruins from fierce bombardment and its garrison exhausted by hunger and at the end of its strength, on July 12, 1191, after a siege lasting two years.[1061]

The Christian victory was followed by the slaughter of Muslim prisoners. Richard of England, devious and greedy,[1062] had thousands of chained Muslims beheaded, sending a signal by this to Salah Eddin as 'a hint to hurry' to meet his terms in paying the prisoners' ransom.[1063] The massacre took place outside the city, on an open space facing Tel Kaisan, where a part of Salah Eddin's army was still encamped.[1064] The victims numbered at least three thousand (2700 according to the contemporary Ambroise who, however pro-English, does not seem proud of it.)[1065] The contemporary Christian source, *Eracles,* claims that the number of the slain amounted to sixteen thousand.[1066] Richard, Oldenbourg notes, would no doubt have massacred sixteen thousand men just as readily.[1067] On that day, the 15th of August, when the Muslims were killed, the Christian chronicler says:

> His (Richard's) soldiers came forward with joy to fulfill his commands, and to retaliate, by Divine Grace, taking revenge on those who had destroyed so many Christians with missiles from bows and arbalists.[1068]

'After Saladin's almost quixotic acts of clemency and generosity,' Lane Poole says, 'the King of England's cruelty will appear amazing. But the students of the Crusades do not need to be told that in this struggle the virtues of civilization,

[1060] Beha Eddin: *Al-Nawadir* (RHOr) iii; op cit; pp. 229-39; in F. Gabrieli: *Arab Historians*; op cit; pp. 215-23.
[1061] Z. Oldenbourg: *The Crusades*; op cit; p. 450.
[1062] P W. Edbury: *The Conquest*; op cit; p. 97.
[1063] W. Durant: *The Age of Faith*; op cit; p. 599.
[1064] Z. Oldenbourg: *The Crusades*; op cit; p. 457.
[1065] Ibid.
[1066] Ibid; p. 458.
[1067] Ibid.
[1068] Jeoff de Vinsauf, IV, 4; in C. R. Conder: *The Latin;* op cit; p. 273.

magnanimity, toleration, real chivalry, and gentle culture, were all on the side of the Saracens.'[1069]

Acre remained one of the rare exploits of the Third Crusade, which eventually failed in its aim to recapture Jerusalem. Although Richard's army marched against Jerusalem twice (at Christmas 1191 and in June 1192) it was not able to take it.[1070] After successfully recapturing Jaffa, and giving up hope of holding Ascalon, Richard signed a peace treaty with Salah Eddin. Richard had already sued for peace in October 1191. In his message, recorded by Beha Eddin, he said:

'I am to salute you and tell you that the Muslims and Franks are bleeding to death, the country is utterly ruined and goods and lives have been sacrificed on both sides. The time has come to stop this. The points at issue are Jerusalem, the Cross, and the land. Jerusalem is for us object of worship that we could not give up even if there were only one of us left. The land from here to beyond the Jordan must be consigned to us. The cross which is for you simply a piece of wood with no value is for us of enormous importance. If the Sultan will deign to return it to us, we shall be able to make peace and to rest from this endless labour.'

When the Sultan read this message he called his council of state and consulted them about his reply. Then he wrote:

> Jerusalem is ours as much as yours; it is even more sacred to us than it is to you, for it is the place from which our Prophet accomplished his nocturnal journey and the place where our community will gather (on the Day of Judgment). Do not imagine that we can renounce it or vacillate on this point. The land was also originally ours, whereas you have only just arrived and have taken it over only because of the weakness of the Muslims living there at the time. God will not allow you to rebuild a single stone as long as the war lasts. As for the Cross, its possession is a good card in our hand and it cannot be surrendered except in exchange for something of outstanding benefit to all Islam.

This reply was sent to Richard by the hand of his own messenger.[1071]

There were further military encounters between the two sides after that, but Richard was unable to recover Jerusalem. The morale amongst his troops had dampened considerably. On their second march on Jerusalem, the "Itinerary" tells:

'This comfort alone sustained them: the hope that they were at last on the point of visiting the Lord's Sepulcher; for beyond measure did they desire to see the city of Jerusalem and finish their pilgrimage ...

But the wiser set of men did not fall in with the too hasty zeal of the common folk. For the Templars, the Hospitallers, and the Pullani, having a sharper view of the

---

[1069] S. Lane Poole: *The Life of Saladin*, op cit, p. 307.
[1070] Z. Oldenbourg: *The Crusades;* op cit; p. 459.
[1071] Beha Eddin: *An-Nawadir* (RHOr); iii; pp. 274-5; in F. Gabrieli: *Arab Historians*; op cit; 225-6.

future, dissuaded king Richard from going towards Jerusalem at that moment; because, they said, if he were to lay siege and set himself with all his might to take Saladin and all the Turks in the city with him, the Turkish army that lay on the mountain heights outside would be making sudden attacks. Thus there would be a double danger in every fight from the enemy in Jerusalem and the enemy outside. Nor, they continued, if they were successful in capturing the city would their success avail much unless they had very stout warriors to whose care they might entrust the city. And this they did not think was likely to be the case, for, in their opinion, the people were showing all eagerness to get their pilgrimage finished, in order that they might get home without delay, being already unspeakably wearied at what they had undergone.'[1072]

In early Autumn of 1192, Richard wrote again to Salah Eddin:

'Now,' he said, 'the time is close when the sea becomes un-navigable and the crests of the waves swell up on high. If you agree to a truce and enable me, I shall fulfill my desire to go; but if you fight and oppose me I shall pitch my tent and fix my dwelling here. Both sides are tired, both companies are exhausted. I have renounced Jerusalem and will now renounce Ascalon... If we persist in our miserable conflict we shall destroy ourselves. So, fulfill my desires and win my friendship; make a pact with me and let me go; agree with me and accept my respect.'[1073]

Salah Eddin assembled his emirs and advisers, and spoke to them:

'We,' he said, 'thanks be to God, are in a strong position and within sight of the victory we have longed for. Our auxiliaries who have migrated to our side are men of faith, nobility and valour. We have become accustomed to fighting the Holy War and in it we have achieved our aim. Now it is difficult to break off what has become customary, and with God's help so far not one has broken with us. We have no other occupation and aim than that of making war, for we are not among those who are beguiled by games and led astray by dissipation. If we give up this work, what shall we do? If we destroy our hope of defeating them, what shall we hope for? I am afraid that with nothing to do death will overcome me; and how will he who is accustomed to being adorned become used to being unadorned? My feeling is to reject the idea of a truce, and in preferring war, to prefer my honour and make it my leader. I do not seek to stand idle if it means wanting my present state to change. This duty has been placed upon me; it is my job, and with God's help I shall take the most determined and resolute course.'[1074]

The emirs replied:

'Divine grace assists you in all bind and loose, all that you give and take away. But you alone have looked to yourself, as one accustomed to happiness, to the desire to serve God, to the acquisition of eternal virtue, to the taking of measures

[1072] *Itinerarium Peregrinorum et Gesta Regis Ricardi (1190-2)*, ed. W. Stubbs, London, 1864, in S. Lane Poole: *The Life of Saladin*, op cit, p. 333.

[1073] Imad Eddin al-Isfahani: *Al fath al-Qusi fi 'l fath al-Qudusi*; Landberg ed; Leiden; 1888; pp. 434; in F. Gabrieli: *Arab Historians*; op cit; pp. 234 ff.

[1074] Ibid; p. 435.

necessary to success, to disdain for idleness and dislike of keeping oneself aloof. In yourself you find force and tenacity, and your indestructible faith marks you out as the one to achieve the aims we strive for. But look too at the state of the country...'[1075]

Then they spoke of the dire condition of the land, and they quoted the verse from the Qur'an: 'And if they incline to peace, incline you also to it' (Qur'an; 8: 61.)

And so the King of England's request for peace was granted. Imad Eddin says he himself helped draw up the treaty and wrote the text, fixing the boundaries and specifying the terms, and this was Tuesday 21 Sha'aban 588, which corresponds to 1 September 1192.[1076]

On October 9, 1192, Richard left the Holy Land.[1077] Less than six months after Richard's departure, Salah Eddin died.

5. Salah Eddin the Statesman and the Man

Crusades literature has given a good place to the two main protagonists of the Third Crusade, Richard and Salah Eddin. Sir Walter Scott's *The Talisman,* covering this period of crusader history, dispels the myth of 'the valorous Christian Knight versus the Muslim beast;' above all, dispelling the myths about the warlike character of Richard I and his extravagant virtues, highlighting, instead, his cruelty and violence.[1078] Richard, other than his infamy at Acre, when he had thousands of Muslim prisoners slain in cold blood, had also acquired a reputation of deceit. He never refrained from attacking civilian caravans against agreed terms.[1079] His reputation of courage suffered when, on one occasion, he dropped his loot and ran off with his soldiers when he learnt that Salah Eddin was approaching.[1080]

When the crusaders encountered Salah Eddin, on the other hand, they came to respect him 'for his unfailing chivalry and his fidelity to his word.'[1081] So endearing to the Christians was Salah Eddin, that even in times of fire and blood, and even amidst the anti Muslim bigotry of the European Middle Ages, his image remained unsullied, and was even romanticised.[1082] This hardly prevented the Christians from committing repeated acts of treachery towards him. After Hattin, Salah Eddin freed most Christian nobility under the oath they would not raise arms against him again. However, once they were safe in Christian Tripoli and Antioch, king and nobles were 'released by the sentence of the clergy from the enormity of their

---

[1075] Ibid.
[1076] Ibid; p. 436.
[1077] Z. Oldenbourg: *The Crusades*; op cit; p. 464.
[1078] Sir Walter Scott: *The Talisman* (1825), J.M. Dent ltd, Everyman's Library, London, 1991; p. 191.
[1079] R. Finucane: *Soldiers of the Faith*; op cit; p. 85.
[1080] A.M. Nanai: L'Image du croise; op cit; p. 24.
[1081] M. Hodgson: *The Venture of Islam;* Chicago University Press; 1979; Vol II, p. 267.
[1082] C. Hillenbrand: *The Crusades*, op cit; p. 195.

promise,' and after that they laid plans of vengeance against him.[1083] King, Guy, was relieved from the oath he had given by the patriarch who absolved him from his oath for it would be to the benefit of Christendom.[1084] It was King Guy who, with an army of men, most of whom had been freed by Salah Eddin after Hattin, put siege first to the city of Acre in 1188. After Salah Eddin sent word to the King accusing him of failing to abide by his oath and the undertakings that he ought not have borne arms against him, and that he had promised he would go overseas, the king replied that he had kept his oath, 'for he had not borne arms against him, though it was true that his horse carried a sword on its saddle, and that he was wearing combat gear.'[1085]

Often, Salah Eddin's spirit of chivalry was excessive, as when following the victory of Jerusalem, his army escorted refugees from the captured cities for the Christian stronghold of Tyre, which reinforced his enemies, and prevented him from capturing it.[1086] Overcoming the Franks was decidedly not easy, Oldenbourg notes, 'Especially when waging a humane war and respecting persons and property as far as possible as Saladin was doing.'[1087]

Salah Eddin also used to send ice and fruits to the enemy in the hope that 'their hearts would melt,' as he used to say.[1088] And their hearts rather than being melted by the sultan's gifts hardened. Soon after he received the gifts from Salah Eddin, which even helped him recover his health, Richard, had the thousands Muslim prisoners beheaded in Acre.[1089] Richard, in fact, according to some accounts, even had the women and children massacred on that occasion.[1090]

Salah Eddin commanded the respect of his foes then and for long after. More importantly, he commanded the respect of his own troops, which is at times even harder to obtain, let alone to maintain, and most of all, he united them in their vast ethnic differences.

> All the strength of Christendom concentrated in the Third Crusade had not shaken Saladin's power [says Lane Poole.] His soldiers may have murmured at their long months of hard and perilous service, year after year, but they never refused to come to his summons and lay down their lives in his cause. His vassals in the distant valleys of the Tigris may have groaned at his constant requirements, but they brought their retainers loyally to his colors; and at the last pitched battle, at Arsuf, it was the division of Mosul that most distinguished itself for valor. Throughout these toilsome campaigns Saladin could always count on the support of the levies from Egypt and Mesopotamia, as well as from northern and central Syria;

[1083] S. Lane Poole: *Saladin;* op cit; p. 246.
[1084] P.W. Edbury: *The Conquest of Jerusalem*; op cit; p. 50.
[1085] Ibid; p. 83.
[1086] J.H. Lamonte: Crusade and Jihad: op cit; p. 180.
[1087] Z. Oldenbourg: *The Crusades*; op cit; p. 436.
[1088] M. Darwish: *Memory for Forgetfulness*; tr. I. Muhawi; Berkeley; 1995; pp. 33-4.
[1089] F. Guizot: *History of France;* London; 1872; 8 Vols; pp. 439 ff. E. Gibbon: *The Decline and Fall;* op cit; VI; p. 119.
[1090] M. Hodgson: *The Venture*, op cit; p. 267.

Kurds, Turkmans, Arabs, and Egyptians, they were all Moslems and his servants when he called. In spite of their differences of race, their national jealousies, and tribal pride, he had kept them together as one host— not without difficulty and twice or thrice a critical waver. But, the shirking at Jaffa notwithstanding, they were still a united army under his orders in the autumn of 1192, as they had been when he first led them "on the Path of God" in 1187. Not a province had fallen away, not a chief or vassal had rebelled, though the calls upon their loyalty and endurance were enough to try the firmest faith and tax the strength of giants. The brief defection, quickly pardoned, of a young prince of his own blood in Mesopotamia only emphasizes, by its isolation, Saladin's compelling influence over his subjects. When the trials and sufferings of the five years' war were over, he still reigned unchallenged from the mountains of Kurdistan to the Libyan desert, and far beyond these borders the King of Georgia, the Catholicos of Armenia, the Sultan of Konia, the Emperor of Constantinople, were eager to call him friend and ally.[1091]

Other than his role as army commander, Salah Eddin had also acquired a reputation for his love and support of learning. We hear indeed of evenings spent in literary discussions, of Salah Eddin's intimacy with the old warrior-poet Usama, of recitations of poetry, and of frequent games at chess, to which the Sultan was passionately devoted.[1092] The Spanish Muslim, Ibn-Jubayr, who visited Damascus in 1184, when Salah Eddin was living there, gave a minute description of the wonders of the great mosque, not least among which was the clock in which 'brazen falcons struck the hours, and a brass door shut for each hour past, whilst at night red lamps marked the time, measured by subsiding water.'[1093] Ibn Jubayr also mentions twenty colleges, two free hospitals, and many monasteries. He reports the high number and varied facilities for foreign students and visitors at the Umayyad Mosque, and he himself encouraged students from Spain to go East for education.[1094] He said: 'Anyone in the West who seeks success, let him come to this city (Damascus) to study, because assistance here is abundant. The chief thing is that the student here is relieved of all worry about food and lodging, which is a great help.'[1095]

Salah Eddin was a builder of madrasas, setting up such edifices wherever he passed, from Syria, to Palestine, to Egypt, to the Hijaz.[1096] He introduced the madrasa system into Jerusalem, and in 1189 (that is two years after he recaptured the city) he endowed the Khanakah Salahiya, then in 1191 the Zawiya

[1091] S. Lane Poole: *The Life of Saladin*, op cit, p. 359.
[1092] Ibid, p. 186.
[1093] Ibn Jubayr: pp. 262-97 in G. le Strange: Palestine; op cit; pp. 249-50.
[1094] Ibn Jubayr in K.A Totah: *The contribution of the Arabs to education;* New York; Columbia University Press, 1926. p. 45.
[1095] Ibid.
[1096] E. Diez: Masjid: *Encyclopaedia of Islam*; 1st ed; vol 3; Leiden Brill; 1936; p. 355.

Khataniya south of al-Aksa for a particular scholar, then more madrasas.[1097] Ibn Jubayr, who also travelled through Egypt in the time of Salah Eddin, speaks of several madrasas in Alexandria and particularly of one beside Al-Shafi's tomb, which looked like a whole town.[1098] Whilst striving to have madrasas built, Salah Eddin also made certain of the survival of the institutions. Whenever a mosque or a school was established, he was in the habit of fixing adequate endowments to pay for the employees' salaries, grants for the students and to keep the establishment in a good state.[1099] When al-Nasiriyyah was established, the sultan endowed it with baths in its neighbourhood, a bakery opposite to it, shops at its back and the Island of the Elephant.[1100]

Salah Eddin, Oldenbourg insists, was one of those men who are always absorbed in some urgent business, incapable of thinking of themselves.[1101] He enjoyed no rest; was as hard a worker as his meanest subject, and sat in the Hall of Justice two days in the week to hear the complaints of his subjects.[1102] Like Caliph Omar, all wrongs that came to his knowledge were speedily redressed; and taxes were lowered at the same time that public works were extended and the functions of government were carried on with efficiency and zeal.[1103] His correspondence was immense, and though he had indefatigable chancellors and secretaries in the Qady al-Fadil, Imad-al-Din, and latterly Baha-al-Din, he must have spent a great deal of time and effort in the dispatches.[1104]

The testimony of Salah Eddin by outsiders does corroborate the statements of those close to him, especially in relation to his modesty and simplicity.[1105] In 1193, just like Caliph Omar centuries before him, building walls and digging trenches round Jerusalem, he carried stones on his own shoulders, so that all, rich and poor, strong and weak, followed his example, even including the scribe 'Imad Eddin and the Qady al-Fadil.[1106] Like Omar, his chief garment was a coarse woollen cloth, his only drink was water.[1107] And just as his predecessor, Nur Eddin, and like Caliph Omar, he esteemed money 'as little as dust,' and left only one dinar in his personal treasury.[1108] When he entered the Fatimid caliph palace in Cairo, he found there 12,000 occupants, all women except the male relatives of the Caliph; and such wealth of jewelry, furniture, ivory, porcelain, glass, and other objects of art 'as could

---

[1097] Ibid.

[1098] Ibn Jubayr: *Rihla*, p. 42 and 48.

[1099] Ibid; 275.

[1100] Al-Maqrizi: *Khitat*; II; p. 400.

[1101] Z. Oldenbourg: *The Crusades;* op cit; p. 469.

[1102] S. Lane Poole: *The Life of Saladin*, op cit, p. 186-7.

[1103] Durant p. 311.

[1104] S. Lane Poole: *The Life*; p. 187.

[1105] Such as Beha Eddin: *The Life of Saladin* (London); op cit.

[1106] Abd al Latif quoted in Ibn Abi Usaybia: *Kitab uyun al-anba fi tabaqat al-atiba;* ed., A. Muller, 2 vols, Konigsberg, 1884. II; p. 206.

[1107] W. Durant: *The Age of Faith*, op cit; p. 310.

[1108] Baron Carra de Vaux: *Les Penseurs de l'Islam*, Vol 1; Geuthner; Paris; 1921; p. 27.

hardly be rivaled by any other dignitary of that era.'[1109] He distributed the Fatimid accumulated treasures, one of which was a seventeen dirham string of sapphires as weighed by Ibn al-Athir in person, among his retainers and troops, keeping nothing for himself.[1110] He gave the palace to his captains, and continued to live in the vizier's chambers a life of fortunate simplicity.[1111] The sum of money he left at his death was not large enough to be submitted to tax; his private charities had absorbed everything.

> He who possessed such abundant wealth left in his treasury [Beha Eddin said] when he died, but seven and forty Nasri dirhems, and a single Tyrian gold piece.[1112]
> He left neither goods, nor house, nor real estate, neither garden, nor village, nor cultivated land, nor any other species of property.[1113]

Salah Eddin was famed for the kindness and softness of his character. So many anecdotes are told by those who knew him, and wrote about his life, where the Sultan showed magnanimity, kindness, and gentleness and a spirit of toleration of human frailty and faults that remained engraved in history.[1114]

> Such gentle, well mannered consideration for subordinates and servants [Hindley says] was, to many observers used to the arrogance and violence of petty despots, one of the most remarkable traits of a remarkable character.[1115]
> Above all things [Lane Poole says] Saladin was a devout Moslem. His religion was all the world to him. In this alone he was fanatical; and the only act of severity, not done in war, that can be alleged against him was the execution of the mystic philosopher es-Suhrawardy, on the ground of heresy. Saladin hated all eclectic philosophers, materialists, and free-thinkers, with a holy horror. His own faith was as rigidly orthodox as it was simple, strong, and sincere. Islam, in its essence and as professed by such a man as Saladin, is a religion of noble simplicity and austere self-sacrifice.... No one was more assiduous in the five daily prayers and the weekly attendance at the mosque; and even when seriously ill, he would send for the Imam and force himself to stand and repeat the fatiguing service of Friday. He delighted in hearing the Koran read to him, but his reader had to be a practiced expert. Saladin would listen till his heart melted and the tears rolled down his cheeks. He had this womanish weakness, yet one

---

[1109] W. Durant: *The Age of Faith*, op cit; p. 311.

[1110] Ibn al-Athir: *Kamil;* vol xi; p. 242; P.K. Hitti: *History;* op cit; p. 652.

[1111] W. Durant: *The Age of Faith*; op cit; p. 311.

[1112] Beha-ed-Din: The Life of Saladin; op cit; reprinted in *The Islamic World and the West;* edited by A.R. Lewis; pp. 53-61; at p. 55.

[1113] Ibid.

[1114] See: Abu Shama: *Kitab al-Rawdatin* in *Receuil des Historiens*; vols IV and V; Beha Eddin; *The Life of Saladin*; H.A.R. Gibb: *The Life of Saladin From the Works of Imad Eddin and Baha Ad Din*; Oxford; 1973; etc.

[1115] G. Hindley: *Saladin*, op cit, p. 185.

likes him nonetheless for his emotional, sensitive nature. "His heart was humble and full of compassion, and tears came readily to his eyes".

It was a grief to him that he was never able to perform the religious duty of pilgrimage; but at least he was a benefactor to the pilgrims. One of his early acts of sovereignty was to abolish the onerous tolls which had for centuries burdened the Faithful who visited Mecca, and his last public appearance was to welcome the returning Hajj. As the pilgrims greeted him, it was noticed how radiant he looked. He had but a week to live.

In nothing did he show his religious zeal more fervently than in the chief and supreme duty of Moslems, the Jihad or Holy War. Naturally averse to bloodshed, even unwarlike, as he was, he was a changed man when it came to fighting the infidels. "I never knew him", says Baha-eddin, "show any anxiety about the numbers and strength of the enemy. He would listen to plans of all kinds and discuss their consequences without any excitement or loss of composure". He used to ride, as we have seen, between the lines of battle, attended only by a page; and once he sat there on horseback surrounded by his staff and listened calmly whilst the sacred Traditions were read aloud to him in face of the enemy. To wage God's war was a genuine passion with him; his whole heart was wrapped up in it, and to this cause he devoted himself, body and soul. During those last years he could hardly speak or think of anything else, and he sacrificed every pleasure, comfort, and domestic happiness, to its service. He even dreamed of wider battles for the faith: when the Franks should be driven out of Palestine, he told his secretary, he would pursue them over the sea, and conquer them, till there should not remain one unbeliever on the face of the earth. "What is the most glorious death?" he asked his friend, who replied, "To die on the Path of God". "Then I strive for the door of the most glorious of deaths", said Saladin. When he was so prostrated with a painful illness at the siege of Acre that he could not come to table, he would yet sit his horse all day before the enemy; and when men marveled at his fortitude, he said, "The pain leaves me when I am on horseback. It comes back only when I dismount". So long as he was doing God's work, he felt no pain; but inaction tortured him.'[1116]

Not long before his death (1193) he gave his son Ez-Zahir instructions:

My son, I commend thee to the Most High God... Do His will, for that way lies peace. Abstain from shedding blood.... for blood that is spilt never sleeps. Seek to win the hearts of thy people, and watch over their prosperity; for it is to secure their happiness that thou art appointed by God and me... If I have become great it is because I have won men's hearts by kindness and gentleness.[1117]

[1116] S. Lane Poole: *The Life of Saladin*, op cit, pp. 372-5.
[1117] Ibid; p. 367.

After his death, one of his contemporaries, 'Abd al-Latif, says:

> Men grieved for him as they grieved prophets. I have seen no other ruler for whose death the people mourned, for he was loved by good and bad, Muslim and unbeliever alike.[1118]

Islam gloried in the integrity and justice of his rule, and Christendom acknowledged in him an 'infidel gentleman.'[1119]

On Friday the 9th of October 1187, only seven days after the recapture of Jerusalem, an immense congregation assembled to pray with Salah Eddin in the sanctuary of Al-Aqsa. The chief Qady of Aleppo preached the sermon, which included:

> Had ye not been of God's chosen servants, he had not honored you by this grace, wherein ye can never be rivaled nor shall any ever share in its perfectness. Blessed are ye, who have fought like those at Bedr, who have been steadfast as Abu-Bekr, victorious as Omar, who have recalled the hosts of Othman and the onslaughts of Ali! Ye have renewed for Islam the glorious memories of Kadisiya, of the Yarmuk, of Khaibar, and of Khalid, the Sword of God. The Almighty recompense you, and accept the offering of the blood ye have shed in his service, and grant you Paradise, happy for ever.[1120]

This noble *khutba*, with its beautiful words, was pronounced with such overwhelming effect, writes the Qady el-Fadil, that

> The heavens almost cracked, not in wrath, but to drop tears of joy, and the stars left their places, not to shoot upon the wicked, but to rejoice together.

The delight of the Muslims at the recovery of the Sanctuary was boundless. Salah Eddin restored it to its former beauty and simplicity, and brought from Damascus an exquisite carved pulpit which Nur-Eddin had had designed at Aleppo twenty years before. It had remained there until recent times, and over the great niche of the Mosque could still be read the inscription:

> In the name of God, the Compassionate, the Merciful! Hath ordered the repair of this holy Mihrab and the restoration of the Mosque el-Aksa, founded on piety, the servant and agent of God Yusuf son of Ayyub Abu-l-Muzaffar el-Melik en-Nasir Salahed-dunya wa-d-din, when that God by his hand had triumphed, in the month of the year [of the Flight] 583: and he prayeth God to endue him with thankfulness for this favor and to make him a partaker in the remission of sins, through His mercy and forgiveness.[1121]

[1118] Cited by B. Lewis: *Islam*; vol I; The Mac Millan Press; Ltd; London; 1974; p. 67.
[1119] W. Durant: *The Age of Faith*, op cit; p. 311.
[1120] S. Lane Poole: *The Life of Saladin*, op cit, p. 237.
[1121] Ibid, p. 238.

From Salah Eddin to Baybars (1193-1248)

The Ayyubid dynasty created by Salah Eddin inherited Egypt and Syria and also parts of Mesopotamia (Al-Jazira) and Lesser Armenia. Before he died, Salah Eddin had his officers and high officials swear allegiance to his children and his successors,[1122] and to each he assigned a certain portion of the Muslim land.[1123] Al-Malik al-Afdal became ruler of Damascus and southern Syria; Al-Malik al-Aziz of Egypt; and Al-Malik al-Zahir of Aleppo and Northern Syria.[1124] In a brief, and certainly ill thought act, one of the rare ones by the Sultan, there was gone the territorial unity that had been built by himself and his predecessors, Imad Eddin and Nur Eddin Zangi. And thus was also gone the common will amongst the Ayyubid elite to finish the job and remove the Franks definitely.[1125] This could have easily been done as the crusader states had now been reduced to only a few ports and a narrow strip of the hinterland.[1126] Instead of pressing home such advantages the heirs to Salah Eddin became engaged in civil wars.[1127] Al-Adil (Salah Eddin's brother) at first wrested power from Salah Eddin's sons.[1128] Following al-Adil's death (in 1218) his sons ruled the separate parts of the empire. Al-Kamil held Egypt; al-Mu'Azzam held Syria and Palestine; and Al-Ashraf governed al-Jazira, that is Upper Mesopotamia.[1129] Al-Adil's heirs soon became involved in armed conflict. Fighting over territorial gains became the main feature of Ayyubid rule which lasted in Egypt until 1250, and most of Syria until 1260.

In the middle of Muslim wars, the will to regain territories from the Franks was abandoned. For al-Adil and the other princes the war against the Franks was not a salient feature at all. Al Adil, for instance, throughout his entire reign undertook only one major campaign against the crusaders, and even this was a punitive expedition rather than a drive for re-conquest.[1130] The concept of Jihad, which was fundamental to the deeds of Nur Eddin and Salah Eddin instantly evaporated upon the latter's death.[1131] The Ayyubids did talk of jihad, in fact, but actually embraced détente.[1132] In their relations with the Franks, members of the Ayyubid family sought peace rather than war, and treated the Christians as rulers with whom to make political alliances and commercial treaties.[1133] They sought the economic

---

[1122] R.S. Humphreys: *From Saladin;* State University of New York Press; Albany; 1977; p. 57.

[1123] Ibn Wasil: *Mufarrij al-Kurub fi Akhbar Bani Ayyub;* ed. G. Shayyal, S.Ashur, and H. Rabi'; 4 vols; Cairo; II; 172-3.

[1124] Ibn al-Athir: *Kamil* (Thornberg); xii. Ibn al-Athir, who flourished during these events offers the best accounts on the distribution of the lands, and the negative effects such distributions had.

[1125] C. Hillenbrand: *The Crusades,* op cit; p. 225.

[1126] R.S. Humphreys, 'Ayyubids, Mamluks and the Latin East in the thirteenth century', *Mamluk Studies Review,* 2 (1998), pp. 1-18.

[1127] W.B. Stevenson: *The Crusaders*; op cit; p. 294.

[1128] H.E. Mayer: *The Crusades*; tr. J. Gillingham; Oxford University Press; 1972; p. 210.

[1129] Ibid.

[1130] R.S. Humphreys: *From Saladin;* op cit, p. 132.

[1131] E. Siwan: *L'Islam et la Croisade*; Paris; Maisonenuve; 1968; pp. 120-4.

[1132] C. Hillenbrand: *The Crusades,* op cit; p. 249.

[1133] Ibid; p. 24.

advantages of maintaining trade routes across Christian territory to the sea.[1134] The Ayyubid period witnessed, in fact, the full integration of the Franks as local Levantine rulers.[1135] Each Ayyubid ruler within the confederacy adopted his own negotiation position with the Franks; each only caring for his portion of territory.[1136] And whilst peace was sought with the Christians, between the Ayyubids themselves, war raged.

During the period of Ayyubids civil wars, no less than six great crusades were launched, four of them against the Muslim world. The first of these was in 1197; then in 1204 (a crusade deviated onto Constantinople); in 1212 against the Albigensians (in the south of France), in 1217; in 1229; and in 1248. There were also countless less grand crusades, and fighting men kept pouring into the Holy Land every year from all parts of Europe (except modern Russia.)

In face of Ayyubid ineptness, Muslim supremacy, and at times, even survival, were in question. In fact the Ayyubids only did what other Muslims were doing elsewhere: that is fighting amongst each other, thus inviting Christian invasion. The crushing of the vast Muslim army by a smaller Christian one at Las Navas de la Tolosa in 1212 signaled the end of Muslim rule on the Iberian Peninsula.[1137] A few decades later all that was left in Muslim hands was Grenada, whilst Christian conquest of North Africa had become both an aim and possible.[1138] The plan was that, once masters of North Africa, Christians would advance east and join with their co-religionists in Palestine.

The encirclement and final subjugation of the Muslim world would, however, in Western view, only be accomplished if the Eastern Orthodox Church and its centre, Byzantium, came under Catholic fold.

> For the medieval crusaders [Cox observes] Byzantium, not less than Syria and Egypt, was a part of heathendom; the people savages to be brought under a yoke as heavy as that of the Western serfs; their patriarchs, their bishops, their priests, and their monks were ministers of a false faith beyond the pale of charity or mercy.[1139]

The second crusade (1148), it was widely felt in the West, would have succeeded if there had been full support from Byzantium, and Holy War against Byzantium was seen necessary for its forcible subjection to the papal see.[1140] Now, in 1204, at last, a great opportunity presented itself when the deposed Byzantine

---

[1134] R.S. Humphreys: Legitimacy and instability in Islam, op cit; pp. 10-11.

[1135] C. Hillenbrand: *The Crusades*, op cit; p. 203.

[1136] R.S. Humphreys: Ayyubids, Mamluks; op cit; p. 7. C. Hillenbrand: *The Crusades*, op cit; p. 225.

[1137] Al-Maqqari: *Nafh Al-Tib;* tr., by P. De Gayangos: *The History of the Mohammedan Dynasties in Spain*; 2 vols; The Oriental Translation Fund; London, 1840-3.

[1138] C.H. Bishko: The Spanish and Portuguese Reconquest, 1095-1492; in *A History of the Crusades*; K.M. Setton ed; The University of Wisconsin Press; 1975; vol 3; pp. 396-456; at p. 435.

[1139] G.W. Cox: *The Crusades*; op cit, pp. 163-4.

[1140] J. Godfrey: *1204 The Unholy Crusade*; Oxford University Press; 1980; p. 32. H.E. Mayer: *The Crusades*; op cit; p. 280.

Emperor's son, Alexius, proposed to the crusaders, on their way to conquer the tottering Ayyubid realm, to reinstate him in return for putting the Orthodox Church under Catholic sway. This offer was enthusiastically taken on. To the crusaders this would mean not just the end of the Christian schism, but also bringing Western Christendom to the frontier of Islam, thus making the chance of a crusade highly successful, especially once Byzantine humane and other resources were put at the service of the crusade as Alexius had promised. The 'fickle' attitude, in crusader view, of the Greeks, prompted the crusaders to storm Constantinople, ransack it, and establish their rule over Byzantium in 1204. (The Greeks eventually rose in rebellion, and helped by the Turks of Anatolia, regained their independence in 1261. Subsequently, in the 14th century, the rise of the Ottomans would foil the Catholic project for centuries to come (until the rise of modern Russia).[1141]

The capture by the Latins of Constantinople in 1204, the success at Las Navas de la Tolosa in 1212, and Ayyubid civil wars, made the moment most opportune to launch a great crusade. Pope Innocent III, as Mayer observes, could have had few doubts about the successful outcome of his plan; he was filled with the quiet certainty that, as was promised in the Book of Revelation, the days of Islam were numbered.[1142] The crusade army that set off towards Egypt in 1217 was one of the largest ever assembled. According to one contemporary, John of Tulbia, it was 100,000 strong.[1143] Gibbon puts the figure at two hundred thousand Franks who were landed at the eastern mouth of the Nile at Damietta.[1144] The choice of Egypt was not fortuitous, of course. When in most of the previous century the country was in Fatimid hands it was seen as an ally, but once it came under Sunni sway, it became the principal foe that needed subjugation. The Fatimids themselves had constantly backed Christian attacks against Muslims, not just in the East during the Crusades but also in North Africa.[1145]

The prospects for success of the 1217 crusade were further enhanced by the arrival of the Mongols, attacking Muslims from the rear. This was the long expected rescue of Christendom by the ally from the East. Already by the mid 12th century reports reaching Europe from the East spread the legend of King Prester John who was expected to come to the aid of the hard pressed Christians of the East.[1146] By the time of this crusade a prophecy referred to by the contemporaries Oliver and Jacques de Vitry predicted that two kings would come, one from the

[1141] T.W. Arnold: *The Preaching of Islam*; Lahore: Sb. M. Ashraf, 1961, p. 151.

[1142] H.E. Mayer: *The Crusades*; op cit; p. 206.

[1143] John de Tulbia; *De Domino Johanne rege Jerusalem*; ed., R. Rohricht; in *Scriptores Minores*; Geneva; 1879; p. 139.

[1144] E. Gibbon: *Decline and Fall;* op cit, vol 6; p. 355.

[1145] M. Canard, 'Une lettre du calife Fatimite al Hafiz (524-544/n30-n49) a Roger II; in *Studi Ruggeriani, VIII Centenario della morte di Ruggero II, Atti del Convegno internazionale di studi ruggeriani (Palermo, 21-25 aprile* 1954) (2 vols, Palermo, 1955), I, pp. 125-46 (reprinted in Canard, *Miscellanea Orientalia,* London, 1973); J. Johns, *Arabic Administration in Norman Sicily,* Cambridge, 2005; pp. 259-65; see also J. Johns: The Norman Kings of Sicily and the Fatimid Caliphate; *Anglo-Norman Studies,* XV (1992), 133-159. C.D. Stanton: *Norman Naval Operations in the Mediterranean;* The Boydell Press; 2011; p. 109.

[1146] H.E. Mayer: *The Crusades*; op cit, p. 216.

west, the other from the east and will subdue the land of the Sultan.[1147] The prophecy seemed to materialize in the wake of this crusade, coinciding with the first Mongol invasion of Islam in 1219-1221.[1148] Fighting alongside the Mongols, themselves under much Christian influence, were large contingents of Armenians and Georgians.[1149] The news of Mongol devastation of the Muslim Eastern provinces reached the crusaders at Damietta, hence seeming to fulfill the prophecy. Genghis Khan, the Great Khan of all Mongols, now stood no more than ten day march from Baghdad as Pelagius, the Pope Legate at Damietta, had reported to the pope.[1150] As a result the Christians refused peace with Sultan al-Kamil even if he offered to return Jerusalem and many other territories to them. They were fully convinced that the end of Islam had indeed arrived. Yet, crucially, for reasons that remain to be elucidated, instead of progressing west and finish off moribund Muslim Syria and the Abbasid caliphate, the Mongols suddenly returned east.

Decades later, in 1248, when under the French King, Louis IX, known as St Louis, a huge crusade set off from Europe, the days of Islam, again, seemed counted, especially now that the Mongol ally was ready to strike at precisely the same time as the crusaders. As he was encamped in Cyprus on his way to Egypt, Louis received two Nestorian Christian envoys from the Mongol headquarters in Persia indicating that a great offensive against Islam was now being mounted by themselves, and simultaneous strikes from east and west should secure final victory over the common, Muslim, foe.[1151] In face of such powerful Christian-Mongol alliance there only stood the divided Ayyubid principalities. Yet, it just happened that no sooner Louis sailed for Egypt, the Mongol supreme leader, Kuyuk (Guyuk), died. This delayed the Mongol attack by another decade.[1152] By the time the Mongols had reformed to launch their war on Islam, there has arisen one of the mightiest figures and legend of Islam: Baybars, the Mamluk.

[1147] Oliver, ch .56, pp. 258-9; Jacques de Vitry: ZKG, XVI, 106-13. The *Annales de Dunstaplia (Annales Monastici*, III, 62. record that Pelagius translated it and sent it to Rome from whence a copy was sent to England.
[1148] P. Pelliot: *Mongols and Popes; 13ᵗʰ and 14ᵗʰ centuries;* Paris; 1922.
[1149] Baron G. d'Ohsson: *Histoire des Mongols*: La Haye et Amsterdam; 1834.
[1150] H.E. Mayer: *The Crusades*; p. 217.
[1151] R. Grousset: *Histoire des Croisades et du Royaume Franc de Jerusalem;* Paris; 1934-5, vol III, p. 520.
[1152] J.J. Saunders: *Aspects of the Crusades*; University of Canterbury; 1962; p. 53.

BAYBARS

Ibn Khaldun writes:

> When the ['Abbasid] state was drowned in decadence and luxury and
> donned the garments of calamity and impotence and was overthrown by
> the heathen Tatars, who abolished the seat of the Caliphate and obliterated
> the splendour of the lands and made unbelief prevail in place of belief,
> because the people of the faith, sunk in self-indulgence, preoccupied with
> pleasure, and abandoned to luxury, had become deficient in energy and
> reluctant to rally in defense, and had stripped off the skin of courage and
> the emblem of manhood—then, it was God's benevolence that He rescued
> the faith by reviving its dying breath and restoring the unity of the Muslims
> in the Egyptian realms, preserving the order and defending the walls of
> Islam. He did this by sending to the Muslims, from this Turkish nation and
> from among its great and numerous tribes, [Mamluk] rulers to defend
> them and utterly loyal helpers, who were brought from the House of War
> to the House of Islam under the rule of slavery, which hides in itself a
> Divine blessing. By means of slavery they learn glory and blessing and are
> exposed to divine providence; cured by slavery, they enter the Muslim
> religion with the firm resolve of true believers and yet with nomadic
> virtues unsullied by debased nature, unadulterated with the filth of
> pleasure, undefiled by the ways of civilized living, and with their ardour
> unbroken by the profusion of luxury. The slave merchants bring them to
> Egypt in batches, like sand-grouse to the watering places, and government
> buyers have them displayed for inspection and bid for them, raising the
> price above their value. They do this not in order to subjugate them, but
> because it intensifies loyalty, increases power, and is conducive to ardent
> zeal. They choose from each group, according to what they observe of the
> characteristics of the race and the tribes. Then they place them in
> government barracks where they give them good and fair treatment,
> educate them, have them taught the Qur'an and kept at their religious
> studies until they have a firm grasp of this. Then they train them in archery
> and fencing, in horsemanship, in hippodromes, and in thrusting with the
> lance and striking with the sword until their arms grow strong and their
> skills become firmly rooted. When the masters know that they have
> reached the point when they are ready to defend them, even to die for
> them, they double their pay and increase their grants, and impose on them
> the duty to improve themselves in the use of weapons and in
> horsemanship, and so also to increase the number of men of their own race
> in the service for that purpose. Often they use them in the service of the

state, appoint them to high state offices, and some of them are chosen to sit on the throne of the Sultans and direct the affairs of the Muslims, in accordance with Divine providence and with the mercy of God to His creatures. Thus, one intake comes after another and generation follows generation, and Islam rejoices in the benefit which it gains through them, and the branches of the kingdom flourish with the freshness of youth.[1153]

These Mamluks, Curtin adds, attained the highest military offices, they saved Egypt at Al-Mansurah, and did most to destroy the French army; their power lay in *esprit de corps* and ambition. Their chiefs rose to dominion in Egypt, and then put a check on the Mongols.[1154] Subsequently, it was these same Mamluks who ended the crusader presence in the East.[1155]

However it is not just Mamluk accomplishments which are remarkable, but rather, as Ibn Khaldun had hinted out, the timing of their arrival which is even more significant. This arrival occurred when Muslim power had already crumbled in the west following the Christian recapture of the whole of Spain except the Grenada enclave, whilst in the east it was about to do so. There, corrupt and weak Ayyubid and Abbasid rules were about to face the greatest onslaught the Muslim world had experienced to date: a grand Christian-Mongol alliance that was about to bring the Muslim realm to near extinction. Far more remarkable, even, were the circumstances of the Mamluk coming and rise to power, helped by a series of circumstances, most particularly the weakness of the Ayyubid rulers, incapable as they were to rise above their fratricidal wars. It was in the 1240s, in the midst of these Ayyubid wars, just prior to the crusade of 1248-1250, that Mamluk power began.

1. Ayyubid Wars and Premises for the Crusade of 1248-1250

In late 1244, the Ayyubid princes, al-Salih Isma'il of Damascus, al-Nasir Dawud of Karak, al-Mansur Ibrahim of Hims and the Christians combined in an alliance against al-Salih Ayyub of Egypt. They confirmed Crusader lordship over Jerusalem, and furthermore pledged a share of booty in Egypt, once Ayyub was defeated.[1156] The Christian army was the largest that was put to the field since Hattin. It included such leaders as Philip of Montfort, Lord of Toron and Tyre, Walter of Brienne, Count of Jaffa, the two grand masters of the Temple and Hospital, many other nobles, and a strong contingent of German Teutonic Knights, as well as the armies of the Ayyubid princes.[1157] Facing them was the Egyptian Mamluk and Turkish Khwarizmian army

[1153] Ibn Khaldun: *Kitab al-Ibar*; v; Cairo: Dar al-Tab'a al-Amira; 1867-8; pp. 379 ff.
[1154] J. Curtin: *The Mongols; A History;* Greenwood Press Publishers; Westport; 1907; p. 258
[1155] See P. Thorau: *The Lion of Egypt*, tr. from German by P.M. Holt; Longman; London, 1987.
[1156] Ibn Wasil, *Mufarrij*; Abu'l-Fida', Mukhtasar *(RHC Hor) I*, 122; Ibn al-Furat, *Ta'rikh* in *Selections,ii*, 1; *Gestes*, 740; Armand of Perigord's letter in Matthew Paris, *Chronica maiora*, IV, 288-91; Rohricht, 'Die Kreuzziige', 88f; Runciman, *Crusades, III, 223.*
[1157] S. Runciman: *A History*; op cit; vol 3; pp. 225-6.

led by the general Rukn Eddin Baybars al Salahi (not Baybars looked at here).[1158] The two sides met at the site known as La Forbie, North East of Ghaza. The battle lasted two days, beginning on the morning of October 17, 1244. The first day, the brunt of the battle was sustained by Baybars' men, who stood firm against the repeated attacks by the Christian-Sultan of Hims' coalition. The second day, the Turkish Khwarizmians went on the counter attack, first crushing the whole army of the sultan of Hims and other Bedouin allies of the crusaders, before turning onto the Christians 'with the relish of men, who, having feasted well, look forward to the sweetmeats at the end of dinner.'[1159] They charged into Christian ranks, and every charge produced 'a mountain of dead horses and dead riders.'[1160] The Khwarizmians drove the Christians against the Egyptian Mamluks which cut them to pieces. In a few hours the whole crusader army was destroyed.[1161] Thirty thousand Christians and their Muslim allies were killed; only the patriarch and the Prince of Tyre escaped with thirty three Templars, twenty six Hospitallers, and three Teutonic Knights.[1162] Seldom had the Latins lost in one battle the two grand masters of St. John and the Temple.[1163] More Christians, in fact, died in this battle than at Hattin, and hundreds were carried prisoners to Egypt.[1164]

Following this Muslim victory, Stevenson notes, the prospects of the crusaders were dark in the extreme.[1165] The Crusader Kingdom had just lost most of its knights and finest leaders. In just one year, Baybars retook most of the territory that the Ayyubids had ceded to them.[1166] Fortunately for the crusaders, Ayyubid rivalries had not ceased, and this gave them a much needed respite.[1167]

In the meantime, in the Christian West, just a few days after the disaster at Ghaza, the patriarch Robert of Jerusalem sent Bishop Galeran of Beirut to Europe to summon Christian rulers of the West to a new crusade.[1168] At the Grand Council of Lyons, the Bishop of Beirut and the Patriarch Albert of Antioch met Pope Innocent IV.[1169] On their urgent insistence on the grave situation in the Holy Land, the pope confirmed the crusading vow of the French King Louis IX (known as St Louis), and had the crusade preached in France.[1170] Louis was the perfect leader the crusade had been longing for decades. His religious zeal was unmatched.[1171] Whilst he was an ardent believer in Christian charity, Louis, Cox points out, burned

---

[1158] RS. Humphreys: From Saladin; p. 456; note 37.
[1159] R. Payne: *The Crusades;* op cit; p. 331.
[1160] Ibid.
[1161] S. Runciman: *A History;* op cit; p. 226.
[1162] C.R. Conder: *The Latin Kingdom;* op cit. p. 318.
[1163] C. Mills: *History of the Crusades;* 2 vols; Longman; London; 1821; vol 2, p. 216
[1164] R. Payne: *The Crusades;* op cit; p. 331.
[1165] W.B. Stevenson: *The Crusaders;* op cit; p. 323.
[1166] A.S. Atiya: *Crusade, Commerce and Culture;* Oxford University Press; London; 1962; p. 90.
[1167] W.B. Stevenson: *The Crusaders;* op cit; p. 324.
[1168] P. Thorau: *The Lion of Egypt;* op cit; p. 33.
[1169] Ibid.
[1170] Ibid.
[1171] G.W. Cox: *The Crusades;* op cit, p. 197.

with the most intense hatred for Muslims.[1172] Louis now set on preparing his mighty crusade that would eventually set off in 1248.

This crusade was perfectly timed. By now, the legend of Prester John, a Christian leader amongst the Mongols, had spread amongst Western Christians 'an almost apocalyptic belief that salvation to Christendom came from the East.'[1173] Everyone knew that the Mongols had fought the Muslims, and that Christian princesses had married into the Mongol imperial family.[1174] The Mongol Great Khan was assumed to be eager to champion Christian ideology against Islam.[1175] The presence in the Eastern background of so mighty a potential ally, Runciman notes, 'surely made the moment seem ripe for a new crusade.'[1176] Christian ambassadors to Mongolia had just returned to the West, and brought with them news that greatly lifted Christian confidence in a decisive victory over the Muslim foe. At the First Council of Lyons (June-July 1245), the returning Christian ambassador to the Mongols, Carpini, gave a letter from the Great Mongol leader, Guyuk, to Pope Innocent IV, agreeing to the Christian-Mongol alliance against Islam.[1177] Louis certainly knew of the message; and in a letter to him (dated between 15-24 May 1248), the Mongol general Aldjigidai, who was Guyuk's envoy in Iran, and also the commander of all Mongol forces in that region, put forward more specific plans.[1178] Aldjigidai stated that he would, in the following year, 1249, attack the Muslim caliphate (that had caused so much harm to Christians, he said in his letter) (it must be pointed out here that Aldjigidai, himself, like most Mongol leadership, including Guyuk, were either of the Christian Nestorian faith, or their wives (or mothers) were.)[1179] Their sympathies were not just passionately for the Christians, they also violently loathed Islam.[1180] In his letter to the French King, Aldjigidai insisted that for the attacks against the Muslims to succeed, it was imperative that he (Louis) disembarked and attacked Egypt at the same time as he attacked in the East so as Egypt would not give support to the Muslims of Iraq. It was with this accord in mind that Louis prepared to attack Egypt.[1181]

Conditions for a new crusade were further aided by the Ayyubid internal wars. In 1247, the Egyptian army operated in Palestine, ravaged the territory of Dawud,

---

[1172] Ibid; p. 199.

[1173] Marinescu: Le Pretre Jean; in *Bulletin de la Section Historique de l'Academie Roumaine;* vol x; Langlois: *La Vie en France au Moyen Age;* vol iii; pp. 44-56.

[1174] Ibid.

[1175] S. Runciman: *A History;* op cit; p. 254.

[1176] Ibid.

[1177] L. Hambis: Saint Louis et les Mongols; in *JRAS;* 1970; pp. 25-33; at p. 28. P. Pelliot: Les Mongols et la Papaute; in *Revue de l'Orient Chretien;* 3rd Series; vol 23; 1922-23; 106 ff. J.J. Saunders: *Aspects of the Crusades;* University of Canterbury; 1962; at pp. 50 ff.

[1178] P. Pelliot: Les Mongols et la Papaute; p. 169.

[1179] Ibid; pp. 165; 169; Aldjigidai had been Christian for a number of years; Guyuk according to Longjumeau (a Christian envoy to the Mongols) was the son of a Christian woman in Pelliot; pp. 169-170.

[1180] J.J. Saunders: *Aspects of the Crusades;* p. 53.

[1181] P. Pelliot: Les Mongols et la Papaute; op cit; p. 169.

and took possession of all his strongholds except the Kerak.[1182] The following year, Hims was besieged for two months and was captured by the army of Al-Malik Al-Nasir of Aleppo.[1183] The Sultan of Hims appealed to Ayyub of Egypt for help, and whilst Ayyub was completing his preparations for a military campaign against his Ayyubid rival, he learned that the French King had landed in Cyprus (September 1248), and was on his way to Egypt.[1184]

2. The 7th Crusade and the Battle of al-Mansurah (1248-50)

Louis had been preparing the crusade for three years. Great sums of money had been raised for the purpose by the clergy and the pope.[1185] On 25th of August 1248, Louis set sail from the South of France to Cyprus. With him, and their armies, was the flower of French nobility: the Queen, herself, his brothers Robert, Count of Artois, and Charles, Count of Anjou; his cousins, Hugh, Duke of Burgundy, and Peter, Count of Brittany, William of Dampierre, Count of Flanders, and many other nobles and barons.[1186] When they arrived in Cyprus, the French King and his followers were joined by the crusader elites of Palestine. All agreed to attack Egypt: it was the richest and also the centre of the Muslim world. Men also remembered that during the fifth crusade, the sultan was willing to exchange Damietta for Jerusalem.[1187] The local Franks also advised that it was better to intervene in Ayyubid family feuds and gain much more, more easily.[1188] The king would have nothing to do with such a scheme. In his view, he had come 'to fight the infidel, not to indulge in diplomacy,' and so he ordered the Templars to break off negotiations with the Ayyubids.[1189]

More importantly, the Mongols had months earlier insisted that in order that the attacks against the Muslims succeed, it was imperative that Louis disembarked and attacked Egypt at the same time as they attacked Iraq and Syria.[1190] The accord received further endorsement when the Mongol ambassadors arrived in Cyprus, late in 1248 to reinforce the Mongol commitment. On Christmas day and Epiphany they heard Mass in the company of the King, who had them guests for dinner. On 25 January 1249, Louis received them in a farewell reception. On 27 January, the Mongol embassy and that which St Louis sent in return, left together Nicosia in direction of the Mongol Empire.[1191] They probably carried there the King's message and plans.

[1182] Abul Feda: *Anales;* op cit; iv; p. 488.
[1183] W.B. Stevenson: *The Crusaders;* op cit; p. 324.
[1184] Ibid.
[1185] Ibid; p. 325.
[1186] S. Runciman: *A History;* op cit; p. 257.
[1187] Ibid; p. 258.
[1188] Ibid.
[1189] Joinville: *Histoire;* op cit; pp. 47; 51; 52; Al-Makrizi: *Histoire* (Blochet); x; pp. 198-9.
[1190] P. Pelliot: *Les Mongols et la Papaute;* op cit; p. 169.
[1191] Ibid; p. 176.

In late Spring of 1249 the large fleet sailed from Cyprus in direction of Egypt.[1192] The crusaders landed on the Egyptian coast on 5 June 1249, and soon began advancing in direction of Damietta. There, the Muslim forces heard that their ruler, Ayyub, was seriously ill, possibly dying, which discouraged any commitment to the defence of the city. According to Ibn Wasil:

'The Muslim army, influenced by al-Malik as-Salih's (Ayyub) serious illness, and with no encouragement or incitement, marched out of Damietta toward Ashmun Tannah... The eastern shore too was without Muslim troops to defend it. The behaviour of the people, of Fakhr Eddin (the Muslim general supposed to defend Damietta) and of the troops was shameful...

On the morning of Sunday 23 Safar (8 June) the Franks appeared before Damietta and found it deserted, with the gates wide open. They occupied it without striking a blow and seized all the munitions, arms, provisions, food and equipment that they found there. It was a disaster without precedent.

There was great grief and amazement, and despair fell upon the whole of Egypt, the more so because the Sultan was ill, too weak to move, and without the strength to control his army, which was trying to impose its will on him instead.'[1193]

Louis had thus, Oman notes, started on his adventure under favourable circumstances.[1194] The crusaders of 1219 had only secured themselves a basis of operation by the capture of Damietta after besieging the place for a year. Their strength was exhausted before they even started on their march up country.[1195] Now they had occupied it without a blow, on the first attempt. What made the situation worse on the Muslim side was that the whole of Egypt was in chaos due to the sickness of Sultan Ayyub (slowly dying from the malignant ulcer on his thigh (caused by poisoning), and there was not a single strong hand at the helm.[1196]

After punishing the generals who had surrendered Damietta, and with immense courage, Sultan Ayyub, surmounting his terrible pain and illness, set out with his army on the direct route for al-Mansurah, where he encamped.[1197] His aim was to block crusader progress toward Cairo. He took up position there on 25 Safar (10 June), galleys and fire ships were brought up, loaded with troops and ammunition, and a great number of irregular infantry and volunteers flocked to the city.[1198] Al Mansurah was the last Muslim bastion in defence of Cairo.

[1192] *Memoirs of the Crusades by Villehardouin and de Joinville* (tr. Marzials); pp. 172-3.
[1193] Ibn Wasil: *Mufarraj*; op cit; fo. 356r-357r; in F. Gabrieli: *Arab Historians*; op cit; p. 284 ff.
[1194] C. Oman: *A History of the Art of War*; op cit; p. 339.
[1195] Ibid.
[1196] Ibid.
[1197] Ibn Wasil: *Mufarraj*; op cit; fo. 357r-v. Also Al-Makrizi: *Histoire* (Blochet); x; pp. 200-1. Al-Aini: *Akd (RHC Or)*; ii; op cit; p. 201.
[1198] Ibn Wasil: *Mufarraj*; op cit; fo. 357r-v

Having began so well, it was incumbent on the French king to utilize his first success and push forward while the Muslims were still in panic.[1199] Instead, to the great fortune of Islam, Louis waited in Damietta for more than five months before he began his march on Cairo.[1200] Very likely the king temporized because he was awaiting news of the Mongol attack on Iraq and Syria. Events in Mongolia, however, had conspired against the great plan for joint assault against the Muslim world. The Mongol leader, Guyuk, had died, and his death, followed by the election of a new ruler considerably delayed Mongol plans.[1201] All this was then unknown to Louis.

There had been panic at Cairo when the news of the fall of Damietta was heard, but the long Christian delay at Damietta enabled the Egyptians to recover the initiative and plan the best means of defence.[1202] The Sultan organised resistance with a clear knowledge of the route which his enemies must take.[1203] As the crusaders waited, Muslims took the initiative and began mounting attacks against their camp, gradually denting their fighting resources.[1204] Every night, Muslim raiders made incursions into the Christian camp and killed their foes wherever they found them sleeping; cut off their heads, which they carried to claim 'a besant of gold for every man's head'.[1205]

On the 20th of November, 1249, at last, the Christian army marched out of Damietta onto Cairo.[1206] At precisely this grave moment, on 21 November 1249, Sultan Ayyub of Egypt, died.[1207] He was the only able ruler amongst the Ayyubids, and his death threatened the Muslims with imminent disaster, for his only son, Turan Shah, was far away in the Jezirah.[1208] A small circle of trusted advisors and generals took over the administration. The dominant figures in this interim group were Shajarat al-Dhurr (Ayyub's former concubine and queen), Fakhr Eddin ibn al-Shaykh (a member of a prominent clan of Khwarizmian-Arab origin and commander-in-chief of the Egyptian army), Beha Eddin ibn Hanna (the vizier) and Jamal Eddin Muhsin (the chief eunuch with authority over the Mamluks).[1209] This group attempted to keep Ayyub's death secret from the bulk of the army and populace until Turan Shah arrived in Egypt.[1210]

[1199] C. Oman: *A History of the Art of War*; op cit; p. 339.
[1200] S. Runciman: *A History*; op cit; p. 263.
[1201] J.J. Saunders: *Aspects of the Crusades;* op cit; p. 53.
[1202] Kemal Eddin in the *Bibliotheque des Croisades;* iv; pp. 451-2.
[1203] C. Oman: *A History of the Art of War*; op cit; p. 340.
[1204] *Memoirs of the Crusades by Villehardouin and de Joinville*; (Marzials); op cit; p. 178.
[1205] Ibid; p. 179.
[1206] William of Nangis; p. 374; R. Payne: *The Crusades*; op cit, p. 346.
[1207] Ibn Khalikan: *Wafayat* (De Slane); op cit; iii; p. 246.
[1208] S. Runciman: *A History*; op cit; p. 264.
[1209] R. Irwin: *The Middle East in the Middle Ages*; Croom Helm; London; 1986; p. 20.
[1210] R.S. Humphreys. *From Saladin to the Mongols;* op cit; pp. 301-20.

The news of Ayyub's death, however, reached the Christians, and encouraged by it, they pressed their march on Cairo.[1211] A letter reached Cairo from Emir Fakhr Eddin warning the people and urging them to join the Holy-War. It was signed with a stamp similar to that of Ayyub to persuade the nation that the letter came from the sultan.[1212] Stirred by the call for jihad, Muslims answered en masse, and marched onto the frontline, and there harassed the Crusaders from all sides, with such vigorous hardiness that it slowed their advance considerably. Four weeks had been occupied in advancing fifty miles.[1213] The Franks camped at Sharamsah and then, on Monday, the 7th of Ramadan (14 December), at al-Faramoun.[1214] Then on Sunday, the 13th of Ramadan (20 December), they came opposite al-Mansurah with Bahr Ashmun in between. On the western bank were the Muslims.[1215]

At this precise spot, the Christian progress was checked by the first formidable watercourse which cuts the way from Damietta to Cairo.[1216] 'The strategic exigencies of the roads' of the Delta had placed Louis and the Egyptians in exactly the same position as was occupied by their predecessors during the fifth Crusade (1218-1221).[1217] The Egyptian army, however, was now a much stronger unit than had been the case in 1220. It was Ayyub who had first organised the celebrated corps of the Circassian Mamluks which was to dominate Egypt for the next six centuries.[1218] The sultan had learned the military worth of the men of the Caucasus, and had been steadily buying Circassian slaves for many years and incorporating them in his guard. The eight or ten thousand Mamluks formed the core of the Muslim army, and to support them were arrayed the horsemen of the Bedouin tribes and the general levy of Egypt, who had marched out at the exhortation of the imams to save Islam.[1219] However, the whole brunt of the war fell upon the heavily-armed and well-mounted Mamluk horsemen.[1220]

Seeing the Egyptians clustering so thick around Al-Mansurah, Louis resolved not to make any attempt to throw his army across the canal by means of his boats, so he decided on a preparatory phase. The Christians set up mangonels and no sooner they were in place the bombardment of Muslim positions began, while their ships stayed opposite them on the Nile, the Muslims' ships being opposite al-Mansurah.[1221] The situation reached a stalemate. A deep discouragement now took hold of the Frankish host as they found themselves pinned to their

---

[1211] Al-Aini: *Akd (RHC Or)*; ii; op cit; p. 207.

[1212] Ibn Wasil: *Mufaraj*; op cit; fo.364r-365r; in Gabrieli: *Arab Historians*; op cit; p. 288.

[1213] C. Oman: *A History of the Art of War*, op cit; p. 340; Ibn al-Furat: *Tarikh*; (Lyons); p. 20.

[1214] Ibn al-Furat: *Tarikh*; (Lyons); pp. 20-1.

[1215] Ibid; p. 21.

[1216] C. Oman: *A History of the Art of War*, op cit; p. 340.

[1217] Ibid. p. 341

[1218] Ibid.

[1219] Ibid.

[1220] Ibid.

[1221] Ibn al-Furat: *Tarikh*; (Lyons); op cit; pp. 20-1.

position.[1222] Then, early in February (1250) fortune smiled on them. The Constable Imbert of Beaujeu found a Copt or a Bedouin who told him that four miles to the east of Mansurah there was a ford over the Ashmun over which to cross onto the Muslim side, deep and difficult indeed but quite practicable for cavalry.[1223] According to Ibn Wasil, it was people from Salamun, who were not Muslims, who gave the information to the Franks.[1224] The Coptic source of the information about the ford is very interesting, Grousset observes, for it confirms the views of many contemporaries of the alliance between the crusaders and the local Copts.[1225]

The army had now been stranded for nearly two months in front of al-Mansurah, and Louis felt that he must leave no device untried, even if it meant crossing a deep ford in face of the Muslims and without possibility of support from his infantry. He accordingly resolved to attempt the passage on the morning of Shrove Tuesday (8th February 1250).[1226]

During the night of the 7th-8th February dispositions were made.[1227] It was confirmed that the Duke of Burgundy and the barons of Palestine and Cyprus with their knights were to remain behind in the camp, and take charge of the great mass of foot-soldiery, and forestall, if necessary, a Muslim counter-attack.[1228] Louis himself, with his three brothers, Charles of Anjou, Robert of Artois, and Alphonso of Poitiers, and the main body of horsemen, were to march to the ford and pass it at daybreak. Once they would reach the southern bank they were to push along it to the Egyptian camp, burst into it, and capture or destroy the engines at the causeway before the Muslims should recover from their surprise.[1229] Once the Egyptian machines which commanded the half-built causeway were captured, the infantry were to complete it (the causeway) in all haste and cross over to join their leader.[1230]

The Battle of Al-Mansurah (February 1250) and the Crushing of Louis' Crusade

On the 8th of February 1250, in a swift and daring move, the crusaders crossed onto the Muslim side, their force including all the available mounted men, in three divisions.[1231] The cavalry corps of the Templars, under their Grand Master, William de Sonnac, rode first. Also crossing with this First Division were Robert

---

[1222] C. Oman: *A History of the Art of War*; op cit; p. 343.
[1223] Ibid.
[1224] Ibn Wasil; p. 208; in R. Grousset: *Histoire*; op cit; p. 458.
[1225] Joinville; p. 215 (in Grousset); Rothelin; p. 603; in Grousset: *Histoire*; op cit; p. 458.
[1226] C. Oman: *A History of the Art of War*; op cit; p. 343.
[1227] *Memoirs of the Crusades by Villehardouin and de Joinville*; op cit; pp. 188-9.
[1228] R. Grousset: *Histoire;* op cit; p. 458; C. Oman: *History of the Art of War*; op cit; p. 343.
[1229] C. Oman: *A History of the Art of War*; op cit; p. 343.
[1230] Ibid.
[1231] Abul Fida: *Annales*; op cit; iv; p. 506.

of Artois (the King's brother), Peter Duke of Brittany, John Count of Soissons, Raoul Lord of Coucy, and the English contingent which William Longsword, the titular Earl of Salisbury, had brought to the Crusade.[1232] They had with them all the king's mounted crossbowmen. In the Second Division (battle) among the Champenois was John of Joinville, who has left us the best account of the campaign. Charles of Anjou, another brother of the King, was probably commander of the corps.[1233] The king and his household knights, with his brother Alphonso of Poitiers and Henry Count of Flanders, rode in the Third Division. Louis had issued strict orders that no knight should straggle from his corps, and that the three divisions should keep close together; the van (First Division) was not to advance till all three had passed the ford.[1234]

The Muslims had kept a careless watch along the canal, and though the ford was only four miles from their camp, at the village of Sahnar, the French reached it unobserved.[1235] The van division, led by Robert of Artois, crossed, not without some difficulty, for the bottom was muddy and the opposite bank scarped and slippery; a few knights lost their footing and were drowned.[1236] As the crusaders crossed in ever larger numbers, the Muslim cavaliers suddenly spotted them, and realised that the passage was lost.[1237] In great panic they rode off to warn their comrades.[1238] Rather than waiting for the other two divisions, flushed with this initial success, and possibly wanting to reach the camp before the Muslims warned their comrades and prepared the defence, Robert of Artois began to move off in pursuit of the Muslims.[1239] The Master of the Temple rode up to him and begged him to stop, but the count would not listen to his remonstrance, and spurred off towards the Egyptian camp. Thinking that he would be shamed if he abandoned his place in the van, the Master unwillingly followed, and after him all the other contingents of the van battle.[1240] Count Robert rode so hard that he came hurtling into the eastern end of the Egyptian camp almost as soon as the fleeing cavaliers whom he was chasing. He and his men found the Muslims in a state of disarray and un-preparedness. The horses were not saddled nor the men armed.[1241] The French rode through the camp, slashing right and left and driving all before them, till they came to the place where the perrières and mangonels commanded the unfinished causeway. They wrought great slaughter on the Muslims.[1242] Ibn Wasil narrates:

[1232] C. Oman: *A History of the Art of War*, op cit; p. 343.

[1233] Ibid. 344.

[1234] Rothelin, Ms. P. 602; in C. Oman: *A History*; op cit; p. 344.

[1235] C. Oman: *A History of the Art of War*, op cit; p. 344.

[1236] Ibid.

[1237] Joinville; p. 224 in C. Oman: *A History*; op cit; p. 344.

[1238] C. Oman: *A History of the Art of War*, op cit; p. 344.

[1239] Ibid.

[1240] Ibid.

[1241] Ibid.

[1242] Ibid; p. 345.

'The Muslims suddenly found that the Franks were in their camp. Emir Fakhr Eddin (the commander in chief of the Muslim army) was washing himself in his bath when he heard the cry go up that the Franks had taken the Muslims by surprise. Frenziedly he leapt into the saddle, without weapons or any means of defending himself, and a band of Franks fell on him and killed him-God have mercy upon him! He was a worthy emir, learned and cultivated, generous and wise, high-minded and magnanimous, without peer among his brothers or any other men.'[1243]

The Count of Artois seeing the Muslims in hopeless disarray imagined that he had gained the day with his own division alone, and thought of nothing but pursuit and slaughter. After a very short breathing space, he ordered a second advance towards the town of Al-Mansurah, into which many of the fugitives were pouring.[1244] The Muslims were in such disarray that Robert of Artois and his followers were able to penetrate within the walls of al-Mansurah and to ride through the town, cutting down the fugitives; some of the knights even emerged at its western gate, and almost reached the Sultan's suburban palace.[1245] The Franks spread through the narrow streets of the town, while the civilian and military population scattered in all directions. Islam was about to suffer a mortal blow, and the Christians were now sure of their victory.[1246] Al-Mansurah, it ought to be reminded, was where the Muslim army in its entirety was concentrated, and should it be destroyed there, this would mean the end of Egypt. And now the crusaders had the town at their mercy. Already fugitives were running away to Cairo carrying the terrible news of the Muslim disaster. Ibn Wasil, again: '(It was heard) that the enemy had attacked Mansurah and a violent battle had followed. That was all, and we and the Muslims were in complete confusion, everyone already imagining disaster for Islam. At sunset Muslim fugitives from the battle arrived, and the Bab an-Nasr stayed open all night, the night of Tuesday to Wednesday. Military and civilians, secretaries and officials entered the city in flight from Mansurah, knowing nothing of the situation after the Franks had entered the town.'[1247]

Meanwhile, at al-Mansurah, after surprising the Muslim camp and killing the top Muslim general, Fakhr Eddin, Robert of Artois swept aside so much the Muslim army that he reached the outer walls of the citadel.[1248] Flushed by his success, he was now determined to capture al-Mansurah and finish off the whole Egyptian army by himself.[1249] In al-Mansurah, however, unknown to him, Robert of Artois

[1243] Ibn Wasil: *Mufaraj*; fo.365v-366v; in F. Gabrieli: *Arab;* op cit; p. 290.
[1244] C. Oman: *A History of the Art of War*; op cit; p. 345.
[1245] Ibid; p. 346.
[1246] Ibn Wasil: *Mufaraj;* fo.365v-366v; in F. Gabrieli: *Arab;* op cit; p. 290.
[1247] Ibid.
[1248] P. Thorau: *The Lion*; op cit; p. 34.
[1249] S. Runciman: *A History;* op cit; p. 266.

came up against the Bahriyya and Jamdariyya Mamluk formations that had not been seized by the general panic.[1250] As Robert of Artois and his division thrust deeper into the city, the Muslims, in the words of Grousset:

> Had the great fortune of finding a leader, not a great general such as Fakhr Eddin, but one of the greatest warriors of all times: the Turkish Mamluk, Baybars Bundukdari, Baybars the arbalester, whose intervention now against the crusaders, just as in ten years time against the Mongols at Ain Jalut, was going to change the course of history.[1251]

Baybars, the ablest of all Mamluks, took control of the situation. He stationed his men at crucial points within the town itself, then let the Frankish cavalry come pouring through the open gate.[1252] Once the crusader forces were in, they scattered in the streets and separated one from another, so that the impetus of their charge and the advantage of combined action were lost.[1253] From the roofs of houses, the Egyptians poured upon them, with deadly effect, burning coals, boiling water, and stones.[1254] They flung darts and tiles upon the knights as they galloped up and down the narrow lanes.[1255] In the meantime, Muslim troops from the camps west of the town, who had not shared in the panic of the rest of the Muslim army, began to pour into Mansurah. They found the Christians scattered in small bands, some intent on plunder, and some on slaughter, but all unprepared to receive a fresh attack.[1256] Rushing out from the side streets, the Mamluks sprang onto them.[1257] The crusaders were not able to deploy their heavy cavalry in the narrow alleys, so the Mamluks cut them to pieces.[1258]

'At the moment of supreme danger,' says Ibn Wasil, 'the Turkish battalion of the Mamluks of al-Malik Al-Salih (Ayyub), Bahrites and Jamdariyya, lions in war and mighty in battle, rode like one man upon the enemy in a charge that broke them and drove them back. The Franks were massacred one and all with sword and club.'[1259]

The Templar Knights were all but for five of them slain. Robert of Artois barricaded himself and his bodyguards in a house, but the Muslims soon burst in and slaughtered them all.[1260] It was a bloodbath amongst Christian warriors. Amongst the knights who fell in the battle were the Earl of Salisbury, and almost all his English followers, the Count of Brienne, the Master of the Temple, the Lord of Coucy, and many barons more.[1261] Only a few knights escaped to bring King Louis

[1250] P. Thorau: *The Lion of Egypt*; op cit; p. 34.
[1251] R. Grousset: *Histoire;* op cit; vol 3; p. 464.
[1252] S. Runciman: *A History*; op cit; p. 267.
[1253] C. Oman: *A History of the Art of War*; op cit; p. 346.
[1254] C. Mills: *History of the Crusades;* op cit; p. 237.
[1255] C. Oman: *A History of the Art of War*; op cit; p. 346.
[1256] Ibid.
[1257] S. Runciman: *A History*; op cit; p. 267.
[1258] P. Thorau: *The Lion of Egypt*; op cit; p. 34.
[1259] Ibn Wasil: *Mufaraj*; 365-6; in F. Gabrieli: *Arab*; op cit; p. 290.
[1260] S. Runciman: *A History*; op cit; p. 267.
[1261] Ibid.

the news of the disaster.[1262] The only route which the fugitives could take lay through the eastern camp of the Egyptians, where the Mamluks were now rallying and getting into battle order.[1263]

Meanwhile, during the hour which Robert of Artois had led his charge, the remainder of the French cavalry had been gradually crossing the Ashmun. Now some of them could see that the Muslims were already rallying, having retired from the tents into the open fields where they were drawing up in line of battle.[1264] The Mamluks mounted a fierce attack on the Second Division, threatening to wipe it out.[1265] Soon there appeared the Third Division with King Louis himself. What was left of the second cavalry division, and the king's third, assembled together, but they were at once assailed by the Mamluks who were now rallied and in good order. A fierce battle began in the outskirts of the camp, and lasted for many hours.[1266] The Muslim onslaught was so violent, and so effective, many of the French knights lost heart and plunged into the Ashmun to swim back to the Christian camp.[1267] Louis had lost, as far as can be calculated, nearly half his cavalry and a still greater number of his horses.[1268] The Christian attack had now lost its impetus, and to the king, the loss was even more personal, that of his brother, the Count of Artois.[1269] Defeat, disaster even, threatened the crusade. To the extremely devout king this was a great shock. As Payne remarks:

> God seemed to have forgotten the Christian army and failed to provide King Louis with military intelligence. A new leader had arisen to take the place of Fakhr Eddin. This was Baybars al-Bundukdari... The defence of Mansurah was now in his hands, and he was more relentless and more pitiless than any Muslim commander had ever been. For the first time since Saladin, the Crusaders were confronted with a military commander of genius.[1270]

Meanwhile, in Cairo, where the first news of the Christian entry into al-Mansurah had caused great distress, Ibn Wasil tells us:

'We remained in suspense until the sun rose on Wednesday and the joyful news of victory reached us. The city prepared for a feast and the glad tidings were announced by a roll of drums. The victory over the Franks caused great joy and exultation. This was the first battle in which the Turkish lions defeated the infidel dogs. The good news reached al-Malik Al-Mu'azzam (Turan Shah, the son of

---

[1262] P. Thorau: *The Lion of Egypt*; op cit; p. 34.
[1263] C. Oman: *A History of the Art of War*; op cit; p. 346.
[1264] Ibid.
[1265] *Memoirs of the Crusades by Villehardouin and de Joinville* (Marzials); op cit; pp. 190-1.
[1266] C. Oman: *A History of the Art of War*; op cit; p. 347.
[1267] Ibid.
[1268] Ibid. 348
[1269] *Memoirs of the Crusades by Villehardouin and de Joinville*; op cit; p. 196.
[1270] R. Payne: *The Crusades*; op cit; p. 348.

Ayyub) while he was on his way, and made him march even faster toward Egypt.'[1271]

The disaster at al-Mansurah and the considerable loss of knights and cavalry forced the Christians to abandon any plan of advance. They, instead, entrenched themselves behind strong defensive positions, south of the Bahr Seghir.[1272] In this camp, outside the walls of Mansurah, the French king and what was left of his army hoped that another miracle would happen.[1273] Things were soon to get much worse, though. Under Baybars' direction, the Egyptians deprived them of their command of the Nile, and cut the lines of communication with Damietta.[1274] In order to accomplish this, Baybars organized the fleet of light ships to be carried on camelback in sections, down on the Nile, then were reassembled, and were sufficiently well equipped when put together to form another army behind the Christian lines.[1275] Soon, the ships suddenly appeared in the waterways between Damietta and al-Mansurah, and from that time the river was in Muslim hands.[1276] The Muslim fleet intercepted the supplies sent from Damietta to the Christians in their camp outside al-Mansurah.[1277] Deprived of supplies by land and by sea, and encircled by the Muslims, the French were threatened with famine.[1278] Now, the king's army could neither advance nor stay where it was.[1279] In the midst of this crisis, Louis found himself obliged to offer peace terms to the Mamluks, but his overtures were rejected.[1280]

The situation in the crusader camp soon deteriorated further. Already starved, the Christian camp was struck by pestilence. Scurvy, typhoid, and dysentery were rampant.[1281] So many of the knights died that the grooms wore their armor and stood guard at points of danger; and so many priests died that there were not enough of them to minister at the altars. The king himself fell ill.[1282] He sent Philip of Montfore to the Egyptians, offering to surrender Damietta to them in exchange for Jerusalem and other places in the Holy Land that had recently fallen into Muslim hands. The Egyptians rejected his offer.[1283]

It was then that Louis ordered a retreat from the camp toward Damietta. This took place on the night of the 5th of April 1250.[1284] The Muslims, however, noticed the

[1271] Ibn Wasil: *Mufaraj*; p. 365; in F. Gabrieli: *Arab*; op cit; pp. 291-2.
[1272] R. Grousset: *Histoire*; op cit; p. 474.
[1273] R. Payne: *The Crusades*; op cit; p. 348.
[1274] W.B. Stevenson: *The Crusaders;* op cit; p. 327.
[1275] R. Payne: *The Crusades*; op cit; p. 348; R. Grousset: *Histoire*; op cit; p. 478.
[1276] R. Grousset: *Histoire*; op cit; p. 478. Al-Aini: *Akd (RHC Or)*; ii; op cit; p. 209.
[1277] R. Payne: *The Crusades;* op cit; p. 348.
[1278] Mathew Paris: *Chronica*; op cit; vi; pp. 193-4; in R. Grousset: *Histoire*; p. 478.
[1279] R. Payne: *The Crusades*; op cit; p. 348.
[1280] *Memoirs of the Crusades by Villehardouin and de Joinville*; op cit; p. 201.
[1281] R. Payne: *The Crusades*; op cit; p. 348.
[1282] Ibid.
[1283] Ibid.
[1284] *Histoire d'Eracles (RHC Occ)* op cit; ii; p. 438.

withdrawal. Very swiftly, they crossed the Bahr al-Saghir in pursuit of the fleeing crusaders.[1285] From all sides the Egyptians attacked the Christians, causing terrible slaughter, and making great many prisoners.[1286] Some of the ships which carried the sick and wounded crusaders escaped but most other vessels were destroyed or captured.[1287] By the time they reached Fariskur the Franks found themselves fully encircled by the Muslims. There took place the ultimate battle. Ibn Wasil narrates:

'On the night before Wednesday 3 Muharram 648/7 April 1250, the Franks marched out with all their forces towards Damietta, which they counted on to defend them, and their ships began to move downstream in convoy.

When the Muslims heard the news they set out after them, crossed to the Frankish bank of the river and were soon at their heels. As Wednesday dawned the Muslims had surrounded the Franks and were slaughtering them, dealing out death and captivity. Not one escaped. It is said that the dead numbered 30,000. In the battle the Bahrite Mamluks distinguished themselves by their courage and audacity: they caused the Franks terrible losses and played the major part in the victory. They fought furiously: it was they who flung themselves into the pursuit of the enemy.'[1288]

The crusaders were slain in their thousands on that day. Those who escaped death were forced to surrender.[1289] Up to 50,000, according to Muslim sources;[1290] between 10,000[1291] and 20,000, according to Western sources.[1292] The mighty army of the seventh crusade was no more. The 'accursed' King of France, in the words of Ibn Wasil, and the great Frankish princes retreated to the hill of Munya, where they surrendered and begged for their lives.[1293] They were all taken to al-Mansurah, where chains were put on the feet of the King of France and his companions.[1294]

It was precisely at this juncture that the Mamluks took power in Egypt. The new ruler Turan Shah, who on his return from al-Jazirah, had assumed power, was weak and self-indulgent. At Fariskur, he built a wooden tower for his residence and abandoned himself to a dissolute and vicious life with his favourites.[1295] Ibn Abd al-Zahir also says:

'Al-Malik al-Mu'azzam (Turan Shah) would not voluntarily mount a horse for battle. Instead he went on board a ship like a spectator. It was his duty to mount,

[1285] P. Thorau: *The Lion;* op cit; p. 36.
[1286] R. Payne: *The Crusades*; op cit; p. 349.
[1287] W.B. Stevenson: *The Crusaders;* op cit; p. 328.
[1288] Ibn Wasil: *Mufaraj*; op cit; fo.369r-370r; in F. Gabrieli: *Arab*; op cit; p. 294.
[1289] William of Nangis, *Gesta* xx; p. 376; P. Thorau: *The Lion;* op cit; p. 36; W.B. Stevenson: *The Crusaders;* op cit; p. 328.
[1290] R. Payne: *The Crusades*; op cit; p. 349.
[1291] G.W. Cox: *The Crusades*; op cit; p. 204; W.B. Stevenson: *The Crusaders;* op cit; p. 328.
[1292] C. Mills: *History of the Crusades;* vol 2; p. 240.
[1293] Ibn Wasil: *Mufaraj*; op cit; fo.369r-370r; in F. Gabrieli: *Arab*; op cit; p. 294.
[1294] Ibid.
[1295] P. Thorau: *The Lion*; op cit; p. 37.

to muster the Mamluks around him, and to display his audacity and sternness.... For if the Mamluks see their king to be undismayed, and he rewards those who show courage, they emulate one another and fight, one for God and the Faith, another for praise and thanks, and yet another for assignment and reward.'[1296]

Turan's inactivity and way of life visibly alienated his army, which expected something else of him.[1297] The Sultan, in fact, saw his dependence on this army which had just freshly defeated the crusaders as a thorn in the flesh.[1298] He began to conduct negotiations for peace with the captive king, Louis, so as to dispense with the military power of his army, and have greater manoeuvre to eliminate the emirs.[1299] He was afraid of Baybars' Mamluks, and he was in the process of reorganising the army and giving high commands to soldiers from the Jazirah.[1300] His father had once written to him in the winter of 1249, giving him two pertinent pieces of advice: first, to keep off alcohol and, second, to be generous to the Bahri Mamluks: 'I strongly recommend them to you... I owe everything to them.'[1301] Turan did the very reverse. When drunk, one evening, he slashed the tops of the tallest candles with his sword, and while doing so, he declared that he would deal with his father's Mamluks, naming his victims in turn.[1302] Ibn Wasil says that when the soldiers, especially the Bahri Mamluks belonging to his father, lost their loyalty to him, a group of them decided to kill him.[1303] On the night of May 2, 1250, while he was entertaining emirs in his tent, he heard a commotion outside, and a moment later Baybars burst into the tent at the head of a small group of army officers. Baybars hit the sultan. Wounded in the hand, Turan escaped to a wooden tower beside the river.[1304] Baybars and his men set fire to the tower. Turan Shah jumped down and ran along the riverbank, until someone hurled a spear, which caught him in the ribs. Trailing the spear, he threw himself into the river. Just then Emir Farid Eddin Aqtay leapt down the bank and plunged a sword into him.[1305] The Muslim historians who describe the event remarked that Turan died three deaths: by fire, by iron, and by water.[1306]

The death of Turan Shah was witnessed by Joinville and King Louis, who were being held on a galley moored in the river. A little while later some thirty Mamluks came on board the galley, drawn swords in their hands and Danish axes hanging from their necks.[1307] The prisoners thought they were about to be put to death. Instead, they were thrown into the hold where they were packed in tightly.

[1296] Ibn Abd al-Zahir: *Al-Rawd al-Zahir fi Sirat al-Malik al-Zahir* (Rawd); ed., A.A. Khuwayter; Riyadh; 1976; pp. 48-9.
[1297] Sibt al-Jawzi: *Mir'at*; op cit; 591.
[1298] P. Thorau: *The Lion*; op cit; p. 37.
[1299] Ibid.
[1300] R. Payne: *The Crusades*; op cit; p. 349.
[1301] R. Irwin: *The Middle East in the Middle Ages*; Croom Helm; London; 1986; p. 22.
[1302] Al-Makrizi: *Kitab al-Suluk*; tr. R.J. C. Broadhurst as *History of Ayyubids and Mamluks*; Boston; 1980; p. 311.
[1303] Ibn Wasil: *Mufaraj*; op cit; fo. 371r-v; in F. Gabrieli: *Arab*; op cit; pp. 295-6.
[1304] R. Payne: *The Crusades*; op cit; p. 349.
[1305] Ibn Wasil: *Mufaraj*; op cit; fo. 371r-v; in F. Gabrieli: *Arab;* op cit; p. 297; R. Payne: *The Crusades;* p. 349.
[1306] R. Payne: *The Crusades*; op cit; p. 349.
[1307] Ibid.

The next morning most of the prisoners, all of them knights or great officers of state, were brought in to discuss terms for their release.[1308]

After a period of captivity, the king's ransom was fixed at a million besants.[1309] This amount was reduced for his liberation. After this, Louis sailed free to Acre, while the rank and file of his forces remained in captivity, and half of the ransom was still due.[1310]

Louis' crusade had been a disaster.[1311] This victory was highly decisive for Islam. According to Grousset:

> Had the crusaders taken al-Mansurah, the road to Cairo would have been opened to the Christians, and Muslim rule there ended, forced to capitulate, and the whole of the Frankish kingdom that had fallen into Muslim hands would have been recovered.[1312]

What is remarkable, however, other than the great Mamluk victory was another fact of crucial significance. It was mentioned above that the Mongols and Christians had agreed to invade simultaneously, the Mongols against Iraq and Syria, and King Louis against Egypt.[1313] Had this happened, it is very likely that a calamity would have struck the Muslim world. Yet, by a remarkable turn of events, just as Louis sailed for Egypt, the pro Christian Mongol Emperor, Guyuk died. His death delayed the Mongol invasion. By the time a new Mongol emperor, Mangku (Mongke), had been put in place, in 1251, Louis crusade was well over.[1314] And by the time the alliance was reformed again for a combined attack, ten years later, by another remarkable turn of events, a new force had risen in Islam, capable of facing them: the Mamluks, and prominent amongst them, Baybars.[1315]

3. Rising Mamluk Power, and Rukn Eddin Baybars

Following Turan's death, Shajarat al-Dhurr, his step mother, was proclaimed queen of the Muslims, and a six year old scion of the Damascus Ayyubids, al-Ashraf Musa, was given the nominal dignity of joint sovereignty. Shajarat was a former Turkish slave who had borne a son to Ayub, a son who died in childhood,

[1308] Ibid.
[1309] A.S. Atiya: *Crusades*; op cit; p. 90.
[1310] *Histoire d' Eracles (RHC Occ)*; op cit; ii; p. 438.
[1311] William of Nangis: *Gesta Ludovoci*; *RHC Occ*; xx; p. 376; Mathew Paris: *Chronica Majora*; ed. H.R. Luard; Rolls Series 57; 7 vols; London; 1872-1883; v; pp. 157-9; 165-8; etc.
[1312] R. Grousset: *Histoire*; op cit; p. 459.
[1313] P. Pelliot: *Les Mongols et la Papaute*; op cit; p. 169.
[1314] J.J. Saunders: *Aspects of the Crusades;* op cit; p. 53.
[1315] P. Thorau: *The Lion*; op cit; p. 36.

and soon she married the Mamluk leader, Aibek, the founder of the Mamluk dynasty.[1316] A new era had just begun: that of the Mamluks.

This swift revolution in Egypt, Saunders reckons, 'spelled the doom of the crusading movement, for it was from the hands of the Mamluks operating from the Nile Valley that the Frankish States were in 1291 to receive their coup de grace.'[1317] In order to accomplish this, the Mamluks were to show qualities which the history of Islam only reveals at its most dramatic moments. Out of the ashes of the moribund Ayyubid dynasty has now risen one of the most formidable forces, which was to oversee the destinies of the Islamic East for many centuries, until, when exhausted, it was replaced by another formidable force: the Ottoman Turks.[1318]

Mamluk power was enhanced by the rise in its midst of probably one of the most able figures that ever lived in history, a sultan, a state builder, and most of all a general of the greatest stature: Baybars. Baybars (ruled 1260-1277) was born a Turkish slave, of Qipchak origin. The Qipchaks were dislodged from their territories when the Mongols invaded in 1219-21.[1319] That Baybars was of Turkish origin is also mentioned in Greek, Latin and Old French sources, such as the 'Tractatus de statu saracenorum' of the Dominican friar William of Tripoli, the 'Chronica minor auctore minorita Erphordiensi',[1320] the Gestes des Chiprois, and the 'Flor des Estoires de la Terre d'Orient' of the Armenian Hethum (Hayton) of Gorigos.[1321] The first two of these historical works were written during Baybars' lifetime, one in the Holy Land, the other in distant Erfurt.[1322]

In Baybars time, when a Mamluk arrived as a young boy from the steppes of southern Russia or the Caucasus, he was housed in barracks in Cairo, and given a tough and thorough education. His curriculum included the study of the Qur'an and the Hadith, and also the arts of war, especially horse riding skills, and using two swords, one in each hand.[1323] Baybars, himself, must have been sold by his captor to a slave dealer, for he was subsequently brought to Syria, where, with another slave, he was offered for sale to the Ayyubid ruler al-Malik Al-Mansur.[1324] An emir of al-Salih, called Rukn Eddin al-Bunduqdari, who had been detained in Hamah (Syria) on account of an offence he had committed, heard of the two slaves, and eventually bought them.[1325] Baybars remained with his new master in Syria until his release, and then accompanied him to Egypt.[1326] Baybars must have displayed his fighting

[1316] F. Gabrieli: *Arab Historians*; note 1; p. 297.

[1317] J.J. Saunders: *Aspects of the Crusades*, op cit. p. 35.

[1318] See D. Ayalon: Aspects of the Mamluk phenomenon in *Der Islam*: Vol 53; 1976; pp. 196-225; p. 196.

[1319] Ibn Taghri Birdi: *Al-Nujum al-Zahira fi Muluk Misr wa'l Qahira;* Cairo; 1938; vol vii; p. 95.

[1320] Chronicon Sampetrinum; ed. B. Stubel, *Geschichtsquellen der Provinz Sachsen*, I, Halle, 1870.p. 98.
William of Tripoli: Tractatus de statu Saracenorum; E.H. Prutz; *Kulturgeschichte der Kreuzzuge*; Berlin 1883; p. 589.

[1321] *Les Gestes des Chiprois*, ed. G. Raynaud (Societe de l'Orient Latin; Serie historique, 5), Geneva 1887; and the '*Flor des Estoires de la Terre d'Orient*' of the Armenian Hethum (Hayton) of Gorigos; Rhar; II..

[1322] W. Wattenbach, F.J. Schmale: *Deutschlands Geschichtsquellen im Mittelalter*, I, Darmstadt; 1976, p. 408.
C. Cahen: *La Syrie du Nord a l'Epoque des Croisades*; Paris; 1940; p. 26.

[1323] C. Hillenbrand: *The Crusades*, op cit; p.446; and 448.

[1324] A.A. Khowaiter: *Baibars the First*; The Green Mountain Press; London; 1978; p. 7.

[1325] Ibid.

[1326] Ibid.

qualities, for he was soon integrated into the Bahri regiment. Gradually, his brave resourcefulness raised him to high command in the Egyptian army.[1327] He distinguished himself at the Battle of Al-Mansurah, in 1250, where his personal bravery, and most of all his qualities of war commander were central to the Muslim victory. He would distinguish himself even more in the next phase.

What is of crucial importance to the destinies of Islam is that Baybars and his compatriots came onto the scene at an hour of great need. Soon, indeed, the very survival of the Muslim entity would be threatened by the most formidable alliance of all: Crusaders, Mongols, and local Christians launching the grandest assault on Islam in history. Had the Ayyubids remained in power in Egypt, the whole realm would have been swept away. Only a force as capable as that of the Mamluks, led by the most able of all men, was strong enough to face such powerful foes and subsequently prevail, most particularly in one of the most determining encounters in history, the Battle of 'Ain Jalut. But this was ten years away.

The Mamluk revolution of 1250 in Egypt was not welcome by the Ayyubids in Syria, though. When the news came that Turan Shah had been murdered, Al-Nasir of Aleppo marched down from Hims on Damascus.[1328] Having taken possession of Damascus in July 1250,[1329] he attempted the conquest of Egypt during the following winter. To secure his aims, he entered into contacts with King Louis in order to form an alliance against the Sultan of Egypt. Louis neither accepted nor rejected his offers.[1330] Louis, instead, used al-Nasir's overtures to put pressure on Egypt. After the Egyptians freed between 700 and 800 prisoners, including the Master of the Hospital, and others they had captured in previous battles, Louis stopped paying the agreed ransom (for his freedom). He also demanded a revision of the treaty he had signed with the Mamluks to obtain his release. This was his price for not allying himself with Al-Nasir.[1331] The Egyptians were thus forced to accept the new conditions, and subsequently, the king's deputies were allowed to make free search in Egypt for all Christian captives and to claim their release.[1332] In the meantime, the army of Damascus began its planned invasion of Egypt. On 2 February 1251, it met the Egyptian army under Aibek at Abbasa, in the Delta. The Ayyubid army of Syria was first successful, but soon a Mamluk regiment of Al-Nasir, deserted his cause in the midst of battle.[1333] The sultan, whose courage was not remarkable, thereupon turned and fled. Mamluk power in Egypt was, thus, saved.[1334]

[1327] W. Durant: *The Age of Faith*, op cit; p. 313.
[1328] Abul Feda: *Al-Mukhtassar fi Akhbar al-Bashar*; in RHOr (Annales); i; p. 131; Ibn Khalikan: *Wafayat*; op cit; ii; p. 446.
[1329] Ibid.
[1330] J. Joinville: *Histoire*; op cit; p. 158; W.B. Stevenson: *The Crusaders*; op cit; pp. 329-30.
[1331] W.B. Stevenson: *The Crusaders*; op cit; p. 330.
[1332] Mathew Paris: *Chronica Majorca*; op cit; v; p. 342.
[1333] Abul Feda: *Annales* (RHOr); op cit; i; p. 131.
[1334] Ibid.

The conflict persisted until the year 1253, when the Abbasid Caliph, al-Mustasim, mediated between the two parties, and peace returned between Syria and Egypt.[1335]

This peace agreement was only a respite, for elsewhere, alliances of powerful foes were gathering momentum, ready to unleash an onslaught on the Muslim world that would nearly terminate its very existence. Playing the leading role in the formation of such an alliance between Christians and Mongols was the French King, Louis.

4. The Christian-Mongol Alliance And the Destruction of the Caliphate (1258) and Syria (1260)

After his liberation (following his capture after the Battle of al-Mansurah, in 1250,) Louis remained in the East for another few years. He was apparently 'stupefied by considering how God could in this manner have abandoned a man who had come to His help,'[1336] his crusade ending in dismal failure.[1337] Louis, however, did not lose his opportunity, and sought to build another crusade against Islam. No sooner was he liberated, he allowed his brothers to return home, and sent with them a letter to the nobles and clergy of France appealing for reinforcements to retrieve the situation.[1338] Louis also used his presence in the East to build powerful alliances. One such alliance was with the Ismailis.[1339] Louis' personal chronicler, Joinville, gives an account of an embassy from the 'Old Man of the Mountain,' or sheikh of the Ismailis, to the French king.[1340] The Ismaili embassy brought expensive gifts to the King, with the request for a closer alliance.[1341] Louis, who had learned of the hostility of the Ismaili Assassins towards Sunni Islam, encouraged their advances and sent Yves Le Breton, who spoke Arabic, to arrange a treaty.[1342] Louis also made the important move to reinforce the links between crusaders and Maronite Christians. Lebanese historians inform us that the Maronites had the privilege to be the only ones to welcome the King of France on visit to Acre in 1250 (shortly after his liberation).[1343] They assert that the Maronites rushed to put at his service between twenty and twenty five thousand fighters.[1344] Louis, in a letter to the Maronite chief dated from 21 May 1250, declared his sympathy and praise for

[1335] Al-Makrizi: *Histoire des sultans Mamluks;* Fr., tr., by M. Quatremere; 2 vols; Paris 1845; I; I; pp. 39; p. 54.
[1336] J.W. Draper: *A History*: op cit; Vol II; p. 74.
[1337] J.H. Lamonte: Crusade and Jihad: op cit; p. 191.
[1338] W.B. Stevenson: *The Crusades*; op cit; p. 329.
[1339] A.S. Atiya: *Crusade;* op cit; p. 90.
[1340] C.R. Conder: *The Latin Kingdom;* op cit; p. 360.
[1341] S. Runciman: *The Crusades;* op cit; 3; p. 279.
[1342] Ibid.
[1343] A. Hoteit: Les Differentes Communautes; in *De Toulouse*; op cit; pp. 41-58; p. 56.
[1344] Ibid.

the Maronite faith as well as 'their union with the successors of Peter, recognising that the 'Maronite nation' was part of the 'French Nation.'[1345]

Even more powerful alliance was built with an eastern foe of Islam: the Mongols. This form of alliance with Eastern people, whether the Mongols, or the Persians, to catch their Muslim foes from the rear has been relied upon by Christianity throughout the centuries.[1346] In subsequent centuries, the Persians would play a central part in breaking Ottoman power and saving Western Christendom.[1347] At this time, in the mid 13th century, the Mongols were at the apogee of their power, and had become the Eastern ally who could help crush the centuries old enemy by an attack from the rear.[1348] They had the military might and ferocity capable and necessary for accomplishing such an aim. The Mongols, moreover, had slain Muslims in great numbers during their first invasions (1219-1221), and this could only be great proof of their loathing of Islam and its followers.[1349] More importantly, the Christian faith had many adherents amongst the Mongols, especially at the highest echelons of command.

Multiple embassies between Mongols and the Papacy had already taken place during the 1240s for coordinated attacks against Islam. Although these had failed due to Guyuk's death, the opportunity for a joint assault offered itself once more. Mongke, yet another pro-Christian emperor, had just been elected, and Mongol generals were ready to march west. They were animated by fierce pro-Christian feelings and equally fierce, or even fiercer, hostility towards Islam. It ought to be reminded how Nestorian Christianity held a great place alongside Shamanism amongst Mongol beliefs.[1350] Hulagu, the commanding general on the western front, and his second in command, Kitbuqa (Kitbugha), had great affinities with Nestorian Christianity.[1351] Kitbuqa was in fact a committed Christian; Hulagu's wife, Dotuz Khatun, was also Christian, and she ferociously loathed Islam.[1352] The wives of other Mongol leaders, Mongke and Kubilai, most particularly, were also Christians, and their role in stirring pro-Christian feelings was decisive for the new campaign.[1353] The Church in Rome laboured hard to stimulate the zeal of these Christian wives, aware of their impact on their husbands.[1354]

The Armenians, who had a large presence amongst the Mongols, also exacerbated both pro-Christian and anti Muslim feelings. The Armenian ruler, Hethoum I, most particularly, had great favours of Mongol rulers, even acting as an ecclesiastic

---

[1345] Ibid.

[1346] G. Sarton: *Introduction;* op cit; ii; p. 37.

[1347] See this author's *The History of Islam;* MSBN Books; 2015.

[1348] B. Spuler: *History of the Mongols;* op cit; p. 1.

[1349] J.M. Fiey: *Chretiens Syriaques;* op cit; p. 5.

[1350] B. Spuler: *History of the Mongols;* op cit; p. 2.

[1351] B. Spuler: *Les Mongols dans l'Histoire*, Payot, Paris, 1961.

[1352] A. Mieli: *La Science Arabe et son role dans l'evolution scientifique mondiale.* Leiden: E.J. Brill, 1938, p. 147

[1353] J. Hayton, Saint Martin Brosset quoted in W. Heyd: *Histoire du Commerce du Levant au Moyen Age;* A.M. Hakkert Editor; Amsterdam; 1967; ii; p. 66.

[1354] J. Richard: *La Papaute et les Missions d'Orient au Moyen Age;* Ecole Francaise de Rome; Palais Farnese; 1977; p. 104.

adviser to the Great Khan.[1355] Hethoum entertained the idea of a great Christian Khanat, which encompassed the Kingdom of Armenia, the crusaders states, and other local Christian territories (that is once Islam had been suppressed by the Mongols).[1356] This dream of a great Christian kingdom was one of the factors, Fiey notes, which incited Eastern Christians to become the agents of the Mongols.[1357]

Louis's aim, just as the Popes', was to make ready such an alliance in the great onslaught on Islam that was now envisaged.[1358] Envoys were sent to the Mongols, carrying messages from popes and King Louis.[1359] In 1253, a report reached Acre that yet another Mongol prince, Sartaq, son of Batu (a brother of Mongke), had been converted to Christianity.[1360] Louis in earnest sent two Dominicans, William of Rubruck and Bartholomew of Cremona, to urge the prince to come to the aid of his fellow Christians in Syria.[1361] The Mongols repeated their promise, as made to Hethoum, the King of Armenia, that they would conquer the Holy Land and give it straight back to the Christians.[1362] Emperor Mongke announced that his brother, Hulagu, was already established in Persia, and had been ordered to capture Baghdad and destroy the caliphate.[1363] The engagement taken by Hulagu to return the Holy City and the old Kingdom of Jerusalem to the Christians was, in fact, the basis for the accord.[1364] The aim of such an accord went further. It meant that the West was about to be released from the fear of Islam by a great Christian army advancing from the Far East, and the time had also come 'for concerted action between the long divided Oriental and Western Christians to crush their common enemy.'[1365] Thus, just three years after the return of Rubruck, the Pope's envoy to the Mongols, Hulagu crossed Persia and attacked Baghdad.[1366]

By the time they were approaching Baghdad, the Mongols had already massacred millions of people further to the east.[1367] Al-Mustasim was the ruling caliph. When his father died, the leading clique placed Al-Mustasim as Caliph in preference to his brother whose energies they feared.[1368] The caliph, as well as his people, Michaud remarks, 'was sunk deep in voluptuous effeminacy, and the pride

---

[1355] J.M. Fiey: *Chretiens;* op cit; p. 7.
[1356] Ibid, 17.
[1357] Ibid.
[1358] C.R. Conder: *The Latin Kingdom*; op cit; p. 346.
[1359] Innocent IV: *Statuta capitulorum generalium ordinis Cisterciensis*, ed. J. Canivez, Vol II, Louvain, 1934, ad. ann. 1245, & 28, p. 294; G. Sarton: *Introduction;* op cit; p. 37.
[1360] C.R. Conder: *The Latin Kingdom*; op cit; p. 371; S. Runciman: *A History*; vol 3; p. 280.
[1361] *William of Rubrouck, Envoye de Saint Louis, Voyage Dans L'Empire Mongol (1253-1255)*, Payot, Paris, 1985.
[1362] J. Hayton; in W. Heyd: *Histoire*; op cit; p. 68.
[1363] S. Runciman: *A History*; op cit; p. 297.
[1364] J. Richard: *La Papaute;* op cit; p. 101.
[1365] R. W. Southern: *Western Views*; op cit; p. 46.
[1366] C.R. Conder: *The Latin Kingdom;* op cit; p. 381.
[1367] E.G. Browne: *Literary History of Persia*, op cit; p. 439.
[1368] Baron G. d'Ohsson: *Histoire des Mongols*; op cit; p. 207.

created by the vain adulation of the Muslims, made him neglect true and available means of defence.'[1369]

The weakness of the caliph was compounded by betrayal around him, in the person of his vizier, Ibn al-Alqami, who sent many secret letters to Hulagu informing him of both his loyalty to him (Hulagu), and talking down the character of the caliph, insisting to Hulagu that the capture of Baghdad would be quite easy, and whilst Hulagu was reticent, Ibn Al-Alqami pressed him to advance on Baghdad.[1370]

Before advancing on Baghdad, Hulagu asked his Muslim astrologer, Nasir Eddin al-Tussi, for his recommendation. Al-Tussi recommended the advance on Baghdad. Hussam Eddin, another Muslim astronomer, sought to dissuade Hulagu, but Al-Tussi was the more convincing of the two, and Hulagu moved on Baghdad.[1371]

On 30th January, 1258, Hulagu opened a massive bombardment of Baghdad. Within three days, the defences of the city were in ruins.[1372] For a week the Mongols waited on the walls, no soldier entering the city.[1373] The Mongols showed favours to Christianity from the moment of their arrival.[1374] This prompted the caliph to choose a Nestorian Christian, Patriarch Machida II, to negotiate the surrender of Baghdad. Hulagu, thereupon, ordered the caliph's army to assemble on the plain outside the walls, where all were massacred.[1375]

In the meantime, the fate of the Muslim population of the city, about, or over a million, was also decided, and betrayal took central stage again. Ibn Al-Alqami went to the camp of Hulagu, then returned to the population of Baghdad, announcing to the nobles and high officials to come out of the city to attend the marriage between the daughter of Hulagu and the caliph. As they came out they were killed en masse.[1376] Then, each Mongol officer was assigned a quarter of the city, with its population, to kill. The whole Muslim population, between 800,000 and one million was, hence, entirely exterminated.[1377] The Dominican, Ricoldo da Monto Groco says

> When the Mongols arrived in Baghdad, where there were many Christians, the Khan (Hulagu) ordered that no Mongol should enter the homes of the

[1369] J.F. Michaud: *The History of the Crusades,* tr., from Fr. By W. Robson, in 3 vols, New York, 1853, vol 3, p. 4.

[1370] G. d'Ohsson: *Histoire des Mongols*; op cit, p. 212.

[1371] Ibid, pp. 225-6.

[1372] J. Glubb: *A Short History*; op cit; p. 207.

[1373] Ibid.

[1374] Y. Courbage, P. Fargues: *Chretiens*; op cit; p. 29.

[1375] J. Glubb: *A Short History*; op cit; p. 207.

[1376] Ibn Taghri-birdi: *Nudjum;* vol 3; in Baron. G. d'Ohsson: *Histoire*; p. 259.

[1377] 800, 000 people according to H.H. Howorth: *History of the Mongols,* London, 1927, in Y. Courbage and Fargues: *Chretiens*; op cit; p. 29. This figure is confirmed by contemporaries, including Joinville, who was the French King St. Louis' personal secretary. D'Ohsson: *Histoire*; op cit; note p. 253.

Christians to cause them any harm, but that they should put to death all the 'Saracens.'[1378]
800,000 of the inhabitants, Arnold tells us, were brought out in batches from the city to be massacred, and the greater part of the city itself was destroyed by fire.[1379]

The news of the destruction of Baghdad, the fall of the caliphate, and the extermination of Muslims made Christianity erupt in exultations, especially when it was found that Christian coreligionists were amongst the chiefs of the conquering Mongol army.[1380]

The Mongol Advance Onto Syria

Following Baghdad, the Mongols marched towards Syria. Eastern Christians and the crusaders, D'Ohsson notes, were jubilant at the impending onslaught against that country.[1381] They were contemplating the ruin of a country, which has 'seen so much Christian blood spilled'. They were already preparing for the gathering of the spoils from the Mongol expedition.[1382]
The subsequent devastation of Syria and the massacre of its population were largely due to the ineptitude of its main Ayyubid ruler: Al-Nasir. Just like the caliph in Baghdad, Malik al-Nasir was weak and undecided; and as in Baghdad, betrayal and divisions amongst Muslims were an encouragement to Hulagu. Prince Al-Nasir had sent to Hulagu his vizier, Zein Eddin al Hafizi, who brought back with him letters of safety to his master. In 1258 he dispatched his son, Aziz, still a boy, with his vizier, a general, and some officers, giving also a letter to Bedr Eddin Lulu, the Armenian prince, who had 'converted' to Islam, and who ruled Mosul.[1383] The envoys, it is said, requested Mongol aid to save Egypt from the Mamluks.[1384]

On learning that Hulagu was at Harran, Al-Nasir consulted his generals and now resolved on resistance. He fixed his camp at Barza, a short distance north of Damascus.[1385] However, in the camp at Barza, according to the contemporary Muslim historian, Ibn Abd al-Zahir, Al-Nasir wasted his time with poetry, although it was his duty to make all necessary preparations for a campaign amongst his warriors.[1386] Baybars, who was in exile in Syria at the time, proposed to take three or four thousand horsemen to hold the fords of the Euphrates

---

[1378] L. De Backer: *Itineraire du Fr. Bieul* (Fra Ricoldo de Monte Croce); 1309; Fr. tr., of Jehan le Long; 1351; pp. 272-356; at p. 294.
[1379] T. W. Arnold: Muslim Civilisation during the Abbasid Period; in *The Cambridge Medieval History*, Cambridge University Press, vol IV; edited by J. R. Tanner, op cit; pp. 274-98; at p. 279.
[1380] Cf, J. Fiey: Chretiens Syriaques entre Francs et Mongols, in *Orientalia Chris. Analecta*, no197, 1974, pp. 334-41.
[1381] G. D'Ohsson: *Histoire;* op cit; p. 285.
[1382] Ibid.
[1383] J. Curtin: *The Mongols; A History*; Greenwood Press Publishers; Westport; 1907; p. 259.
[1384] Ibid
[1385] Ibid; pp. 261-2.
[1386] Ibn Abd Al-Zahir: Al- *Rawd al-zahir fi sirat al-malik al-zahir;* ed., A.A. Khuwaiter, Riyadh; 1976; 61-2; pp. 61-2.

against the Mongols, but Al-Nasir refused.[1387] During a discussion of the policy to be adopted towards the approaching Mongols, seeing Al-Nasir's alarm, Al-Hafizi extolled Hulagu's might and advised submission. Indignant at this, Baybars rushed towards the vizier, struck him, cursed him, and proclaimed that he was a traitor seeking the destruction of Islam.[1388] The vizier reported the incident to al-Nasir who decided to act on his side. Baybars and a group of Mamluks took, as a result, the decision to murder al-Nasir.[1389] That same night, a group of Mamluks led by Baybars attacked Al-Nasir in a garden. They had determined to cut him down immediately, and choose a new Sultan. Al Nasir survived and fled to the citadel, but returned later on to the camp.[1390] Baybars, who realized that nothing was to be expected from Al-Nasir, hurriedly left for Gaza from where he sent an officer named Taibars to Al-Mansur, the new sovereign of Egypt, pledging his oath of fidelity.[1391] Al Mansur was only a nominal sovereign, the true ruler, in fact, being Qutuz (Kutuz, and other spellings), the Mamluk leader.

In the meantime, on the Mongol-Christian side, King Hethoum of Lesser Armenia advised the capture of Aleppo, first, for, by taking it, the road to the rest of Syria was open.[1392] Hulagu followed the advice. On 18 January 1260 the city was besieged. King Hethoum, like his crusader son in law, Bohemond VI of Antioch-Tripoli, assisted Hulagu in the siege and, eventually, the storming of the city with an army of Christian warriors.[1393] The city was bravely defended, though.[1394] The walls of Aleppo were strong, and the city disposed of a good stock of weapons. The besiegers, however, made in one night a firm counter wall; and twenty catapults were trained on the city, which was taken by assault on January 25, 1260.[1395] The results of the capture were horrifying. When it had been sacked during five days and nights, and most of the inhabitants had been cut down, Hulagu proclaimed an end to the massacre. The streets were blocked up with corpses.[1396] As elsewhere, Runciman notes, the Muslim citizens were slaughtered en masse whilst the Christians were spared except for some Orthodox, whose church had not been recognised in the heat of the carnage.[1397] Of those who survived, it is said that one hundred thousand women and children were taken as slaves.[1398] The conquest of

---

[1387] Ibid; Al-Yunini: *Dhayl mir'at al-zaman*; 4 vols; Hyderabad; 1954-61; 3:243; Kutubi, *Fawat al-wafayat* (Bulaq, 1299/1881-2), 1:86; Safadi, at- *Wafi bi'l-wafayae*, ed. H. Ritter *et* al. (Wiesbaden, 1931), 10:332.

[1388] Ibn al-Furat, *MS*. Vatican, fol. 220a-b; Al-Makrizi: *Kitab al-suluk*; ed. M.M. Ziyada and S.A.F. Ashur; Cairo; 1934-73; 4 vols; in 12 parts; 1:419. G. d'Ohsson: *Histoire des Mongols*; op cit; p. 311.

[1389] G. d'Ohsson: *Histoire des Mongols*; op cit; p. 311.

[1390] J. Curtin: *The Mongols*; op cit; p. 262.

[1391] Ibid.

[1392] Bar Hebraeus: *Chronography*; op cit; p. 555.

[1393] P. Thorau: *The Lion;* op cit; p. 67.

[1394] J. Glubb: *A Short History*; op cit; p. 207.

[1395] J. Curtin: *The Mongols*; op cit; p. 265.

[1396] Ibid.

[1397] S. Runciman: *A History;* op cit; p. 306.

[1398] J. Glubb: *A Short History;* op cit; p. 207.

Aleppo was followed by that of the important fortress of Harim on the route from Aleppo to Antioch, a fall which also ended in massacre of the Muslims.[1399]

Meanwhile the Mongols advanced on Damascus. The city gave in without a fight. At its taking, on 1 March 1260, three Christian leaders (the Mongol commander Kitbugha (Kitbuqa), the King of Armenia and the Crusader Count Bohemond VI of Antioch) rode through the streets and forced the Muslim population to bow to the cross.[1400] Bohemond VI, whose father in law, the King of Armenia, had convinced him to join with the Mongols, had Mass sung in the Mosque of the Umayyad; the other mosques he had defiled by donkeys, wine was scattered on the walls, with grease of fresh pork, and salt, and the excrement of his men.[1401] The Christian population of the city had bells rung, went in procession through the streets, drank wine publicly during Ramadhan, and insulted and humiliated the Muslims.[1402]

Hulagu, meanwhile, had received news of the death of Mongke, the Grand Khan, and decided at once to return to Mongolia. This came soon after Hulagu resolved to invade Palestine.[1403] He made Kitbuqa commander of the armies in Syria, then marched homeward.[1404] However, before he left Tabriz in Iran, his base, he learned that his brother, Kubilai, had been elected, and this stopped his journey.[1405] Hulagu could now contemplate his and his Christian allies' accomplishments. By the end of the Summer of 1260, a vast territory stretching from Iran to the frontiers with Egypt was under Mongol-crusader control. With the three great cities of Baghdad, Damascus and Aleppo fallen to Christian-Mongol rule, it seemed, as Runciman notes, that the end of Islam had arrived.[1406] Should Egypt fall, Muslim power was finished. And Hulagu was determined to make an end of her.[1407]

> Round about 1260 [Saunders remarks] the world stood at one of the cross-roads of history. The whole future of Asia and Europe would have been altered but for certain accidents. The mind is staggered at the fantastic possibilities that opened out. A vast drama was played out against an appalling background of blood and ruin such as the world had not seen since the days of the Assyrian massacres.[1408]
>
> Islam was doomed; scriptural prophecies were being fulfilled; five centuries of Muslim oppression were ended! In those spring days of 1260 a

---

[1399] P. Thorau: *The Lion;* op cit; p. 67.
[1400] J.J. Saunders: *A History*; op cit; p. 182.
[1401] J. Richard: *La Papaute et les Missions d' Orient*; op cit; p. 99.
[1402] P. Thorau: *The Lion*; op cit; p. 68.
[1403] J. Curtin: *The Mongols*; op cit; p. 267.
[1404] Ibid.
[1405] Ibid.
[1406] S. Runciman: *A History*; op cit; p. 308.
[1407] C. Dawson: *The Mongol Mission*; Sheed and Ward; London; 1955; p. xxvi.
[1408] J.J. Saunders: *Aspects of the Crusades*; op cit; p. 50.

new era seemed dawning for eastern Christendom. Persia and Iraq had passed out of Muslim hands, the Caliphate had gone, Syria was being overrun, the Latin Crusaders held the coastlands, and within a few weeks, it was thought, the Mongols would be in Jerusalem and Cairo. The conquest of Egypt would open the road to North Africa, and the Christians of Spain might meet the advancing Mongols somewhere in Morocco. Islam would be obliterated. Two things clouded this hopeful prospect: the death in 1259 of the Great Khan Mongke in distant China, and the spirited and unexpected resistance of the new Mamluk régime in Egypt.[1409]

5. The Battle of Ain Jalut (September 1260) and its Impact

From the beginning of his reign, the Mamluk leader of Egypt, Qutuz (Kutuz and other spellings), had pursued an unequivocal anti-Mongol policy. Qutuz's resolve was reinforced by the steady influx of troops from Syria as al-Nasir's army began to disintegrate in the late winter and spring of 658/1260. Of even greater importance was the return of Baybars to the Mamluk fold, in spite of the hatred occasioned by Qutuz's role in the murder of Farid Aqtay, former leader of the Bahriyya regiment, and a close friend and ally to Baybars.[1410] But now in the face of the Mongol threat, past differences were forgotten. Qutuz needed Baybars' leadership abilities and his following of Bahris.[1411] Baybars, for his part, now understood that his continued allegiance to al-Nasir or any other Ayyubid prince in Syria was worthless. After sending a trusted subordinate and obtaining an oath of safety, he made his way to Egypt from Gaza, reaching it on 7 March 1260, at the time when the Mongol raiders were harrying Palestine.[1412] Following his return to Egypt, Baybars strengthened Qutuz's resolve and denigrated the might of the Mongols.[1413]

Hulagu had now decided to attack Egypt, and before doing so, sent an embassy of forty people to Cairo with a letter which stated that: 'God has raised the House of Genghis Khan, and whoever has resisted has been wiped out. Our armies are invincible. If you do not submit, and do not bring tribute in person to my camp, prepare for war.'[1414]

Whilst the rest of Islam was gripped with terror, to the summons for surrender sent by the Mongols, the Mamluks answered much differently.[1415] The Mamluk

---

[1409] Ibid; pp. 55-6.

[1410] R. Amitai-Preiss: *Mongols and Mamluks*; Cambridge University Press; 1995; p. 35.

[1411] Ibid.

[1412] R.S. Humphreys: From Saladin to the Mongols, Albany; 1977; 345-8; A.A. Khowaiter, *Baibars the First* (London, 1978), 18-20; Thorau, *Baybars*, op cit; 65-6.

[1413] Al-Yunini: *Dhayl*, op cit, 1:365; Ibn al-Furat, MS. Vatican, fol. 238b.

[1414] G. d'Ohsson: *Histoire des Mongols;* op cit; Note 2; p. 332.

[1415] C. Cahen: *Orient et Occident*; op cit; p. 198.

leadership met in council, and the Khwarizmian general Nasir Eddin, the princes of Irbil and Acre, and Baybars, decided for war.[1416] Qutuz then said:

>Well then, we will go to war; winners or losers, we would have done our duty, and the Muslim nation will not call us cowards.[1417]

And as a further measure of defiance, it was also decided that Hulagu's ambassadors be put to death.[1418]

The Muslim army left Cairo about the middle of Sha'ban 658 A.H. (end of July, 1260).[1419] They left for Salihiyya, the staging area some 120 km to the north-east of Cairo.[1420] The Muslim force, 120,000 men strong, included the Mamluk Egyptian army, Syrians who had passed to Egypt, and also Turkmen.[1421] There were also Bedouins and Shahrazuriyya Kurds, who had also come to Egypt.[1422] The Ayyubid ruler of Hamah, Al-Mansur Mohammed, had left his city to join al-Nasir at Damascus, but when the latter had failed to fight the Mongols, Al-Mansur had made his way to Egypt with his army.[1423] The army of Hamah now constituted a major force within the Mamluk ranks. Qutuz had also sent an envoy to demand aid of al-Ashraf of Hims, the chief governor of Syria under Hulagu's orders, and al-Said Hasan, ruler of Banias and al-Subayba.[1424] Al-Said abused the Mamluk envoy, but Ashraf received him, and in private prostrated himself in his presence through respect for Qutuz.[1425]

After marching for some days, Qutuz sent Baybars with a contingent forward to Ghaza to locate the Mongol army.[1426] On hearing of his approach, the Mongols, who were encamped there, moved to a place in al-Ghaur, presumably considering their position at Ghaza not favourable for a battle.[1427] Baybars, thus, occupied Ghaza. Qutuz soon reached Ghaza with the bulk of the army and after a stopover of one day moved up the coast to Acre.[1428]

[1416] G. d'Ohsson: *Histoire des Mongols;* op cit; p. 332.
[1417] Ibid.
[1418] Ibid.
[1419] A.A. Khowaiter: *Baibars the First*; The Green Mountain Press; London; 1978; pp. 20-3.
[1420] Ibn al-Dawadari: *Kunz al-Dura;* ed. U. Haarmann; Freiburg; 1971, 8:49; Yunini: *Dhayl*, 1:365; Ibn al-Furat: *Tarikh*, MS. Vatican, fol. 244b.
[1421] J. Curtin: *The Mongols*; op cit; p. 269.
[1422] Ibn al-Furat: *Tarikh*, MS. Vatican, fol. 244b (whence Makrizi, 1:429, but he omits the Kurds). For a further discussion of the composition of the army, see Amitai-Preiss, 'Ayn Jalut Revisited; *Tarikh*; 2; 1991; pp. 119-50, 126-7.
[1423] Ibn Wasil: *Mufaraj al-Kurub*; MSS. Bibliotheque Nationale ar. 1702-3 [two separate Mss of the same work]; Ms 1703; fols 150a, 151 a-b. Ibn Kathir: *Al-Bidaya wa'l nihaya fi'l tarikh*; rprt Beirut; 1977; 14 vols; 13:220, 226, says that the majority of the Syrian army entered Egypt; see also Ibn al-Suqa'i: *Tali Kitab wafayat al-Ayan*; ed.; and tr. J. Sublet; Damascus; 1974; 168.
[1424] J. Curtin: *The Mongols*; op cit; p. 269.
[1425] Ibid.
[1426] Ibn al-Furat: *Tarikh*, MS. Vatican, fol. 245a (=ed. Lyons, 1:51).
[1427] A.A. Khowaiter: *Baibars the First*; op cit; pp. 20-3.
[1428] Ibn al-Furat: *Tarikh*; Ms Vatican; fol. 245 a (Lyons; 1:51).

As soon as Kitbuqa discovered that the Muslim army was camping on the plain before Acre, he moved down the Jordan Valley.[1429] He was first to reach 'Ain Jalut. 'Ain Jalut ('Goliath's Spring') is an all-year spring at the foot of the northwest corner of Mt. Gilboa, about 15 km north-northwest of Baysan.[1430] There is little doubt that the Mongols were the first to arrive at the site and take up position: when subsequently Baybars reached a nearby hill he found the Mongols already camped there.[1431] This contradicts the suggestion made by some scholars that the Muslims arrived at the location first and set up an ambush.[1432] For the Mongols, this was a good place to await the Muslims. Along the northern foot of the Gilboa runs Wadi or Nahr Jalut, which provided water for their horses, and the adjacent valley offered both pasturage and good conditions for cavalry warfare, which suited them.[1433] The Mongols could also exploit the proximity of the Gilboa to anchor their flank, and it also offered an excellent vantage point, as did the nearby Hill of Moreh.[1434]

The exact position of the Mongols was not known to the Muslims at first, and so Qutuz had dispatched Baybars with the vanguard to locate the enemy, whilst he followed with the main part of the army.[1435] After riding continuously Baybars came upon the Mongols' vanguard which he attacked and defeated.[1436] Then, finding the main Mongol army at 'Ain Jalut, he sent word to Qutuz.[1437] During the night while waiting for Qutuz to join him with the rest of the Muslim troops, he took up a position on the mountain overlooking the plain where the Mongol camp was, and kept watch, coming down during the day to engage in skirmishes.[1438]

Ibn al-Dawadari, a descendant of a Turkish family which had held important offices under the late Ayyubids and early Mamluks, wrote his chronicle, the *Kanz al-durar,* in the first third of the 14th century.[1439] According to him, Baybars skirmished repeatedly with the Mongol vanguard, attacking them again and again only to retreat on each occasion.[1440] In this way he lured the Mongols to the very place the Muslims wanted in 'Ain Jalut, an ideal battlefield with its wooded ridges, water supply and adjacent plain.[1441] The choice of an appropriate place and the attempt to draw the enemy by tactical manoeuvre into an unfavourable position were requirements set by Mohammed ibn 'Isa in his *Manual of War* for superior

---

[1429] P. Thorau: The Battle of Ayn Jalut: a Re-Examination; in P.W. Edbury: *Crusade and Settlement*; Cardiff; 1985; pp. 236-41; p. 238.

[1430] R. Amitai-Preiss: *Mongols and Mamluks*; op cit; p. 40.

[1431] Baybars al-Mansuri: *Kitab al-tuhfa al-Mulukiya fil al-dawla al-Turkiya;* ed. A.R. Hamdan; Cairo; 1987; 43.

[1432] P. Thorau: The Battle of Ayn Jalut, 236-9.

[1433] R. Amitai-Preiss: *Mongols and Mamluks;* op cit; p. 40.

[1434] R. Amitai-Preiss, "Ayn Jalut," 132-3.

[1435] P. Thorau: The Battle of Ayn Jalut; p. 238.

[1436] A.A. Khowaiter: *Baibars the First;* op cit; pp. 20-3.

[1437] Al-Safadi: *Al- Wafi bi'l Wafayat;* ed. Ritter et al; Wiesbaden; 1931-; 20 vols to date; 10:332; Ibn al-Furat: *Tarikh*, MS. Vatican. fol. 245b; cf. Makrizi: *Kitab al-Suluk*, 1:430.

[1438] A.A. Khowaiter: *Baibars the First;* op cit; pp. 20-3.

[1439] Ibn al-Dawadari: *Kunz al-Durar*; ed. U. Haarmann; Freiburg; 1971; Intr. pp. 11-22.

[1440] Ibn al-Dawadari; viii; 49; Ibn al-Furat: *Tarikh*; Ms Vatican Arab. 726; fol. 245v.

[1441] P. Thorau: The Battle of Ayn Jalut: a Re-Examination; op cit; p. 238.

military leadership.[1442] It is obvious that Qutuz and Baybars as commander of his vanguard met his standards. It is therefore appropriate to speak of this tactical manoeuvre as a trap, not as an ambush, notes Thorau.[1443]

After Baybars had informed him about the Mongol location, Qutuz joined him with the main army, and soon the two armies were facing each other on the plain of 'Ain Jalut.[1444] At 'Ain Jalut, on Friday 25th of Ramadhan, 658 A.H. (3rd September, 1260),[1445] the Muslim and Mongol armies fought one of the world's most decisive battles.[1446]

Just before the fighting began, early in the morning, the two armies were drawn up in order of battle on the plain facing one another, the Mongols having positioned themselves at the foot of the mountain.[1447] It would seem that the armies were drawn up more or less from north to south.[1448] It appears that the Muslim army rode in from the northwest along the Jezreel Valley. The sun just rose. The valley was full of fighting men; from everywhere were heard the cries of people, and the continuous sound of beating drums of the Muslims.[1449]

The fighting was fierce from the onset, a fight for the destinies of the entire Muslim world. Qutuz led the charge in person, pushing through Mongol ranks, encouraging his army to follow suite.[1450] The battle initially did not go well for the Muslims. The Mongols responded to the Muslim assault by attacking them. The extent of their attack is unknown but it must have at least included the Mongol right, since the Muslim left was defeated and disintegrated.[1451] Qutuz noticed this. He encouraged and drove on his troops, and himself with the other emirs fought fiercely.[1452] The left wing of the Muslim army that had first weakened, seeing its leaders thrusting forward, rallied to fight. The Muslims fought with fury, forcing forward, aiming to break the ranks of the Mongols.[1453] Baybars' biography singles out the courage he displayed on the occasion: his bravery and determination inspiring the troops to press against the enemy.[1454] Baybars' courage and his top

[1442] Mohammed Ibn Isa: *Nihayat al-su'l wa'l ummiya fi taliim al-furusiya*; British Museum Add; Ms 18866; fols 208-9 cited in G. Tantum: Muslim Warfare; in R. Elgood; ed., *Islamic Arms and Armour*; London; 1979; p. 199.
[1443] P. Thorau: The Battle of Ayn Jalut: a Re-Examination; op cit; p. 238.
[1444] J. Curtin: *The Mongols*; op cit; p. 270.
[1445] G. Deyedan: *La Chronique Attribuee au Connetable Smbat*; op cit; 106; Sarim al-Din Ozbeg in G. Levi della Vida ed., and tr. *L'Invasione Tartari in Siria nel 1260*; Orientalia; 4; 1935; pp. 253-76, in Ibn al-Furat: *Tarikh*, fol. 247a (= Levi della Vida, "L'Invasione," 366); For the time of the battle, see Amitai-Preiss, 'Ayn Jalut,' 133-6; and P. Thorau, *Baybars*, 77 and 86, n. 21.
[1446] J.J. Saunders: *Aspects of the Crusades*; op cit. p. 67.
[1447] A.A. Khowaiter: *Baibars the First*; op cit; pp. 20-3.
[1448] For a detailed discussion of the position of the two armies, see Amitai Preiss, 'Ayn Jalut," 134-8.
[1449] Al-Makrizi: *Histoire* (Quatremere); p. 104.
[1450] G. d'Ohsson: *Histoire des Mongols*; op cit p. 339
[1451] R. Amitai-Preiss: *Mongols and Mamluks*; op cit; p. 41.
[1452] A.A. Khowaiter: *Baibars the First*; op cit; pp. 20-3.
[1453] J. Curtin: *The Mongols*; op cit; p. 270.
[1454] A.A. Khowaiter: *Baibars the First*; op cit; pp. 20-3.

leadership are also supported by Frankish sources.[1455] His and other emir's leadership and courage surely inspired the men to fight a foe that had struck terror in Muslim hearts, more importantly, even, this day of battle was a holy day of Ramadhan, greatly stirring Muslim valour and commitment to the cause of their faith. The Muslim attack was so fierce, the Mongols began to lose ground, especially after losing many of their leaders.[1456]

To the Muslim attack, the Mongols responded with a second, fiercer, assault, and again the Muslims were close to defeat. But Qutuz was not disconcerted, and he again rallied his troops- if the reports are to be believed, with several cries of "Oh Islam! O Allah! help your servant Qutuz against the Mongols!" He then launched a frontal attack. As the two armies violently clashed, Mamluk fighting skills began to prevail. With their maces and axes, they slashed and cut through Mongol ranks. It was probably during this second attack that the Mongol general Kitbuqa was killed.[1457] According to some accounts he was killed by a certain Djemal Eddin Accoush.[1458] (In al-Makrizi's version of the battle, he was captured and put to death by the Mamluks.)[1459] The death of their general was a serious blow to the Mongols. But they were not finished. They sought to reorganise their ranks for another attack. As a Mongol division tried to entrench itself in a neighbouring hill, and began to gather, Baybars led an attack on them and cut them to pieces.[1460] The fierce fight the Muslims were putting on was disconcerting to the Mongols, who had not met similar stern opposition hitherto; the loss of their general had also caused them to begin to disintegrate as a fighting force.[1461] All over the vast battle field scores of them began to waver and even flee in disorder and panic. As soon as he saw this, Baybars led in the chase after them, and in their flight the Mongols were killed in large numbers, only a few managing to escape.[1462] Some hid in the surrounding thick vegetation. This may be a reference to reed beds in either the Wadi Jalut area or the vicinity of the Jordan River.[1463] Qutuz ordered the place to be set alight, and the Mongols hidden there were consumed by fire.[1464] Al-Makrizi writes that at this stage contingents of Mongols regrouped at Baysan and launched a counter-attack, which almost defeated the Mamluks until Qutuz was able to reorganise and launch the attack which decided the day.[1465] This report, however, is an incorrect summary of a larger account of events as told by Ibn al-Furat. The latter author only writes of two rounds of the same battle near 'Ain Jalut; there was no second battle at Baysan, as stated by al-Makrizi.[1466]

[1455] *Gestes des Chiprois* in RHC, Ar, 2:753, cited in Thorau, 'Ayn Jalut,' 240 n. 24.

[1456] G. D'Ohsson: *Histoire*; op cit p. 339.

[1457] R. Amitai Preiss: *Mongols and Mamluks*; op cit; p. 43.

[1458] G. d'Ohsson: *Histoire*; op cit; p. 339.

[1459] Al-Makrizi: *Sultans* (Quatremere); op cit; pp. 104-6.

[1460] G. D'Ohsson: *Histoire;* op cit; p. 339.

[1461] R. Amitai-Preiss: *Mongols and Mamluks;* op cit; p. 43.

[1462] G. D'Ohsson: *Histoire*; op cit; p. 339.

[1463] R. Amitai-Preiss: *Mongols and Mamluks*; op cit; p. 43.

[1464] G. D'Ohsson: *Histoire*; op cit; p. 339.

[1465] Al-Makrizi: *Kitab al-Suluk*, op cit; 1:431.

[1466] Ibn al-Furat: *Tarikh*, MS. Vatican, fols. 247b-248a; see Amitai-Preiss, "Ayn Jalut," 142-3, for further discussion of this.

As the battle drew to its conclusion, of the impressive Mongol-Christian army little was left on the ground except the dead or dying. Surviving bands of Mongols and their allies were now fleeing north, mainly in direction of Armenian territory.[1467] Setting in their pursuit was Baybars with his men, capturing and killing most of them. Those who escaped Baybars were caught and slaughtered by local Palestinian villagers.[1468] Only small numbers made it to friendly territory. The field of battle itself was a revolting shamble of the slain. Little mercy had been shown by Muslims; no account speaks of Mongol prisoners. Contemporary Christian sources claim that 100,000 Mongols were killed.[1469] Victory secure, Qutuz dismounted his horse, and prayed two rakaas (prostrations) to thank God.[1470] Prince al-Said Hasan, ruler of Banias and al-Subayba, who had fought on the side of the Mongols, now came to surrender. On dismounting he went to the Sultan to kiss his hand, but Qutuz kicked his mouth, and commanded an equerry to cut his head off immediately.[1471]

The Muslim victory was total. Al Ayni writes that most of the Mongols were killed in the battle.[1472] The few Mongol survivors who had fled north to the Armenian territory received friendly treatment, and would soon be re-equipped for further campaigns.[1473] Qutuz dispatched a force under Baybars after the routed Mongols. Baybars chased them up through northern Syria, and at Hims caught up with a group of them, along with their women and children, and dealt them another blow.[1474] There are also reports that Baybars met a fresh contingent of Mongols there, numbering 2000 troopers, sent by Hulagu to reinforce Kitbuqa.[1475] Ibn Abd al-Zahir writes that Baybars reached as far as Hàrim and Afamiya, where the Mongol reinforcements were defeated.[1476] Other writers state that Baybars reached as far as Aleppo before turning back to join the main Mamluk army, now camped at Damascus.[1477]

The victory over the Mongols had a great impact on the Muslims.

> For the first time in history [Loewe remarks] the Mongols were fairly and indisputably beaten in a decisive battle. The effect was magical. Wherever the news of the Mamluk victory became known, men gave themselves up to the

---

[1467] J. Richard: *The Crusades c.1071-c.1291;* Cambridge University Press; tr., from the French; 1999; p. 415.

[1468] Ibn Wasil: Mufarraj; op cit, MS. 1703, fol. 160b; Al-Yunini: Dhayl, op cit, 1:361; 2:35.

[1469] 'L'Estoire d'Eracles empereur et la conqueste de la Terre d'Outremer', *RHC Or.,* ii, 444,638; 'Annales S. Justinae Patavini', *MGHS*, xix 191; 'Maius Chronicon Lemovicense', *RHGF*, xxi, 59.

[1470] G. D'Ohsson: *Histoire*; op cit; p. 339.

[1471] J. Curtin: *The Mongols;* op cit; p. 270.

[1472] Al-Ayni: *Iqd al-Juman fi tarikh ahl al-Zaman*; ed. M.M. Amin, 2 vols; Cairo 1987-8; Also partial ed., and tr., in RHC or, II.; fol 76a.

[1473] J. Richard: *The Crusades c.1071-c.1291;* op cit; p. 415.

[1474] R. Amitai-Preiss: *Mongols and Mamluks*; Cambridge University Press; 1995; p. 44.

[1475] Abu Sháma: Kitab, op cit, 209; Ibn al-Dawadari: Kunz, op cit, *8:59—60;* Al-Yunini: Dhayl, 1:366; Ibn al-Furat, MS. Vatican, fol. 251a; Al-Ayni: Iqd, fol. 76a.

[1476] Ibn Abd Al-Zahir: Al- *Rawd al-zahir*, op cit, 65.

[1477] Ibn Wasil: Mufarraj, MS. 1703, fols. l60b—161a; Al-Dhahabi: *Kitab Duwal al-Islam*, MS.Laud 305, fol.254a.

wildest transport of rejoicing. The spell was broken at last, and it was clear that the superhuman power, claimed by the Mongol boasts and credited by the fears of their victims, was a myth.[1478]

On 27 Ramadhan, 5 September 1260, two days after 'Ain Jalut, the news of the Mamluk victory reached Damascus. The Ayyubid vizier, Zein Eddin al-Hafizi, whom Baybars had once struck and cursed, now working as governor for the Mongols, with those close to him, left the city hurriedly for the Mongol court in Iran.[1479] He and his followers were harried by local villagers, robbed and a number amongst them were killed.[1480] As the news of the Muslim victory spread in Damascus, the Muslims directed their ire at the Christians, and to some extent at the Jews.[1481] Altogether thirty Christians were hanged, and the Christian population was fined for its collaboration with the Mongols 150,000 drachmas.[1482] Next came the turn of Muslims who had been partisans and agents of the Mongols; these were massacred without pity.[1483] The same happened in Hamah and Aleppo.[1484] All of Hulagu's officials were executed there and in other towns and cities.[1485]

The Mongol defeat, understandably, spread consternation amongst Christians.[1486] King Henry III of England was informed of the issue of the battle in 1261 by a letter from Florence, Bishop of Acre.[1487] The Bishop lamented a lost opportunity.[1488] It was his opinion that since 'the time of Godfrey of Bouillon, never had the Christians had such an opportunity of aid against the Saracens.' This opportunity had been missed.[1489] The 13th century Muslim historian, Abu'l Fida, says:

> We had despaired of beating the Mongols, seeing them the masters of all Muslim provinces. Never had they entered a country and failed to subjugate it, and never had they fought battle and failed to win it.[1490]

The Mongols have not just been defeated, the Muslim victory was one of the most defining events in history.[1491] As Runciman writes:

[1478] H.M. J. Loewe: The Mongols; op cit; p. 643.
[1479] Al-Yunini: *Dhayl*, 1:366; Ibn al-Dawadari: *Kunz*, 8:51; Ibn al-Furat: *Tarikh*, MS. Vatican, fol. 250a.
[1480] Ibid.
[1481] P. Thorau: *The Lion*; op cit; p. 78.
[1482] G. D'Ohsson: *Histoire des Mongols;* op cit; p. 343.
[1483] J. Curtin: *The Mongols*; op cit; p. 271.
[1484] Ibn Wasil: *Mufaraj*, MS. 1703, fol. 162b; Abu 'l-Fida', 3:215; Sarim al-Din, cited in Ibn al-Furat: *Tarikh*, MS. Vatican, fol. 247b (= Levi della Vida, "L'invasione," 366); cf. Rashid al-Din, ed. Quatremere, 352 (cf. ed. Alizadah, 3:76 and n. 6), who writes that the Mongol officials were massacred everywhere but in Damascus.
[1485] G. D'Ohsson: *Histoire des Mongols*; op cit; p. 342.
[1486] *Annales monasterii de Osenia*, s.a. 1261, in *Annales Monastici;* op cit. ed., Henry Richards Luard (London, 1869); iv; pp. 129-30.
[1487] *Diplomatic Documents Preserved in the Public Record Office; 1101-1272;* ed. Pierre Chaplais (London, 1964), i. No 343; pp. 241-2.
[1488] J. Paviot: England and the Mongols (1260-1330); *JRAS;* Series 3; 2000; pp. 305-318; at p. 307.
[1489] Ibid
[1490] Abu'l Fida; p. 144 in Grousset: *Histoire*; op cit; 3; p. 606.
[1491] See Al-Makrizi: *Al-Suluk fi Ma'rifat Duwal al-Muluk;* tr. M. Qatremere as *Histoire des Sultans Mamluks de l'Egypte*; Paris; 1845; vol I; pt. 1; pp. 98; 104.

The Mamluk victory saved Islam from the most dangerous threat that it ever had to face. Had the Mongols penetrated into Egypt there would have been no great Muslim state left in the world east of Morocco (it must be remembered that by 1260, Muslim rule in Spain, with the exception of Grenada, had just been ended). The Muslims in Asia were far too numerous to be ever eliminated but would no longer have been the ruling race. Had Kitbuqha, the Christian, triumphed, the Christian sympathies for the Mongols would have been encouraged, and the Asiatic Christians would have come into power for the first time since the great heresies of the pre-Muslim era... The Mamluk victory at Ain Jalut made the Mamluk sultanate of Egypt the chief power in the Near East for two centuries till the rise of the Ottoman Empire. By strengthening the Muslim and weakening the Christian element it soon induced the Mongols that remained in western Asia to embrace Islam. And it hastened the extinction of the Crusader states, for as the Teutonic Grand Master foresaw, the victorious Muslims would be eager now to finish with the enemies of the faith.[1492]

Given unity, a better organisation and improved techniques, Muslim armies could at least hold the Mongols in any future battle.[1493] Baybars, in particular, ambitious as he had always been, must have felt confident that a Muslim force equipped and trained in accordance with his own ideas could restore their lost territories to the Muslims. The victory brought renewed assurance also to the inhabitants of the Muslim lands, especially to Syria, where people now began to return to their homes.[1494]

******

On his way back to Egypt from Damascus, Qutuz was slain by a group of emirs led by Baybars. There are many reasons for the discord between the two men. One of them was that Qutuz refused to grant the governorship of Aleppo to Baybars, which he had initially promised him.[1495] Another was that Baybars proposed to Qutuz to attack crusader Acre directly after the Battle of 'Ain Jalut, but Qutuz refused on the ground that he had passed an armistice with the Christians.[1496] Baybars, Michaud remarks, reproached the sultan with a criminal moderation towards the enemies of Islam.[1497] This latter reason is certainly the real one for the act, knowing Baybars' enmity to the Franks and his commitment to total war. It must also be borne in mind that Qutuz had had Baybars' closest allies and friends decapitated some years before, and that it was the Mongol danger that had brought Baybars back with Qutuz.

[1492] S. Runciman: *A History;* op cit; p. 313.
[1493] A.A. Khowaiter: *Baibars the First*; op cit; pp. 203.
[1494] Ibid.
[1495] Abul-Feda: *Annales (RHC Or)*; i; p. 144.
[1496] William of Tripoli: *Tractatus de Status Saracenorum;* in H. Prutz: *Kulturgeschichte der Kreuzzuge*; Berlin, 1883. p. 586.
[1497] J.F. Michaud: *The History of the Crusades,* tr., from Fr., by W. Robson, in 3 vols, New York, 1853, vol 3, p. 7.

Taking over Qutuz, Baybars was crowned sultan in 1260.[1498]

> This revolution [Michaud remarks, again] gave the Muslims the sovereign
> most to be dreaded by the Christians. Baybars was named the pillar of the
> Muslim religion and the father of victories; and he was destined to merit
> these titles by completing the ruin of the Franks. He had scarcely mounted
> the throne before he gave the signal for war.[1499]

From that time until his death in 1277, he personally led the Muslims into many
battles against the combined armies of Crusaders, Mongols, and their local allies,
and unlike his predecessors, he showed little pity or quarter.[1500] Stirred by victory
and under his leadership, the Muslim fight back against the crusaders and their
allies was going to reach a new pitch of intensity. As Thorau notes:

> The Franks had long experience of reaching accommodation with the
> Ayyubid principalities which emerged after the death of Saladin, and a
> political equilibrium had come into existence. Even the invasion of Syria by
> the Mongols under Hulagu had never seriously put in question the
> continued presence of the remaining Frankish states in the Holy Land. But
> a new political order was to arise from the Mamluk victory at Ain Jalut
> which in time was to bring Frankish rule in Syria to an end and was to help
> shape the history of the Near East for almost 300 years.[1501]

BAYBARS SULTAN (1260-1277)

> During the seventeen years of his reign (1260-1277), Baybars [Mayer
> points out] undertook 38 campaigns, travelled about 25,000 miles, and
> personally fought in fifteen battles. He banished the double threat to the
> Muslim Middle East which was posed by the Franks and Mongols. He
> fought nine times against the Mongols, five times against the Armenians,
> three times against the Assassins of Syria, most of all, he had defeated the
> Franks twenty one times. They had lost all the strong points which they
> held in the interior of the country. All that was left to them now (after his
> death) was the coastline from Athlit (Caste of the Pilgrims) south of Mount
> Carmel, to Lattakieh in the north.[1502]

As the existence of many small Muslim independent (often conflicting)
principalities had contributed to the great success of the First Crusade, Thorau
remarks, so had the Ayyubid confederacy of rulers after Salah Eddin's death

---

[1498] C. Hillenbrand: *The Crusades*, op cit; p. 230.
[1499] J.F. Michaud: *The History of the Crusades*, op cit, p. 8.
[1500] For a good account of Mamluk wars see: Ibn Al Furat: *Tarikh* (Lyons); op cit.
[1501] P. Thorau: The Battle of Ayn Jalut: a Re-Examination; p. 236.
[1502] H.E. Mayer: *The Crusades*; tr. J. Gillingham; Oxford University Press; 1972; p. 272.

favoured the continued presence of the Crusader states.[1503] As long as the Franks in the Holy Land were able to form alliances with one or other, or more, of the often mutually hostile Ayyubid princes as allies of comparable strength, their existence was not seriously threatened. 'But when Baybars combined in a single hand the rule over Syria and Palestine,' Thorau adds, 'the Franks had little to set against him apart from their castles and fortified cities.'[1504] During his sultanate from 1260 till 1277, he broke the power of Prince Bohemond of Tripoli, captured Antioch, the crusader stronghold; shattered the Templars by taking the castles of Safed and Burdj Safitah; annihilated the Knights of St. John by capturing their strongest fortress Hisn al-Akrad; and even more, made the once so dangerous Ismailis 'submit to the all powerful sultan.'[1505] Their fortresses, Maysaf, Kadmus, Kahf, Khawabi, Manika, Ullaika surrendered one after the other.[1506] Baybars also ended the hostile state of lesser Armenia, repeatedly crushed the Mongols until they no longer constituted the threat they once did, and finally brought the Maronite Christians to heed. His remarkable accomplishments, thus, paved the way to his successors in ending the Crusader presence in the East.

These are the accomplishments of this remarkable figure examined in the following, beginning with his role as a state builder.

6. Baybars and the Formation of the Modern State

Baybars was not just one of the most formidable generals in history, he was also one of the greatest state builders ever known. He had realized that in order to establish Muslim power, not only he had to thoroughly defeat, if not utterly destroy, Islam's enemies, he also needed to build a powerful state to allow its long survival. When he became sultan, he ruled a state stretching from the Nile to the Euphrates but as yet quite fragile and vulnerable to both internal and external foes. Externally it was threatened by Mongols and Crusaders and their Armenian allies, and how Baybars dealt with them would be seen further on. Internally there were still more or less autonomous enclaves, and many foes, whether former Ayyubid claimants of some sort or another, Ismailis, Maronites, and other groups. These forces could easily undermine a weak, shaky power structure and administration. The state Baybars found had been undermined by the destruction caused by the Christians and Mongols; Syria, in particular, had born the brunt of crusader-Mongol destruction, besides Ayyubid incompetence and internecine wars.[1507] Although he had at the start of his rule to cope with insubordinate governors, threatening the newly united state of Egypt and Syria, and had also to defend

[1503] P. Thorau: *The Lion of Egypt*; tr., into English by P.M. Holt; Longman; London; 1992; p. 150.
[1504] Ibid.
[1505] M. Sobernheim; Baybars I; in *Encyclopaedia of Islam*; vol 1; first ed; 1913; p. 589.
[1506] Ibid.
[1507] P. Thorau: *The Lion of Egypt*; op cit; p. 102.

himself against attacks directed against his person, he nevertheless began immediately to restore the internal structures through bold measures.[1508] Methodically he set up a smoothly functioning administration and a powerful army.[1509] On the foundations which he laid, he inaugurated a development that was going to last for centuries.[1510] His re-organisation of the state, Wiet observes:

> Manifests an exceptional harmony and equilibrium. Beyond his actions, which one can establish by deeds and dates, Baybars gives the impression of a man who dominates events with an imperturbable optimism.[1511]

In priority, he devoted very particular attention to the construction of a powerful army and system of defence. He realised that despite the victory at Ain Jalut, the Mongol danger persisted. They were still extremely powerful, and except for the Golden Horde, they had a fierce hatred for Islam, and were based in nearby Iran. The Crusader states along the Syrian coast also posed a problem especially as more armed men kept pouring in from the West. Armenia was also a thorn on the Muslim side. Unlike the Ayyubids, Baybars knew that the external danger was ever present, especially when there were internal foes always plotting and collaborating with the external enemies. 'The seriousness with which he took these dangers and his own efforts to develop his army's striking power,' Thorau remarks, 'is indicated not only by its numerical increase and organisational development, but also by his attempts to increase its fighting power by new branches of the service.'[1512] A strongly increasing tendency towards militarisation, Humphreys also notes, is clear in the organisation of the civil service and court officials.[1513]

Among Baybars main endeavours was his aim to construct a war-fleet such as Egypt had formerly possessed, and also his attempt to introduce fighting elephants-a plan which, however, proved not feasible.[1514] The attempt to create an effective war-fleet not only would enable energetic action to be taken against attacks by sea, but also trade in the goods necessary to Egypt.[1515] The import of more Mamluks from the regions north of the Black Sea was also borne in mind, and their travel by sea markedly shortened and simplified the journey.[1516] Baybars thus reconstructed entirely the arsenals, and had warships and cargo vessels built.[1517] Subsequently the Mamluk fleet would grow very strongly, and only the scarcity of timber, and hampering of its imports by Christian pirates and

[1508] Ibid; p. 98.

[1509] Ibid; p. 150.

[1510] Al-Makrizi: *Al-Mawaiz wal Itibar fi Dikr al-Khitat wal Athar* (Khitat); 2 vols; Bulaq; 1853-4; II; p. 375; 380-1.

[1511] G. Wiet: Baybars I; *Encyclopaedia of Islam*; vol 1; new ed.; 1960; p. 1125.

[1512] P. Thorau: *The Lion of Egypt*; op cit; p. 99.

[1513] R.S. Humphreys: The Emergence of the Mamluk army; *Studia Islamica*; 45; 1977; pp. 66-99.

[1514] Ibn Abd al-Zahir: *Al-Rawd al-Zahir fi Sirat al-Malik al-Zahir*; (Rawd); ed. A. Khwaiter; Riyadh; 1976; p. 449.

[1515] P. Thorau: *The Lion of Egypt*; op cit; p. 101.

[1516] Ibn Abd al-Zahir: *Rawd*; pp. 89-93; Ibn Shaddad: *Tarikh al-Malik al-Zahir*; ed., A. Hutait; Wiesbaden; 1983; pp. 339-61.

[1517] G. Wiet: Baybars I; op cit; p. 1125.

Papal embargo, would centuries later hinder its challenge to more powerful Western fleets.[1518]

Baybars period, Wiet also remarks, cannot but recall that of Salah Eddin: the achievement of a unity of command, and the victorious war against the Franks.[1519] These are two elements of the comparison which are to the advantage of Baybars.[1520] Moreover, Salah Eddin's offensive, of which the title to glory is the capture of Jerusalem, was 'a clap of thunder without consequence.' In this respect the advantage lies with Baybars, whose forced marches, rapid and unexpected, were not without method: every inch of conquered land was put immediately in a state of defence.[1521] From the year 659/1261 the Sultan consolidated the key points of his future offensives. Every citadel which had been destroyed by the Mongols, from Hims to Hawran, was repaired and provided with food and material of war.[1522] The fortifications of Damascus, al-Salt, 'Ajlun, Salkhad, Busr, Ba'labakk, Ubayba, Shayzar and Shumaymis, which had been partially or completely demolished during the Mongol conquest of Syria, were restored and strengthened.[1523] Everywhere he ensured that the castles captured by Muslims from the Franks were carefully repaired and put into a state of readiness.[1524] The fortress erected by al-Salih Ayyub on the island of Rawda in the Nile had been demolished by the first Mamluk ruler, al-Mu'izz Aybak; Baybars ordered its rebuilding, and stationed a garrison in it.[1525] The fortifications of Alexandria, which had already twice seen the attack and withdrawal of a Frankish invasion of Egypt, were strengthened. A watch-tower was erected at the harbour of Rosetta to facilitate the early identification of hostile shipping.[1526]

In Baybars' eyes these military precautions were insufficient. He took particular trouble to see that he obtained news quickly, for this enabled him to react with unexpected speed.[1527] He insisted on being informed of every piece of news as soon as it was received, regardless of the situation he was in.[1528] It would even happen that the sultan received information in a state of almost complete nakedness, which, according to Wiet, tended to increase the zeal of his functionaries.[1529] He also insisted upon being able to dispatch orders with the same speed.[1530] For Baybars's highly-organised system of travelling in secret meant that he could well be present when he was thought to be far away.[1531] For

---

[1518] See W. Heyd: *Histoire du Commerce du Levant au Moyen Age*; Leipzig; 1885-6; reedit; Amsterdam 1967.
[1519] G. Wiet: Baybars I; op cit; p. 1125.
[1520] Ibid.
[1521] Ibid.
[1522] Ibid.
[1523] P. Thorau: *The Lion of Egypt*; op cit; p. 101.
[1524] H.E. Mayer: *The Crusades*; op cit; p. 269.
[1525] P. Thorau: *The Lion of Egypt*; op cit; p. 100.
[1526] Ibid; p. 101.
[1527] H.E. Mayer: *The Crusades*; op cit; p. 269.
[1528] G. Wiet: Baybars I; op cit; p. 1125.
[1529] Ibid.
[1530] Ibid.
[1531] A. Khowaiter: *Baybars the First*; op cit; p. 38.

military purposes, Khowaiter notes, secrecy was an integral part of almost every operation carried out by Baybars; the destination of a raiding or besieging force was concealed sometimes even from the commander of the force himself, who would receive his instructions for the next stage of his operation at a given place *en route* from the hands of another officer.[1532] Often, nobody knew Baybars' destination with the army until the last moment, and at times he disguised his moves seeming to be going on a hunting party before he suddenly launched a military assault on an important objective, such as Caesarea in 1265.[1533]

Fully aware that the Muslim world thronged with internal enemies, always ready to betray, Baybars also set up a secret service of the first order, possibly the first of its genre. What is remarkable was the use of this service not to control or repress the people, as no excesses are known out of it, but a network keeping a watch on the Mongols and crusaders, and their internal agents. The remarkable working of this service, its efficiency, and most of all some instances of its work are well summed up by Khowaiter.[1534]

For the better administration of the greatly enlarged Muslim territory, and the more rapid transmission of intelligence, particularly about the movements of the hostile Mongols and Crusaders, a scholar is said (according to al-'Umari) to have told Baybars about the forgotten postal service, and Baybars took up the idea.[1535] He immediately organised the post *(barid)* along every route to allow regular and relatively swift communication-four days-between the Mamluk capitals of Cairo and Damascus and the more distant cities of his realm.[1536] Extra relay stations were provided on the route, with fresh horses amounting to ten horses a day; salaries were paid to the men and largesse were showered on them.[1537] And, of course, whenever a dispatch arrived, Baybars would attend to it in person immediately. Just as the Pony Express operated in the western United States in the 19th century, Sims observes, the solitary Mamluk *barid* riders usually took ways that were more direct but more arduous and with fewer amenities.[1538] Like the caravans, however, the *barid* required stations for rest, water and stabling, and at its inception, it made use of existing caravanserais wherever possible. One such example is at Qara Khan, midway between Damascus and Hims, where Baybars carved his emblem, a running panther, on its entrance corridor.[1539] Thanks to this sophisticated system, intelligence reached Damascus [from Cairo] in four days and

---

[1532] Ibid.

[1533] P. Thorau: *The Lion of Egypt*; op cit; p. 160.

[1534] A. Khowaiter: *Baybars the First*; op cit; pp. 38 ff;

[1535] Al Umari: *Al-Tarif bi'l Mustalih al-Sharif*; Cairo 1895; p. 187.

[1536] E. Sims: Trade and Travel: Markets and Caravanserais; in G. Michell ed., *Architecture of the Islamic World*; Thames and Hudson; London; 1978; pp. 97-111; at p. 103.

[1537] Ibn Shaddad, *op.cit*, Vol. II, f. 223.

[1538] E. Sims: Trade; op cit; 103.

[1539] Ibid.

returned in four days. Answers to letters were not delayed longer than it took to write them in Damascus or Cairo.[1540]

Following the devastation of war and neglect, works for repair to affected civilian structures became an urgency.[1541] Immediate attention was given to the Dome of the Rock in Jerusalem, which was threatening with collapse.[1542] In the province of Jiza the sultan had work carried out on the dike of Shubramant to enable the inundation of the neighbouring lands to be regulated.[1543] Syria and Palestine witnessed a great upsurge of construction of water supplies; the Sultan, emirs, and governors taking charge of providing water to places large or small.[1544] Baybars also ordered the partial closure of the Nile mouth at Damietta to make impossible the entry of large enemy vessels as happened with Louis' crusade. Since during previous crusades against Egypt (1217-1219, in particular), the Crusaders had been put in a very precarious situation through the flooding of the land, Baybars had the branch of the Nile at Ashmum dredged as it was in danger of silting up.[1545]

These necessary measures stimulated the economy, provided employment, and increased the revenue of the state through a higher tax-yield.[1546] This not only gave a new lease of life to an economy that had been torn by war, the increased revenue allowed the financing of the war effort, and was much more efficient than just taxing an already impoverished population. The oppressive taxes which Qutuz had, thus, introduced to enable him to finance his campaign against the Mongols were abolished, and the high expenditure of the court on entertainments was suppressed.[1547] Popular confidence in the state grew as conditions became stable, and confidence grew even more as the sultan imposed on his officials to pay in fill without any undervaluation the prices asked by merchants for goods supplied to the court and army.[1548] Only a figure with Baybars's stature, just like Imad Eddin Zangi and Caliph Omar, could give such orders, and break recalcitrant officers or officials ready to bypass the rules. The sultan's interest in the economy, in a well-regulated state, appears in a decree issued in Jerusalem in 661/1263: No one was to encroach on cultivated land, and the sultan also wiped out any traces of feudalism, and freed the peasantry.[1549]

In spite of all the sultan's measures, in February 1264 Egypt was threatened with famine, and a sharp depreciation of the currency resulted. However, while the

[1540] Ibn Abd al-Zahir: *Rawd*; op cit, p. 95.
[1541] P. Thorau: *The Lion of Egypt*; op cit; p. 100.
[1542] Ibid.
[1543] H. Halm: *Agypten nach den mamlukischen Lehensregister*; Wiesbaden; 1979; I; 205 ff; p. 237.
[1544] I.M. Lapidus: *Muslim Cities in the Later Middle Ages*; Harvard University Press; Cambridge Mass; 1967; p. 71.
[1545] P. Thorau: *The Lion of Egypt*; op cit; p. 101.
[1546] Ibid.
[1547] Ibn Abd al-Zahir: *Rawd*; p. 77.
[1548] Ibid, pp. 77-9.
[1549] Ibn Wasil: *Mufarraj al-Kurrub fi akhbar banu Ayyub;* (Mufarrij);Paris; Bibliotheque Nationale; BN 1702; ff. 41r-418v. Baybars al-Mansuri: *Zubdat al-fikra fi tarikh al-Hijra*; (Zubdat); London; British Library; Ms Add. 23325; f. 59r. G. Wiet: Baybars I; *Encyclopaedia of Islam*; vol 1; new ed; 1960; p. 1125:

crisis lasted, the needy were supplied from the state granaries, and the state dignitaries and wealthy merchants were called upon to contribute similarly from their means to the support of the poor. Through these measures, the worst effects of famine were thus averted.[1550]

In order to check the danger of infection, and for their own benefit, Baybars decided (probably towards the end of 1266) to assemble the incurably sick, and then isolate them from the populace. He had those sick 'with gaping wounds in their limbs and visible bones' (leprosy is suggested) conveyed to the oasis of the Fayyüm and provided with the necessities of life.[1551]

> Justice, religious foundations and public works admittedly characterized the pious Islamic ruler, not Baybars alone [Thorau says.] The measures taken by Baybars for the strengthening and restoration of the state, however, went already far beyond the demands of the ideal picture of a ruler by reason of his purpose and effect.[1552]

7. Baybars' Military Campaigns (1260-1267)

Baybars distinguished himself as one of the greatest warriors of jihad and defenders of the Muslim world.[1553] This turned him into a legendary figure, whose exploits lived on in the popular folk epic *Sirat Baybars*. He led many battles against the combined armies of the crusaders, Mongols, Maronites, Armenians and Ismailis, and prevailed on each occasion.[1554] His success, Sobernheim remarks, was chiefly due to his power of organisation, his speed of action, and his 'reckless daring.'[1555] The network of post routes brought news from the seats of the governors to Cairo with almost incredible swiftness, and the Sultan with his cavalry moved equally quickly. He often appeared before a town in Syria whose inhabitants believed him to be still in Cairo.[1556] His boldest deed was a reconnaissance raid with 40 men against the powerful fortress of Hisn al-Akrad (Krac des Chevalliers), and the story seems to us almost incredible that Baybars, disguised as a Sheikh, took part in an embassy to the crusader leader, Bohemond of Tripoli, to get an idea of the strength of this town.[1557]

[1550] Baybars al-Mansuri: *Zubdat*; f.63; Al-Makrizi: *Kitab al-Suluk li Ma'arifat al-Muluk*; (Suluk); ed., M.M. Ziyada and S.A.F. Ashour; 4 vols; Cairo 1956-1972; partial tr. E. Quatremere: Histoire des Sultans Mamlouks; 2 vols; Paris 1845; partial tr. R.J. C. Broadhurst: *A History of the Ayyubid Sultans of Egypt*; Boston; Mass; 1980; I/ii; pp. 506-8.

[1551] Baybars al-Mansuri: *Al-Tuhfa al-mulukiya fil al-duwla al-Turkiya*; ed. Abd al-Hamid Salih Hamdan; Cairo; Cairo; 1987; (*Tuhfa*) p. 59.

[1552] P. Thorau: *The Lion of Egypt*; op cit; p. 102.

[1553] C. Hillenbrand: *The Crusades*, op cit; p.230.

[1554] For a good account of Mamluk wars see: Ibn Al Furat: *Tarikh* (Lyons); op cit.

[1555] M. Sobernheim; Baybars I; op cit; p. 589.

[1556] Ibid:

[1557] Ibid:

Unlike the Ayyubids, Baybars' objective was to remove the crusaders permanently from Muslim soil. In the Summer of 1262, he sent an army to Aleppo and the Euphrates region. It then turned west and devastated and plundered the region of Antioch, even threatening the city. When King Hethoum of Armenia arrived with a relieving force of Armenians and Mongols, the Mamluk army had already withdrawn to Cairo in August 1262.[1558] Prince Bohemond of Antioch and King Hethoum of Armenia, who had helped the Mongols during their conquest of Syria, Thorau notes, 'were soon to feel Baybars' anger, and receive a foretaste of what they had to expect.'[1559]

During 1263, Baybars' movements are those of a general who surveys his field of operations, seeking to know the strength and disposition of the enemy.[1560] He entered Palestine about the beginning of March with the immediate result that the Count of Jaffa hastily released Muslims he held prisoners for the sake of peace.[1561] The sultan made his headquarters at Jebel al-Tur where he was speedily visited by representatives of the Christian military orders and envoys of the principal crusader states who were dismissed without ceremony.[1562] In mid April of the same year, he threatened Acre and devastated the city's neighbourhood.[1563]

In 1264, King Hethoum I of Armenia assembled his army which he reinforced with Bedouins of the Banu Kilab tribe, and advanced to 'Ayn Tab. Baybars learned at once of the invasion through his efficient intelligence service, and ordered the troops stationed at Hamah and Hims to move off towards Aleppo. There were limited encounters between the two armies, in which the Muslims had the upper hand. Hethoum called on the Mongols to assist him, and pushed forwards towards Harim.[1564] He was soon joined by mounted troops dressed in Mongol attire with the intention of causing panic amongst the Muslims, knowing the dread the latter still caused. However, heavy falls of snow and rain compelled the attackers to retreat as their supplies of food were becoming exhausted.[1565] Once winter was over, Hethoum marched again into Muslim territory, whereupon Baybars transferred troops from Damascus to the north, and in the following encounters, the Armenians were so beaten they were compelled to retreat.[1566]

In 1265 Baybars happened to be on a hunting expedition in the vicinity of Arsuf when he received news of a Mongol attack on the important town and fortress of al-Bira on the Euphrates. He dispatched 4,000 light cavalry from Syria, whilst he himself set out for Cairo. The Franks had informed the Mongols that at the time (January 1265) the Muslim soldiers were dispersed over the country, the horses

[1558] Abu Shama; *Tarajim rijal al-qarnayn al-sadis wa'l sabi'*, Cairo, 1947 (repr. Beirut 1974); 214; 219.
[1559] P. Thorau: *The Lion of Egypt*; op cit; p. 142.
[1560] W.B. Stevenson: *The Crusaders*; op cit; p. 336.
[1561] *Estoire d' Eracles* (Receuil His occ); op cit; ii; p. 447.
[1562] *Estoire d'Eracles* (Receuil); op cit; ii; p. 447. Al-Makrizi: *Sultans* (Quatremere); op cit; I; I; p. 190.
[1563] Al-Makrizi: *Sultans* (Quatremere): I; I; pp. 228 ff.
[1564] P. Thorau: *The Lion of Egypt*; op cit; p. 151.
[1565] Ibn Wasil: *Mufarraj* (BN 1702); f. 422 r. Ibn Abd al-Zahir: *Rawd*; pp. 191-3.
[1566] Ibn Abd al-Zahir: *Rawd*; 196-7.

were at pasture, and hence the Egyptian army would be unable to mount a campaign.[1567] However, on 25 January Baybars left Cairo at the head of his army, to relieve al-Bira. Surprised by his sudden appearance, the Mongols took flight. Baybars could operate without fear of an attack in his rear, and could therefore use his army to attack the Franks in the south.[1568] Without disclosing the details of his further intentions, he invited the officers to a great hunt in the woods near Arsuf, thereby getting a close look at the defences of Arsuf and Caesarea.[1569] At the same time there was set up in front of the sultan's tent another of even greater size. There, in two days and a night five catapults of Hispano-Moroccan construction were secretly erected. Additional siege equipment, stonemasons and carpenters were brought in from the surrounding fortresses, and the soldiers prepared scaling-ladders.[1570] In the night 26-27 February 1265, the army was called to arms.[1571] Before dawn Baybars set out for Caesarea. There to the alarm and surprise of the Christians he suddenly appeared after a few hours' march, and the city was immediately encircled and stormed by the Muslim army.[1572] The details of the operation and Baybars personal involvement are told by Ibn al-Furat:

> Baybars immediately encircled the city, and the Muslims attacked it, throwing themselves into its trenches, using iron horse pegs together with tethers and halters on to which they clung, they climbed up from all sides and set up their banners there. The city gates were burnt and its defences torn away, while the inhabitants fled to the citadel. The sultan then set up his mangonels against the citadel.
>
> The citadel was one of the most strongly fortified and finest of its kind. It could not be mined because of the granite columns used crosswise in its construction, and even were it undermined it would not fall. However, the Muslims continued to bombard it with their mangonels..
>
> The sultan remained steadfastly at the front of the fighting. He remained in the company of the crossbowmen shooting away and preventing the Franks from climbing to the top on the citadel. At times he would go on one of the siege engines fitted with wheels, being drawn along beneath it up to the walls where he could see the saps for himself. One day he fought with a shield in his hand...
>
> Then, on the night of Thursday, half way through Jumada I (5 March 1265), the Franks came out and surrendered the citadel with its contents. The Muslims climbed up to it from the walls, burned its gates and entered it

---

[1567] P. Thorau: *The Lion of Egypt*; op cit; p. 158.

[1568] Abul Feda: *Annales* (RHOr); i; p. 150; Al-Aini: *Akd* (RHOr); ii; pp. 219-21.

[1569] P. Thorau: *The Lion of Egypt*; op cit; p. 160.

[1570] Al-Makrizi: *Suluk*; op cit, I; ii; 526.

[1571] R. Rohricht: *Geschicte des Konigreichs Jerusalem*; Innsbruck 1898; p. 925.

[1572] P. Thorau: *The Lion of Egypt*; op cit; p. 160.

173

from above and below, while the call to morning prayer was made from its
top.'[1573]

The garrison was allowed to go free but the town and castle alike were rased to
the ground.[1574] This was done probably in order to prevent once and for all
Caesarea ever again being used as the bridgehead for a Crusading army.[1575]

A few days later Baybars' troops appeared before Haifa. Those of the inhabitants
who were warned in time fled to boats in the anchorage, abandoning both the
town and the citadel, which were destroyed.[1576] Soon after, on 19 March, Baybars
set out from Caesarea, again keeping his objective secret. Two days later he
appeared with his army before Arsuf.[1577] The Hospitallers had garrisoned and
provisioned it well. Baybars had timber felled in the vicinity of Arsuf to meet the
needs of the siege. Breastworks and canopies were prepared for the protection of
the attackers. The advanced fortification trenches of both the town and the
citadel, which held no water, were linked together (probably in the north, where
they almost touched) by two branch trenches.[1578] By means of these approach
trenches, the Muslims were able to reach a forward position. Then the attack was
launched. The lower town fell on 26 April after its walls had been broken down
by the Sultan's siege-engines, and three days later the commander of the citadel
who had lost a third of his knights surrendered.[1579] On 29 May 1265 the
victorious sultan made his entry into Cairo with scores of Frankish prisoners,
with broken crosses around their necks, a symbol of crusader demise.[1580]

In 1266, during early summer, Baybars attacked on all fronts simultaneously.[1581]
Two Mamluk armies set out from Egypt, one, under the sultan himself, appeared
before Acre on 1 June. But the regiment maintained there by Louis IX had recently
been reinforced from France. Finding the city strongly garrisoned, Baybars
marched suddenly on Safad, 'because it was a lump in Syria's throat, and an
obstacle to breathing in Islam's chest,' says the contemporary, Ibn abd al-
Zahir.[1582] From its huge castle the Templars dominated the Galilean uplands. The
fortifications had been entirely reconstructed some twenty-five years before, and
the garrison was numerous. Baybars appeared before the stronghold on 8
Ramadan/13 June and set siege to the fortress. Siege equipment was brought
along from Damascus, arriving before Safad on 21 Ramadan/26 June.[1583] As the
bombardment with rocks and fire began, the sultan's soldiers started mines,

---

[1573] Ibn al-Furat: *Tarikh* (Lyons), op cit; pp. 70-1.

[1574] S. Runciman: *A History*; op cit; p. 318.

[1575] Ibn Abd al-Zahir: *Rawd;* 229-31. Baybars al-Mansuri: *Tuhfa;* 53.

[1576] S. Runciman: *A History*, op cit, p. 318.

[1577] Ibn Abd Al-Zahir: *Rawd*; op cit; p. 235.

[1578] P. Thorau: *The Lion of Egypt*; op cit; p. 161.

[1579] S. Runciman: *A History*; op cit; p. 318.

[1580] Al-Shafi: *Husn al-Manaqib al-Sirriya al-muntaza'a min al-sira al-zahiriya* (Husn); ed. A. Khwaiter; Riyad; 1976; 97.

[1581] H.E. Mayer: *The Crusades*; op cit; p. 269.

[1582] Ibn Abd al-Zahir: *Rawd*; op cit, pp. 253-4.

[1583] Baybars al-Mansuri: *Tuhfa*, op cit, p. 57.

which were answered by the counter-mines of the defenders. The first assault on 7 July was beaten back, but there followed six weeks' siege and sixteen days of hard fighting.[1584] At length, one Friday (we quote an Arab chronicle), says Michaud, the Qadi of Damascus was praying for the combatants, when the Franks were heard to cry from the top of their half-dismantled towers:
"O Mussulmans, spare us, spare us!"
The besieged had laid down their arms, and fought no longer — the gates were immediately opened, and the standard of the Muslims floated over the walls of Safad.[1585] Like most other captured castles, Safad was not demolished but became a Mamluk fortress, fully supplied with provisions and military equipment, and garrisoned.[1586]
In the wake of Baybars' recent victories the fate of the crusader kingdom seemed bleak, which inspired the Templar troubadour, Ricaut Bonomel, to write a bitter poem complaining that 'Christ seemed now to be pleased by the humiliation of the Christians.'[1587] The troubadour appears 'to reproach Providence with the defeats of the Christians of Palestine.'[1588]

> He is then mad who seeks a quarrel with the Saracens, when Jesus Christ opposes them in nothing, as they have obtained victories, and are gaining them still (which grieves me) over the Franks, the Armenians, and the Persians. Every day we are conquered; for he sleeps, — that God that was accustomed to be so watchful: Mahomet acts with all his power, and the fierce Bibars seconds him.[1589]

Despite these successes, Baybars was constantly aware of the threats from within, the Ismailis, in particular, and their independent principality in Karak.[1590] In 1262 an envoy of the Ismailis appeared before the sultan. He handed over a letter in which the two leaders of the sect made demands, accompanied with threats, for the return of the territories which they had formerly possessed under the Ayyubid Sultan, al-Malik al-Nasir Dawüd.[1591] The Ismailis, to whose daggers many had in the past fallen victim, and who had twice sought to murder Salah Eddin, clearly misjudged Baybars, Thorau remarks.[1592] It appears that they trusted in their power and their fame, and had little fear of the Mamluk sultan. Baybars appeared to accept their demands.[1593] Baybars, however, feared neither the sect's power nor its threats, scornfully stating in one of his letters that 'they can do nothing with their daggers against the Mamluks' swords, whose iron

[1584] R. Rohricht: *Beitrage zur Geschichte der Kreuzzuge*; 2 vols; Berlin; 1874-78. II, 287. Al-Aini: *Akd* (RHOr); ii; pp. 222-3; Al-Makrizi: *Sultans* (Quatremere); I; ii; pp. 28-30. S. Runciman: *A History*; op cit; p. 321.
[1585] J.F. Michaud: *The History of the Crusades*, op cit, p. 14.
[1586] P. Thorau: *The Lion of Egypt*; op cit; p. 171.
[1587] Bonomel's poem is given in Bartholemew: *Poesie provenziale;* ii; pp. 222-4.
[1588] J.F. Michaud: *The History of the Crusades*, op cit, p. 28.
[1589] Ibid, p. 29.
[1590] Ibn Wasil: *Mufarraj*; (BN 1702); f. 397v.
[1591] P. Thorau: *The Lion of Egypt*; op cit, p. 164.
[1592] Ibid.
[1593] Ibid.

shields offer better protection than the paper of their letters.'[1594] Subsequently, when he had dealt with other foes, Baybars would remove the Ismaili threat entirely.

The Mongols, although defeated at Ain Jalut, still represented, possibly, the greatest danger. At the end of 1261, their Christian general, Samgadou, besieged Mosul. D'Ohsson outlines the subsequent events:

> The city expected reinforcements from Egypt, but a terrible sandstorm blowing in direction of the Egyptians helped the Mongols to beat them. In June 1262, Mosul surrendered after Samgadou promised the lenient treatment of its inhabitants. He first destroyed the city's defences, and then had the whole population slain in a massacre which lasted nine days. Only few people who had escaped to the mountains survived. Prince Salih, who had defended the city, was taken to the residence of Hulagu in Tabriz, and there was wrapped in a sheep-skin for a month, exposed to the summer heat until he died. His son of three years was cut in half, before both parts were hanged at the city's main doors.[1595]

This was one of Hulagu's last deeds. In 1264, a year before his death, he sent a Mongol embassy to the Vatican, which was received by Pope Urban IV, the Mongol ambassador expressing Hulagu's wish to be baptised as a Christian.[1596] Possibly as a result, many Christian ambassadors came to give him blessings.[1597] Hulagu confessed to the Armenian Monk, Vartan, his love for Christianity, and Vartan assured him that 'all Christians living on this earth and on the seas were devoted to him with their hearts, and never refrained from praying for him.'[1598]

In 1265 Hulagu died. His passing was sorely lamented in Christendom. The contemporary Christian chronicler, Bar Hebraeus (Ibn al- Ibri of the Arabs) wrote of his 'wisdom, greatness of the soul, and admirable deeds, without comparison.'[1599]

And when soon after, Dotuz Khatun, Hulagu's wife, died, Bar Hebraeus lamented:

> Immense sadness has fallen upon Christians all over the world after the loss of these two great lights who had made Christianity triumphant.[1600]

Vartan, the Armenian, for his part, said:

> The pious Queen Khatun left us to be in the company of Christ; and Christian nations fell into despair and grief, overwhelmed by pain and sorrow, for during the life of this princess, the wound (from the loss of

---

[1594] Ibid.

[1595] G. D'Ohsson: *Histoire des Mongols*; op cit; pp. 371-4.

[1596] D. Ashby cited in J. Richard: Mongols and Franks; in *Journal of Asian History*; Indiana University; III. I. 1969; pp. 45-57; at p. 53; n. 32; J. Richard: Les Missions chez les Mongols aux XIIIem et XIV em siecles; Ch IV de l'*Histoire Universelle des Missions Catholiques;* I, Monaco; 1957; p. 192.

[1597] Extracts from Histoire Universelle de Vartan; tr. E. Dulaurier; in *Journal Asiatique*; V. XVI; 1860; pp. 273-322; esp. pp. 300-5.

[1598] Ibid.

[1599] Bar Hebraeus: *Chronography*; p. 444; in J.M. Fiey: *Chretiens*; op cit, p. 32.

[1600] Ibid.

Hulagu) had begun to heal. She had hoped to see Christianity rise and sparkle in all its splendour. All that Hulagu accomplished was owed to her.[1601]

For the Armenian historian, Stephen Orbeian:

> The great and pious king, the master of the world, the hope and stay of the Christians, Hulagu Khan, died in the year 1265. He was soon followed by his respected wife Dokuz Khatun. The Lord knows they were not inferior in well-doing to Constantine and his mother Helena.[1602]

In the meanwhile, Baybars was campaigning against the main Mongol-Crusader ally: Armenia. Baybars had never forgiven the Armenians for their alliances with the Mongols and their role in the massacres of Muslims in previous years. The Armenians had also maintained their hostile intentions as much as the Franks and the Mongols. In the winter of 1263-64 and during March of 1264 King Hethoum had taken the offensive. On both occasions he had been routed by Mamluk units.[1603] In 1266, in the wake of his successes against the crusaders, Baybars felt strong enough to launch a counter-offensive. The possibility of an intervention by the Mongols in Asia Minor did not deter his move as the victories against them at Ain Jalut, Hims, and more recently at al-Bira, had increased the confidence of the Syro-Egyptian forces.[1604] Still, he calculated his move. He decided to hit the Armenians via his emirs, whilst he kept a watch on both Mongols and Crusaders, the two more dangerous foes. Baybars ordered his general, Qalawun (Qalau'n), and the Sultan of Hamah, Al-Mansur, to inflict the now overdue retribution on the Armenians. Their combined armies, first raided territories around Tripoli during which the forts of Qulaiat and Halba and the town of Arqa were captured. The combined troops then marched towards Aleppo, and then turned westward into Cilicia, in Armenian territory.[1605] King Hethoum had expected a Mamluk attack, and in the spring of 1266, knowing that it was imminent, he set out for the Court of the Mongols in Tabriz.[1606] While he was there seeking Mongol help, the Muslim forces attacked in Cilicia. The Armenian army led by Hethoum's two sons, Leo and Thoros, waited by the Syrian Gates, with the Templars at Baghras guarding its flanks. The Mamluks and their Hamah allies, however, turned northward to cross the Amanus Mountains near Sarventikar, where the Armenians hastened to intercept them as they descended into the Cilician Plain. A decisive battle took place on 24 August, and in the ensuing fight, the Armenian army was cut to pieces. Of the two Armenian princes Thoros was slain, and Leo taken prisoner.[1607] The victorious Muslims swept

[1601] Extracts from Histoire Universelle de Vartan; op cit; esp. p. 309.
[1602] Quoted in Howorth, *Hist of the Mongols*, III, 210.
[1603] P. Thorau: *The Lion of Egypt*; op cit, p. 173.
[1604] Ibid; p. 174.
[1605] Abul Feda: *Annales* (RHOr); i; p. 151; Al-Aini: *Akd* (RHOr); ii; p. 222.
[1606] S. Runciman: *A History*; op cit; p. 322.
[1607] Ibid.

through Cilicia. While Qalawun and his Mamluks sacked Ayas, Adaima and Tarsus, al-Mansur advanced by way of Karanjil, Sarvantikars and Tell Hamdün to Hamus, which was set alight.[1608] He crossed the Jayhan, and finally stood before the great stronghold of the Teutonic Order, Adamodana (al-'Amudayn).[1609] There great numbers of refugees had fled, including the garrison made of knights of the Teutonic Order and Mongols among others, who were put to the sword, whilst women and children were made captive.[1610] After the castle had been demolished, the Mamluk army marched past Mamistra to the Armenian capital at Sis where 'it plundered the palace, burned down the cathedral, and slaughtered some thousands of the inhabitants.'[1611] At the end of September the victorious troops retired to Aleppo with nearly forty thousand captives and immense booty.[1612] King Hethoum hurried back from the Mongol court with a company of Mongols only to find 'his heir a captive, his capital in ruins, and his whole country devastated.'[1613] The Cilician kingdom never recovered from the disaster, and was no longer able to play more than a passive part in the politics of Asia.[1614]

Clement IV (Pope 1265-1268) wrote to the king of Armenia to console him 'for the evils he had suffered by the invasion of the Mamluks,' and to announce to him that the Christians of the East were about to receive powerful support.[1615] Abaga (Abaqa), khan of the Tartars, who was then prosecuting a war against the Turks of Asia Minor, sent ambassadors to the court of Rome, and to several princes of the West, proposing to attack the Mamluks in concert with the Franks, and drive them from Syria and Egypt.[1616] The pope received the Mongol ambassadors with great solemnity; he told them that an army, led by a powerful monarch, was about to embark for the East, that 'the hour fatal to the Muslims was come, and that God would bless His nation, and all the allies of His nation.'[1617]

Whilst in the background the anti Muslim alliance was in preparation, on the ground a frenetic diplomatic movement was in motion. Throughout the end of 1266 and 1267, envoys came from every quarter to sue for peace, and recognise Baybars' authority. First to arrive were the Armenians seeking to obtain Leo's release, attempts which were not successful.[1618] In February-March 1267 envoys came from the Ismaili Assassins, and delivered to Baybars a considerable sum of money. They declared to him that it was the amount which they previously paid as tribute to the Franks, but that henceforward they would contribute it to the Egyptian state treasury, to be used 'for the Holy War against the infidels.' Ibn 'Abd

---

[1608] R.T. Boase: *The Cilician Kingdom of Armenia*; Edinburgh and London; 1978; p. 179.

[1609] Abd al-Zahir: *Rawd*; op cit, 270.

[1610] P. Thorau: *The Lion of Egypt*; p. 174.

[1611] S. Runciman: *A History*, op cit, p. 322.

[1612] Al-Makrizi: *Sultans* (Quatremere); I; ii; p. 34; Abul Feda: *Annales* (RHOr); i; p. 151. S. Runciman; op cit; p. 322.

[1613] J. Hayton: *Flor des Estoires*; op cit; pp. 177-8.

[1614] Ibid.

[1615] J.F. Michaud: *The History of the Crusades,* op cit, p. 26.

[1616] Ibid.

[1617] Ibid.

[1618] Baybars al-Mansuri: *Tuhfa;* op cit, p. 59.

al-Zahir proudly remarks that previous kings and princes had paid tribute to the Assassins, but under Baybars' rule the situation was reversed.[1619]

On Saturday, 18 March 1267 Baybars left Cairo in the company of only a few officers. His mere departure from Egypt caused a mood of panic in Acre, as may be gathered from a letter of the papal legate, Simon.[1620] Envoys from Acre sought out the sultan in Gaza, bringing with them gifts and a number of their Muslim captives.[1621] Soon after envoys from the Kingdom of Armenia and from Beirut arrived in Safad delivering Muslim prisoners to the Sultan and restoring money that had been stolen from Muslim merchants.[1622]

Whilst 1267 seems to witness a lull in hostilities, soon after the Sultan went on the offensive again.

8. Baybars' Military Campaigns (1268-1277)

Early in 1268 Baybars set out once more from Egypt. The only Christian possessions south of Acre were the Templar Castle of Athlit and John of Ibelin's town of Jaffa. John, who had always been treated with respect by the Muslims, died in the spring of 1266.[1623] His son Guy did not have the same prestige, but he had hoped that the Sultan would honour the truce that his father had made.[1624] Baybars' answer was not encouraging, though:

> The man with whom I have made the peace treaty is dead. Also, I have heard that the people of Jaffa are taking provisions to Acre, though this traffic is forbidden. They have set up a tavern in Jaffa and put a number of Muslim women into it, and they have deliberately undertaken other things that are not covered by truce terms.[1625]

Baybars also answered the envoys of the Count of Jaffa:

> The time is come in which we will endure no more injuries; when a cottage shall be taken from us, we will take a castle; when you shall seize one of our labourers, we will consign a thousand of your warriors to chains.[1626]

When the Mamluk army appeared on 7 March, Jaffa was in no state to defend itself. After twelve hours of fighting it fell to the Sultan.[1627] Many of the ordinary people were killed during the storming of the city. But when the citizens who had fled to the citadel agreed to surrender both city and citadel on condition that they

---

[1619] Shafi b. Ali: *Husn al-Manaqib alsirriya al-muntaza'a min al-sira al-Zahiriyya.* (Husn,) 117.

[1620] Selections, II, 218, n. 2 to p. 101.

[1621] P. Thorau: *The Lion of Egypt;* op cit, p. 177.

[1622] *Gestes des Chiprois;* 766; Ibn abd al-Zahir *Rawd;* 280-1. P. Thorau: *The Lion of Egypt;* p. 178.

[1623] S. Runciman: *A History;* op cit; p. 324.

[1624] Ibid.

[1625] Ibn al-Furat: *Tarikh;* op cit; pp. 107-8.

[1626] J.F. Michaud: *The History of the Crusades,* op cit, p. 17.

[1627] *Histoire d'Eracles* (Receuil); ii; p. 456.

should be allowed to go free with their possessions and their children, the condition was agreed.[1628] They left unhindered for Acre with the garrison under the protection and guard of an escort provided by Baybars.[1629] The castle was destroyed, and its wood and marble were sent to Cairo to serve as material for the great new mosque that Baybars was building there.[1630]

After Jaffa, Baybars set his aim on the Castle of Beaufort. On 4 April he appeared before the stronghold, which was already surrounded by Muslim troops. Siege equipment and war machines had already been brought up from Damascus.[1631] When the sultan arrived, his commanders had already opened up the weak points in the defences, so that on the following day, 12 April 1268, the bombardment began.[1632] As in other sieges, imams and ulamas were installed in the camp in order to raise the moral and religious strength of the soldiers.[1633] In the meantime, on the Christian side, in order to concentrate the defence effort on the castle itself, the Templars gave up the outer works of the stronghold.[1634] They had these erected only after the acquisition of Beaufort in 1260, probably to prevent the setting up of hostile siege engines near the stronghold.[1635] So on the following day Baybars had catapults erected on the walls of these outer works, and continued the bombardment from very close proximity. Under constant heavy bombardment the garrison surrendered after a few days. The women and children were sent free to Tyre, but the men were all kept as slaves.[1636] Due to its strategic role, the castle was repaired and strongly garrisoned by the Muslims.[1637]

On 14 May, 1268, Baybars launched his attack on one of the principal crusader strongholds: Antioch. The campaign against Antioch had extra significance because its ruler, Bohemond, had played a leading part in the alliance with the Mongols and the massacres of Muslims in Syria eight years earlier.[1638] In order to capture the city, Baybars divided his forces into three. One army went to capture Saint Symeon, thus cutting off Antioch from the sea; the second moved up to the Syrian Gates to prevent any reinforcements coming from Armenian Cilicia, and the third, and main force, was commanded by Baybars himself.[1639] With this army he took the direct route to Antioch, where the three corps were to reassemble. He advanced by Apamea (Afâmiya), crossed the Orontes below the twin castles of La Garde, and on the morning of 1 Ramadan/15 May 1268 halted a short distance

---

[1628] Ibn al-Furat: *Tarikh*; op cit; p. 108.
[1629] Shafi': *Husn;* op cit, 124-5.
[1630] Al-Makrizi: *Sultans* (Quatremere); I; ii; pp. 50-1.
[1631] P. Thorau: *The Lion of Egypt*; op cit; p. 188.
[1632] Ibn al-Furat: *Tarikh;* op cit; p. 111.
[1633] P. Thorau: *The Lion of Egypt*; op cit; p. 188.
[1634] Ibid.
[1635] *Selections*, II, 221, n.1 to p. 110.
[1636] S. Runciman: *A History*; op cit; p. 324.
[1637] Al-Aini: *Akd* (RHOr); ii; pp. 227-8.
[1638] S. Runciman: *History*; op cit; p. 316.
[1639] Ibid; p. 324.

before Antioch. Baybars sent a negotiator to the city demanding an annual tribute of 1 dinar per head of the population.[1640] Although the city had hitherto paid this sum to the Mongols, and by accepting this condition would have in fact been saved from the threatened doom, the city's envoys, who trusted the strength of their walls, refused.[1641] On the morning of Friday 18 May, Baybars surrounded the city on all sides, and the following day, he warned the Christians that he was about to attack the city. After he had sent the priests and monks back, the general storming of Antioch began.[1642] This attack is lengthily described by the contemporary Ibn al-Furat,[1643] but Runciman's description has the merit of depicting the event from both Muslim and Christian sources:

'Prince Bohemond was at Tripoli; and Antioch was under the command of its Constable, Simon Mansel, whose wife was an Armenian, related to Bohemond's Princess. The Constable had rashly led out some troops to try to dispute the investment of the city, and had been captured by the Mamluks. He was ordered by his captors to arrange for the capitulation of the garrison; but his lieutenants within the walls refused to listen to him. The first assault on the city took place next day. It was beaten back, and negotiations were opened once again, with no greater success. On 18 May the Mamluk army made a general attack on all sections of the walls. After fierce fighting a breach was made and the Muslims poured into the city. Even the Muslim chroniclers were shocked by the carnage that followed. By order of the Sultan's emirs, the city gates were closed, that none of the inhabitants might escape. Those who were found in the streets were slaughtered at once. Others, cowering in their houses, were spared only to end their days in captivity. Several thousands of the citizens had fled with their families to the shelter of the huge citadel on the mountain top. Their lives were spared, but their persons were divided amongst the emirs. On 19 May the Sultan ordered the collection and distribution of the booty. The number of captives was enormous. Many of the leading dignitaries of the government and of the Church were killed or were never heard of again.'[1644]

The principality of Antioch, the first of the states that the Franks founded in Outremer (Overseas), had lasted for 171 years. Its destruction was a terrible blow to Christian prestige, and it brought the rapid decline of Christianity in northern Syria. The Franks were gone, and the native Christians fared little better. It was their punishment for their support, not of the Franks but of those more dangerous foes to Islam, the Mongols.'[1645]

[1640] Primat Chronique traduite par jean du Vignay; in *Revue des Historiens de Gaule et de France*, ed., M. Bouquet et al; 24 vols, Paris; 1737-1904; 20.

[1641] P. Thorau: *The Lion of Egypt*; op cit; p. 191.

[1642] Ibid.

[1643] Ibn al-Furat: *Tarikh;* op cit; pp. 121-6.

[1644] *Histoire d'Eracles* (Receuil); ii; pp. 456-7. Al-Makrizi: *Sultans* (Quatremere); I; ii; pp. 52-3.

[1645] S. Runciman: *A History*; op cit; pp. 325-6.

After the fall of Antioch, nearby castles could no longer be held, thus causing the immediate collapse of crusader rule in Syria. The garrisons of Dargous, Kafr Dubbin and Cavea Belmys capitulated at the end of May, and were put into captivity. The Templars gave up the castles of Gaston (Baghras), Port Bonnel (Hisn Rusas) and La Roche de Roissol without a fight or even negotiation.[1646] The stronghold of Cursat (al-Qusayr), belonging to the Catholic patriarch of Antioch, quickly passed within Muslim territory, and thus became a last Frankish enclave in northern Syria. A treaty was made with Baybars, in which half of the territory of Cursat was awarded to him.[1647] The crusaders now only retained Tripoli, and their so-called Kingdom of Jerusalem was reduced to a slender coastal state consisting of Haifa, Acre, Tyre, Sydon and Beirut.[1648] King Hethoum of Armenia, for his part, in order to obtain peace from Baybars, promptly restored to the Muslims Behesna, Darbassak, Ra'ban, and other places, which the Armenian-Mongol alliance had won him years before.[1649]

Pleased with his military success, Baybars took a break to make his pilgrimage to Makkah.[1650] No sooner that was accomplished, he resumed his military campaign. In the summer of 1269, he moved north, to Syria, to check continuous Mongol attacks there.[1651] Baybars was most particularly weary of new developments which sought to bring Mongols and crusaders into closer alliance again. After Hulagu's death, his son, Abaqa, had succeeded him.[1652] Like his father, Abaqa had a Christian wife, Maria, married to him by the Patriarch of Constantinople.[1653] And like his father, Abaqa fervently supported the alliance with Christendom against the Muslims.[1654] To the Christians, in the words of Bar Hebraeus:
'God had gifted him with understanding and wisdom, a good nature and forbearance... He was loved by all people of his realm.'[1655]
A Georgian chronicler, likewise, writes:
'He was kind and good, gentle and just, charitable to the poor, and very lenient.'[1656]
In August 1267, Pope Clement IV wrote to him to praise him for his supposed conversion to Christianity.[1657] He was also assured by the same pope that 'the hour fatal to the Muslims was come.'[1658] The pope was referring to a new crusade, and Abaqa's role was central to it.

[1646] P. Thorau: *The Lion of Egypt*; op cit; p. 192.
[1647] Baybars al-Mansuri: *Tuhfa,* op cit, 62-4.
[1648] J. Glubb: *A Short History*; op cit; p. 211.
[1649] Al-Makrizi: *Sultans* (Quatremere); I; ii; p. 54 ff.
[1650] W.B. Stevenson: *The Crusaders*; op cit; p. 344.
[1651] Ibid.
[1652] B. Spuler: *The Muslim World: The Mongol Period*; tr., by F.R. C. Bagley; Leiden; Brill; 1960; p. 26.
[1653] J.M. Fiey: *Chretiens*; op cit; p. 33.
[1654] B. Spuler: *The Muslim World*; op cit; p. 30.
[1655] Bar Hebraeus: *Chronography*; op cit; p. 445.
[1656] Cited by J.B. Chabot: Histoire du patriarche Jabahaba III et du moine Rabban Cauma; tire a part de la *Revue d'Orient Latin*; vol I and II; Paris; 1895; p. 44; n.4.
[1657] C.R. Conder: *The Latin Kingdom;* op cit; p. 389.
[1658] Ibid.

During a visit to Alexandria, in November 1269, Baybars learned of the king of Aragon's impending crusade and his alliance with Abaqa.[1659] The new situation in Spain explains this first Spanish crusade to the Holy Land. Muslim rule in Spain, with the exception of Grenada, had now just ended. The Muslims had lost to the Christians the Balearic Islands between 1229 and 1235, Cordova in 1236, Valencia in 1238, Murcia in 1243-4, Jaen in 1246, and Seville, the Muslim capital, had fallen in 1248.[1660] King James I of Aragon had already distinguished himself in his wars against Muslims, and received the name of 'the Conqueror'. Now his anti Muslim ardour was directed to the Holy Land. In the spring of 1267 a Mongol embassy appeared in Perpignan (in modern southern France), and promised him Abaqa's friendship and support.[1661] Perhaps also to appease the pope, Clement IV, who was angered by an illicit sexual act of his, James resolved to take the cross. This had a favourable effect on the Pope since also at this time there occurred Baybar's run of victories against the Christian territories in the Holy Land.[1662] The timing was also right now that King Louis IX of France was making preparations for a new crusade.[1663] To safeguard the project from a military point of view, James sent Jaime Alarich of Perpignan as ambassador to Abaqa in the middle of 1267. Jaime returned after two years with ambassadors from the Mongol ruler, who repeated his earlier assurances of a combined attack on Baybars.[1664] On 4 September 1269 the fleet carrying the crusader army set sail from Barcelona. On his way, the King sent envoys to Abaqa informing him of his arrival, and that their paths should converge by Sis (Lesser Armenia).[1665] The plan for the meeting of the two armies in Lesser Armenia is confirmed by King James himself in his diary.[1666] Bad weather and storms, however, partially wrecked and scattered the Spanish fleet. James, who had to seek shelter in the harbour of Aigues Mortes, gave up his plan of going on crusade, and returned to Aragon. This was a serious setback, which weakened the crusade considerably. However, the situation was not all lost, the King's bastard sons, Fernando Sanchez and Pedro Fernandez, set sail again with part of the fleet and army for Acre, where they landed at the end of October.[1667] The Aragonese crusaders were received in Acre with great joy, especially as they had brought abundant provisions and horses, which were hardly obtainable in the Christian kingdom. Since too at this juncture the Mongols

---

[1659] Ibn al-Furat: *Tarikh;* VI; f. 179.

[1660] H.C. Lea: *The Moriscos of Spain*; Burt Franklin, New York; 1901; 1968 reprint. Al-Maqqari: *Nafh Al-Tib.* Translated by P. De Gayangos: *The History of the Mohammedan Dynasties in Spain* (extracted from *Nafh Al-Tib* by al-Maqqari); 2 vols; The Oriental Translation Fund; London, 1840-3. J. Read: *The Moors in Spain and Portugal*; Faber and Faber, London, 1974. S.P. Scott: *History of the Moorish Empire*; op cit.

[1661] P. Thorau: *The Lion of Egypt*; op cit; p. 199.

[1662] Rohricht: Der Kreuzzug des Konigs Jacob I, von Aragonien; *Mitteilungen des Instituts fur Osterreichiche Geschictsforschung*; (MIOG) 11; 1890; 372-78.

[1663] Ibid.

[1664] P. Thorau: *The Lion of Egypt*; op cit; pp. 199-200.

[1665] Ibn al-Furat: *Tarikh;* op cit; p. 137.

[1666] *Historia del Rey d'Aragon Don Jaime I. el conquistador*; ed. A. de Bofarull; Valencia 1848; ch. 282.

[1667] Ibid.

invaded northern Syria and thrust into the neighbourhood of Aleppo, new optimism arose in Acre.[1668] Baybars, on being informed of the arrival of the Aragonese and the appearance of the Mongols on his northern frontier, took the necessary measures to meet the twofold danger. He first sent emir 'Ala' al-Din al-Bunduqdar to Syria with an army corps to keep an eye on the Mongols' movements and, if necessary, to advance further north.[1669] On 18 November 1269 himself left Cairo with only a very small force, marched in very wet weather by Gaza to Damascus, where he arrived on 4 December. The sultan's confidence had not deceived him: at the report of his imminent arrival the Mongols retreated.[1670] The sons of James I and the crusaders were, however, extremely confident in their strength and determination to fight the Muslims and left Acre, in front of which they were stationed. Baybars received a report of the Franks' movements, and assembled with all speed the units stationed in Palestine.[1671] He crossed Jacob's Ford, and brought his troops in a night march close up to Acre. He ordered two emirs to attack the Christians with their troops, then to feign flight and to lure the enemy into the vicinity of Toron Saladini, where he, Baybars, lay in ambush with the main fighting force. On the way back to Acre, the crusading force of Oliver of Termes and Robert of Creseques with their men encountered the units of the two armies (18 December).[1672] Oliver of Termes thought it best not to get into a fight, but to retreat to Acre as quickly as possible. Robert of Creseques, however, insisted on fighting, since he had come to the Holy Land 'to fight for God's honour.' Baybars' stratagem had worked.[1673] In the ensuing fierce hand to hand fight, the Christians were utterly crushed; their losses amongst the nobility included the nephew of the King of Aragon, the deputy of the French King at Acre, and countless numbers of captives.[1674] The Christian army stationed before Acre did not dare get involved in the fight but withdrew behind the security of the city walls.[1675] Such was the dread of Baybars the Christians did not risk going outside the gates of Acre to bury the fallen until days later. The surviving crusaders, who had been welcomed with so much hope, made no further attempt to fight, and in the following spring they returned to Spain.[1676]

In the summer of 1270, there was launched another mighty crusade led by Louis IX, seconded by his brother, Charles of Anjou. Its destination was Tunisia. The subjugation of the Muslims in Africa, Mills points out, was seen not just as an enterprise aimed at restoring Christianity in North Africa, it was also to be a

---

[1668] Rohricht: Der Kreuzzug des Konigs Jacob I, von Aragonien; op cit, p. 378.
[1669] P. Thorau: *The Lion of Egypt*; op cit; p. 200.
[1670] Ibid.
[1671] Ibid.
[1672] Ibid.
[1673] Ibid; p. 201.
[1674] Ibn al-Furat: *Tarikh,* op cit, p. 137.
[1675] Yunini: *Dhayl;* op cit, II; c31.
[1676] Rohricht: Der Kreuzzug des Konigs Jacob I, von Aragonien; op cit, pp. 378-9.

necessary preliminary to success in Palestine.[1677] The excuse given for the crusade against Tunis, Michaud explains, was that the kingdom of Tunis

> Covered the seas with pirates, who infested all the routes to Palestine; it was, besides, the ally of Egypt, and might, if subdued, be made the readiest road to that country.[1678]

It was also of importance to the king of Sicily that the coasts of Africa should be brought under European subjection.[1679] Louis also believed it possible to convert the king of Tunis, and thus bring a vast kingdom under the Christian banners.[1680] Those who advocated the conquest of Tunis argued that the passages of the Mediterranean would be opened, and the power of the Mamluks would be weakened; and that after that conquest the army would march through Tunisia and modern Libya, and 'go triumphantly into either Egypt or Palestine.'[1681] Al-Makrizi says:

> It happened that this Frenchman (Louis IX), after escaping from the hands of the Muslims decided to attack Tunisia in the land of Africa, profiting by the plague and famine that were rife there, and he sent to summon the Christian kings to arms. He also sent to the pope who wrote calling on the Christian kings to join the campaign with Louis, giving them a free hand with the Church's wealth. Thus, Louis was joined by the Kings of England, Scotland, Toulouse, Barcelona, and whole host of other Christian princes. The Tunisian ruler, Al-Mustansir bi-llah sent ambassadors with 8,000 dinars to sue for peace, but they took the money, and did not make peace. Instead, they attacked Tunisia on 21 July 1270, disembarking in Carthage.[1682]

The Christians had reached the first object of their hopes; landing in Tunisia, and the camp and town of Carthage were their first gains.[1683] In response, from all parts of Africa the Muslims marched to assist the Tunisians.[1684] Preparations were likewise made in Egypt to meet the invasion of the Franks, and in the month of August, Baybars announced he was about to march to the assistance of Tunis.[1685] The troops which the sultan of Cairo maintained in the province of Barka received orders to set forward.[1686] Events, however, developed in such a manner as to render the Sultan's march unnecessary. Al Maqrizi again:

> The Muslims (in Tunisia) kept up the fight until the end of August, with violent battles in which many of both sides died. The Muslims were almost defeated when God liberated them. One morning (in August), the King of

---

[1677] C. Mills: *History of the Crusades*; op cit; p. 262.

[1678] J.F. Michaud: *The History of the Crusades*, op cit, p. 34.

[1679] Ibid.

[1680] Ibid.

[1681] Ibid, p. 36.

[1682] Al-Makrizi: *Kitab al-Suluk;* ed., M. Ziyade; Cairo; 1934; pp. 364-5.

[1683] C. Mills: *History of the Crusades*; op cit; p. 263.

[1684] J.F. Michaud: *The History of the Crusades*, op cit, p. 40.

[1685] Ibid.

[1686] Ibid.

France was found dead. Succeeding events led to the signing of the peace treaty and the departure of the Christians.[1687]

During his illness, Mills remarks, Louis did not cease to praise God, and supplicate for the people whom he had brought with him.[1688]

King Louis' death before Tunis relieved Baybars from marching to the assistance of the Tunisian sultan.[1689] He could now re-organise his war aims, and resume his fight against local foes. For months already he had been preoccupied with eliminating the Ismailis 'always the foci of a special kind of unrest,' Mayer says.[1690] Baybars had already dispatched an army corps to the castle of Masyaf, which was occupied in mid March 1270.[1691] The castle of Ullayqa was taken on 23 May 1271, and provided with a garrison.[1692] The Ismaili leader, Al-Rida died in a Cairo prison. In June, Mamluk units attacked the Assassins' castle of al-Rusafa and took possession of it.[1693] Already after the loss of Masyaf, the main Ismaili leader, Najm al-Din and his son, Shams al-Din, had asked the sultan for forgiveness, and appeared before him. For the future an annual tribute of 120,000 dirhams was imposed on the father, and Baybars prudently detained the son as a hostage.[1694] Once again the sultan had humbled the sect's prestige and further reduced its power. Since it was indeed of importance to him to completely destroy the Ismailis' political power, it was only a matter of time before he proceeded against them once more. No sooner had the danger of a crusade by Louis IX been averted, and the strongholds of Krac des Chevaliers and 'Akkār seized from the Christians, than Baybars accused Najm al-Din's son (who had been freed) of secret accords with the Franks.[1695] Baybars made preparations to take the field against him. Thereupon Shams al-Din once again submitted, but he was arrested and brought to Egypt. In October 1271 the Ismaili garrisons of al-Khawabi and al-Qulay'a surrendered their castles to the sultan's representatives.[1696] In May 1273 the castles of al-Maniqa and al-Qadmus followed suit, and on 10 July 1273 one of the sultan's emirs compelled al-Kahf to surrender.[1697] With the capture of this, the last of their castles, Baybars had finally crushed the once dreaded power of the Ismailis. Henceforward the sect no longer played an independent political role, and their territory was absorbed in the unified Mamluk state.[1698]

[1687] Al-Makrizi: *Kitab al-Suluk;* ed., M. Ziyade; op cit; pp. 364-5.
[1688] C. Mills: *History of the Crusades*; p. 263.
[1689] S. Runciman: *A History*; op cit; p. 333.
[1690] H.E. Mayer: *The Crusades*; op cit; p. 269.
[1691] Baybars al-Mansuri: *Tuhfa*; p. 68.
[1692] Ibn Abd al Zahir: *Rawd*; 384.
[1693] Ibid. 390.
[1694] Yunini: *Dhayl*; II; p. 432.
[1695] P. Thorau: *The Lion*; 202.
[1696] Ibn Abd al-Zahir: *Rawd*; 393-4.
[1697] Shafi': *Husn*; op cit, p. 151.
[1698] Qalaqashandi: *Subh al-asha fi sina'at al-Insha;* ed. M.A. Ibrahim; 14 vols; Cairo; 1918-1922; IV; 143; 202; Gaudefroy-Demombynes: *La Syrie a l'Epoque des Mamlouks;* Paris; 1923; 77; 182.

Baybars, in the meantime, had not set aside his primary objective: the final removal of Frankish power. In February 1271, he marched on the huge Hospitaller fortress of Krac des Chevaliers, Qalat al-Hosn. It was the principal retreat of the Knight Hospitallers, and probably 'the most beautiful military monument of the Middle Ages.'[1699] It had been in crusader hands since 1110, and even Salah Eddin was not able to capture it.[1700] Baybars opened the siege between 18 and 21 February.[1701] On 15 March, after a brief but heavy bombardment, the Muslims forced an entry into the gate-tower of the outer defence.[1702] A fortnight later they broke their way into the inner defence, killing the knights that they met there and taking the native soldiers prisoners. Many of the defenders held out for ten more days in the great tower at the south of the enceinte.[1703] The stronghold capitulated to Baybars on 8 April after successfully resisting all previous sieges. The garrison was permitted to withdraw to Tripoli.[1704] The capture of Krac, which had defied even Salah Eddin, gave Baybars control of the approaches to Tripoli.[1705]

Impressed by Baybars' latest conquests, the Templars of Tortosa, like the Hospitallers, asked for peace, which the sultan granted. It was to be valid for Tortosa and Marqab with the exclusion of the region of Chastel Blanc. The Hospitallers were forbidden from reinforcing the walls of the stronghold, and had to cede half of the territory of Marqab to the sultan.[1706] The Hospitallers were also required to give up all the revenues which they had hitherto drawn from Muslim areas. The Hospitallers' castle of Toron de Belda (Balda) with its territories was also to be ceded to the sultan, which caused the Order to strip Balda and the tower of Qarfis of all supplies and demolish them.[1707]

Now Baybars set about seizing from Bohemond VI the stronghold of Gibelacar (Hisn 'Akkr), near Tripoli. The siege began on 29 April, and catapults were installed on 2 May. In order to bring them across the trackless open country, it was first necessary to construct level roadways.[1708] Once the siege engines were in place, the bombardment began. After nine days of heavy bombardment, part of the eastern wall collapsed. The defenders offered to surrender in return for their safety, which was granted to them. On 12 May the garrison surrendered Gibelacar to Sultan Baybars, and withdrew to Tripoli.[1709]

[1699] P.K. Hitti: *History;* op cit; p. 657.

[1700] Ibn al-Furat: *Tarikh;* op cit; pp. 144-5.

[1701] D.J. Cathcart King: The Taking of Le Krak des Chevaliers in 1271; *Antiquity;* 23; 1949; 83-92; at pp. 88-92.

[1702] S. Runciman: *A History;* op cit; p. 334.

[1703] Al-Makrizi: *Sultans* (Quatremere); I; ii; pp. 84-5; Estoire d'Eracles (Receuil); ii; p. 460.

[1704] P. Deschamps: *Les Chateaux des Croises; Le Crac des Chevalliers;* Paris; 1934; 133. *Selections,* II. 239; n. 9 to p. 145.

[1705] Al-Makrizi: *Sultans* (Quatremere); I; ii; pp. 84-5; *Estoire d'Eracles;* ii; p. 460.

[1706] P. Thorau: *The Lion of Egypt;* op cit, p. 205.

[1707] *Selections,* II. 240; n. 1 to p. 147. Yunini: *Dhayl:* II; p. 448.

[1708] P. Thorau: *The Lion of Egypt;* op cit; p. 205.

[1709] Yunini: *Dhayl;* II; 448.

Later in the same year, 1271, a new crusade, that of Edward of England, arrived in the East. Edward was 'brave and provident, and owed his success to his skill and courage. But, he was not less cruel than any preceding hero of the holy wars, and once in the East, he would give 'a dreadful earnest of that savage implacability which Scotland afterwards so often rued,' says Hemingford.[1710] King Edward wanted to do what Louis IX first intended, to winter in Sicily and to go to the Holy Land in 1271 and re-conquer it with the help of the Mongols.[1711] Mongol envoys had arrived at Tunis after Louis' death.[1712] They could have come back to the east with Edward (who was part of Louis' crusade), which could explain why, soon after his arrival, Edward sent Brother Reginald Rossel, Godfrey de Waus and John le Parker in embassy to Abaqa.[1713] The latter answered from Maragha, in Iran, on 4 September 1271.[1714] A Mongol assault against Syria was imminent any time. Local Christians also joined the alliance. Edward, first, with 7,000 men attacked and took Nazareth, causing a massacre 'as pitiless as any which had sullied the chronicles of the crusades.'[1715] 'The barbarities which stained the entry of the Christians into Jerusalem two centuries before were repeated in a smaller theatre of cruelty in Nazareth,' says Mills.[1716] It was his first and last 'victory' in Palestine.[1717] In response to his call, in mid October 1271, 10,000 Mongol horsemen were sent to him. They devastated Syria, but on hearing of Baybars' advance in their direction, fled back to Iran.[1718] Discouraged by this, Edward signed a truce with Baybars and left the Holy Land.

On 28 November 1272 a report reached the sultan of a new Mongol attack on the Euphrates frontier.[1719] He immediately ordered one of his commanders to advance to the Hārim district with a contingent of Egyptian and Syrian troops. Another was sent out with a further corps, backed up by a contingent of Bedouin irregulars; Baybars followed with the main fighting force.[1720] After the Mongols had crossed the Euphrates, one of their armies proceeded to besiege al-Bira, while the other advanced on al-Rabba. Baybars therefore divided his army similarly. He seized the fishing-boats on lake Qadas near Hims, which were loaded on camels, and brought along for possible use in constructing a bridge of boats. When they heard of his advance, the Mongols stationed outside al-Rabba withdrew and took up position in a fortified camp on the further side of the

---

[1710] Hemingford, iii, 590; in C. Mills: *History of the Crusades*; vol 2; p. 265.

[1711] Cf. Richard: *St Louis;* pp. 558-566; esp. pp. 562-3.

[1712] *Chronicon Hanoniense quod dicitur Balduini Avennensis*; ed. J. Heller, in *Monumeta Germaniae Historica, Scriptores*, vol 25, ed., Georg Waitz (Hanover, 1880 repr. 1974); p. 463.

[1713] J. Paviot: England and the Mongols (1260-1330); *JRAS;* Series 3; 2000; pp. 305-318; at p. 309.

[1714] *De antiques legibus liber: Cronica maiorum et vicecomitum Londoniarum*, ed. Th. Stapleton (Camden Society, xxxiv), London, 1846; p. 143.

[1715] G.W. Cox: *The Crusades;* op cit, pp. 208-9.

[1716] Hemingford, iii, 590, in C, Mills: *History of the Crusades*, op cit, p. 265.

[1717] S. Runciman: *A History;* op cit; p. 336.

[1718] G. D'Ohsson: *Histoire;* op cit; pp. 459-60. S. Runciman: *A History*; p. 337.

[1719] Yunini: *Dhayl*, op cit, III; 2.

[1720] P. Thorau: *The Lion of Egypt*; op cit; p. 223.

Euphrates. Baybars, advancing from Manbij, arrived on 11 December, and ordered a bridge to be constructed. With his usual speed, and in order not to leave any time to the enemy, he gave orders to his army to ride through the river, on the assumption that the Mongols would keep watch on the ford, where the crossing was easiest. The enemy commander, Chinqar, however, anticipating Baybars' thinking, had deliberately chosen a place that was not shallow. When the sultan realized this, it was already too late-the Mamluk army found itself in midstream, and the soldiers had to swim across beside their horses, exposed to the shots of the enemy. Since to retreat would have caused confusion and panic owing to the continuing pressure of troops from the rear, and could have ended in disaster, Baybars repeated the order to attack the Mongols, who must have numbered in thousands.[1721] The difficulty of delivering an attack from the water against an opponent in a fortified position on the shore was considerable. Yet, under the exhortations of Baybars, two Mamluk commanders succeeded in reaching the bank in the foremost line of the army, followed by Baybars, who stormed the camp at the head of his troops. The two emirs on the wings succeeded in overthrowing the enemy positions. The Mongol army suffered utter defeat; Chinqar fell, and Baybars claimed the victory.[1722] Fearing now an attack in the rear, the second Mongol army (which according to the Persian chronicler, Wassãf, was twice as strong as the sultan's) broke off the siege of al-Bira. Leaving behind the military equipment and all its supplies, it retreated speedily.[1723]

Having checked both Mongol and crusader threats, Baybars now turned his attention back to the Armenians. The sultan's formal declaration of war against King Leo III of Armenia followed at the end of 1274 or beginning 1275. Since succeeding his father, the King of Armenia had repeatedly broken the Mamluk-Armenian treaty of 1268.[1724] Baybars accused Leo of failing to deliver the tribute imposed on the kingdom, and in addition of having permitted attacks on Muslim trading caravans.[1725] Baybars set out north from Cairo on 1 February 1275, and joined forces in Damascus with Syrian units.[1726] To stop an attack by the Mongols in the rear, an army corps under the emir al-Ayntabi raided out to Ra's al-Ayn.[1727] Baybars seized the bridge over the Jayhan at al-Massisa, and the town itself was captured.[1728] Then on 29 Ramadhan/28 March 1275, the sultan stood in front of the Armenian dominant city of Sis. There a fierce fight took place. The Sultan, once more, crushed his foes. The city was captured, and in the King of Armenia's palace, Baybars celebrated Eid al-fitr (the end of Ramadhan).[1729] King Leo could

---

[1721] Ibid.
[1722] Ibid.
[1723] Ibid.
[1724] Ibid.
[1725] Ibn Abd Al-Zahir: *Rawd;* op cit; p. 432.
[1726] Ibid; pp. 432-6.
[1727] Ibid.
[1728] P. Thorau: *The Lion*; op cit; p. 233.
[1729] Ibn Abd al-Zahir; *Rawd;* pp. 432-6; P. Thoreau: *The Lion*; op cit; p. 233.

only look on helplessly on the devastation of his country by Baybars.[1730] On his way back, passing by the territory of Antioch, Baybars seized the last crusader stronghold in Muslim territory: the Castle of Cursat (Al-Quysar), which surrendered to him on November 1275; the garrison was allowed to go freely.[1731]

In late 1275, Baybars launched military campaigns against the Mongols of Anatolia whose troops were stationed in the Seljuk realm.[1732] Anticipating his arrival, the Mongol leader Abaqa ordered the attack on the Mamluk stronghold of Al-Bira, which was besieged. The Mongol siege failed despite heavy bombardment as the fortifications had been reinforced by Baybars.[1733] Then, on hearing of Baybars' arrival, the Mongol army fled from the field.[1734]

It was in the spring of 1277 that Baybars made his final preparations for the main campaign against the Mongols. On his march to Syria, he, first, defeated Bedouin tribes allied with the Mongols. He then defeated an advanced Mongol corps on 12 April 1277.[1735] Two days later, he was able to look down from the heights of Elbrus on the main Mongol army, which had set out against him, encamped in the plain of Albistan beyond the Jayhan.[1736] The following day one of the most decisive battles between Mamluks and Mongols took place: The Battle of Albistan. On the morning of that day, the left wing of the Mongols opened the battle with an attack on the centre of the Mamluk army.[1737] The Mongols thrust deep into Mamluk ranks, broke through the centre, and attacked the Mamluk right wing from the flank. Baybars who was following the battle from the rear saw the danger of a flank attack, and hastened to the help of the threatened wing. In the meantime the Mongol right wing had come to blows with the Mamluk left, which it was about to break. At this critical moment, Baybars ordered the Syrian prince of Hamah, his ally, to get into the fight.[1738] The prince put himself at the head of the corps and mounted a counter attack on the Mongol right wing. As the fortune of battle turned in favour of the Mamluks, the Mongol general Tatawun dismounted his troops, on the one hand to prevent them from fleeing on horseback, on the other to force his Muslim opponents to fight a closely ranked infantry in a constricted space. His strategy failed, and the Mongol army was utterly destroyed in fierce hand to hand combat.[1739] Mongol losses were considerable.[1740] In the wake of this victory, Baybars made a triumphant entry into

[1730] P. Thorau: *The Lion*; op cit; p. 234.
[1731] Ibn Abd Al-Zahir: *Rawd*; op cit; 443-4.
[1732] Ibn Shaddad: *Tarikh al-Malik al-Zahir*; ed., A. Hutait; Wiesbaden; 1983; p. 107.
[1733] P. Thorau: *The Lion*; op cit; p. 236.
[1734] Al-Yunini: *Dhayl mir'at al-zaman*; 4 vols; Hyderabad; 1954-61; III; 165-6 etc.
[1735] P. Thorau: *The Lion*; op cit; p. 238.
[1736] The best account of this battle is by Ibn Shaddad: *Tarikh al-Malik al-Zahir*; op cit.
[1737] Ibn Shaddad: *Tarikh*; p. 182.
[1738] P. Thorau: *The Lion*; op cit; Appendix 6; p. 267.
[1739] Ibid; p. 239.
[1740] Ibn Shaddad: *Tarikh al-Malik al-Zahir*; op cit; pp. 171-2.

the capital of the Seljuks of Rum on 22 April 1277.[1741] Soon after this great victory, which literally broke Mongol power, Baybars' life ended.

Baybars died on 1st July 1277. Runciman's eulogy of him, although not affectionate, still acknowledges:

> His (Baybars) death removed the greatest enemy to Christendom since Saladin. When Baybars became Sultan the Frankish dominions stretched along the coast from Gaza to Cilicia, with great inland fortresses to protect them from the East. In a reign of seventeen years he had restricted the Franks to a few cities along the coast: Acre, Tyre, Sidon, Tripoli, Jebail and Tortosa, with the isolated town of Lattakieh and the castles of Atlilit and Marqab. He did not survive to see their entire elimination, but he had made it inevitable. Personally he had few of the qualities that won Saladin respect even from his foes. He was cruel, disloyal and treacherous, rough in his manners and harsh in his speech. His subjects could not love him, but they gave him their admiration, with reason, for he was a brilliant soldier, a subtle politician and a wise administrator, swift and secret in his decisions and clear-sighted in his aims. Despite his slave origins he was a patron of the arts and an active builder, who did much to beautify his cities and to reconstruct his fortresses. As a man he was evil, but as a ruler he was amongst the greatest of his time.[1742]

To Baybars' qualities, Stevenson adds:

> His swift secret movements were the wonder of his subjects. He had all the qualities of a brave soldier, a competent general and a clear sighted statesman. His valour and success gained him respect and fear. His capture of Antioch is itself sufficient to preserve his memory, and his achievements against the crusaders will always shed lustre on his name.[1743]

THE END OF THE CRUSADER EAST (1277-1291)

Baybars was succeeded by one of his sons, who made himself very unpopular and stepped down after two years (17th August 1279).[1744] His successor was a brother who was deposed in three months by Saif Eddin Qalawun (Qalaun) on 26th November 1279, who eventually succeeded Baybars.[1745] Qalawun, like Baybars, was a Qipchak Turk who had been brought to Egypt as a slave boy and sold to the Sultan Malik al-Salih Ayyub.[1746] Qalawun, Al-Makrizi says, was a strong, handsome figure,

[1741] P. Thorau: *The Lion*; op cit; p. 239.

[1742] S. Runciman: *History*; op cit; p. 348.

[1743] W.B. Stevenson: *The Crusaders*; op cit; p. 346.

[1744] Al-Makrizi: *Sultans* (Quatremere); I; ii; p. 171.

[1745] Abul Feda: *Annales*; op cit; v; p.50.

[1746] Al-Makrizi: *Sultans* (Quatremere); II; part three; p. 1.

who inspired respect, who spoke Turkic, but knew very little Arabic.[1747] Qalawun's rise to power was not without the customary problems following the death of a strong figure. He was in earnest challenged by Sunkur Al-Ashkar, who proclaimed himself sultan of Damascus early in 1280.[1748] Qalawun, however, retook the city soon after. The defeated Al-Ashkar sought Mongol help, and they took possession of Aleppo and its neighbourhood in October 1280.[1749] Taking advantage of the situation, the crusader knights of Al-Markab allied themselves with the Mongols, and raided the neighbourhood of Safitha, and defeated the emir of Hisn al-Akrad.[1750]

The Mongols based in Iran, whose power had been severely curtailed by Baybars, remained a threat, indeed. During the 1270s, prior to the advent of Qalawun, they constantly strived to strengthen their alliance with the Christian monarchs. In 1270, when Louis IX was on the crusade against Tunisia, Abaqa wrote to him pledging Mongol support as soon as the crusaders appeared in the Holy Land (which they failed to do). Then, in the following year, he exchanged embassy with Henry III of England.[1751] In mid October 1271, in the wake of Edward of England's crusade, Abaqa sent 10,000 Mongol horsemen in support.[1752] Edward's crusade failed, but two years later, in 1273, Abaqa sent a letter to Acre, addressed to Edward, asking when his next crusade would take place. Edward sent a friendly answer, but regretted that neither he nor the Pope had decided when there could be another expedition to the East.[1753] Mongol envoys appeared next year, 1274, at the Second Council of Lyons, and two of them received Catholic baptism from the Cardinal of Ostia, the future Pope Innocent V.[1754] In the autumn of 1276 two Georgians, the brothers John and James Vaseli, landed in Italy to visit the Pope, with orders to go on to the Courts of France and England. They carried a personal letter from Abaqa to Edward I, in which the former apologised that his help had not been more effective earlier in 1271.[1755] King Edward sincerely hoped to go on another crusade, but neither he nor Philip III of France were ready yet to do so.[1756] These efforts to rebuild the crusader-Mongol alliance were somehow hindered by the conversion to Islam of the Mongols of the Golden Horde (based in southern Russia), under Sultan Berke, which led to conflict with Abaqa's Mongols.[1757] It was, however, Baybars, who, with his incessant attacks and victories on the ground, had managed to break the power of both crusaders and Mongols and prevent any repetition of their earlier successes.

[1747] Ibid p. 111.
[1748] W.B. Stevenson: *The Crusaders*; op cit; 346.
[1749] Al-Makrizi: *Sultans* (Quatremere); II; i; p; 26.
[1750] Abul Feda: *Annales;* op cit; v; p. 54.
[1751] J. Richard: *Mongols and Franks*; op cit; p. 53-4.
[1752] S. Runciman: *A History*; op cit; p. 337.
[1753] Ibid; p. 347.
[1754] Ibid.
[1755] Ibid.
[1756] William of Nangis: *Gesta Ludovici* VII; in RHF; xx; op cit; pp. 540-64.
[1757] H.H. Howorth: *History of the Mongols*; op cit; iii; pp. 218-25.

Following Baybars' death, hopes for a fresh alliance were high again, and in 1280, at last, another Mongol-Christian coalition was in place ready to strike at the Muslim world. Abaqa sent an army into Syria, which was reinforced by the armies of Leo III of Armenia.[1758] Abaqa's aim was to strike against the Mamluks before Qalawun was able to consolidate himself.[1759] At the end of September 1280, the Mongol army, divided in three corps, crossed the Euphrates and occupied Aintab, Baghras and Darbsaq.[1760] On 20 October, the main army entered Aleppo. The population was killed en masse, the city was looted, many prisoners were taken, whilst colleges, hospitals, shops, mosques and houses were set aflame.[1761] Of the population, only those few who hid in caves and underground escaped the massacre.[1762] As the Mongols raided Syria, the Hospitallers of Marqab went on the attack in the Buqaia, penetrating almost to Krak and, on their return, defeated near Maraclea the Muslim army sent against them.[1763]

It was when the tide seemed to be turning against Islam, again, that a decisive battle was fought near Hims, in Syria, between the Muslims and the Christian-Mongol alliance. This followed the advance of two Mongol armies into Syria in September 1281. One, commanded by Abaqa in person, slowly reduced the Muslim fortresses along the Euphrates frontier. The second Mongol army, under his brother, Mangu Timur, first made contact with Leo III of Armenia, then marched down through Aintab and Aleppo into the Orontes Valley.[1764] The Hospitallers of the Castle of Marqab joined with the Mongols and the King of Armenia.[1765] The news reached Cairo that an enemy force, 80,000 strong (50,000 Mongols, and 30,000 Georgians, Armenians, and Franks,) was marching on Syria.[1766] Qalawun, who had already gone to Damascus, assembled his troops, and rushed northward to meet them.[1767] On 30 October 1281 the two armies met just outside Hims for a battle that was to determine the destinies of Syria.[1768] The fighting started at dawn. For long moments, the contest was fierce and the issue undecided, until summoning all their reserves of bravery, strength, and determination, the Muslims took the upper hand. The fight ended in a crushing defeat for the Christian-Mongol coalition, lamented by Armenian sources, in particular.[1769]

[1758] J.M. Fiey: *Chretiens;* op cit; p. 39.
[1759] S. Runciman: *A History*; op cit; p. 390.
[1760] Al-Makrizi: *Sultans* (Quatremere); p. 25.
[1761] Ibid.
[1762] Ibid.
[1763] S. Runciman: *A History*; op cit; p. 390.
[1764] Ibid; pp. 391-2.
[1765] Ibid.
[1766] Al-Makrizi: Sultans (Quatremere); p. 33; p. 35.
[1767] S. Runciman: *A History*; op cit; pp. 391-2.
[1768] Al-Makrizi: Sultans (Quatremere); p. 34 ff. S. Runciman: *A History*; op cit; pp. 391-2.
[1769] Table Chronologique de Hethoum; in *Receuil des Historiens Armeniens des Croisades*; I; p. 487.

In 1283, two years after the defeat of the Mongols, Qalawun removed the Maronite obstacle by taking their stronghold: Ehden et Hadat.[1770] After this success, all Christian lords of the southern Latin cities rushed to make treaties with him.[1771]

On May 25, 1285, Qalawun attacked the last great defence of the crusaders: the Castle of al-Marqab. This castle had been a major source of worry for the surrounding Muslim region. It looked like 'a dreadnought crowning a hill' near Tartus, and overlooking the sea.[1772] After yet another fierce fight, the Muslim standard rose over the battlements and 'a universal chorus of blessing was raised, and from the heights of the citadel the call to prayer resounded with praise and thanks to God.'[1773]

In February 1289, Qalawun attacked the crusader stronghold of Tripoli. With his combined Egyptian and Syrian armies, he besieged the city on the first Friday of the month of Rabi' I/25 March.[1774] Most of the city being surrounded by sea, the only approach by land was along a narrow bridge of land.[1775] In the attack, Qalawun used nineteen catapults and employed 1,500 artillery men and bombardiers.[1776] Al-Makrizi says that the city received support from the King of Cyprus, but the sultan kept up the intense bombardment, pressing the attack on the walls until at the seventh hour of Tuesday 4 Rabi II, after a siege of thirty four days, the city was taken by storm.[1777] By the time Qalawun departed, there was nothing left in the city.[1778] Following the fall of Tripoli, the main stronghold left in crusader hands was Acre.

It was early in April 1291 that the Muslim armies congregated outside Acre. According to the contemporary, Abu'l Mahasin:

'The siege of Acre began on Thursday [early in April]. Warriors from every country fought there. Such was the enthusiasm of the Muslims that the numbers of volunteers far surpassed that of the regular troops. Many machines were set up against the town; a few came from those which had already been taken from the Franks; some were so large that they hurled stones weighing a hundredweight and even more.'[1779]

The battle for Acre was fiercer than elsewhere, but in the end the city, half in ruins, yielded. An amazing coincidence occurred, notes Abu'l Feda:

'The Franks seized Acre from Salah Eddin at midday on 17 Jumada II 587, and captured and then killed all the Muslims therein; and God in His prescience

[1770] Duwayhi; p. 146; in A. Hoteit: Les Differentes communautes; op cit; p. 52.
[1771] J.H. Lamonte: Crusade; op cit; p. 195.
[1772] P.K. Hitti: *History*; op cit; p. 657.
[1773] Anonymous: *Tashrif al-Ayyam wal Usur bi Sirat Sultan al-Malik al-Mansur*; Ms Paris; Ar. 1704; pp. 149r-160r; in F. Gabrieli: *Arab*; op cit; p. 334 ff.
[1774] Abul Feda: *Mukhtassar* (RHOr); i; op cit; p. 162.
[1775] Ibid.
[1776] Al-Makrizi: *Kitab al-Suluk*; Ziade's ed.; op cit; p. 746.
[1777] Ibid.
[1778] J.H. Lamonte: Crusade; op cit; p. 195.
[1779] R. Pernoud: *The Crusades;* op cit; 281.

destined that this year (Friday 17 Jumada 1/18 May 1291) it should be re-conquered at the hand of another Salah Eddin, the Sultan al-Malik al-Ashraf.'[1780]
According to Ludolph of Suchem:
'When the glorious city of Acre thus fell, all the Eastern people sung of its fall in hymns of lamentation, such as they are wont to sing over the tombs of their dead, bewailing the beauty, the grandeur, and the glory of Acre even to this day. Since that day all Christian women, whether gentle or simple, who dwell along the eastern shore of the Mediterranean dress in black garments of mourning and woe for the lost grandeur of Acre, even to this day.'[1781]

The fall of Acre signaled the end of the Crusader East.[1782] On 19 May, al-Ashraf (Qalawun's son and successor) sent a large contingent of troops to Tyre.[1783] It was the strongest city of the coast, impregnable against an enemy that lacked command of the sea. In the past its walls had twice thwarted Salah Eddin himself. A few months earlier the Princess Margaret, to whom it belonged, had handed it over to her nephew, the King's brother, Amalric. But its garrison was small; and, as soon as the Muslims came on sight, Amalric's Bailli, Adam of Cafran, lost his nerve and sailed away to Cyprus, abandoning the city without a struggle.[1784]

At Sidon, the Templars determined to make a stand. Tibald Gaudin was there, with the treasure of the Order; and the surviving knights had elected him Grand Master to succeed William of Beaujeu, who had died in Acre.[1785] They were left in quiet for a month, then a large Muslim army appeared led by the emir Shujai. The knights were too few to hold the town; so they retreated with many of the leading citizens to the Castle of the Sea, built on an island rock a hundred yards from the shore, refortified not long before. Tibald at once set sail for Cyprus to raise troops for the castle's assistance. But once he was there he did nothing, either from cowardice or despair.[1786] The Templars in the castle fought bravely, but when the Muslim engineers began to build a causeway across the sea, they gave up hope and sailed away up the coast to Tortosa. On 14 July Shujai entered the castle and ordered its destruction.[1787]

A week later Shujai appeared before Beirut. Its citizens had hoped that the treaty made between the Lady Eschiva and the Sultan would protect them from attack. When the emir bade the leaders of the garrison to come and pay their respects to him, they complied and were made prisoners.[1788] Without its leaders the garrison

[1780] Abul Feda: *Annales (RHC Or)*; op cit; i; pp. 163-4.
[1781] Ludolph of Suchem: Description of the Holy Land (Brundage); op cit; p. 271.
[1782] Ibid; p. 270.
[1783] S. Runciman: *Histoire;* op cit; p. 421.
[1784] *Gestes des Chiprois;* op cit; p. 254; Abul Feda: *Annales (RHC Or)*; i; p. 164.
[1785] S. Runciman: *A History*; op cit; p. 422.
[1786] *Gestes des Chiprois*; pp. 256-7; Abul Feda: *Annales (RHC Or);* p. 164.
[1787] Ibid
[1788] S. Runciman: *A History*; op cit; p. 422.

could not contemplate defence, and so they took to their ships and fled, carrying with them the relics from the Cathedral. The Muslims entered the city on 31 July.[1789]

Haifa had been occupied without opposition the day before, on 30 July (1291).[1790] There still remained the two Templar castles at Tortosa and Athlit, but in neither was the garrison strong enough to face a siege. Tortosa was evacuated on 3 August and Athlit on the 14th. All that was left to the Templars was the island fortress of Ruad, some two miles off the coast opposite Tortosa. There they maintained their hold for twelve more years.[1791]

After the fall of Acre and other towns, the Kingdom of the Crusaders was ended.[1792] The religious dimension of the campaign was stressed at every stage of the way.[1793] It was seen and celebrated as 'the removal of the infidel from Muslim soil and the triumph of Islam over Christianity.'[1794]

> With these conquests [Abu'l-Feda concludes] all the lands of the coast were fully returned to the Muslims, a result undreamed of. Thus were the Franj, who had once nearly conquered Damascus, Egypt, and many other lands, expelled from all of Syria and the coastal zones. God grant that they never set foot there again![1795]
>
> For a century to come [Runciman says] the great ladies of Cyprus, where the Christian refugees from the Holy Land fled, when they went out of doors, wore cloaks that stretched from their heads to their feet. It was a token of mourning for the death of Outremer (Overseas Christendom).[1796]

[1789] *Gestes des Chiprois*; pp. 257-8; Abul Feda: *Annales (RHC Or)*; p. 164.
[1790] S. Runciman: *A History*; op cit; p. 422.
[1791] *Gestes des Chiprois;* p. 259; Abul Feda: *Annales (RHC Or)*; p. 164.
[1792] J.H. Lamonte: Crusade; op cit; p. 195.
[1793] C. Hillenbrand: *The Crusades*, op cit; p. 240.
[1794] Ibid.
[1795] In A. Maalouf: *The Crusades;* op cit; p. 259.
[1796] S. Runciman: *A History;* op cit; p. 423.

CAESAREA

ICONIUM

BAYBARS TAKES
CAESARIA 1277

TAURUS MOUNTAINS

ALBISTAN

BAYBARS DEFEATS
MONGOLS 1277

CILICIA

Mongol-Armenian
devastation of Syria
and Iraq 1258-1260

TARSUS

ALEPPO

R. Euphrates

MUSLIM CAPTURE
OF ANTIOCH 1268

ANTIOCH

CYPRUS
(LUSIGNAN)

HAMA

WADI AL-KHAZINDAR

HIMS

MUSLIM CAPTURE OF
TRIPOLI APRIL 1289

TRIPOLI

ANTIOCH-TRIPOLI

QALAWUN CRUSHES CRUSADER/
MONGOL ARMY 1281

Mediterranean
Sea

BEIRUT

SIDON

SYRIA

DAMASCUS

KINGDOM OF JERUSALEM

PRINCE EDWARD
LANDS AT ACRE 1271

TYRE
ACRE

SAFAD

CHRISTIAN-MONGOL ARMY
STORM DAMASCUS IN 1260

MUSLIM CAPTURE
OF ACRE 1291

HAIFA

MAMLUK VICTORY AT
AIN JALUT SEPT 1260

MUSLIM CAPTURE
OF JAFFA 1268

JAFFA

AL MANSURAH

JERUSALEM

GAZA

KHWARIZMIAN TURKS RECAPTURE
JERUSALEM FOR ISLAM 1244

EGYPT

MAMLUK VICTORY AT
AL MANSURAH FEB 1250

BATTLE OF
GHAZA 1244

CAIRO

R. Nile

MAMLUK
SULTANS:
Baybars   1260-1277
Qalaun   1279-1290

Mongol devastation
of eastern Islam 1219-1222

0   100   200   300   400   500 Miles
0   200   400   600   800 KM.

Overview of the second century of the Crusades (1194-1291)

THE CRUSADES: OUTCOMES AND NEW PLANS

In the words of Housley:

> 'The news of the Mamluk conquest of Acre had been received in the West with consternation rather than horror. Characteristically, recrimination was the order of the day, so that Thaddeo of Naples, who was present at the siege and wrote a valuable description of the city's fall at Messina at the end of 1291, criticized the behaviour of Henry II, the Italian merchants, and others. But it would be wrong to conclude that contemporaries were unaffected by the disaster, or that they regarded the Muslim occupation of the Holy Land as irreversible.[1797]

Indeed, the defeat of the crusaders and their removal from the Muslim East only constituted a phase in history, and the confrontation between the Christian West and Islam was by no means over. The conflict was to stretch for centuries and involve further regions of Christian-Muslim contact in military encounters, equally violent and bloody.

Crusading was also to take new forms, more complex and more sophisticated, consisting not just in sending armies, but also in imposing economic blockades on the Muslim world, beginning with Mamluk Egypt, the centre of Muslim power.[1798] The strategy also aimed at the capture of North Africa and bringing its population under Christian fold. This was seen both as a recuperation of a former Christian land and a pre-requisite for the conquest of the Holy Land.[1799]

As this grandiose scheme was put into action, there arose a new obstacle: Ottoman Turkey. Just, as the rise of the Mamluks took place at a time when Ayyubid power could no longer respond to the Christian-Mongol alliance, the rise of the Ottomans took place precisely at a time when the Muslim world had begun its long road to decline. The East had just been devastated by two centuries of crusader-Mongol wars, a devastation which, in places, it would never recover from. North Africa was divided into feuding local dynasties, and Muslim Spain, with the exception of Grenada, had just fallen under Christian rule.[1800] Turkey, therefore, became the primary objective of continuous crusader attacks by land and sea. As early as the 1330s, a wide alliance of Christian fleets and armies were

---

[1797] N. Housley: *The Later Crusades*; Oxford University Press; 1992; p. 22.

[1798] A.S. Atiya: *The Crusade in the Later Middle Ages*; Methuen; London; 1938.

[1799] R. Lull: *De Acquisitione Terrae Sanctae* (1309); in E. Kamar, 'Projet de Ramon Lull "De Acquisitione Terrae Sanctae", in *Studia Orientalia Christiana Collectanea* no. 6 (Cairo, 1961). R. Lull: *Liber de Acquisitione Terrae Sanctae*, Munich MS. Lat. 10565 ff.. 89 ro-96 vo. See also Longpre, in *Criterion* (Barcelona, 1927), III, 266-78.

[1800] C.H. Bishko: The Spanish and Portuguese Reconquest, 1095-1492; in *A History of the Crusades*; K.M. Setton ed; The University of Wisconsin Press; 1975; vol 3; pp. 396-456; Ch. E. Dufourcq: Un Projet Castillan du XIIIem siècle: La Croisade d'Afrique, *Revue D'Histoire et de Civilisation du Maghreb*, I (1966), pp. 26-51.

directed against Turkish positions in the Aegean.[1801] A decade later, in 1344, in response to a crusade preached in 1343, a combined papal, Venetian, Hospitaller and Cypriot fleet attacked Smyrna (Izmir).[1802] Many more attacks were carried out, most principally the crusades of Nicopolis in 1396 and Varna in 1444.

It was in the midst of Christian crusading and Ottoman counter crusading that the fate of Byzantium was decided.[1803] Byzantium and the Greek Orthodox Church were caught between both Catholic Christendom wish to terminate the Orthodox 'heresy,' and the Ottoman dread of a Catholic Byzantium at their door. In the view of Western Christendom, as explained above (The crusade of Constantinople of 1204), crusades against the Muslims would only succeed if the 'Greek heretics' were put under Catholic sway. According to the Dominican, Burcard's (14th century), for instance, in his *Directorium ad Philippum Regem,*[1804] 'the conversion to Catholicism of the Greeks, Nestorians and Jacobites was a sufficient incentive for the crusade.'[1805] When the Byzantine ruling elites, seeking to keep their political and other privileges, signed The Act of Union of the two Churches in 1439, and consecrated it in 1452, the fate of Byzantium was sealed. The act was reviled by both Greeks and Ottomans alike. One Greek dignitary, Lucas Notaras said:

> It would be better to have in Constantinople the rule of the Turkish turban than the Latin mitre.[1806]

To the Ottomans, the Union of the two Churches meant that Turkey would be attacked by land and sea by a more aggressive, united, Christendom.[1807] In 1453 the Ottomans captured Constantinople. By this they ended Byzantine existence as a ruling power, but in fact secured the survival of the Greek Orthodox Church under their rule for centuries to come until the rise of modern Russia, and subsequently the Soviet Union, secured its continuity.

These are the themes to be explored in the next volume.

[1801] P.E. Edbury: The Crusading Policy of King Peter I of Cyprus, 1359-1369; in *The Eastern Mediterranean Lands in the Period of the Crusades*; P.M. Hold Editor (Aris and Phillips Ltd; Warminster; 1977), pp. 90-105, at p. 91.

[1802] Ibid.

[1803] See Doukas: *Decline and Fall of Byzantium to the Ottoman Turks*; Wayne State University Press; 1975.

[1804] See: J. Delaville Le Roulx: *La France en Orient au XIV em Siecle;* Ernest Thorin Editor, Paris; 1886; pp. 89 ff. See Fr tr., by J. Mielot of Lille; B.N. fr. 5593 and 9087.

[1805] A.S. Atiya: *The Crusade in the Later Middle Ages;* op cit; p. 99.

[1806] M. Doukas: *Historia Byzantina*; ed., by I. Bekker (*Corpus Scriptorum Historia Byzantinae*;) Bonn 1834; p. 264.

[1807] Doukas: *Decline and Fall of Byzantium*; op cit, p. 181.

BIBLIOGRAPHY

-Abu al-Fadail: *Tarikh al-Mansuri* in *Bibliotheca Arabo-Sicula*; Second Appendix; Leipzig; 1887.

-Abu'l Fida (Abul Feda and other spellings): *Al-Mukhtassar fi Akhbar al-Bashar* (Annales); in *Receuil des Historiens Des Croisades; Historiens Orientaux* (RHC Or); Paris; 1841 ff. vol 1; pp. 1-186.

-Abu'l Fida: *Taqwim al-Buldan*; ed., Reinaud and De Slane; Paris; 1840.

-Abul-Fida: *Annales Muslemici*; ed., Reiske; vols iv and v; 1792-1794.

-Abu Shama: *Kitab al-Rawdatayn*; ed., M.H.M. Ahmad; 2 vols; Cairo; 1954.

-Abu Shama: *Kitab al-Rawdatayn*; in (RHC Or); vols iv-v

-Abu Shama; *Tarajim Rijal al-Qarnayn al-Sadis wa'l Sabi'*, Cairo, 1947 (repr. Beirut 1974);

-Al-Ayni: *Iqd al-Juman fi Tarikh Ahl al-Zaman*; ed. M.M. Amin, 2 vols; Cairo 1987-8; Also partial ed., and Fr. tr., in RHC Or, II; pp. 183-250.

-*The Alexiad of Anna Comnena,* tr. E.R.A. Sewter; Harmondsworth; 1969.

-M. Amari: *La Storia dei Musulmani di Sicilia,* 3 vols, Florence; 1854-1872.

-Ambroise: *The Crusade of Richard Lion-Heart by Ambroise;* tr. M.J. Hubert, with notes by L.L. La Monte; Columbia University Press; 1941; reprinted 1976.

-R. Amitai-Preiss: *Mongols and Mamluks*; Cambridge University Press; 1995.

-Anonymous: *Tashrif al-Ayyam Wal Usur bi Sirat Sultan Al-Malik Al-Mansur*; Ms Paris; Ar. 1704.

-T.A. Archer: *The Crusades*; T. Fisher Unwin; London; 1894.

-T.W. Arnold: *The Preaching of Islam*; Lahore: Sb. M. Ashraf, 1961.

-A.S. Atiya: *Crusade, Commerce and Culture*; Oxford University Press; London; 1962.

-A.S. Atiya: *The Crusade in the Later Middle Ages*; Methuen; London; 1938.

-A.S. Atiya: *The Crusade of Nicopolis*; Methuen & co. Ltd; London; 1934.

-M.W. Baldwin: *Raymond III of Tripolis and the Fall of Jerusalem (1140-1187)*; Princeton University Press; 1936.

-Baybars al-Mansuri: *Zubdat al-Fikra fi Tarikh al-Hijra*; Ms British Library Add 23325;

-Baybars al-Mansuri: *Kitab al-Tuhfa al-Mulukiya fil al-Dawla al-Turkiya*; ed. A.R. Hamdan; Cairo; 1987.

-Beha Eddin: *An-Nawadir al-Sultaniya* in RHC Or; iii.

-Beha Eddin: *Al-Nawadir al-Sultaniyya,* ed., J. El-Shayyal; Cairo; 1964.

-Beha Eddin: *The Life of Saladin*; London, Palestine Pilgrim's Text Society, 1897.

-Bellaguet, ed., *Chronique du Religieux de Saint-Denys, Contenant le Règne de Charles VI, de 1380 a 1422,* I (Paris, 1839).

-C.H. Bishko: The Spanish and Portuguese Reconquest, 1095-1492; in *A History of the Crusades*; K.M. Setton ed; The University of Wisconsin Press; 1975; vol 3; pp. 396-456.

-J.A. Brundage: *The Crusades*; The Marquette University Press; 1962.

-C. Cahen: *Orient et Occident au Temps des Croisades*, Aubier Montaigne, 1983.

-*The Cambridge Medieval History*, vol IV; edited by J.R. Tanner, C.W. Previte; Z.N. Brooke, 1923.

-John of Plano Carpini: *History of the Mongols*; IV; tr., by a nun of Stanbrook Abbey in *The Mongol Mission,* C. Lawson; New York; Sheed and Ward; 1955.

-J.L. Cate: The Crusade of 1101, in *A History of the Crusades;* ed., by K.M. Setton; University of Pennsylvania Press; 1955; vol 1; pp. 343-67.

-M. Chehab: *Tyr a L'Epoque des Croisades,* 2 vols, Paris, 1979.

-M. Ben Cheneb: Ibn Taimiyya: *Encyclopaedia of Islam*, 1st edition, Leyden; 1913.

-Paul E. Chevedden, «Fortifications and the Development of Defensive Planning during the Crusader Period», in *The Circle of War in the Middle Ages*, ed. Donald J. Kagay and L. J. Andrew Villalon, Woodbridge, UK, 1999, pp. 33-43.

-Paul E. Chevedden, «The Invention of the Counterweight Trebuchet: A Study in Cultural Diffusion», *Dumbarton Oaks Papers*, no. 54 (2000), pp. 71-116.

-Paul E. Chevedden, «Une innovation militaire decisive», *Qantara*, no. 41 (Autumn 2001), pp. 50-55.

-Paul E. Chevedden, «Black Camels and Blazing Bolts: The Bolt-Projecting Trebuchet in the Mamluk Army», *Mamluk Studies Review,* no. 8/1 (2004), pp. 227-277.

-*Chronicon Hanoniense Quod Dicitur Balduini Avennensis*; ed. J. Heller, in *Monumeta Germaniae Historica, Scriptores*, vol 25 ed., Georg Waitz (Hanover, 1880 repr. 1974).

-C.R. Conder: *The Latin Kingdom of Jerusalem;* The Committee of the Palestine Exploration Fund; London; 1897.

-Y. Courbage, P. Fargues: *Chretiens et Juifs Dans L'Islam Arabe et Turc*, Payot, Paris, 1997.

-G.W. Cox: *The Crusades*; Longmans; London; 1874.

-J. Curtin: *The Mongols; A History*; Greenwood Press Publishers; Westport; 1907.

-N. Daniel: *The Arabs and Medieval Europe*; Longman Librarie du Liban; 1975.

-C. Dawson: *The Mongol Mission*; Sheed and Ward; London; 1955.

-*De Toulouse a Tripoli*, Colloque held between 6 and 8 December, 1995, University of Toulouse; AMAM, Toulouse, 1997.

-M. Defourneaux: *Les Francais en Espagne aux 11 et 12em Siecles*; PUF; 1949.

-J.P. Donavan: *Pelagius and the Fifth Crusade*; University of Pennsylvania Press; 1950.

-M. Doukas: *Historia Byzantina*; ed., by I. Bekker (*Corpus Scriptorum Historia Byzantinae*;) Bonn 1834.

-Doukas: *Decline and Fall of Byzantium to the Ottoman Turks*; Wayne State University Press; 1975.

-J.W. Draper: *A History of the Intellectual Development of Europe*; George Bell and Sons, London, 1875.

-Ch. E. Dufourcq: Un Projet Castillan du XIIIe siècle: La Croisade d'Afrique, *Revue D'Histoire et de Civilisation du Maghreb*, I (1966), pp. 26-51.

-W. Durant: *The Age of Faith*, Simon and Shuster, New York; 6th printing; 1950.

-Al-Duri: *Tarikh al-Iraq*; Baghdad; 1948.

-P. W. Edbury: *The Conquest of Jerusalem and the Third Crusade*, Scolar Press, 1996.

-N. Elisseeff: *Nur al-Din: Un Grand Prince Musulman de Syrie au Temps des Croisades*; Damascus; 1967.

-*Encyclopaedia of Islam*, Leyden; Brill.

-*Epistolae Innocenti III* (ref as Inn. Ep); ed. Baluze, 1683, Publ J. Migne in *Patrologia Latina,* vols 214-217, Paris 1855.

-M. Erbstosser: *The Crusades;* David and Charles; Newton Abbot; first published in Leipzig; 1978.

-*Extraits de l'Histoire des Patriarches d'Alexandrie Relatifs au Siege de Damiette*; tr. E. Blochet, *ROL.* XI (1908).

-Fidenzio of Padua: '*Liber Recuperationis Terrae Sanctae,*' edition G. Golubovich: Bibliotheca bio-bibliografica della Terra Santa; 5 vols; Florence; 1906-27.

-J.M. Fiey: *Chretiens Syriaques Sous les Mongols;* Louvain; 1975.

-J.M. Fiey: Chretiens Syriaques entre Francs et Mongols, in *Orientalia Chris. Analecta*, no197, 1974, pp. 334-41.

-R. Finucane: *Soldiers of the Faith*; J.M. Dent and Sons Ltd; London, 1983.

-*The Chronicles of Froissart*, tr. J. Bourchier, Lord Berners; London: D. Nutt, 1903.

-Fulchert of Chartres: *A History of the Expedition to Jerusalem 1095-1127*; tr., by F. Rita Ryan; Knoxville: University of Tennessee Press; 1969.

-F. Gabrieli: *Arab Historians of the Crusades*; London; Routledge; 1957.

-D. Geanakoplos: Byzantium and the Crusades 1354-1453; in K.M. Setton ed., *A History of the Crusades*; op cit; pp. 69-103

-*Gesta Francorum et Aliorum Hierosolimitanorum*, ed. K. Mynors, tr. R. Hill; London, 1962.

-*Les Gestes des Chiprois*, ed. G. Raynaud (Societe de l'Orient Latin; Serie historique, 5), Geneva 1887.

-Al-Ghazali: *Manaqib al-Turk*; tr. Harley-Walker.

-E. Gibbon: *The Decline and Fall of the Roman Empire*; vol 5; ed. W. Smith; London, 1858.

-S.J. Joseph Gill: *Byzantium and the Papacy 1198-1400*; Rutgers University Press; New Jersey; 1979.

-J. Glubb: *A Short History of the Arab Peoples*; Hodder and Stoughton, 1969.

-J. Godfrey: *1204 The Unholy Crusade*; Oxford University Press; 1980.

-V. Goss Editor: *The Meeting of Two Worlds;* Medieval Institute Publication; Kalamazoo; Michigan; 1986.

-A. Gottron: *Ramon Lulls.. in Ahbhandlungen zur Mittleren...* ed. G.W. Below; H. Finke u; F. Meinecke, Heft 39; Berlin; 1912.

-R. Grousset: *Histoire des Croisades et du Royaume Franc de Jerusalem;* Paris; 1934-5.

-W.Z. Haddad: The Crusaders Through Muslim Eyes: *The Muslim World;* vol 73; pp. 234-52.

-L. Hambis: La Legende du Pretre Jean; in *La Tour St Jacques;* No 8; Jan-Feb 1957; pp. 31-47.

-L. Hambis: Saint Louis et les Mongols; in *JRAS;* 1970; pp. 25-33.

-J. Hayton: La Flor des Estoires de la Terre d'Orient, in *Receuil des Historiens des Croisades Armeniens;* vol ii; Paris; 1906; pp. 111-253.

-Hayton: *Histoire Orientale ou des Tartares;* tr., by N. Falcon: in *Receuil des divers voyages curieux faits en Tartarie, en Perse et ailleurs;* ed., by M. Molther; 1829.

-Bar Hebraeus: *The Chronography of Abu'l Farradj... Bar Hebraeus;* 2 vols; English tr. E.A. Budge Wallis; Oxford University Press; 1932.

-Baron Henrion: *Histoire generale des missions Catholiques depuis le XIII siecle jusqu'a nos jours* (1846).

-C. Hillenbrand: *The Crusades, Islamic Perspectives,* Edinburgh University Press; 1999.

-R. Hill: The Christian view of the Muslims at the time of the First Crusade; in *The Eastern Mediterranean Lands in the Period of the Crusades;* P.M. Hold Editor; Aris and Phillips Ltd; Warminster; 1977.

-P.K. Hitti: *History of the Arabs;* MacMillan and Co. Ltd; London; 1937.

-N. Housley: *The Later Crusades;* Oxford University Press; 1992.

-R.G. Hoyland: *Seeing Islam as Others Saw It;* The Darwin Press, Inc; Princeton; New Jersey; 1997.

-R.S. Humphreys: *From Saladin to the Mongols;* State University of New York Press Albany; 1977.

-R.S. Humphreys, 'Ayyubids, Mamluks and the Latin East in the thirteenth century', *Mamluk Studies Review,* 2 (1998), pp. 1-18.

-Ibn al-'Adim (Kemal Eddin): *Zubdat al-Halab Fi Tarikh Halab,* S. Al-Dahan, Damascus; 1955.

-Ibn al-'Adim (Kemal Eddin): *Muntakhabat Min Tarikh Halab;* in *RHC Or;* vol iii.

-Kemal Eddin: *Zubdat al-Halab Fi Tarikh Halab;* tr., as Histoire d'Alep de Kamal Ad-Din by E. Blochet; in *Revue de L'Orient Latin* (ROL); vols 3-6.

-Ibn Abd al-Zahir: *Al-Rawd al-Zahir fi Sirat al-Malik al-Zahir* (Rawd); ed., A.A. Khuwayter; Riyadh; 1976. Partial ed., and tr. F. Sadeque: *Baybars I of Egypt;* Dacca; 1956.

-Ibn al-Athir: *Kitab al-Kamil;* ed., K.J. Tornberg; 12 vols; Leiden; 1851-72.

-Ibn al-Athir: Kamil in *RHC Or;* vol i.

-Ibn al-Athir: *Tarikh al-Dawla Al-Atabakiyya;* ed. A.A. Tulaymat; Cairo; 1963.

-Ibn al-Athir: Tarikh al-Dawla; in *RHC Or* vol ii.

-Ibn al-Dawadari: *Kunz al-Dura;* ed. U. Haarmann; Freiburg; 1971.

-Ibn Al-Furat tr., by U. and M.C. Lyons: *Ayyubids, Mamluks and Crusaders, Selection from the Tarikh al-Duwal wal Muluk of Ibn al-Furat*; 2 vols, W. Heffer and Sons Ltd, Cambridge, 1971.

-Ibn al-Furat: *Tarikh al-Duwal wal Muluk;* ed. M.F. El-Shayyal; unpublished Ph.d. thesis; University of Edinburgh; 1986.

-Ibn Iyas: *Badai al-Zuhur fi Waqa'i al-Duhur*; Bulaq; 1311.

-Ibn Jubayr: *The Travels of Ibn Jubayr*; tr. R.J.C. Broadhurst; London; 1952.

-Ibn Khaldun: *Kitab al-Ibar*; Cairo: Dar al-Tab'a al-Amira; 1867-8.

-Ibn-Khaldun, *Histoire des Berberes*, tr. de Slane, III (Paris, 1934).

-Ibn Khalikan: W*afayat al-Ayan wa-Anba Abna al-Zaman*, Maymunyah Press, Cairo, 1888.

-Ibn Khalikan: *Wafayat (Biographical Dictionary)*, tr., M. De Slane Duprat, Paris and Allen & Co., London, 1843.

-Ibn Kathir: *Al-Bidaya wa'l nihaya fi'l tarikh*; rprt. Beirut; 1977; 14 vols.

-Ibn al-Qalanisi: *The Damascus Chronicle of the Crusades*, tr., of Ibn al-Qalanisi, H.A. R. Gibb; London, Luzac and Co, Ltd, 1932.

-Ibn al-Qalanisi: *Dayl Tarikh Dimashk;* ed. H.F. Amedroz; Leiden; 1908.

-Ibn Shaddad: *Tarikh al-Malik al-Zahir;* ed. A. Hutait; Wiesbaden; 1983.

-Ibn al-Suqa'i: *Tali Kitab Wafayat al-Ayan;* ed., and tr. J. Sublet; Damascus; 1974.

-Ibn Taghri-Birdi: *Al-Nujum al-Zahirah fi Muluk Misr wa'l Qahira;* ed. T.G.J. Juynboll; vol 2; Leyden; 1855.

-Ibn Taghri- Birdi: *Al-Nujum al-Zahira fi Muluk Misr wa'l Qahira;* Cairo; 1938; vol vii.

-Ibn Taymiyya: *Lettre a un Roi Croise*; tr., J.R. Michot; Louvain; 1995.

-Ibn Wasil: *Mufarrij al-Kurub fi Akhbar Bani Ayyub;* ed., G. Shayyal, S. Ashur, and H. Rabi'; 4 vols; Cairo, 1954-62.

-Ibn Wasil: *Mufarrij al-Kurub fi Akhbar Bani Ayyub*; MSS. Bibliotheque Nationale ar. 1702-3 [two separate Mss of the same work]; Ms 1703; fols 150a, 151 a-b.

-Ibn Zafir: *Akhbar al-Duwal al-Munqati'a;* ed., A. Ferre; Cairo; 1972.

-Imad Eddin al-Isfahani: *Sana al-Barq al-Shami*; summarized by al-Bundari; ed. F. al-Nabarawi; Cairo; 1979.

-Imad Eddin al-Isfahani: *Al Fath al-Qusi fi 'l fath al-Qudusi*; Landberg ed., Leyden; 1888.

-H. Inalcik, The Ottoman Turks and the Crusades; 1329-1451; in K. Setton ed., *The Crusade*; op cit.

-Al-Jahiz: *Opuscula*, tr. Walker, *JRAS*, 1915.

-J. Joinville: *Histoire de St Louis*; ed., de Wailly; Paris; 1874.

-J. Joinville: *Memoirs of the Crusades by Villehardouin and de Joinville* tr., by Sir Frank Marzials; published by J.M. Dent; London and Toronto; 1908.

-N. Jorga: Latins et Greeks d'Orient; *Byzantiniche Zeitschrift*; XV; 1906; pp. 179-222.

-N. Jorga: *Notes et Extraits Pour Servir a L'Histoire des Croisades au XVem Siecle*; Paris; Ernest Leroux; 1899; and 1902.

-N. Jorga: *Philippe Mezieres (1327-1403) et la croisade au XIVem siecle*; Bibliotheque de l'Ecole des Hautes Etudes. Fasc 110. Paris; 1896.

-A.A. Khowaiter, *Baibars the First;* The Green Mountain Press; London, 1978.

-M.A. Kohler: 'Al-Afdal und Jerusalem-was versprach sich Agypten vom ersten Kreuzzug 7', *Saeculum,* 37 (1986), pp. 228-39.

-A.C. Krey: *The First Crusade: The Accounts of Eyewitnesses and Participants*, Princeton University Press; 1921.

-Kutubi, *Fawat al-Wafayat,* Bulaq, 1299/1881-2.

-J.H. Lamonte: Crusade and Jihad: in N.A. Faris ed., *The Arab Heritage*, Princeton University Press, 1944; pp. 159-98.

-S. Lane Poole: *Saladin and the Fall of the Kingdom of Jerusalem*; Beirut; Khayats; 1964.

-G. Le Strange: *The Lands of the Eastern Caliphate*; Cambridge University Press; 1930.

-Kervyn de Lettenhove, ed., *Oeuvres de Froissart,* XIV (Brussels, 1872).

-H.M. J. Loewe: The Seljuqs: in *The Cambridge Medieval History*, vol IV; edited by J.R. Tanner et al; 1923; pp. 299-317.

-J.P. Lomax: Frederick II, His Saracens, and the Papacy, in *Medieval Christian Perceptions of Islam,* edited by J.V. Tolan; Routledge; London.

-R. Lull: *De Acquisitione Terrae Sanctae* (1309); in E. Kamar, 'Projet de Ramon Lull "De Acquisitione Terrae Sanctae", in *Studia Orientalia Christiana Collectanea* no. 6 (Cairo, 1961).

-R. Lull: *Liber de Acquisitione Terrae Sanctae,* Munich MS. Lat. 10565 ff.. 89 ro-96 vo. See also Longpre, in *Criterion* (Barcelona, 1927), III, 266-78.

-Guillaume Machaut: *La Prise d'Alexandrie ou Chronique du Roi Pierre 1er de Lusignan;* ed. Mas de Latrie; Soc de l'Orient Latin; Geneva; 1877.

-Al-Makrizi (Al-Maqrizi): *Al-Mawaiz wal Itibar fi Dikr al-Khitat wal Athar* (Khitat); 2 vols; Bulaq; 1853-4.

-Al-Makrizi: *Al-Mawaiz wal Itibar...;* ed., by A.A. al-Mulaiji. 3 Vols. Beirut: Dar al-Urfan. 1959.

-Al-Makrizi: *Kitab al-Suluk li Ma'arifat Duwal al-Muluk*; (Suluk); ed., M.M. Ziyada and S.A.F. Ashour; 4 vols; Cairo 1956-1972; partial tr. E. Quatremere: Histoire des Sultans Mamlouks; 2 vols; Paris 1845; partial tr. R.J.C. Broadhurst: *A History of the Ayyubid Sultans of Egypt*; Boston; Mass; 1980;

-Al-Makrizi: *Kitab al-Suluk,* translated as Histoire de l'Egypte de Makrizi by E. Blochet; *Revue de l'Orient Latin;* vols viii-xi; Paris.

-Mathew Paris: *Chronica Majorca*; ed., Luard; Rolls Society; 7 vols; London; 1872-84.

-H.E. Mayer: *The Crusades*; tr. J. Gillingham; Oxford University Press; 1972.

-D. Metlitzki: *The Matter of Araby in Medieval England*, Yale University Press, 1977.

-C. Mills: *History of the Crusades*; 2 vols; Longman; London; 1821; vol 2.

-Mudjir Eddin: *Al-Euns al-Jalil bi Tarikh el-Qods wa'l Khalil*, tr., into French as Histoire de Jerusalem et Hebron, by H. Sauvaire; Paris; Ernest Leroux; 1875; and 1926.

-Awad Munis: *al-Rahhala Al-Awrubiyyun Fi Al-Bayt Al-Maqdis*, Cairo, 1992.

-D.C. Munro, "Urban and the Crusaders", Translations and Reprints from the *Original Sources of European History*, Vol 1:2, 1895, pp. 5-8

-D.C. Munro: The Western attitude toward Islam during the period of the Crusades; *Speculum* vol 6, No 4, pp. 329-43.

-Al-Nuwayri: *Nihayat al-Arab fi Funun al-Adab*; XXVIII; ed. S.A. Al-Nuri; Cairo; 1992.

-Nicetas Choniates: *Historia,* ed., I. Bekker; 1835.

-Al-Nuwairi: *Al-Ilmam Bil'lam...* al-Askandaria; vol 1; in 2 parts; Berlin Mss. We. 359-60 and vol 2; Cairo; Ms.; Hist; 1449.

-Baron G. d'Ohsson: *Histoire des Mongols*; 3 vols; La Haye et Amsterdam; 1834.

-Z. Oldenbourg: *The Crusades*; tr., from the French by A. Carter; Weinfeld and Nicolson; London; 1965.

-C.W.C. Oman: *A History of the Art of War in the Middle Ages*; 2 vols; London; 1924.

-C.W.C. Oman: *A History of the Art of War*; Methuen; London; 1898.

-Jean Cabaret d' Orville: *La Chronique du Bon Duc Loys de Bourbon,* ed. A.M. Chazaud, Paris, 1876.

-Oliver of Paderborn: *The Capture of Damietta*; tr. J.J. Gavigan; University of Pennsylvania; 1948.

-Mathew Paris: *Chronica Majorca*; ed., Luard; Rolls Society; 7 vols; London; 1872-84.

-*Patrologia Latina*, ed. J.P. Migne; Paris, 1853.

-R. Payne: *The Crusades*; Wordsworth Editions; London; 1986.

-P. Pelliot: *Mongols and Popes; 13th and 14th Centuries*; Paris; 1922.

-P. Pelliot: Les Mongols et la Papaute; in *Revue d'Orient Chretien*; 1923-1924; and 1931-2.

-P. Pelliot: Mellanges sur l'Epoque des Croisades; *Memoires de l'Academie des Inscriptions des Belles Lettres*; 44; 1960.

-R. Pernoud: *The Crusades;* tr. E. McLeod; Secker &Warburg; London; 1962.

-H. Prutz: *Kulturgeschichte der Kreuzzuge*; Berlin, 1883.

-Qalaqashandi: *Subh al-Asha fi Sina'at al-Insha;* ed. M.A. Ibrahim; 14 vols; Cairo; 1918-1922.

-*Receuil des Historiens des Croisades;* Imprimerie Nationale; Paris; 1841 ff.

-*Historiens occidentaux (RHC Occ);* 5 vols; Paris; 1844-1895.

-*Historiens Orientaux (RHC Or);* 5 vols; Paris; 1872-1906.

-*Historiens Grecs (RHC Greek);* 2 vols; Paris; 1875-1881.

-*Historiens Armeniens (RHC Arm);* 2 vols; Paris; 1869-1906.

-*Revue des Historiens de Gaule et de France*, ed., M. Bouquet et al; 24 vols, Paris; 1737-1904.

-P. Riant: *Expeditions et Pelerinages des Scandinaves en Terre Sainte au Temps des Croisades;* Paris; 1865.

-R. Rohricht: Die Kreuzzuge der Grafen Theobald von Navarra und Richard von Cornwallis, in *Forschungen zur deutschen Geschichte*, 26 (1866).

-R. Rohricht: Der Kreuzzug des Konigs Jacob I, von Aragonien; *Mitteilungen des Instituts fur Osterreichiche Geschictsforschung;* (MIOG) 11; 1890.

-R. Rohricht: *Forshungen zur Deutschen Gescghichte*; XVI; 1876.

-R. Rohricht: Zur innen Geschichte des Kreuzzuges,' in *Studien zur Geschichte des Funften Kreuzzuges*; Innesbruck, 1891.

-R. Rohricht: *Zeitschrift fur Kirchengeschichte (ZKG)*; vols 1406; 1894-6; vol XV (1895).

-R. Rohricht: *Geschichte des Konigreichs Jerusalem*; Innsbruck 1898.

-R. Rohricht: *Beitrage zur geschichte der Kreuzzuge*; 2 vols; Berlin; 1874-78.

-R.A. Rotz on J.J. Saunders: *A History of Medieval Islam*; Routledge; London; 1965.

-S. Runciman: *A History of the Crusades*, in 3 vols; Cambridge University Press, 1962.

-S. Runciman: *The Fall of Constantinople 1453*; Cambridge University Press; 1965.

-Al-Safadi: *Al- Wafi bi'l Wafayat;* ed. Ritter et al; Wiesbaden; 1931-; 20 vols to date.

-M. Sanudo: *Liber secretorum...*; edited by Bongars; Gesta Dei per Francos; T II; Hanover; 1611.

-J.J. Saunders: *Aspects of the Crusades*; University of Canterbury Publishing; Canterbury; 1962.

-J.J. Saunders: *The History of the Mongol Conquests;* Routlege & Kegan Paul; London; 1971.

-K.I. Semaan ed., *Islam and the Medieval West;* State University of New York Press/Albany; 1980.

-K. M. Setton: *A History of the Crusades*; K.M. Setton ed., The University of Wisconsin Press; 1975; vol 3.

-Al-Shafi: *Husn al-Manaqib al-Sirriya al-muntaza'a min al-sira al-zahiriya* (Husn); ed. A. Khwaiter; Riyadh; 1976.

-E. Siberry: *The New Crusaders*; Ashgate; Aldershot; 2000.

-Sibt al-Jawzi: *Al-Muntazam Fi Tarikh Al-Muluk Wa'l Umam*; X; Hyderabad; 1940; VIII/ 2.

-Sibt al-Jawzi: *Mir'at al-Zaman;* Partial edition by Jewett; Chicago; 1907.

-E. Siwan: *L'Islam et la Croisade*; Paris; Maisonenuve; 1968.

-E. Siwan: La Genese de la Contre Croisade; *Journal Asiatique*; 254 (1966), pp. 199-204.

-V. Slessarev: *Prester Jean: The Letters and the Legend;* 1959.

-B. Spuler: *History of the Mongols*; London, Routledge & Kegan Paul, 1972.

-B. Spuler: *The Muslim World: The Mongol Period*; tr., by F.R. C. Bagley; Leyden; Brill; 1960.

-B. Spuler: Die Mongolen und das Christentum, in *Internationale Kirchichte Zeitschrift;* Bern; 28; 1938; pp. 156-75.

-W.B. Stevenson: *The Crusaders in the East*; Cambridge University Press; 1907.

-R.W. Southern: *Western Views of Islam in the Middle Ages*, Harvard University Press, 1978.

-Al-Sulami: Un Traite Damasquin du debut du XIIem siecle, ed., E. Siwan, *Journal Asiatique*, 1966.

-J.W. Sweetman: *Islam and Christian Theology*; Lutterworth Press; London; 1955; Vol I; Part II.

-Thaddeo of Naples: *Hystoria de Desolacione...* in AD MCCXCI; ed. Comte Riant; Geneva; 1873.

-P. Thorau: *The Lion of Egypt;* tr., by P.M. Holt; Longman; London; 1992.

-P. Thorau: The Battle of Ayn Jalut: a Re-Examination; in P.W. Edbury: *Crusade and Settlement*; Cardiff; 1985; pp. 236-41.

-J.V. Tolan ed., *Medieval Christian Perceptions of Islam*; Routledge; London; 1996.

-A.S. Tritton tr., with notes by H.A.R. Gibb: The first and second Crusades from an Anonymous Syriac Chronicle; *Journal of The Royal Asiatic Society (JRAS)* 1933; pp. 69-101.

-The First and second crusades from an Anonymous Syriac chronicle: tr., by A.S. Tritton and notes by A.H. R. Gibb: *JRAS*: Part two: April; pp. 273-305.

-William of Tyre: *A History of Deeds Done Beyond the Sea*; 2 vols; tr., and ed., by E. Babcock and A.C. Krey; Columbia University Press; 1943; repr. 1976.

-Al-'Umari: *Al-Ta'arif bi al-Mustalah al-Sharif*; Cairo; 1312.

-Usama Ibn Munqidh: *Kitab al'Itibar;* tr., P.K. Hitti; Beirut; 1964.

-Extracts from Histoire Universelle de Vartan; tr. E. Dulaurier; in *Journal Asiatique*; V. XVI; 1860; pp. 273-322.

-G. de Villehardouin: *Constantinople sous les Empereurs Francais*; Paris, 1657; 67-74. Other eds: Constantinople... Societe de l'Histoire de France; Paris; 1838;

-G. de Villehardouin: *La Conquete de Constantinople*; De Wailly ed.; Paris; 1872.

-William of Tyre's history entitled *L'estoire de Eracles Empereur et la Conquete de la Terre d'Outremer*, RHC. Occ. II. 323.

-William of Nangis: *Gesta Ludovoci; RHC Occ*; xx.

-*William of Rubrouck, Envoye de Saint Louis, Voyage Dans L'Empire Mongol (1253-1255)*, Payot, Paris, 1985.

-Al-Yunini: *Dhayl Mir'at Al-Zaman*; 4 vols; Hyderabad; 1954-61.

Made in the USA
Las Vegas, NV
12 January 2023